No Turning Point

C&C

CAMPAIGNS & COMMANDERS

GREGORY J. W. URWIN, SERIES EDITOR

No Turning Point
The Saratoga Campaign in Perspective

Theodore Corbett

University of Oklahoma Press : Norman

Also by Theodore Corbett

The Clash of Cultures on the Warpath of Nations: The Colonial Wars in the Hudson-Champlain Valley (Fleischmanns, N.Y., 2002)

The Making of American Resorts: Saratoga Springs, Ballston Spa, and Lake George (New Brunswick, N.J., 2001)

This book is pubished with the generous assistance of the Kerr Foundation, Inc.

No Turning Point: The Saratoga Campaign in Perspective is Volume 32 in the Campaigns and Commanders series.

Library of Congress Cataloging-in-Publication Data

Corbett, Theodore, 1941–
    No turning point : the Saratoga campaign in perspective / Theodore Corbett.
        p.   cm.
    Includes bibliographical references and index.
    ISBN 978-0-8061-4276-0 (hardcover : alk. paper)
    1. Saratoga Campaign, N.Y., 1777. 2. Social conflict—New York (State)—Saratoga Region—History—18th century. 3. Ethnic conflict—New York (State)—Saratoga Region—History—18th century. 4. Land tenure—New York (State)—Saratoga Region—History—18th century. 5. Allegiance—New York (State)—Saratoga Region—History—18th century. 6. New York (State)—History—Revolution, 1775–1783—Social aspects. I. Title.

The paper in this book meets the guidelines for permanence and durability of the Committee on Production Guidelines for Book Longevity of the Council on Library Resources, Inc. ∞

To Christine Brooks-Corbett

*As she and I both know, there are things
far more important than history books.*

CONTENTS

ILLUSTRATIONS

PREFACE AND ACKNOWLEDGMENTS

This book had its origin in 1965, when I had a summer job as a seasonal ranger at Saratoga National Historic Park. While I enjoyed showing visitors around the park, I put Saratoga aside and went on to take a PhD in European history and follow a much different direction. By the 1980s I was back in the Hudson-Champlain region, and as director of Historic Cherry Hill, I was able to probe the role of the Van Rensselaer family in the War of Independence. In 2000 I published a book on the region's resort life and a year later one on its role in the colonial wars. I needed to carry the saga of the latter book forward to the War of Independence, and the best way of doing this was to put the Burgoyne Campaign in context. When I attended conferences that covered the Burgoyne Campaign, I surprised myself by pointing out that from the local standpoint the Battles of Saratoga were not a turning point. The local audience knew exactly what I was talking about, for they immediately responded that my perspective was logical but that nobody had looked at it in depth.

Over the years, I have been in debt to the archives and individuals who facilitated this project. Locally these include Sally and Joe Brillon, Al Cormier, Winston Adler, Marie Butler, Jim Corsaro, and exceptional students like Loretta Bates. Further afield in 2001, I was awarded a Gilder Lehrman Foundation fellowship to work at the New-York Historical Society and New York Public Library on the participants in the battle. To see the other side, I traveled to the Canadian National

Archives and Library in Ottawa several times. Earlier, I had worked at the British Museum and Public Record Office in London before its successors the British Library and the National Archives were created.

As the manuscript took form, Eric Schnitzer, historian of Saratoga National Park, became the first reader of my very sloppy draft. Much later, Gavin Watt, the dean of Loyalist historians, was ever ready to point out that I had confused one Loyalist with another. My brother, Jim Corbett, has been enthusiastic about the project throughout. These three saved me from many embarrassments.

The University of Oklahoma Press made me trim the manuscript considerably, and while the process was painful, this is a better book because of it. Anyone who wants to know more about the region during the Revolutionary War can certainly contact me. I was honored to have the manuscript added to the Press's Campaigns and Commanders series, which maintains the highest standards. John Gilkes and I worked long and hard on the maps, which reflect his uncluttered lines, achieved even though he was in Britain. And, saving the best for last, I want to gush at the way the Press's editor-in-chief, Chuck Rankin, carried me through the development of the manuscript and yet somehow left all the final decisions to me.

New Castle, Delaware
July 25, 2011

PROLOGUE

A party of eight Iroquois, probably Mohawks, had been raiding in
the area north of Albany, east of the Hudson River. Their leader
was Le Loup, French for "wolf," a name that resulted from his time
in one of the Iroquois-dominated Canadian missions. These Indians
were allies of the British army, commanded by Lieutenant General John
Burgoyne, which had invaded the Hudson-Champlain region from
Canada in the summer of 1777. At Salem, New York, the Mohawks
had been driven back from the village's makeshift fort and one of
their warriors had been killed. The seven survivors decided to move
north to Fort Edward and seek captives to replace their dead comrade.[1]
On the way they took the required male captive for their villages, but
sought others too, as well as plunder and scalps. On July 25, near
what became South Argyle, they stumbled on John Allen's farm—
perhaps having rejected other, more strongly held farms in the area.
Allen and his helpers were in the fields harvesting his wheat crop,
so the Mohawks decided to hold their attack until the extended family
came together in the house for their noonday meal.

John Allen, his wife, and three children, all under the age of four,
had moved to the Argyle Patent in 1774, and he had built a one-room
log house and a barn, cleared sixteen acres, and sowed wheat.[2] By
July 1777 his crop was ready to be harvested. Allen was an outspoken
Loyalist in the ongoing war between Great Britain and thirteen of
its North American colonies, and so, he believed, were most of his

neighbors. In early July Reverend Thomas Clark of Salem had preached a Presbyterian service in Allen's barn—signifying that he was not bothered by Allen's Loyalism. Rumor had it that the rebels in Salem and Hebron were coming to get Allen because of his and his neighbors' convictions, but he was more concerned with having help harvesting his wheat. To aid him with the harvest, his father-in-law, George Kilmer, had sent his black slave, Tom; two additional slaves, one named Sarah; and Mrs. Allen's sister. On that day, July 25, they were called to the house at noon for dinner. And as they sat down to dinner, the Mohawks struck.

There is no record of what happened next, for there were no known survivors. Allen was found between his house and barn, having probably escaped through the house's back door or window. His wife, her sister, and the youngest child were found in the same direction, but closer to the house, as if they had followed behind him. The other two children had hid in a bed, where they had been killed. The slave Tom was found lying with his neck across the threshold, his head protruding out the open front door; he had many wounds and his lips had been skinned. All of the victims had been scalped.[3] No record exists of the other two slaves' bodies having been found; most likely they were taken captive by the Mohawks.

Kilmer had expected his daughter and the slaves to return in the evening, but when they failed to appear, he assumed the harvest was not yet complete.[4] When they still failed to appear by the morning of the third day, however, he sent a young slave to the Allen house to investigate. The boy had a hard time approaching the house, as his horse was spooked by the smell of blood. Upon discovering the bodies, he raced back to the Kilmore farm and mill. An armed party of Argyle patentees went to the farm and placed the bodies in two graves, one for the whites and the other for Tom.

News of the slaughter led most Argyle patentee families to search out their relatives and neighbors to see if they were safe. No sign of further Indian depredations was found, but most patentees abandoned their houses in fear of Indian raids and camped in the woods or, in one case, on an island in Cossayuna Lake. The family of Argyle settler Eunice Reid did not feel safe remaining in their house, and so "at first we slept in the hay barrack but not deeming this a secure retreat, we withdrew to a thicket of hemlocks that grew a piece north of the house and there slept night after night."[5] The Reids and ten patentee families then sought protection with Burgoyne's army at Fort Edward. There the group of twenty persons was crammed into "a tiny house, 14 feet wide and a little more in length, with a sleeping loft." At least two mothers and a daughter died, probably because of the exertions of their retreat and the conditions within the tiny house, where "the air was so confined and impure." Despite the risks, the Reid party was followed by many other patentees.

The Allen Massacre was a small but typical incident in the warfare of the Saratoga Campaign. Burgoyne did not realize that his plans would have to be imposed upon an already existing and confusing civil war, and that it would be difficult to separate friend from foe. The white settlers of both sides feared and suffered the indiscriminate destruction of their farms by the Mohawks, who operated independent of their British allies. The rebel commander, Major General Philip Schuyler, had ordered all inhabitants in the area to abandon their homes and retreat to Albany, an order the Allens and their neighbors clearly had not followed.[6] By remaining, the Allens identified themselves as Loyalists. From Burgoyne's standpoint, the Allen Massacre was a blot on his reputation because both the Allens and the Mohawks were nominally, at least, his allies. Burgoyne's long-term problem was that he could not exercise enough control over his Indian allies to have them discriminate as to whether a family was Loyalist or rebel.

While Burgoyne's concern was to protect all civilians from Indian depredations and to prevent scalping, especially of women and children, he probably never learned the details of this incident. We know he had, however, received tidings about similar incidents, such as the murder of Jane McCrea, fiancée of a Loyalist officer. In the McCrea case, he tried to punish his Indian allies for the murder, requiring them to have a British officer with them when they raided.[7] As a result he lost the support of some of them. On the plus side, however, the resulting movement of the Argyle patentees toward his army for protection fit well with his plans for winning the countryside for the king. Even if he could not control the continuing civil war, Burgoyne recognized the need to influence and participate in it.

The motives of John Burgoyne as commander of the invading British army are critical to our story. Being in the Hudson Valley in the summer and fall of 1777 was a vindication of his plans and the efforts of Lord North's ministry in London. Those plans shaped the formal war that would lead to the Battles of Saratoga. At the end of 1776, Burgoyne had left Canada for London to present news of Governor Guy Carleton's successful expulsion of the rebels from Canada and of his invasion of Lake Champlain. Burgoyne also wanted to lobby for a command independent of Carleton. Burgoyne fancied himself a military strategist and desired a detailed review of his ideas by the colonial secretary in charge of military policy, Lord George Germain—who was no friend of Carleton. Burgoyne had an audience with King George III, and on February 28 he presented Germain with an updated plan for the invasion of Lakes Champlain and George in 1777. The monarch was persuaded by Germain to favor Burgoyne, and it was decided that he, rather than Carleton, should lead the proposed lakes expedition in the summer.[8]

The strategic thoughts Burgoyne presented did not form a clear-cut plan but rather a discussion of possibilities, and thus they were and still are open to differing interpretations. Control of Lake Champlain was the first priority, to be achieved by returning to the lake with a fleet and army.[9] Then Fort Ticonderoga was to be taken and would become the base for further action. The next move depended on the decision of the ministry in London: should Burgoyne's army move south to Albany, to meet with an army coming up the Hudson River from New York City, or should he cooperate with the British army in Rhode Island and advance into New England to control the Connecticut Valley? Burgoyne also proposed a secondary invasion by way of the Mohawk Valley to draw off support and weaken Albany's defenses. Finally, if a lack of resources prevented any of this from happening, the Canadian army, he suggested, should be transferred by sea to join General William Howe in New York City. Burgoyne did not propose a line of posts to hold the Hudson-Champlain valley and isolate New England from the other colonies—a goal emphasized by many historians. His most logical object was merely to effect a junction with an army from New York City by capturing and occupying the pivotal city of Albany, giving him control of the region north of that city.

Burgoyne's plan was that of a professional soldier, one who was also schooled in the intrigues of ministerial and parliamentary politics. Sitting in London as he wrote, Burgoyne expected the North ministry to produce an overall plan that defined the nature of his cooperation with General William Howe in New York City. Implementing such a plan would be Germain's responsibility, and one he let slip by, rather than execute, leaving Howe to make other plans.[10] Burgoyne was also unaware of the civil war already raging in the region, although he would make an effort to pacify the inhabitants. All this did not bode well for executing his plan.

Burgoyne's ultimate surrender had as much to do with incidents like the Allen Massacre that contributed to the civil conflict as to the rebel army that would corner him at Saratoga. But after his army had disappeared from the scene, civil war continued unabated, and a much reduced Continental Army could not confront the British in the region. The combined military and civil conflict continued for the rest of the war, and the British were consistently victorious, maintaining dominance of strategic Lakes Champlain and George. In the Hudson-Champlain valley, therefore, it is difficult to regard the Battles of Saratoga as a turning point.

PART I

SETTING THE SCENE

1

SETTLEMENT IN THE HUDSON-CHAMPLAIN VALLEY

The Hudson-Champlain region, through which Burgoyne would travel, extended from the British base at Ile aux Noix on the Richelieu River in the north to the environs of the Hudson River city of Albany, famous for its Dutch fur-trading oligarchy. North of Albany, the Saratoga area would become the critical site of Burgoyne's final defeat. The region included eastern New York, western Vermont, western Massachusetts, and the Montreal area of Canada. By 1777 this region was no longer the wilderness it had been during the colonial wars. Much of it was being cleared and farmed and becoming populated by a prosperous class of yeomen farmers and a few plantation owners. Most of the land along water courses was settled, and only the areas most distant from streams lacked cultivated open spaces. As this agricultural hinterland expanded, the small city of Albany became less influential, vastly outnumbered by the population in the surrounding countryside on which it depended for its market produce, foodstuffs, and exportable staples like lumber and wheat. Thus Burgoyne found the Saratoga area developed, so that for a while his army could supplement their own supplies with food taken from the land. It was also a countryside worthy of being pacified to support the king's cause.

When Burgoyne's army appeared at the Hudson River in Kingsbury, the officers noted that the level area along the river was settled and thriving with crops. Between Fort Ann and Fort Edward, as German

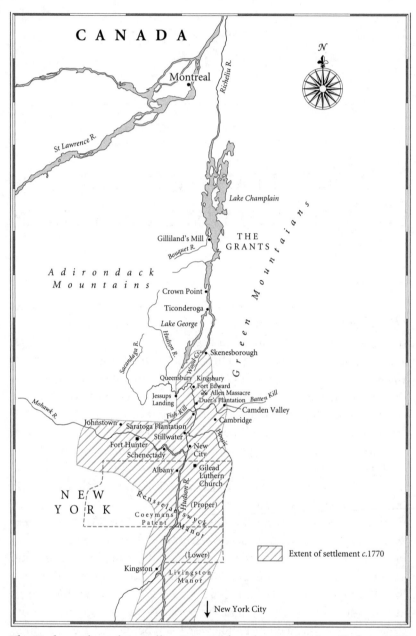

The Hudson-Champlain Valley. Extent of settlement in New York, c. 1770

surgeon's mate, J. F. Wasmus commented, they "had the pleasure of seeing the first rye fields in America; they almost were like those in Germany. We passed several settlements, whose inhabitants had all fled. The houses were built in German [log cabin] style and covered with shingles. The farther we advanced, the more pleasant was the countryside; the one today was the most beautiful we have seen in America. The main road seemed to be quite passable. We have not been used to marching on such a road."[1] At Fort Edward, British lieutenant William Digby wrote: "On the whole, the country thereabout wore a very different appearance from any we had seen since our leaving Canada . . . the land improves much, and no doubt in a little time will be thickly settled."

Below Fort Edward in early August, Wasmus continued to rhapsodize, although the farms were apparently abandoned:

> We found both sides of the river settled with rather well-built houses . . . which were all empty; the families had fled into the wilderness with all their belongings just for fear of the Germans. The beautiful wheat and rye fields were going to ruin; they were all ripe. We passed several bridges and places where the enemy had camped. We also saw grapes, although not ripe, as well as many [blueberries], raspberries and blackberries on both sides of the well laid-out military road. It was noon when we entered the camp at Fort Miller. . . . On a height on our left, one saw a magnificent building [William Duer's house], several respectable houses, as well as various saw mills and gristmills, which were all empty.[2]

Below Fort Edward, another German, Brig. Gen. Johann Friedrich Specht, was more concise, noting, "This region is quite well settled with habitations and the corn in most fields is ready for the harvest."

Landlord Philip Schuyler's plantation at Saratoga was immortalized by the nineteenth- century German-American artist Emanuel Gottlieb Leutze as a center of productivity that could have fallen into the hands of the British.[3] To prevent this, the artist portrayed Mrs. Philip Schuyler as burning the wheat fields around the house—an incident that in reality never took place. Thus in both fact and fiction the area along the region's rivers was renowned as farmed and bountiful.

Below Schuyler's Saratoga plantation, on September 15, two days before the Battle of Freeman's Farm, the luxuriant farms continued to impress the foreigners. A German corps "landed in a mown field where large sheaves of wheat and rye provide camp straw for almost the entire army. . . . Fields of considerable size were planted in [corn], that were as productive as any farmer could wish."[4] The observers were seeing the best farms along the Hudson River, but even inland, the clearings of less developed farms were causing the forest to recede. Away from the Hudson on the New York–Vermont border, historian Philip Lord, who has steeped himself in the land use and settlement pattern, has rated the farms caught in the midst of the Battle of Walloomsac in August 1777 as being a step above the lowest hardscrabble type. This last type of farm had only a few acres of field cleared, where crops grew among the tree stumps and a tiny log cabin with some minimal rail fencing completed it.[5] Instead, the three farms at the Walloomsac bridge had fifty acres or more in fields, some for pasture, some for cultivation, and some in the process of being cleared. An original log cabin had been expanded, and a log barn now housed the livestock so they wouldn't wander. A well was a necessity, and a variety of fences surrounded the entire property. This more advanced type of farm dominated the Saratoga area.

The Battles at Saratoga on September 19 and October 7 involved cultivated locations, Freeman's Farm and the Barber wheat field, a sign of this development. John Freeman, Sr., who held a 150-acre farm on lease forever from landlord Philip Schuyler, had settled in 1766, and by the time of the war he had cleared 50 to 60 acres and had erected a frame house and barn. One British soldier concluded that fighting at Freeman's Farm caused "a plantation, with large crops of several sorts of grain, thriving and beautiful in the morning," to be "before night reduced to a scene of distress and poverty!"[6]

The Flow of Migration

How did the Hudson-Champlain region become a populous and rich farming area by the time of Burgoyne's invasion? The settling of the lands above Albany had been delayed because the region was exposed to hostile Native American and Canadian forays during King George's and the Seven Years' Wars. Before the 1740s and 1750s, settlement was limited to the Saratoga plantation at the mouth of Fish Creek and the

Hoosic Valley, where Albany and Schenectady Dutch families had gathered.[7] With the Peace of Paris in 1763, most of the earlier settlers returned to the region, and Albany County became more populated than ever. True, the Schaghticoke Indians never returned to their Hoosic Valley reserve, but this indicated that Native Americans could not cohabit with the growing number of settlers.

The flow of migration to the Upper Hudson region came from two directions. From the south it began in New York City, where immigrants from the British Isles or German states landed and stayed before moving to the middle areas of the Hudson Valley. The colony's immigrants were mainly Scots-Irish and Scottish—chiefly Presbyterians—and Quakers or German Palatine and Brunswick settlers.[8] The religious sectarianism of many of these ethnic groups contributed to their desire to move, as they sought to establish a godly community in the wilderness. The process of their movement to the region north of Albany might take a decade or more and involve a second generation that was born in New York. Also involved in settlement was a new generation of the Albany, Schenectady, and Kingston Dutch, whose families had previously attempted to settle the area but had been expelled during the colonial wars.

A second wave of settlers came to New York from the east—that is New England—originating chiefly in Connecticut and Massachusetts. These migrants would settle in the New Hampshire Grants but also spill over into New York as they moved further west. They came as result of overpopulation and diminishing resources in eastern and southern New England. As the eighteenth century wore on, it had become increasingly difficult for fathers to have enough acreage to provide each son with sufficient land for a farm.[9] This was not as disastrous as it sounds—in fact, it was an act of renewal. Ignoring primogeniture and partible inheritance, parents chose to provide their children according to abilities and needs, often before a will ever was made. As one of the chief options, children, especially mature sons, were provided with the wherewithal to move to a new settlement where land was cheaper and society more fluid. Early destinations were the western townships of Connecticut or Massachusetts, but by the 1770s New York and the New Hampshire Grants were favored. Thus, the pressure of population growth on limited resources in Connecticut and Massachusetts spearheaded the movement of New Englanders into the region.

Religious motives also led New Englanders to migrate to the region in groups. The covenanted Congregational Church was the established church of Massachusetts and Connecticut, and that powerful church would even appear in New York at Stillwater and Granville. But not all New Englanders were Congregationalists. Viable Anglican, Baptist, Presbyterian, and Methodist churches appeared in New England by the mid-eighteenth century, and their communicants looked upon New York and the New Hampshire Grants as places where they could practice their faith without the restraints of the established Congregational Church.[10]

As a result of these two distinct waves of immigration, Albany County more than doubled its population, the census of 1771 showing 38,829 white and 3,877 black persons.[11] This was about one-quarter of New York colony's entire population—much larger than New York City, by far the colony's most populous political unit.

The Insignificant Population of Cities

By 1777 only three very small cities existed, and none of them held newly arrived immigrants for long because they were attracted to farming in the countryside. Albany was clearly the dominant community, but with less than 3,000 inhabitants within its stockade, it was no more than an overgrown village.[12] The other sizable places, Schenectady and Kingston, had only about 500 residents each. All three were commercial centers, having once been fur trading posts, and had made the transition to dealing in lumber and foodstuffs, clearly depending on their hinterlands for these products. While they had a need for craftsmen, servants, stevedores, and laborers, most of these positions were held by black slaves and existing freemen, whom the patrician oligarchs favored over immigrants. Hence, while an immigrant might look for work in Albany, once he had a little money his chief goal was to find a suitable farm. Thus the cities were at best temporary magnets for growth, instead serving as a source of migrants and development for the countryside, conditions that blunted their own influence and population size.

Albany Patricians Lead in Resettling the Region

Traditional histories of the colonies point out that New York's land was full of manors, supposedly vestiges of the European Middle Ages that forced new settlers to become tenants and retarded settlement because they could not own land in fee simple.[13] This view is based on later Jeffersonian ideas about the virtue of independent farmers, not the actual mentality of eighteenth-century settlers. Most migrants to New York sought not the outright landownership that impressed New Englanders but rather favorable terms from a landlord, especially a lease of long duration, ninety-nine years being ideal. They also wanted to be paid for their improvements when the lease ended or they sold the lease. Newcomers chose such an alternative to fee simple because it was closer to what they had experienced in Europe and offered them a greater degree of security. In turn, landlords were to be indulgent about collecting rents and also provide benefits such as seed, tools, housing, and amenities during the first years of establishing a farm. European immigrants, at least, regarded New York as an attractive place to settle because of the competing offers of the various landlords. Thus, capitalistic rivalry in developing estates and plantations, not the conditions of the medieval manor, spurred settlement in New York.

The great patrician families of Albany had extensive country houses that were not centers of leisure or academic gardening but rather engines for the settlement of the hinterland. The houses, in fact, were centers of plantations and seats of enterprise that required considerable management.[14] Country houses were built to provide the city with dairy and foodstuffs and to support the wheat or lumber trade down the Hudson to New York City. The urban commercial interests of Albany were driven by their ability to settle and develop the countryside around their houses.

The Van Rensselaer Family and the Manor

The Van Rensselaer family had inherited the largest manorial grant in New York colony, which came to be the Manor of Rensselaerswyck. Rensselaerswyck dated from a seventeenth-century Dutch grant that was confirmed by English authorities like the Duke of York in 1678 and Governor Thomas Dongan seven years later.[15] The boundaries comprised most of present-day Albany and Rensselaer Counties, as well as large tracts around Claverack in Columbia County. The manor's vast acreage actually surrounded the city of Albany, which made developing land immediately beyond the city difficult, because of the manorial obligations.

The manor founder, Killian Van Rensselaer, was born in 1663 and brought up in Albany. He had political influence because he represented the manor, which had its own seat in the New York Assembly, and he was a member of the Governor's Council and a commissioner of Indian affairs.[16] But despite his advantages, he was never an entrepreneur but rather a landed squire, who preferred to rest on his political laurels. Before his death in 1718, he did take the honorary title of "patroon" or fatherly landlord, which would continue in the family into the nineteenth century.

Not all the branches of the Van Rensselaer family were rich like the patroon. Killian's younger brother, Henry, had modest manorial property on the east side of the Hudson and to the south, at Claverack. Yet, until his death in 1740, he scarcely visited his Claverack holdings. Like his brother, he preferred to be a gentleman, living alternatively in his Greenbush country home, Crailo, and a townhouse in Albany.[17] Henry's youngest son, Killian, was born in 1717 and inherited an even more modest estate in Greenbush, across from Albany on the east side of the river. He could not provide much of an inheritance for the next generation, but he could use the illustrious family name to find wealthy husbands for his daughters: William Ludlow, of a New York City merchant house; Abraham Lansing, of a rising Albany shipping family; and Leonard Gansevoort, of one of Albany's patrician families. Killian's sons were also urged to marry women with wealth: Killian, Jr., married his cousin Margaret, who was an heir of Scotia's Sanders family and Philip took as his wife Maria, the daughter of merchant Robert Sanders of Albany. Through intermarriage with Albany patricians and their connections, the Van Rensselaers formed alliances that perpetuated their influence in Albany as well as the city's expansive hinterland. Killian's sons would also make names for themselves as rebel officers in the War of Independence.

In 1714, after eighty years of existence, Rensselaerswyck had only 82 tenants. Subsequently, however, the manor grew moderately, and with the end of the Seven Years' War it boomed, reaching about 1,000 tenants by 1779. The first major influx of German Protestant refugees, the Palatines, dated from 1710, when 2,500 arrived in New York City, after a perilous voyage in which many perished. Initially most were settled on Livingston Manor, where they were engaged in the production of naval stores, especially pitch. At first they lived in camps, not really prospering until the 1730s, when they left the Livingstons and dispersed, some going to the Schoharie and Mohawk Valleys, while others moved north into Rensselaerswyck's east manor.

A decade later, additional German immigrants came and named their east manor hamlet Brunswick, after Duke Ferdinand of Brunswick, who commanded British troops in the Seven Years' War. It is likely that some of the Germans were veterans of Brunswick's command.[18] By 1757 these immigrants had erected a log structure, which became the first Gilead Lutheran Church. At the same time, Germans settled as tenants within the jurisdiction of Rensselaerswyck on the west side of the Hudson River in the Coeymans Patent. This was the case of the farming and slave-holding family of Johannes Waltermyer, who spoke German and would become a legendary Loyalist in the War of Independence.

As noted, the Van Rensselaers were not interested in the detailed management of their manors. To overcome this deficiency in the 1760s and 1770s, Abraham Ten Broeck was brought in, to become the most industrious and well-connected figure in the management of their manors. Related to both the Van Rensselaers and Livingstons, he was a political leader of the Albany patricians. Born in 1734, as a youth Ten Broeck was sent to New York City to work in the counting house of his brother-in-law, Philip Livingston.[19] The Livingstons, lords of the Hudson Valley manor south of Rensselaerswyck, were already related to important families like the Schuylers. When Abraham's father, Dirck Ten Broeck, died, seventeen-year-old Abraham was sent to Europe to learn international trade and gain polish. After a year he returned to Albany, residing with his widowed mother, Margarita, in the family homestead.

Abraham became involved in the lumber trade, clearing acreage on the Hudson River north of Albany and exporting the boards, while importing goods to sell in his store. His property came to include an Albany lumberyard and private dock on the Hudson. During the Seven Years' War, he was a commissioned officer in the provincial militia, the beginning of a militia career that would carry into the War of Independence. By 1759 he was also an Albany alderman, and four years later he married Elizabeth Van Rensselaer, the only daughter of the region's richest person, Stephen Van Rensselaer, the patroon. In 1769, following the death of Stephen, Ten Broeck was named co-administrator of Rensselaerswyck, representative for the manor in the New York Assembly and guardian of the four-year-old heir, Stephen, Jr. He was now the most powerful figure in Rensselaerswyck.

As co-administrator of the manor, Abraham Ten Broeck controlled more resources than anyone in Albany, and he used them to develop Rensselaerswyck's vast territory. He maintained seven sawmills and three gristmills, most of them being operated on lease.[20] Those he managed were run by his skilled black slaves—of which, by the 1760s, Rensselaerswyck had more than any other part of the Albany area. He also brought in new English and Dutch tenants, settling them in the area north of Albany. More than any member of the extended Van Rensselaer family, he deserved credit for developing the extensive manors, and when the War of Independence came, he would be one of the most prominent rebels.

PLANTATIONS

Beyond the region's three cities and Rensselaerswyck, three plantations stood out as not just farms but centers of enterprise like milling, flax production, and in one case a bloomery for iron production. The three plantation landlords were Philip Schuyler at Saratoga on the Hudson River, Sir William Johnson at Johnstown near the Mohawk River, and Philip Skene at Skenesborough on Wood Creek at the southern end of Lake Champlain. These entrepreneurs rented out their land, and to attract tenants, had to give them the best possible terms. Immigrants were most likely to take their promise of land on easy terms and accept a paternal attitude. By 1775 few other places in the countryside could match the size and productivity of these manors.

A Patrician Plantation

Substantial in economic potential was Philip Schuyler's plantation. The Albany patrician Schuylers were the leading family in the settlement of the Saratoga area, developing their lands on both sides of the Hudson River. Their plantation was located on the south bank of Fish Kill, where it emptied into the Hudson, near what was to be the site of Burgoyne's surrender on October 17, 1777. About a month before the surrender, British volunteer Thomas Anburey described Schuyler's plantation as having "a handsome and commodious dwelling-house, with outhouses, an exceedingly fine saw-and grist-mill, and at a small distance a very neat church, with several houses round it. . . . On the grounds were great quantities of fine wheat, as also Indian corn; the former was instantly cut down, threshed, carried to the mill to be ground, and delivered to the men to save our provisions; the latter was cut for forage for the horses."[21] Certainly, Philip Schuyler had made a success of his plantation.

The early history of the Schuyler plantation shows that it was an independent family development. John Schuyler's farm, house, mills, lumber, and slaves had been destroyed or taken by a Canadian raid in 1745, a blow that discouraged the family from rebuilding the plantation for fifteen years—until after the Seven Years' War.[22] It was left to John's great-nephew, Philip, to succeed to 1,900 acres of the estate and to decide to resurrect it. He had married well, in 1755, to Catherine Van Rensselaer, her father, John, being the landlord of Claverack Manor. While Philip was not a manorial landlord, his mother was a Van Cortlandt and Catherine tied him to the Van Rensselaer family, so he was part of the network of patrician families that dominated Albany County. In the 1760s Philip restored the saw- and gristmills, built himself a house near the foundations of the old one, erected storehouses and outbuildings, and introduced the growing and processing of flax for linen and oil. When he built his mansion in Albany, the wooden planks for the structure were sawed at the plantation.

Schuyler sought tenants, attracting them by allowing rents to be paid in produce and profitable quarter sales when they sold their leases, and his rent rolls in 1773 and 1774 show he was able to recruit Dutch and Scottish tenants.[23] He attracted some to work at his enterprises and others to be his tenants, but altogether they probably numbered only about a hundred, not much of an improvement over his Uncle John's Saratoga plantation of 1745. For the convenience of his tenants and himself, he operated a store, which sold rum, staples, and dry goods. Like his uncle's household, his own workforce consisted largely of black slaves.

Philip Schuyler had gained some military experience in the Seven Years' War, serving in the Albany commissary under Brigadier John Bradstreet, who settled in Albany after the war and remained a friend of the young patrician. The fact that Schuyler took a supply position in the British army was respected by British officers because he was a patrician gentleman "of ability, activity, and ambition," not the usual money-grubbing wagoner.[24] When Schuyler built his Albany mansion in 1766, it was constructed in Georgian, rather than Dutch style, copying Bradstreet's own mansion—a sign that he was now an Englishman. Here were the origins of the rebel general and patrician who would be most familiar with the Hudson-Champlain valley.

An Irish Landlord in Albany County

The Johnson family, from Sir William to Guy and Sir John, are usually thought of as lords of the Mohawk Valley, too far removed from the realm of Albany politics and military affairs. In fact, they were highly involved in both and rivals for power with the Schuylers and other Albany patricians. William Johnson came to New York in 1738 and in the next year developed a small farm on the north bank of the Mohawk River, a farm that was soon expanded into a plantation, which he called Mount Johnson.[25] The Mohawk Valley was part of Albany County until 1772, and thus William Johnson held county offices, including the colonelcy of the Albany County militia. Beginning in 1750 he also become the dominant figure in Indian affairs, especially with the neighboring Mohawks, taking this responsibility away from the Albany Indian Commissioners, a body the Schuylers and other Albany patricians had used to control the lucrative fur trade. Johnson was a definite imperialist, who threatened the communal and independent activities of the Albany Dutch patricians, in contrast to the patricians, who during the early colonial wars had no scruples about trading with Britain's enemies like the French merchants of Montreal.

Sir William Johnson developed additional lands ten miles north of the Mohawk River, which he named Johnstown—the seat in 1772 of newly created Tryon County—and, above it, Johnson's Bush. He aimed in the next year to secure Scottish Highland migrants, of whom three hundred had been gathered from Knoydart and Glen Garry and who sailed from Fort William for New York on a Royal Navy ship.[26] Their leaders sought offers of settlement that would allow the group to keep "as close and united as possible," and they hoped to join Johnson in the Mohawk Valley. A year later, Johnson outbid other landlords by attracting fifty Scottish families to his land, numbering about four hundred persons. The clansmen received fifty or one hundred acres, the gentlemen two hundred. They paid no rent until their farms were established, and then it was fixed at £6 per hundred acres.

These Macdonnells—from Glen Garry, Glen Moriston, Glen Urquhart, and Strathglass in Scotland—farmed their holdings, bringing their grain to be ground at Johnson's mill. Their militaristic society and Roman Catholicism intimidated the Mohawk Valley's Palatine German, Dutch, and English settlers. These Highland tenants seemed content, but in only three years, they would follow their landlord and their priest John MacKenna farther to Canada.

A British Officer's Plantation

Serving with Jeffrey Amherst's forces in the Seven Years' War, Philip Skene was impressed by the region's potential for settlement, especially near the southern end of Lake Champlain—present-day Whitehall. After the capture of Fort St. Frédéric on Lake Champlain in 1759, he was given an important role in the construction of the new fort, Crown Point, involving him in the distribution of building material and supplies. With Amherst's blessing and some of these materials, he began to recruit settlers in the Whitehall area, even though he had yet to obtain title to the land.[27] To get land, Skene ignored both the granting authority of the governments of New York and New Hampshire but in 1759 wrote directly to Amherst, asking him to present a petition to the monarch to obtain a patent on his emerging Lake Champlain property.

While the crown's attitude was positive, the petition only received preliminary confirmation in 1764.[28] Still, Skene went ahead and industriously placed tenants on his property, from a variety of sources. Some were captives, British American subjects held in Canada by mission Indians and who were purchased from the Indians by General Thomas Gage in 1761 and 1762. Others were immigrants from Ireland, where Skene's wife, Katherine, recruited them. Still others were British soldiers who had served with him at the capture of Havana, Cuba, in 1762. Finally, he also brought some of the twenty-three black slaves he purchased while serving in the West Indies. These tenants and slaves were not all there when he returned to Lake Champlain in 1763, but the expense he incurred in settling them and in building a sawmill helped support his claim to the patent. His wife and his children arrived in 1765, confirming that a soldier could be not only a developer, but also a settler. Clearly his friendship with Amherst allowed him to cut through the normal legal and political procedures

Philip Skene's house and barn as they looked before they were sacked by Samuel Herrick in May 1775. Conception by Wayne Latrell in Doris Begor Morton, *Philip Skene of Skenesbourgh* (Granville, N.Y., 1959).

and avoid the conflict over the New Hampshire grants. Locals knew him as "a large, fine looking person, with a pleasant countenance and an affable deportment." He was an ideal settler because he was more interested in creating a plantation than in becoming a land speculator.

By the 1770s, however, Skene was aware that his development at Skenesborough was not meeting his economic expectations. The soil was not as fertile as his tenant-recruiting broadsides claimed, and by April 1771 he was thinking "of sending to Canada for some wheat to subsist my inhabitants that lost their bread by the worms last year."[29] Most payments to him were made in kind, so he was continually short of cash. With minimal rental income because of the liberal terms he used to attract tenants, Skene's sources of profit were limited to his mills, bloomery, and the sale of cattle and horses. He was dependent on agents—Thomas Gamble in New York City and, after 1773, Barry Bloom in Albany—to obtain specie and manufactured goods. Skene did think in terms of transatlantic trade; he built a sloop of red cedar, on which he hoped to carry sawed lumber to Montreal and also export horses to the West Indies. However, most of the livestock he raised, including oxen, were sold locally. Before the War of Independence, then, he was in the thick of the region's development, and he understood the need for heavy and innovative investments to make a property profitable. What he did not realize was that his plantation would be a pivotal—and often occupied— site to both armies in the coming hostilities.

Plantations Being Realized

Some plantations had been recently established and were not fully developed by the time Burgoyne's army invaded. In Albany, Philip Schuyler had convinced William Duer to purchase land north of his Saratoga plantation at Fort Miller and establish his own plantation. Born in 1743 in Devonshire, as a young man Duer had served briefly in India and then managed the family estate in Dominica. He came to New York City from the West Indies in 1768 with a contract in hand to provide the Royal Navy with spars and masts. He might have fallen under William Johnson's sway, but he chose to associate himself with Schuyler's development at Saratoga. Across the Hudson at Fort Miller, from 1773, Duer built a sawmill, warehouses, and store, from which he supplied the local farmers. He constructed a house that looked like the seat of a West Indies planter. A German veteran of the Saratoga campaign in 1777 described it as "the first house built in good taste that we had seen . . . of two stories, and was covered with an Italian roof; a pavilion was built on each side of it in which were the kitchen and pantries; by means of a covered gallery, they were connected with the main building." [30] Unfortunately, he also observed that the fortunes of war had damaged it and left it almost empty.

Lumber was the chief commodity of Duer's plantation, and he gained a small contract to supply it to the Royal Navy. However, even a trip to London in 1772 could not procure an additional Royal Navy contract, so most of his lumber trade was with his West Indies connections. [31] He married late in life, at the age of thirty-six, to Cathe- rine Alexander, the daughter of William Alexander, Lord Stirling— later a Continental general. Duer had a gambler's delight for land development that led to speculation, and after the war he spent seven years in a debtor's prison on account of his transgressions.

Of course, New York had land speculators, who patented many parcels but never personally settled on the acreage, hoping that the market would raise their value so they could be sold to another speculator. Some did attempt to find settlers, usually foreign immigrants, for portions of their land. Such a speculator in the Hudson-Champlain valley was James Duane of New York City, an attorney who was impeccably connected to New York's leading families.[32] His father, an officer in the Royal Navy, had left the navy and contracted two marriages to important New York City merchant families. When he died in 1747, fourteen-year-old James became a ward of Robert Livingston, the lord of Livingston Manor. When James grew up he married Livingston's eldest daughter and in 1767 was made attorney general of New York. When the War of Independence came, Duane honored his family connections and hesitantly became a rebel. After the British captured New York City in 1776, he was forced to move his family up the Hudson River to Livingston Manor. From 1774 to 1784 he was New York's consistent representative to the Continental Congress, where he was known for his effort to reconcile the colonies with the mother country and his opposition to punishing Loyalists.

Before this, Duane was an active speculator, so successful that his detractors called him a "swivel-eyed genius." He purchased grants cheaply from veterans of the Seven Years' War, holding several parcels in the New Hampshire Grants as well as New York. In the mid-1760s he bought into the Princeton Grant, which covered the source of the Batten Kill River and involved him in dealings in the New Hampshire Grants.[33] In all, Duane spent £3,363 to obtain 67,000 acres in eastern New York. Later he secured land in the military grants in Charlotte County's Camden Valley, where from 1769 he encouraged the settlement along the Batten Kill of a group of Palatine Irish Methodists led by Philip Embury. Duane was the agent for the purchase of the Turner Patent, which became Salem, and encouraged Dr. Thomas Clark to bring his Scots-Irish congregation there. In the late 1790s he retired to his country estate at Duanesburg, south of Schenectady, where he a developed a community around his house, showing that a speculator could become a settler.

Tenants and Slaves

Overall, the Albany patricians, imperialists like Skene and Johnson, and New York City developers like Duer attempted to extend the

Anglo-Dutch society that already existed in the Hudson Valley to Albany's northern reaches. With long-established manors and rapid water transport of staples like wheat and lumber to New York City, it was an economy based on tenantry, supplemented by black slave labor, and it became a system that was perpetuated even in the Saratoga area above Albany, where Dutch traditions weakened. A substantial number of tenants would lease their land from one of the influential landlords. The lease was an effective tool for settling land because the renter was less likely to fall into debt. Potential farmers needed help in establishing farms in the wilderness, and their burden could be eased by leasing land as a tenant rather than buying it. In Charlotte County north of Albany, an area with no tradition of manorial tenure, lists of electors—those men who met the property qualification to vote—for a portion of it in 1790 show that a substantial minority of the electors were still leaseholders. Twenty-two percent of the wealthiest men were leaseholders, and as the county grew rapidly, the number of lease-holders increased rather than lessened.[34] Thus, landlord tenure was persistent and strong in the most recent areas of settlement.

Strong pockets of slavery existed, chiefly along the Hudson and Mohawk Rivers. The greatest number of slaves were spread throughout Rensselaerswyck or concentrated in the city of Albany. In Charlotte and Saratoga Counties, on the banks of the Hudson River, Dutch farmers raised a wheat staple with black slaves as field hands.[35] After the War of Independence when the first figures appear, seven Easton Town households on the east side of the Hudson had four or more slaves, and that of Daniel Winne had an extraordinary ten slaves. Opposite Easton, on the west bank, the towns of Stillwater and Saratoga had the area's greatest percentage of slaves and the largest number of slaveholders, including by then John Bradstreet Schuyler, the son of Philip, with fourteen slaves at the Saratoga plantation.

THE SMALLER PLACES

Below the large-scale patrician and landlord developments were numerous smaller communities without direct ties to them. Many of the exuberant accounts of the productivity of the region were actually observations of these lesser known places, especially hamlets that were devoted to serving farmers. In choosing New York communities to describe, the focus will be on those located on the route of Burgoyne's army.

The Kingsbury Patent and Fort Edward

As Burgoyne's army moved southward on their way to Fort Edward, they first viewed the Hudson River at Kingsbury. The Kingsbury Patent was granted in 1762 to a number of proprietors from Connecticut, the most prominent being New Milford's James Bradshaw. Lots were laid out and divided amongst the proprietors. Bradshaw actually came to Kingsbury in 1763, and two years later he brought his family. Others followed, and a wing dam and sawmill were constructed at what is today Hudson Falls.

Another early family was that of the widow Sarah Dunham Jones. Originally from Leamington, New Jersey, and then Connecticut, she settled in the northeast of the town, near present-day Patten Mills. She had six sons: John, Jonathan, Dunham, Daniel, David, and Solomon. John and Daniel served as heads of the family and developed prosperous farms on Bond's Creek. The widow Jones's house was substantial enough to have Burgoyne choose it as his headquarters in 1777. Kingsbury was described by Burgoyne's officers as having "Other beautiful houses . . . as well as a mill in good condition. We also saw many maple trees from which they had drawn sugar in the spring."[36] The sons were friends with nearby families like the McCreas and Wings. Daniel married Deborah Wing, daughter of Abraham and Anstis Wing, the founders of Queensbury. He also bought land from the land developers Ebenezer and Edward Jessup of Albany. In 1777 David would be betrothed to Jane McCrea, an engagement that brought two of the area's leading families together. She would be the heroine killed by Burgoyne's Indians.

South of Kingsbury was Fort Edward. In the colonial wars, it had been fortified because of its strategic location at the head of Hudson River navigation, where two overland routes diverged: one to the northwest toward Lake George, the other to the northeast toward Lake Champlain. Both routes required portages, and it became the "Great Carrying Place," where the traveler had to commence on roads. By 1766 the fortifications were in such a state of disrepair that the British army abandoned them. Six years later, however, Fort Edward won the contest to become the county seat of newly created Charlotte

County.[37] Henceforth, the place gained the reputation of being "Royalist Fort Edward," since its citizens prospered by the royal appointments that derived from being the county seat.

No one prospered more from receiving royal plums than a recently arrived Irishman, Patrick Smyth. Originally settled in Albany where he practiced law, he had spent time at Fort Edward from 1762 and became custodian of the fort after it was abandoned by the British army.[38] Having decided to make Fort Edward his primary home, in 1772 he built a large wood-frame, gambrel-roofed house. So scarce were housewrights that he had to send to Salem for men to raise the building's frame. He stocked his cellar with barrels of pork, beef, shad fish, and wine. The same year, he also bought land from Philip Schuyler. In 1768 he was an agent for the Albany interests of Henry Cuyler, and when Charlotte County was formed in 1772, he was made road commissioner and, a year later, county clerk and justice of the peace. His brother, Dr. George Smyth, joined him and resided in Fort Edward at this time, though his medical practice soon drew him to Claverack in the Rensselaer Manor.

Another Fort Edward extended family was the Sherwoods, headed by Seth and Adiel. The families migrated from Stratford, Connecticut, in the mid-1760s and settled near the dilapidated fort. Seth's land was unfortunately the victim of many overlapping patents, including those of Argyle and Saratoga, and at first he had difficulty in confirming the title to the property.[39] While he attempted to purchase his land and clear it of conflicting claims, in October 1770 he was committed to an Albany jail over his claims. Evidently Patrick Smyth, as the agent of Henry Cuyler, had a hand in arresting him, and this was the beginning of a falling-out between the two settlers. During his trial, Seth called fellow Connecticut developer, and now resident of Albany, Edward Jessup to vouch for his character. In the future, Jessup would be a Loyalist and thus his enemy.

Seth Sherwood did not gain a clear title until the War of Independence, when he chose to be a rebel, while most of his neighbors were Loyalists. Seth had served in the Seven Years' War in a Connecticut provincial regiment and would expand on this background as a Charlotte County militia officer in the War of Independence. His brother, Adiel, also had military interests and joined the Charlotte County militia as a lieutenant in 1775. As war clouds gathered, he tried to repair the defenses of Fort Edward and remount its aged ordnance.

Jessups Landing

On the northern reaches of the Hudson River, the Jessup brothers, Ebenezer and Edward, made an entrepreneurial effort to develop the land that focused on Jessups Landing. Coming to the area after the Seven Years' War, the Jessups were newcomers from Stamford, Connecticut, who settled in Albany and then became developers of its hinterland. They were wealthy and Anglican, gaining crown offices to feed their interest in land speculation and development.

Their story began in 1744, when the extended Jessup family had moved from Connecticut to the Upper Nine Partners Patent, Dutchess County.[40] The brothers prospered there, but they did not sever their ties with Stamford. Sixteen years later, Ebenezer and Edward went back to the town of their birth to marry their cousins, the sisters Elizabeth and Abigail Dibble, who crucially brought to the marriage contracts for one hundred acres each. Edward had served in the Seven Years' War as a volunteer from 1755 to 1758, then, a year later, he raised a provincial company, serving as its captain in Amherst's campaign that captured Ticonderoga and Crown Point. This experience would serve him well when he became a Loyalist officer.

With the Seven Years' War over, in 1764 the Jessup brothers moved from Dutchess County to Albany, bringing with them their parents, Joseph and Abigail Jessup, and another brother, Joseph.[41] They became members of Albany's St. Peter's Church, once the church of the British garrison, where Henry Munro was the rector. In 1773 the Jessup brothers gave two large tracts of land in trust to support the Society for the Encouragement of the Established Religion, which had been unsuccessful in another effort to make the Anglican faith the established church of New York colony. A trained surveyor, Ebenezer worked in Albany's Royal Land Office as deputy to Alex Geldon, the surveyor, and in 1775 he was named a justice of the peace of Albany City and County.

Like the Albany patricians, the Jessup brothers saw the future in investing in lands beyond the city. Their first investment was in a farm on the Hudson at Fort Miller, but it soured and they sold it by 1771, just as Duer was beginning to make an impression there.[42] To contain speculators in New York, the crown had placed limitations on the amount of land an individual could purchase, so the Jessups had to recruit fourteen to fifteen associates to invest jointly in land speculation, including leading New York City merchants like Isaac Low. Three years earlier, as representatives of this association, the brothers had purchased two tracts, where the Sacandaga River flowed into the Hudson, totaling 40,000 acres. They called the ferry site on the Hudson Jessups Landing, and it became the center of their real estate empire. The land they held also technically belonged to the Mohawks, and in 1771 the Jessups visited Sir William Johnson with a map of the grant and requested that the Indians sell it so they could obtain a certificate of permission. Acting as an agent for the Mohawks, Johnson was cooperative and set a price, but despite the growing friendship, in an economy where cash was scarce the Jessups never had enough to meet the price. Furthermore, many of their associates complained about the quality of the land in the townships and were uncooperative.

Regardless, the Jessups were able to build a hunting lodge at Jessups Landing in 1772, surveyed town lots around it to be distributed to the members of the association, and referred to it as "Jessupborough." The lodge may have been more than a cabin, for it was described as "magnificently and tastefully furnished, boasting costly paintings and engravings, fine linen, and massive plate."[43] Five years later the brothers claimed to own more than 100,000 acres, and their seasonal residence at Jessups Landing and efforts to prepare it for settlement shows them to be more interested in actual settlement than the usual speculator. From the standpoint of the Saratoga Campaign, the chief role of the Landing would be as a way station for Loyalists on the move. Ebenezer and Edward would spend the Saratoga Campaign with Burgoyne's army.

Stillwater

Below the Argyle Patent and Schuyler's Saratoga plantation on the Hudson was Stillwater, technically an Albany County district that stretched inland to Saratoga Lake. It was a goal for Burgoyne's army that he would come close to but never reach. Stillwater developed with a diversity of settlers and religious convictions. In 1762 John Bemis had established a tavern at the bottom of Bemis Heights, a place that would play a crucial role in the Battles of Saratoga. On the heights themselves, in 1775 John Neilson leased 150 acres of land and soon built a small frame house. He had come to Stillwater three years earlier, working the farm of Abner Quitterfield, and when he left for Bemis Heights, his new wife was Lydia, Abner's daughter. [44]

A newcomer to Stillwater in 1774 was retired captain Daniel McAlpin of the 60th Royal American Regiment, who had purchased 1,000 acres on the west side of Saratoga Lake and begun to improve it.[45] He built a log-planked house in 1775 and another a year later, and by the summer of 1777 he had 170 acres in cultivation, employing as many as twenty-nine indentured servants. He had hundreds of bushels of wheat in his barn, a substantial number of stock, and valuable furniture within the houses. McAlpin also had land beyond his home farm, in 1775 purchasing 125 acres from the Jessup brothers. McAlpin's extensive farm shows that land a considerable distance from the Hudson River was now being developed.

Cambridge's Diverse Development

Southeast of Stillwater, Cambridge in 1777 would be Lieutenant Colonel Friedrich Baum's most important stop before he reached the Walloomsac River, where he would attempt to pacify the inhabitants, who were much divided. The Cambridge Patent, held by several New York City speculators, had initially been settled from 1761 to 1763, each of thirty families receiving a hundred acres from the patentees.[46] The families settled in dispersed farms, rather than in a village, tending at first to spread out along the Owl Kill. Cambridge remained part of Albany County, and in 1772 it was named a military district of the county.

Many of the first settlers were originally immigrants from Scotland and Ulster who had settled in Massachusetts and Connecticut. From Coleraine in north-central Massachusetts came some Scots-Irish, who because of Indians had found Coleraine too difficult and dangerous for planting and harvesting crops, and because of the established Congregational Church had lacked freedom to worship in the way they had in Ireland. [47] Faced with this bleak future in Coleraine, they decided to move to the Cambridge Patent, and in 1775 they were led there by Major James Cowden and Colonel Absalom Blair. Thus, New England proved to be the source of Cambridge's Scots-Irish settlers.

Four other Cambridge settlers—Phineas Whiteside, George Gilmore, Simeon Covel, and John Younglove—of Scots-Irish origin would involve themselves in politics. While of the same ethnic background, the politics of the four men form no pattern. Whiteside was born in County Tyrone, Ulster, in 1716, where he was brought up as a Presbyterian and initially settled in Lancaster County, Pennsylvania.[48] In 1766 he purchased eight hundred acres in the Cambridge Patent southeast of Cambridge center and leased six hundred more. He prospered so much that he was able to provide each of his many sons with a two hundred-acre farm. George Gilmore had also come from Ulster, immigrating in 1774 or 1775 and settling on a farm between Cambridge and Coila. Soon his farm produced several hundred bushels of wheat annually, of which some was taken by Lieutenant Colonel Baum. Simeon Covel was the first supervisor of the town in 1774 and 1775, and as such he was delegated to carry the early town meeting inquiries to the provincial legislatures. The town meetings were held at his house in the White Creek area, which was then part of Cambridge. He would become Cambridge's most renowned Loyalist, a captain in the Queen's Loyal Rangers. The other settler, and a Presbyterian, was John Younglove, who before 1775 established a farm east of Waite's Corners, also in the White Creek area. He would become Cambridge's most important rebel leader during the War of Independence.

Methodists in the Camden Valley

Irish Methodists were convinced by James Duane to settle in the Camden Valley. Their origins were as Palatines, Calvinist and Lutheran refugees who had been driven from their homeland in Germany in 1709 and were welcomed by Queen Anne to the British Isles to strengthen Protestantism. While some immigrated to New York at that time, many choose to settle in Ireland on the estates of Protestant gentry like that of Sir Thomas Southwell near Limerick, where they were exposed to rising Methodism.[49] After a generation in Ireland in the 1760s, the Methodist families of Philip Embury, Paul Heck, Peter Miller, and others left Southwell and immigrated to New York City.

By 1768 Philip Embury had become the pastor of the city's John Street Methodist Church. However, he was seeking a place outside the city to develop a purely Methodist community. He already held a patent near the Camden Valley, and he found the valley an ideal for his community. The Southwell immigrants, along with Edward Carscallen's family, left the city and came to the valley in 1770, where their settlement flourished with subsistence farming.[50] Unfortunately,

Embury was not up to the rigors of farming; while haying in 1773, he died of overheating at the age of forty-five.

After Embury's passing, Edward Carscallen became one of the leaders of the Camden Valley Methodists. He was a Scots-Irish soldier who had been stationed in Ireland at Althorne near Southwell and may have known the Irish Palatines. In 1756 he had been ordered, with his wife, Elizabeth, to take ship to New York City and serve in the Seven Years' War. After twenty years of service in the British army, Carscallen was discharged in 1763. As a retired soldier and follower of Embury's Methodism, he developed a flourishing farm on the Batten Kill River of over three hundred acres, the second largest in the Camden Tract.[51] In his Loyalist Claim, he listed his possessions as one yoke of oxen, three horses, one yoke of steers, one cow, eleven hogs, utensils, clothes, furniture, and tools, identifying him as a substantial farmer. He needed his five sons—John, James, Luke, George, and Edward—and two daughters—Elizabeth and Ann—to run his farm.

Embury's Methodists were not alone in their development of the Camden Valley. In the summer of 1769, prosperous Thomas Ashton and his wife left Ireland, immigrating to New York City. Thomas was a Methodist, and like Embury he hoped to found a Methodist colony in New York.[52] To this end he purchased property in the Schermerhorn Patent, directly west of Duane's Camden Valley Tract, where Philip Embury, Edward Carscallen, and other Methodists were already settling. Thomas Ashton may have met Embury in Ireland or in New York City, when he was in charge of the Methodist mission.

Ashton established his settlement of Ashgrove in the Camden Valley, while Embury had taken a farm a few miles away, so the two new friends created what they called a "Christian neighbourhood."[53] In 1770 Embury was the preacher and class leader, while Ashton was the steward and leading layman, in what was the first Methodist church north of New York City. Later Thomas's brother James joined him at Ashgrove, but he was not as devoted a Methodist as his brother. When war came in 1775, Camden Valley Methodists like Edward Carscallen, Andrew Embury, Dana Dulmage, Paul Heck, Philip Switzer, Valentine Detlor, and Peter Detlor were Loyalists, since Methodism was still a reform within the Anglican Church and their English guiding light, John Wesley, supported the king.

Walloomsac Bridge

At the hamlet at Walloomsac River bridge in northeastern Albany County, the family farms in 1777 belonged to Obadiah Beardsley, Hazard Wilcox, and the Widow Whipple.[54] The farms must have been settled in the late 1760s, when log cabins were built with second-floor lofts. By 1777 there were four outbuildings between the families, probably their barns. Beardsley's farm was family run, with a wife and two half-grown sons, who were in charge of taking the cows to pasture. He also claimed six oxen, although they may have been owned jointly with his neighbors. Beardsley was a pacifist who had strenuously avoided military service in the Seven Years' War and would hold these views in the War of Independence. Wilcox was perhaps the richest of the three, and he must have farmed with slaves or hired labor. He would become a notorious Loyalist organizer. Very little is known about the Widow Whipple, except that her house would be burned in the Battle of Walloomsac, the only structural casualty of the three. Such was the makeup of this ordinary hamlet that for a day in August 1777 would be the center of military conflict.

Resettlement of the Hoosic Valley

The city of Albany had held a land reserve on the Hoosic River since the early eighteenth century, acting as a landlord.[55] On the northern border of the Van Rensselaer manor, the Hoosic River valley had been settled in the 1720s by Albany Dutch plebeians, who, however, were driven out when Canadian raiders burned the area in 1746 and 1754. Still, a few settlers held on tenaciously through the Seven Years' War. The Hoosic settlers were not among the leading Dutch patricians but rather from families in the city's middle class, lured by the possibilities of having a farm without manorial obligations.

The area south of the Hoosic River and above Rensselaerswyck attracted newcomers like Francis Pfister, originally from Braunschweig, Germany.[56] Similar to Skene in Skenesborough or McAlpin in Stillwater, Pfister was a former British officer, specifically in the king's 60th Regiment, having risen from ensign to engineer. During the Seven Years' War, this unit had been organized and commanded by British officers, but the men were raised in the colonies. A surprising number of Burgoyne's regular and Loyalist officers in the Saratoga Campaign had originally served in this most American of British regiments. Pfister participated in Jeffery Amherst's expedition against Canada in 1760 and worked on the defenses of Fort Stanwix two years later. While on half-pay in the 1760s, he spent time at Johnson Hall, helping Sir William Johnson with Indian relations. Pfister and other reduced British soldiers must have taken advantage of the Royal Proclamation of October 1763 that offered land to discharged soldiers in the upper Hudson Valley. War veterans were entitled to free land on a graduated scale according to rank: 50 acres for privates, up to 5,000 acres for those with the rank of major or above.

In 1766 Pfister purchased a land grant with New York City speculator James Duane, checking with William Johnson to see if Indian claims existed so they would not cloud the title.[57] Evidently they did not, and Pfister occupied the patent of 1,275 acres at Nepimore Vale, a stream that runs into the Hoosic River near Johnsonville. The area contained stands of pine that were harvested for naval lumber, staves, and shingles, and thus it was referred to as Shingle Hollow. His house was commodious and unusual in that it was painted white, an expensive color that was regarded as gaudy. Pfister spoke German, and many of his nearby friends were Brunswicker or Palatine German settlers, who lived in or close to the eastern corner of the Van Rensselaer manor.

Pfister married Anne, the daughter of merchant and county judge John Macomb of Albany. His father-in-law was also a nearby developer of a country estate in Hoosic. He was Scots-Irish, once a Belfast merchant, and had decided to follow army contracts to New York during the Seven Years' War. With his wife, Jane, his two young sons and Anne, Macomb had embarked from Belfast for New York City. He had settled in Albany, which during the war was the hub for expeditions against the French in Canada. Macomb could provide British and provincial officers with luxury goods, wines, books, and snuff, as well as procure a good mistress—if it was their desire. However, as a Scots-Irish merchant he was discriminated against by Dutch patricians, who included the Schuylers and Ten Broecks, who assessed him at a higher tax rate than for comparable patrician merchants. He complained, "Ever since we came here we have been charged double our proportion of all public charges."[58] When he inquired as to why his charges were so high, he was told there was no possibility of redress. Nonetheless, despite patrician hostility he prospered, putting his profits into the development of his Hoosic estate. In 1766, however, Albany's own Liberty Boys, a group of colonists who rebelled against the British, led the protest and prevented him from taking the post of agent for the revenues of the Stamp Act. When the War of Independence came, both Pfister and Macomb would be Loyalists.

Much of the Hudson-Champlain region had become a developed area in the decade after the Seven Years' War, and by 1777 Burgoyne's soldiers saw the area north of Albany as a land of milk and honey. Settlers came from three sources: the Hudson Valley, New York City, and New England. New York was divided by landlord patents, even though the terms sometimes approached fee simple ownership. Landlords like the Van Rensselaer, Schuyler, Johnson, and Skene families were responsible for large-scale development by offering terms that attracted New York's many immigrants. Tenants, however, were a substantial minority of the population, and where they were lacking, especially along the Hudson River, black slaves did much of the fieldwork. Land tenure was confusing and landlordism was ever present, as even the City of Albany acted as a landlord in the Hoosic Valley. Settlers needed the help of a landlord to develop farms, meaning that land ownership in fee simple was only desirable for some. Many Presbyterian Scots-Irish migrants, like those from Coleraine, had already settled in Massachusetts, but were restless because of the authority of the Congregational Church and the lack of fertile land, so that New York offered an improvement in their condition. Diversity certainly describes the nature of settlement of the Hudson-Champlain region, and one must look closely at each community to identify what conditions led it to react to an invading army.

2

SETTLEMENT OF THE GRANTS
A Cause of Discord with New York

The towns of the New Hampshire Grants were settled at the same time as the patents of New York, and they contributed to the settlement of the Hudson-Champlain region. Although the name implies that New Hampshire was the source of settlers, in fact the Grants, especially in the Hudson-Champlain valley, were populated chiefly by people from Massachusetts and Connecticut, which is where the bulk of the rebel Continentals and militia that would fight in the Battles of Saratoga would come from. The Grants were an area north of Williamstown, Massachusetts, that before the War of Independence was claimed by New Hampshire, New York, and Massachusetts. While the crown eventually awarded the area to New York, its jurisdiction was never secure.

As early as 1749, Benning Wentworth, the governor of New Hampshire, had begun laying out town grants in the disputed territory.[1] He named each town, set aside lots for the Anglican Society for the Propagation of the Gospel, and reserved lots for himself, making a profit when groups of proprietors purchased the land. He knew very well that the area was disputed territory and admitted from the beginning that his grants would be void if the crown decided against them. He also ignored his instructions from the crown on his appointment as governor, which required that he grant no lands until fifty families were ready to begin settlement and which prevented a township from exercising its privileges until one hundred families were settled. The

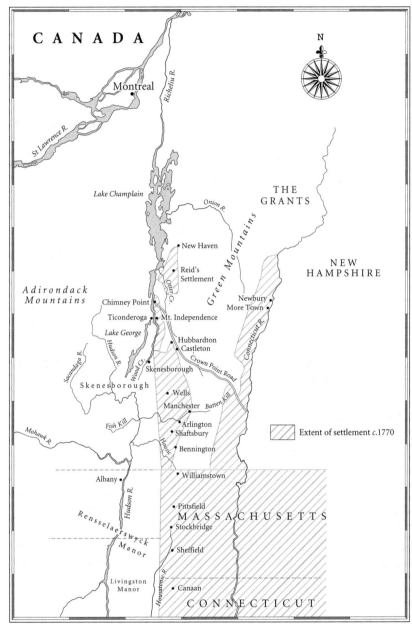

The Grants and Western New England. Extent of settlement in New England, c. 1770

crown also forbade him to make large grants to proprietors who were
not going to settle the land. Regardless, Wentworth enjoyed making
a tidy sum by awarding grants to groups of investors, friends, and relatives, not bothering himself as to whether the grants were actually
cultivated and settled. As a result, by 1764 the Grants contained
many acres of ungranted land, and most of the land granted to proprietors had not been developed. It has been estimated that in that
year no more than 2 percent of what became Vermont had actually
been settled.[2]

In April 1765 Wentworth finally admitted that his grants were
in jeopardy because the territory belonged to New York. The year before,
the Board of Trade in London had recommended to the crown that
New York's claim over the Grants territory was best, setting the
Connecticut River as the boundary between New York and New
Hampshire.[3] The legality of Wentworth's New Hampshire grants was
now in question, and clearly the people who held them were upset.

It became crucial as to how New York would handle this situation. If New York recognized the existing Wentworth grant titles—
and it appeared that that was going to happen—would the confirmation
of the deeds be an opportunity for New York to charge an additional
fee?[4] Also, would actual settlement of land play a role in a dispute
over land titles because only a minimal number of grants could claim
that? Governor Cadwallader Colden and the Council of New York
responded that occupants of land granted by New Hampshire who
settled before May 22, 1765, would be favored in disputes over the
titles. While New York wanted to confirm these grants, confirmation could not be issued because the distribution of stamps to vali-
date the documents had been prevented. In opposition to the Stamp
Act as a tax, New York City's Liberty Boys destroyed the stamps.
The king's role in settling the dispute became crucial, as most Grants
leaders and towns petitioned him directly to avoid New York authorities and gain favorable confirmation terms. In 1771, for example, 185
male heads of household in the town of Pownal petitioned George III,
asking that their grants be recognized without any additional fees.

Before it became clear that the New Hampshire Grants belonged to
New York, some settlements had been made under Wentworth's grants.
The accounts of settlement are varied, as in New York, and empha-
sis will be on the towns that would figure in Burgoyne's invasion.

ARLINGTON

Located on the Batten Kill River, Arlington was settled in 1764 by families that knew each other before they left three western Connecticut hill towns: Newtown, New Milford, and Woodbury.[5] These upland towns had less agricultural productivity and commercial enterprise than the more populous towns of Long Island Sound and the Connecticut River Valley, and a corresponding decline in available land made it difficult for fathers to perform the duty of settling farms upon their sons. In 1760 Newtown and New Milford families began to look for a new town site, and they eventually decided upon the newly surveyed town of Arlington in the New Hampshire Grants.[6] The land was located on the banks of the Batten Kill River, a stream that began in the Green Mountains at East Dorset and then flowed to Arlington, where it abruptly bent to the west and entered New York on its way to the Hudson River.

The Newtown and New Milford families did not deal with Governor Wentworth, instead purchasing titles from numerous proprietors, who saw a Grants township as an investment. The Searls—Isaac, John, William, and Gideon—proprietors and land speculators in Williamstown, Massachusetts, had laid out Arlington as a town in 1762.[7] They offered two lots of one hundred acres each to sixty-six proprietors that included, as required, lots for Governor Benning Wentworth of New Hampshire and members of his family. Each proprietor was to provide $400 in cash toward the cost of laying out the town. The Searls were chiefly interested in encouraging the sale of land in Arlington; only one, William's son, William, Jr., actually settled in Arlington in the 1770s. Thus, the first Connecticut families purchased lots from the proprietors and traveled from Newtown and New Milford to Arlington in 1763, to be followed the next year by a second wave. Some returned from clearing land in Arlington to winter in Connecticut, and permanent settlement was not achieved until the late 1760s.

Those Connecticut families that bought lots in Arlington were already part of a kinship network, consisting of Hawleys, Briscos, Hards, Canfields, and others.[8] Focus is on the Hawley family, headed by Jehiel Hawley, but other related families play a supporting role based on their intermarriage with the Hawleys. The Hawleys must have known other Vermont settlers in Connecticut—like the Warners, Bakers, and Allens. Jehiel's brother Josiah married Hannah Warner of Woodbury, the daughter of Benjamin Warner and eldest sister of Seth Warner, the future Green Mountain Boy. The Warner and Baker families of Woodbury were intermarried in the late 1730s and early 1740s, producing not only Seth Warner but his first cousin, Ethan Allen, and another cousin, Remember Baker.[9] When the Allens resided near Woodbury, eight miles from New Milford, they visited their relatives, and Ethan's father, Joseph, may have attended Woodbury's Anglican Christ Church, where Ethan was probably married to Mary Brownson in 1762. The Hawleys also favored this church. In 1764 Remember Baker responded to an Arlington Proprietor's Meeting notice, which offered land in exchange for establishing needed saw- and gristmills in the new settlement. Future Green Mountain Boys like Warner, Baker, and Allen came to be on the edge of the Hawley kinship network.

The patriarch of the Hawleys, Jehiel, was born in 1712 and raised in Newtown.[10] Twenty years later, having married Sarah Dunning in Litchfield, he moved to New Milford, Connecticut, where all of his children were born and he became a leading citizen. In 1764, at the age of fifty-two, he led his extended family and kin to Arlington. With him came Abra (his second wife), his ten children, his father Ephraim—age seventy-three—and three of his brothers, Abel, Josiah, and Gideon, with their families. Jehiel Hawley would remain as influential in Arlington as he had been in Connecticut.

As a patriarch, deference to Jehiel was shown in that he was addressed as "captain," a title of respect from his early years in the Connecticut militia. On Sundays Jehiel held Anglican worship services in his homestead. In May 1764 he was elected moderator of Arlington's proprietors' meeting, which then consisted of seven settlers (including his son Andrew) in Arlington and an equal number from neighboring Sunderland. He was charged with "the care of the public rights."[11] A year later the town sent him to Boston and Portsmouth, New Hampshire, to purchase the shares of the remaining absentee proprietors, who had no intention of settling in Arlington. Now most of the town property could be locally owned.

Through his purchase of land from William Searls, Jehiel was a New Hampshire grantee. His Arlington grants totaled 3,000 acres, making him one of the area's chief landowners. He wanted to develop it primarily in terms of prosperous farms and mills, for he was not a speculator. His farms were managed by his middle son, Jeptha, who kept a "flax book" of the family's dealings.[12] Routine household enterprises included the drying and salting of meat, the sawing of oak and pine boards, the tanning of moose skin, and the manufacture of potash to trade in the Arlington area. In his twenties and early thirties, Jeptha developed a separate farm of 250 acres, which Jehiel provided for him in "Considn of Love & Affection."[13] By 1775 Jeptha had cleared 90 acres, built and furnished a frame house and barn, raised a stock of cattle and horses, and purchased farming implements. What set him off, as a well-to-do-farmer, was his ox team, providing the animal power that allowed him to clear and farm so much land. He not only used his team in his own fields, he rented it out to neighbors to pay family debts and earn extra income. Clearly, the oxen made the Hawleys serious farmers.

Families like the Hawleys of Arlington had farms developed well beyond the hardscrabble stage of their neighbors. They not only exploited the forest but succeeded in clearing enough land to be successful farmers. Their work routine was on a seasonal basis of spring planting, summer cultivation, and fall harvesting and milling. They had oxen to support their enterprises. The Hawleys harvested corn, oats, rye, wheat, hay, potatoes, turnips, and flax.[14] From the heading of Jeptha Hawley's book it appears this last crop was important because it was a chief source of homespun textiles. The difficulty of transport, however, prevented flax from being a staple like wheat and flour were in the Hudson Valley. The Hawleys created a farm that was more productive than most in Arlington, exchanging their produce and skills locally, using their family skills and labor, along with the mutual help of their neighbors.

The Settlement of Bennington

To the south of Arlington, the village of Bennington was established in 1761 as a religious sanctuary—a "Republic of Saints." By the time of the War of Independence, a British regular described Bennington as "the first place that we have met in [Vermont] that has the least appearance of a town. It consists of a meeting house . . . and 12 or 14 dwelling houses. In England it would scarcely be entitled to the name of village."[15] For the Grants, Bennington was large, but it did not compare with Albany or Schenectady; it was more comparable to Saratoga Plantation, Skenesborough, Salem, or Arlington.

The guiding light in the settlement of Bennington was Samuel Robinson, Sr. Born in 1707 in Cambridge, Massachusetts, by 1721 he had gravitated westward to Worcester County, where he became a carpenter and house builder.[16] After marriage to Mary Leonard, he obtained land in Hardwick Township, where he was elected clerk and selectman, the beginning of an important political career. He was also a small-time speculator, holding more acres for sale than those covered by his farmstead.

In the 1730s Robinson became involved in the Separatist and New Light reform of the Congregational Church. By 1746 he and another future Bennington settler, John Fassett, Sr., were deacons of the Hardwick Congregational Church, but as Separatists they were secretly holding religious services on Robinson's farm.[17] They believed in an elect religious body made up of only those who had gone through an individual experience in which they were saved. This they doubted had happened to very many in the established Congregational Church or to its educated ministry, and therefore they refused to attend or financially support the established church. They petitioned the local Congregational authorities and then the General Court, asking that they be exempt from support of the established church. In both cases they were rejected and threatened with confiscation of their property and a term in jail if they failed to pay support for the church. Under such conditions, Robinson, Fassett and the other Separatists decided to look for a place where they could practice their demanding, disciplined, and elitist faith.

Robinson had already been to the Hudson-Champlain region during the Seven Years' War. He had served under Hardwick's Brigadier General Timothy Ruggles at the Battle of Lake George in 1755, raised troops to break the siege of Fort William Henry two years later, participated in General James Abercromby's debacle at Ticonderoga in 1758, and a year later been at Amherst's capture of the same post.[18] Robinson, Fassett, and other Separatists were able to purchase the Township of Bennington from its numerous proprietors, who were also land speculators in their own right. Robinson's land right came from wealthy proprietor Sir William Pepperell of New Hampshire, the famed conqueror of Louisbourg in 1745. The other major proprietors belonged to the Williams family of Hampshire County, Massachusetts, who dominated the Connecticut River Valley to the extent that they were known as the River Gods.

After several exploratory trips were made to Bennington, in June 1761 Robinson led families from Hardwick to Bennington, establishing Vermont's first permanent settlement.[19] Over the next years, the new settlers cultivated land along the Walloomsac River and several drained ponds. The proprietors' investment meetings gradually gave way to town government, and Robinson became moderator of the town meeting. In 1764 the Bennington militia was formed, with John Fassett, Sr., as captain and James Breakenridge as lieutenant.

That same year Samuel Robinson was appointed a justice of the peace by the New Hampshire Assembly, and he rode with friends who had purchased land in Governor Wentworth's town of Pownal to drive out settlers with New York titles.[20] Dutch families like Hans Jurry Creiger's had come to Pownal in the 1730s and lived in the Hoosic Valley for decades under New York's Walloomsac Patent, which had been confirmed in 1664. On August 3 Robinson and his party arrived and expelled Creiger and his family from their farm, seizing his Indian corn and cattle. This was followed by ejections of the families of Peter Voss and Bastian Deal from their Hoosic Valley farms. The arrival of the sheriff of Albany County with two New York justices of the peace and thirty men put an end to their depredations, and Robinson and his colleagues were arrested and escorted to Albany, where they were placed in jail. Governor Wentworth of New Hampshire protested, but his action was for show; he knew that he had caused this situation and had simply been feathering his own nest. Robinson was released on bail, and for the first time he must have realized that he had been bamboozled by Wentworth and that his and other Bennington land titles might be worthless. Robinson would spend the rest of his life shoring up the claims of New Hampshire grantees like himself.

SHAFTSBURY AND NEW HAVEN

With Arlington and Bennington established, the area between the Batten Kill and Walloomsac Rivers was ready for settlement, and Shaftsbury first drew settlers there in 1767. These included the Bothums, Elijah and Dorothy and their five children—Dorothy, Sarah, Elijah, Jr., Simon, and Lemuel—all Baptists from Norwich, Connecticut.[21] Elijah's New Hampshire grant was in the hills, a difficult area for cultivation, but he developed a farm known for the quality of its sheep.

In the winter of 1771–72, another Connecticut immigrant, Justus Sherwood, bought a hundred-acre New Hampshire grant, north of

Arlington, in Sunderland. Born in 1747, Justus had lived in Stratford and then Newtown, Connecticut, until he moved through Shaftsbury to Sunderland. [22] He was the nephew of Seth and Adiel Sherwood, who had recently settled in Fort Edward, New York. A twenty-five-year-old surveyor, Justus was determined to do well in the lumber and potash trade. He also began to court the Bothums' daughter Sarah, and early in 1774 they were married in Shaftsbury by a Baptist elder approved of by the Bothums. Moreover, from 1770 Justus was both allied with the Allen family and an active Green Mountain Boy, demonstrated by his participation in the rescue of Remember Baker from New York authorities.

Not long after his marriage, Justus Sherwood put a tenant on his Sunderland farm and purchased a New Hampshire grant in New Haven, ninety miles further north, near Otter Creek. With Sarah, his three slaves, and his cattle, he set out for his new grant. He raised a log house, and a son, Samuel, was born before the year was out. Justus was elected proprietors' clerk, responsible for keeping the town meeting records.[23] We see Justus as a Baptist, landlord, slaveholder, prosperous farmer, town clerk, and Green Mountain Boy, a combination that was exceptional among Grants settlers. Among the Green Mountain Boys, he distanced himself by accepting the necessity of the British closing the port of Boston because of the destructiveness of the Boston Tea Party. Here was a hint that he would become one of the region's leading Loyalists.

CASTLETON TO THE NORTH

North of Arlington, Manchester, and Dorset was strategically located Castleton, which would come to mark the northern frontier of Vermont's thin settlement. It was a small village established at an important crossroads, where a road along the Castleton River to Skenesborough and the older military road to Ticonderoga crossed. The town's New Hampshire grant was chartered in 1761, and its first settlers, Colonels Amos Bird and Noah Lee of Salisbury, Connecticut, arrived six years later.[24] Bird built a sawmill in 1772 at Castleton Falls, now Hydeville, but he died in the process, and the first boards sawn at the mill were, ironically, for his coffin. A gristmill was built the following year. Just outside of the village was Remington's Tavern, which would be the chief meeting place in the area. In 1770 there were only three families there, but in 1777 it was described by a German soldier as having "seventeen miserable houses," or perhaps thirty people. A majority of the houses in the Castleton area were described as incomplete, with "no partitions, glass windows or stoves." During Burgoyne's Campaign, Castleton would be the scene of a pacification meeting between Loyalists, neutrals, and rebels.

Lake Champlain, the Greatest Potential

The low, level, and fertile lands on both sides of 109-mile-long Lake Champlain offered great opportunities for settlement. The growing season of over 150 days was the longest in the Grants, a result of the protection of the Green Mountains, the low elevation, and the proximity to the lake.[25] The earliest settlement above Crown Point on the New York side came into being with William Gilliland, later named a justice of the peace for the entire Grants, and his tenants at the falls of the Bouquet River. Access to the lake had become much better in 1759, when General Jeffrey Amherst took Crown Point from the French and decided to build a military road from there all the way across the Green Mountains to the Connecticut River—an engineering feat typical of Amherst. John Stark commanded the road builders, who cut a path from Chimney Point toward Otter Creek, reaching it close to Brandon, then following the creek by Rutland, until the road moved eastward toward Fort no. 4 in New Hampshire. There is an indication of the Lake Champlain's potential productivity in 1779, when the Vermont Board of War ordered troops to the lake, which was now abandoned to the enemy, to secure or destroy the wheat and grain that was growing unattended on the edge of the lake.

However, distance from markets and controversy over land claims precluded significant settlement before 1777. Seven years earlier, Governor Wentworth had sold Ethan Allen a lot on the Onion River, a totally illegal transaction considering how the crown required him to distribute land.[26] Two years later, Ethan, three of his brothers, and Remember Baker had formed the Onion River Land Company and bought more land along the lake, hoping that the area would prosper as a route to Montreal. Their violent activities against holders of New York titles who had settled there led to the serious retardation of settlement along the lake. This was especially detrimental because the Allens and their company had very limited resources for settling and sustaining towns along the lake.

In protecting their titles, the Allens did not hesitate to destroy an Otter Creek settlement of the transplanted Scot John Reid, which had flourished briefly from 1769 until 1773. Reid had served in the Seven Year's War and risen to the rank of lieutenant colonel of the 42nd Royal Highland Regiment.[27] With Amherst in the campaign of 1759, he, like Philip Skene, had first seen the possibilities of land along Lake Champlain. His ties to the east side of Lake Champlain became closer in 1760 when, like William Duer, he married one of the five daughters of William Alexander, Lord Stirling, who was surveyor general of New York and New Jersey. Susana brought the Otter Creek property to John as part of her dowry, to which John added more land, the total patent coming to 50,000 acres. John now being retired, the development of this land became his pet project. What Reid did not know was that New Hampshire grantees had occasionally occupied some of the same land and had refurbished a sawmill constructed earlier on Otter Creek. This mill probably dated from Amherst's occupation of the area in August 1759, when his army was involved in the construction of the military road across the Green Mountains to the new fort at Crown Point. Amherst sent several parties to explore the creek in search of mill sites and "ordered three forts to be built there."

Reid visited and took up his land, including the sawmill and two houses he found unoccupied. He left Donald Macintosh as his agent to protect the property. True to the New York patent stipulation that he would settle the land, in 1769 Reid recruited and transported tenant families from New Jersey to Otter Creek.[28] They found a lone mill operator running the sawmill, and though Reid offered to buy the mill, the operator refused and left. Reid's settlement prospered for the next three years, until the summer of 1772, when a party of Green Mountain Boys under Seth Warner and Remember Baker used strong-arm tactics to drive out the tenants. Defensive, Ethan Allen claimed that a few Grants "inhabitants" had been terrified by Reid's efforts to settle the area and yet asserted that he had convinced a few of Reid's tenants to stay under a New Hampshire title. Reid, however, felt he had a clear title to the property, was making definite efforts to settle it with families, and had made every attempt to

The falls of Otter Creek, Lake Champlain, with a sawmill, 1766, by Thomas Davies. First erected by order of Jeffery Amherst, this probably was the mill burned down by the Green Mountain Boys in 1773 to prevent it from being used by Reid's Scottish settlers. Reproduced with permission of the Royal Ontario Museum © ROM.

deal fairly with the New Hampshire grantees on the land. He began recruiting another group of tenants to settle at Otter Creek.

In June 1773 several Scottish immigrants arrived in New York City, met with Reid, and agreed to settle on his Lake Champlain patent.[29] Reid stepped in and personally led a dozen Scottish families from Albany to settle on Otter Creek. When he and his tenants arrived, he found three of the Allens' representatives occupying what he felt was his land. They agreed to leave if Reid would purchase their crop for a full price, which he did. Reid provided cows and provisions for his tenants, fixed up the now dilapidated mill and existing houses, and with the plantation on its feet, he returned to New York City.

But Reid had not reckoned with the continuing hostility of the Green Mountain Boys. Barely had he left in August, when Ethan Allen, Remember Baker, and Seth Warner arrived with over a hundred Green Mountain Boys and threatened to skin the Scottish families alive.[30] The Scots offered to settle the dispute honorably by meeting the intruders with broadswords, but Baker declined, for his followers knew only bush fighting. The Green Mountain Boys evicted the tenants, burned the mill and broke the stone, fired six houses and all the crops, and drove off the livestock. Allen stated that New York had no authority at Otter Creek; the only authority was his as "captain of that mob." Allen preserved his title, and thus Lake Champlain remained an area of a few widely dispersed seasonal mills and houses.

The Green Mountain Boys: Continuing Violence

In the controversy over conflicting land titles in the Grants, the case of Charles Hutchinson is typical. He had served as a corporal in Montgomery's Highland Regiment during the Seven Years' War and had seen the fertility of the land north of Albany. With the peace, Hutchinson settled in Hebron, New York, where he farmed his two hundred-acre New York grant. On October 29, 1771, he was one of the first victims of the violence that challenged New York's land titles.[31] He had built a log house and was working on the farm when nine armed Green Mountain Boys—including Ethan Allen, Remember Baker, and Robert Cochran—seized him, burned his home, cursed New York's governor and council, cursed the king, and ordered him to get off his grant. They added that they would kill any constable who came after them. Cochran claimed that Hutchinson was trespassing on his New Hampshire grant in Rupert, where he had begun minor improvements, though in reality Hutchinson's land was immediately adjacent to, not on, Cochran's grant. Other New York grantees may have settled on Cochran's land, but he choose to drive out Hutchinson because he had cleared considerable acreage and his farm was flourishing. Niceties, such as who could improve land the best, did not impress the Green Mountain Boys, who were most concerned to protect their New Hampshire titles.

Hutchinson was also not the first to be shocked that Allen "Denys the Being of a God," asserting that it was Allen's hedonism that made him so destructive.[32] The Hutchinsons and eight other evicted families fled to Salem. Alexander McNaughton of Argyle issued a warrant for Allen's arrest and delivered it to Constable John Reid, ordering him to raise a posse and proceed to Rupert and arrest the culprits, but Reid failed to put the posse together. Governor Tryon and his council declared Allen, Baker, Cochran, and the others outlaws and offered a reward for their arrest. This event was one of many in the violent conflict over land titles between New York and the Grants that began in the late 1760s.

Hutchinson was not aware of it, but the Green Mountain Boys had been established in Bennington in 1770, when nearly one hundred New Hampshire grantees came together and resolved to form a paramilitary force to resist New York's court orders and Grants settlers who held New York titles.[33] Members of the group were dispersed in the western part of the Grants, radiating from Bennington north to Shaftsbury, Arlington, and Sunderland. While the Green Mountain Boys often carried weapons, they were never a formal military unit, operating like an illegal police force, usually succeeding by using intimidation rather than outright bloodshed. Still, there is no question that they often destroyed property and humiliated their victims. Their enemies viewed them as an anarchistic mob, and they appeared to enjoy and perpetuate that image.

Ethan Allen was the undisputed leader of the Green Mountain Boys. He was born in 1738 to Joseph and Mary Baker Allen in Litchfield County, Connecticut.[34] He grew up mostly in Cornwall, a town of stony soil that his father had helped to found. When Ethan was seventeen, his father died, and he became head of a family consisting of his mother, six brothers, and two sisters. Over the next dozen years he ran iron and lead mines, tried subsistence farming, and speculated in land, but was a failure at all of them. Over six feet tall, he was reputedly of stocky build, although no actual likeness of him was ever made. Ethan married Mary Brownson, a pious woman who did not appreciate his emerging deism. Nor were his views appreciated by the inhabitants of Northampton, Massachusetts, who warned him out for conducting boisterous religious disputes in a tavern. He quickly went through Mary's inheritance, leaving her destitute to support their three children because he often left home to hunt and trap in the Grants. She and the children were taken care of by Ethan's brother Zimri at his farm in Sheffield, Massachusetts. Finally she went to live with her brothers, the Brownsons of Sunderland, north of Arlington.

Allen was no settler. He came to the Grants to establish a fur trade, a hope that was dashed by the lack of fur-bearing animals. He began to move there anyway, alternating between a family home in Salisbury, Connecticut, and Bennington, where he rented sporadically from 1769 to 1775.[35] As noted, in 1770 he started buying land in the Grants, and two years later, he, three of his brothers—Ira, Heman, and Zimri—and cousin Remember Baker formed the Onion River Land Company to speculate in the northern Champlain Valley. Within two years, largely using credit, the company had acquired more than one hundred square miles of land near the lake. In June 1770, when holders of New Hampshire grants faced the Albany ejectment trials, the speculating proprietors of Connecticut hired Ethan Allen to defend their land titles in court. No attorney, Allen lost the case in the New York courts. Thus, Allen entered politics as a land speculator concerned to defend New Hampshire land titles.

Ethan Allen was a master at organizing an ad hoc movement, to which he applied his considerable skills as an orator and stamina that allowed him travel constantly for a cause.[36] While he sought a military command, he was really not cut out for such a job; his temperament was too undisciplined and volatile, and he never became a Continental officer. Allen and his Green Mountain Boys operated outside of existing authorities like town government and even the emerging rebel committees of safety. While he resided in Bennington and used it as his base of operations, he held no town offices and was not supported by Bennington's town leaders. The meetings he called were spontaneous and made up usually of his relatives and friends, not within the framework of any existing government.

One of Allen's followers, Seth Warner, would play a greater role than he in defending the Grants during the Burgoyne Campaign. In 1763, at the age of twenty, Warner had come with his parents from Connecticut to settle in North Bennington among the Separatist Congregationalists.[37] While his father was a physician and probably provided him with the basics of reading and writing, he appears to have had no formal education. Like Ethan Allen, as a young man he loved to hunt. But he was always portrayed as being level headed, in contrast to the volatile Allen.

Warner was an active Green Mountain Boy. In August 1771 he led the group to the home of a New York grantee living near Bennington, calling the farmer and his family outside their house, which his followers then pulled down.[38] A year later, at his own expense, Warner formed a paramilitary group based in Bennington that supported the Green Mountain Boys. Warner's "army" held several public reviews, which were reputedly meant to overawe Benningtonians. His "army" was completely separate from Bennington's militia company, which was commanded by John Fassett, Sr., the original settler and Congregational Separatist. Warner was the only prominent Green Mountain Boy who did appear on the Bennington tax lists as a resident. Although he may not have been a successful farmer, he even held some minor town offices.

Warner was soon participating in a series of Green Mountain Boy incidents. In March 1772 he rode to New York Sheriff John Munro's House in Shaftsbury, and when Munro tried to take him, he knocked Munro down.[39] Five months later Warner was amongst those who drove John Reid's Scottish settlers from Otter Creek, and in the next year he was a "judge" at the trials of New York appointed justices of the peace Benjamin Spencer and Jacob Marsh. Spencer was accused of "cuddling with the land-jobbers of New York" and was forced to recognize the titles of New Hampshire grantees when "the court" threatened to burn down his house. Unlike the Allen brothers, Warner was not a land speculator. During the War of Independence, the Vermont legislature awarded him land for his outstanding service in the Continental army, but it led to nothing because it was inaccessible and of such poor quality that it was almost worthless.

CONCERN OVER VIOLENCE

The title of Bennington Mob was given to the Green Mountain Boys by New Yorkers who wanted to emphasize the group's violence.[40] However, New Yorkers were not really in a position to know how and where the violence was organized. Despite Bennington's reputation as the home of the Green Mountain Boys and mob rule, the community's leaders tried to distance themselves from a reputation for anarchy.

The Bennington Committee of Safety was formed in 1772 and would create policies independent of Allen's paramilitary organization and use of violence. The committee took on the role of negotiating for the Grants with New York. Members were John Fassett, Sr., Robinson's sons—Samuel, Jr., and Moses—Samuel Safford, Simon Hathaway, Henry and Ebenezer Walbridge, and Jonas Fay.[41] Clearly Robinson's sons continued their father's perspective and none of the members were associated with Green Mountain Boy activities. Jonas Fay's family was among the Separatists who came from Hardwick, Massachusetts, to settle in Bennington, and Fay would never be a favorite of the Allens. A physician, Fay did eventually work with Ethan Allen as the clerk of the early conventions, and eventually he was secretary of the Constitutional Convention of 1777.

The Bennington Committee of Safety was open to peacefully settling the Grants controversy with New York. In June 1772 they sent Jonas Fay and his father, Stephen, to meet with Governor William Tryon in New York City.[42] They were cordially received, and a truce between the two sides was formulated. Tryon agreed to follow the crown's stipulations in bending over backwards to accept New Hampshire grants that were actually settled. New proprietors were to take this stipulation into account in any claims they made. The Fays told the governor plainly that the existing proprietors could not afford to pay any fee to transfer their grants.

A truce was put into effect, but it lasted only two months because Allen was completely against the Bennington accommodation effort. In writing to Governor Tryon in August, Allen claimed that the Fays were only messengers, "not authorized to . . . complete articles of public faith for their constituents."[43] And while Allen admitted that at a public meeting in Bennington on July 15 the truce was recognized and "a sacred bond of friendship formed," all this was thrown over, he claimed, because of a report that a New York surveyor was laying out lots in the northern Grants. The real problem was that Allen had no part in these negotiations because he little influence with the Bennington Committee of Safety. In fact, it is unclear as to what group Allen represented in writing to Tryon. Allen went ahead with his program of paramilitary violence to make sure the truce would be broken. The Allen family were speculators, after all, and they never accepted the concept that land had to be permanently settled to meet the obligations of a grant. Crucially, Ethan Allen broke with the Fays and the Bennington Committee of Safety by opposing peaceful negotiations.

PROTEST IN ARLINGTON

Other Grants leaders supported the compromising effort of the Bennington Committee of Safety. Jehiel Hawley, the prominent Arlington patriarch, could not avoid being drawn into the Grants controversy with New York. He had political experience in Connecticut, where he had served as New Milford's representative in the General Assembly.[44] He also had the makings of a Green Mountain Boy, for he was threatened by New York's assertion that his 3,000 acres of New Hampshire grants were worthless and he had ties to Seth Warner's extended family. Yet he was not to be associated with the anarchy and violence that had become the favored tactic of the Green Mountain Boys.

In the 1760s and 1770s, several incidents establish Hawley's perspective on the Grants controversy. In 1765 Hawley, like Robinson, entertained James Duane on his inspection of his property in the Grants. Through New York's Princeton Patent, Duane claimed to own most of the land in the Arlington area, including Hawley's own property. He was sympathetic with Hawley's plight as a New Hampshire grantee, promising him that his improved property could be sold or leased to him under a New York claim.[45] Duane, however, could not eliminate a New York fee for confirmation of New Hampshire titles, which upset Hawley. In 1769 Hawley represented Arlington by signing a petition to Governor Benning Wentworth of New Hampshire that condemned ejection suits coming from New York courts, which Hawley felt were driving New Hampshire grantees from their land.

Hawley wanted confirmation of New Hampshire titles like his own, though he was willing to accept the jurisdiction of New York if its legislature would confirm them with a more reasonable fee. In

October 1772 he and James Breckenridge were elected by the proprietors to take a ship to London and present a petition to the Privy Council to convince them that the region favored the jurisdiction of New Hampshire over New York's claims.[46] But Jehiel apparently did not go. Instead, he tried to resolve the problem locally in a compromise with New York. He wrote Philip Skene, the landlord developer of Skenesborough, saying he favored recognition of Skene's own claims by New York. He also played to Skene by suggesting that Skenesborough was the best trade center and place for the county seat of newly designated Charlotte County. Lastly, he warned Skene about the increasing violence of the Green Mountain Boys headed by Ethan Allen.

Allen's violent action reached Arlington, when some Hawleys acted as Green Mountain Boys to support their New Hampshire grants. Remember Baker, the first cousin to Ethan and Ira Allen, had taken the Arlington proprietors' mill offer and settled there in 1764. Eight years later, New York sheriff and Shaftsbury landholder John Munro captured Baker at his Arlington home and began to take him to Albany to stand trial as a ringleader of the violent opposition.[47] However, Baker's wife, Desire, called on her neighbors to save him, and he was rescued in New York by a group of Green Mountain Boys from Arlington and Sunderland that included Curtis Hawley, Jehiel's son, Abel Castle, Jr., Jeptha's brother-in-law, and Justus Sherwood, the friend of the Allens and nephew of the Sherwoods of Fort Edward.

Unfortunately, New York authorities continued to ignore Jehiel Hawley's compromising overtures. On January 11, 1774, he, his brothers Abel and Gideon, and his cousin Reuben joined Ethan Allen and Laird Castle in a warning to Benjamin Spencer to purchase a New Hampshire title.[48] Spencer was a New York justice of the peace in the western grants who had been mobbed by the Green Mountain Boys a year earlier. Allen, who drafted the warning letter, referred to Jehiel and his family as respectable gentlemen who would assist Spencer in purchasing a New Hampshire title at a reasonable price.

Two months later, a meeting of Grants' committees of safety was held at Jehiel's frame house to protest a sweeping statute enacted by New York's Governor William Tryon that made it a felony punishable by death to hold assemblies, to oppose law officers, or to refuse to disperse if involved in a mob.[49] Tryon was aiming at retaliation for the strong-arm tactics of the Green Mountain Boys and wanted to encourage the acceptance of New York's legal authority. A few weeks after the illegal assembly at Jehiel's home, a petition was readied announcing the grantees' determination to defend their land until the king's opinion over the dispute between New York and New Hampshire was known. They would protect any of their neighbors indicted by the New York government. They would also act in accordance with the law in civil cases and criminal prosecutions and would assist the officers appointed for that purpose. Respect for the crown's role as "political father" in arbitrating the dispute was unquestioned, not only by Hawley, but by most of the committees of safety. The tenor of the entire document shows their reluctance to use violence, even if it was "justified by the Law of God and Nature." This was written less than a year before the outbreak of hostilities at Lexington and Concord, when it was clear the grantees again wanted George III to settle the claims controversy. Hawley's name was affixed to this latest petition.

The New Hampshire Grants controversy added an additional dimension to the development of the Hudson-Champlain region. The Grants were chiefly settled at the whim of Governor Benning Wentworth of New Hampshire, who sought to line his pockets from township grants. Settlers were lured to the valleys within the Green and Taconic Mountains, where the growing season was short and mixed farming was precarious. While there were successful farmers like the Hawleys of Arlington or the Bothums of Shaftsbury, most settlers exploited land merely for its forest products, like lumber and potash. It was a land speculator's paradise because of the possibilities of selling land at increasingly higher prices without ever developing it. The clash between New York and the Grants over land titles became violent, thanks to the emerging Green Mountain Boys headed by Ethan Allen, who were willing to destroy settlements made by New Yorkers. Thus settlement would spawn civil war, a conflict that began well before the War of Independence and continued beyond it.

Neither the peaceful petitions nor the violent actions of the proprietors and Green Mountain Boys would ensure recognition of their land titles. While the king remained the favored arbitrator until 1775, his influence would wane and be eliminated by the Declaration of Independence. The creation of an independent Vermont in 1777, separate from both Great Britain and the United States, would be the result of this land issue and a background to British invasion from Canada.

PART II

CIVIL CONFLICT
IN THE MAKING

3

NEW ALLIANCES AS THE WAR
OF INDEPENDENCE BEGINS

Civil war appeared as the era of settlement unfolded. The volatile
mix of squatters' rights, religious separatism, and the claims of
New Hampshire grantees affected the growing movement for independence from Great Britain. The organs of protest in the port cities
that had developed over taxes and trade with Britain were lacking in
the region, with the possible exception of Albany. In 1775 concilia-
tion was still the watchword, and the natural rights of the Declaration
of Independence still seemed more like theory than reality. Most
leaders of both sides still favored compromise, hoping that a change
of ministry and policy in the motherland would turn the clock back.

Fort Ticonderoga on Lake Champlain had been a French and then
a British stronghold during the Seven Years' War. In the era of settlement that followed, it was neglected and lightly garrisoned with
British regulars, although it still had a large number of cannons in
various states of repair. The idea of capturing Fort Ticonderoga did
not originate in the New Hampshire Grants. It was the brainchild of
rebel leaders in distant Connecticut and Massachusetts whose motive
had to do with the British army bottled up in Boston, which it was
impossible to drive out without more and better artillery. Massachusetts and Connecticut leaders wanted the fort's cannons and
munitions for the siege of Boston, a situation that would not be
remedied until ordnance was transported to Boston.[1]

In the Grants, support for capture of the fort also existed, but the leaders of the Green Mountain Boys were not inspired by what was happening in Boston. The Allens viewed the fort's capture in terms of their land title conflict with New York, seeing the capture of the fort as a means of providing them with recognition as military activists and thus enhancing their political role in the region. They especially needed to prevent New Yorkers like landlord Philip Skene from increasing their influence over Ticonderoga and Crown Point. Ethan Allen would use the opportunity to strike back at his rivals in the Grants controversy.

The earliest enthusiasts who sought to rally public and private support for the capture of the fort were Silas Deane, Connecticut delegate to the Continental Congress, and Samuel Holden Parsons, militia officer and Connecticut legislator. From Parsons's position in the legislature, he promoted the taking of the fort and gathered commitments for public and private funds to underwrite the expedition.[2] They and Edward Mott of Connecticut gained the sum of £300 from the Hartford Committee of Correspondence, which had borrowed the money from the Connecticut Treasury. Mott raised sixteen recruits, including Ethan Allen's brothers, Levi and Heman Allen, though it was clear a larger force was needed.

On May 1 Mott joined Major John Brown and Colonel James Easton at the latter's tavern in Pittsfield, Berkshire County, Massachusetts. At the tavern, Mott suggested that more recruits could be found in the Grants among those led by Ethan Allen. The three conspirators went north to Bennington to convince Ethan to join Levi and Heman in the capture of Ticonderoga. Ethan Allen had been talking about the possibility since March, when he had made it clear that the Green Mountain Boys would support the rebels if war came. Allen controlled 100 to 150 Green Mountain Boys, just what his three visitors needed. He was pleased to listen to the visitors and formulate plans to seize the fort. It did not bother him that he would be attacking His Majesty's fort, for unlike most grantees, he had never assumed that George III would settle their quarrel with New York.

The four conspirators decided to assemble closer to Ticonderoga in Richard Bentley's house in Castleton, where all the parties came together and formed what they called the Board of War on May 8, 1775.[3] In addition to Ticonderoga, the Board designated three other objectives: Crown Point, Skenesborough, and Fort Edward. The latter two were no longer or had never been fortifications, but were, rather, emerging population centers, and no functioning artillery pieces existed at either place. As noted, the two places had rivaled each other to be the seat of Charlotte County. Fort Edward had won and was now the location of the crown's Charlotte County court. After debate, Fort Edward was dropped from the conspirators' objectives, but Skenesborough was retained.

While Mott was elected chairman of the Board of War, he declined to lead the force, letting the men pick their own commanders. Elected were Ethan Allen as colonel and James Easton as lieutenant colonel, reflecting the presence of men from both the Grants and Massachusetts. John Brown, whom Allen called an "attorney at law," was passed over. Samuel Herrick of Bennington was asked to command the force that was charged with capturing Skenesborough, including Skene's watercraft, which were to be sent to Ticonderoga to ferry Allen's men over the lake to the fort. If this failed, bateaux were to be hired at Crown Point to ferry the troops across the lake. Supplies were needed for the raid, and at this time the conspirators gained the support of the Bennington Committee of Safety. About a week before the raid on Ticonderoga, representatives from the Bennington Committee of Safety went in secret to the Albany Committee of Correspondence, asking for "a supply of flour" to feed the men.[4] They got it because of their ties to the Albany Committee, so that even New York did its part in supporting the raid.

All the planning seemed to have fallen into place, and the raiding force moved to Shoreham, a bit north of the fort on the east side of the lake. Suddenly, Benedict Arnold burst in on the scene. Arnold was at the beginning of a career that would prove him to be a talented soldier, one who would be a figure of immense stature in the Saratoga Campaign. From New Haven, Connecticut, he was one of a long line of mostly distinguished Arnolds.[5] In Rhode Island the family had been wealthy and one Arnold had become governor. However, Benedict's father had come to Norwich, Connecticut, as a mere cooper, although he had married well and prospered as a merchant by the time of Benedict's birth in 1741. His father could not sustain his success, however, and soon took to excessive drinking, besmirching the family name. It was no wonder that Benedict became obsessively concerned with his and his family's honor. He moved to New Haven and became a prosperous merchant and apothecary, and by the mid-1760s he was a ship owner. He went to sea on his own vessels, trading in the West Indies and Canada, where his specialty was horses, earning him the designation of "horse trader." His early experience trading in Canada was to serve him well in the War of Independence.

A man on the make, Arnold became a Freemason, and in 1774 he joined an elite militia unit, the Second Company of Governor's Foot Guards.[6] Membership was limited to the wealthy and well born, and it was fitting that their uniform was scarlet, with buff facings and silver buttons, something that no ordinary man could afford. When word of Lexington came to New Haven, the fifty-eight members of the guards voted to join the militia besieging Boston. However, as a social club they had no arms or ammunition and the selectmen of New Haven found their plan too radical, forbidding them access to the local magazine. Under Arnold, the guards confronted the magistrates, demanding the keys to the magazine, threatening that they would break in if they were not given up. The magistrates were forced to hand the keys over, and the guards were soon marching to Boston. Arnold had shown his decisiveness in his first political confrontation, and on the way to Boston he met Samuel Holden Parsons, who was promoting the idea that Ticonderoga should be taken so its ordnance could contribute to the siege of Boston.

In Boston, Arnold convinced the Massachusetts General Court to appoint him colonel of an expedition against Ticonderoga. The Massachusetts authorities also wanted Ticonderoga's ordnance for the siege of Boston. They granted him authority to recruit men, ammunition, and powder.[7] Arnold began recruiting in Massachusetts but moved ahead of his men to Castleton and then Shoreham. There he confronted Ethan Allen on his way to capture Ticonderoga with his Green Mountain Boys and Easton's and Mott's recruits. Audaciously, Arnold, in his guards' uniform, demanded command of the expedition, which Allen's men immediately rejected, as they had already elected their officers. Allen was more conciliatory. After all, Arnold had a legitimate commission from Massachusetts, while Allen really had no military authority. He agreed that Arnold should share the command at his side. Allen, of course, held the overall command, because he had recruited most of the two hundred men at Shoreham from nearby Bennington, Manchester, and Castleton. In this way, the various parties came together for the capture of Ticonderoga.

SKENESBOROUGH: TO EMBEZZLE EVERYTHING

Ethan Allen's motives in seeking to seize Skenesborough were his own, for the Massachusetts and Connecticut men were interested only in the bateaux needed to cross Lake Champlain. The developer Philip Skene, who had been looking for allies because he felt that Skenesborough had unfairly lost the contest to Fort Edward to become the Charlotte County seat, had recently dealt with Allen on the possibility of creating a separate province. It would belong to neither New York nor New Hampshire but be an independent colony. Skene and Allen appeared to be friendly, despite the fact that Skene had received warnings about the violence of the Green Mountain Boys.[8] While Allen wrote a letter sympathetic to Skene's desire to have the county seat, he stopped short of a full endorsement because Skenesborough was not within the Grants. In 1774, as part of the plot by Skene, Allen, and Jehiel Hawley to unite Skenesborough with the New Hampshire Grants, Skene went to London to propose a new province along these lines. There, on March 16, 1775, Skene wrote to Hawley that he had moved a step closer to this goal by being named lieutenant governor of Crown Point and Ticonderoga. Skene never really assumed this position, and it is unclear as to what the title meant. It may have been limited to the role of maintaining the crumbling defenses of the two forts, a position common in England for the military but one that had no civil authority.

Allen betrayed Skene and Hawley, for he was not about to see Skene with any implied power over the Grants, even if he were to recognize the claims of the New Hampshire grantees. And while Skene was preparing to leave England with his newfound authority, Allen was planning to take his home from him.

On May 9, 1775, the day before Ethan Allen's raid on Fort Ticonderoga, Captain Samuel Herrick and thirty men arrived at Skenesborough. Not only interested in confiscating Skene's watercraft, they also sacked his entire estate. Herrick was already showing himself to be a soldier in the mold of Ethan Allen. From Norwalk, Connecticut, forty-three-year-old Herrick had settled in 1768 in Bennington, where he kept a tavern. His orders said he was to take into custody "Colonel Skene's family, servants, tenants and boats."[9] In fact, Herrick was never able to deliver Skene's bateaux or schooner to Allen at Hand's Cove for the crossing to Ticonderoga. The orders also imply that the

Board of War was unaware that Skene could not be taken prisoner, for at the time he was aboard ship en route from England.

Herrick's men surprised the Skene's stone house, taking his aged sister and daughters prisoner.[10] In addition they violated Mrs. Skene's coffin, for she had been buried in the cellar of the house—a not unusual practice in her native Ireland. The lead cover of her coffin was ripped off, supposedly to make bullets, and her remains were later reburied in the yard. The men drank the contents of Skene's wine cellar and carried off his forty slaves, who as spoils seem to have disappeared from the record. On May 12 Herrick reported that his prisoners included the colonel's son, Andrew; his two daughters, Mary and Katherine; the aged sister; and an overseer, John Brooks.

The Skene family was sent under guard over two hundred miles to Salisbury, Connecticut. On the way they stayed overnight with Mrs. Philip Schuyler, who treated them hospitably. In Hartford the Connecticut Assembly wanted nothing to do with an act they treated as a depredation, so Andrew petitioned for the family's return to Skenesborough.[11] The Assembly decided the daughters were to return with Brooks, who was once more to take charge of the estate. So they went back to Skenesborough, protected from Herrick's marauders by an escort of Connecticut militia. Andrew was later released.

Back at Skenesborough, the daughters decided to leave for the more hospitable political environment of Canada, and in June 1775 Benedict Arnold, claiming he knew nothing about why Skenesborough had been sacked, was their host on the way north at Crown Point. The daughters were welcomed in Canada and loaned money. Skene claimed the girls were forced to travel the distance to Quebec, mainly on foot, as he put it "with scarce a change of apparel and exposed to every insult and mortification from a licentious people."[12] Skene, of course, saw Herrick's men as "armed banditti," destroying property without any authority. Since the Connecticut Assembly distanced itself from the affair, what little authority that could be surmised came from five citizens of the Hartford Committee of Correspondence that had borrowed funds for the capture of Ticonderoga.

The sack of Skenesborough is usually treated as a footnote to the taking of Ticonderoga. However, it had political ramifications equal to the capture of the fort, and it became a blot on the leadership of the Allens. Two years after the event, in April 1777, Ethan Allen's brother Heman claimed that Ethan, who was then in a British prison, was being detained there because Skene's "family [were] imprisoned, and his schooner, Iron works &c put into the employ of the United States," and that Skene remained "his implacable enemy," only because Allen "boldly maintained his landed interest."[13] Although Herrick rather than Ethan Allen was responsible for the depredation, the latter would be held accountable by Skene for violently destroying his property and influence in the region.

TICONDEROGA TAKEN

The day after Skenesborough was looted, Allen was able to transport only eighty-three of his two hundred men across Lake Champlain in two trips, using a single bateau, as no other boats were found. He led the men entering the fort and captured its garrison of forty-eight regulars, in the name of "the Great Jehovah and the Continental Congress."[14] A day later Seth Warner seized Crown Point, a ruin that was garrisoned by ten men and an equal number of women. Both conquests were bloodless achievements in which the garrisons were caught by surprise, making resistance impractical in the dilapidated fortifications.

After he captured Fort Ticonderoga, Ethan Allen had no idea of what to do with it or of how to maintain a garrison. In the week after the capture, he sought help from three authorities: the Albany Committee of Correspondence—claiming "your county is nearer than any other part of the colonies"—the Massachusetts General Court, and Jonathan Trumbull, governor of Connecticut. He begged them to support his occupation of the forts with ammunition, supplies, and reinforcements.[15] His force of no more than 150 was itching to return home for spring planting.

Only a year earlier, Allen and the Green Mountain Boys had issued a decree to the people of Albany and Charlotte Counties, warning that the New Hampshire grantees "are under necessity of resisting, even unto blood, every person who may attempt to take us as felons or rioters," reducing the Grants to a "disagreeable state of anarchy and confusion." Now the leader of the Green Mountain Boys was asking for Albany's support.[16] Despite the past, the Albany Committee of Correspondence responded to Allen's plea with food, and after a delay in raising them, two companies of militia for Ticonderoga's garrison. But powder and ammunition were unavailable because they had already been supplied to New England militia.

Philip Schuyler in Command of the Continental Army

In Albany the military authority of the Continental Congress first appeared in June 1775, when Philip Schuyler was named a major general of the Continental Army, which Congress had placed under the command of George Washington. Schuyler ranked third among Congress's major generals, exceeded only by Artemus Ward and Charles Lee. Washington had named Schuyler commander of the New York Department, a position that would be expanded into commander of the Northern Department.[17] When Schuyler met with Washington in New York City, he was instructed only to put the Lake Champlain posts in order and watch the efforts of Guy Johnson in bringing the Iroquois to support the British. To these orders would soon be added a more aggressive direction from Congress, which wished him to invade Canada—if he had the resources and found that the Canadians would be receptive to the invasion.

Schuyler's talent was as a master of supply. During the Seven Years' War, he had never held a combat position, but he had the experience of being a quartermaster under John Bradstreet. As an entrepreneur, he knew what resources were necessary to create an army and how to prepare armies in Albany.[18] Turnips and potatoes for the Northern Department often came from his own Saratoga plantation. His Albany patrician family also had long experience in New York's Indian affairs, so he was certainly ably equipped to seek their support.

Schuyler and Washington had bonded from their first meeting, for both still felt that further war with Britain might be avoided. Schuyler's perspective on the possibility of reconciliation with the mother country would continue to be held until after Canada was invaded. He wrote that the conquest of Canada might bring the "Ministry of [George III] to reasonable terms" and that heaven might still "reunite us in every bond of affection and interest; that the British Empire may become the envy and admiration of the Universe and flourish until the Omnipotent Master thereof shall be pleased to put his fiat on all earthly empires."[19] To him the British Empire was still viable, for its armies had driven the Catholic French from Canada, and the events that precipitated the conflict were the result of mismanagement by the king's overbearing ministers. These sentiments still prevailed among New York's leadership for the next seven months, even when a five-man congressional committee, which included Thomas Jefferson, began to write the Declaration of Independence.

Furthermore, Schuyler would not accept the sack of Skenesborough by Herrick's Green Mountain Boys as a rebel victory. Instead, he would make an effort to compensate and restore the property to Skene.[20] As would the authors of the Declaration of Independence, Schuyler valued the rights of property and felt that the looting of private investment had no place in opposing the crown. He correctly viewed Herrick's action not in terms of the crisis in Boston but as a continuation of the grantees' effort to discredit New York land titles.

Schuyler set about to restore Philip Skene's property to him. In June 1775 he argued that Skene's property had been seized by "a set of people" from the Grants, whose aim was "to embezzle everything." He ordered that the property be returned to Skene's agent, Patrick Langan, and required a reckoning of the property's accounts, so "that no disgrace may be brought on our cause."[21] He asserted that the war being waged by Congress was defensive and that neither persons nor property should be damaged unless it was necessary for the safety and protection of the army.

At first, the damages at the Skenesborough estate were accounted for by the very people who had done the deed.[22] Ironically Noah Lee, who had been part of Herrick's force that sacked the place, was placed in charge of the estate. His compatriot Elisha Phelps was the commissary for Connecticut and Massachusetts in Albany, a position that would soon be integrated into the Continental Army's Commissary. Lee and Phelps made Brooks leave as overseer, because he had worked for the Skenes. As late as December 1775, Patrick Langan was sending estimates to Schuyler, which he passed on to Congress, for items taken by the rebels such as sails, a crane, a French canoe, a burned barn, and a broken scow and even making claims for Skene's property that had been burned at Crown Point. Investigation showed that certain Green Mountain Boys had appropriated Skene's property. Herrick had seized Skene's double-barreled gun, while Warner had later taken a canoe. Captain Nathaniel Dickerson had carried one of Skene's slaves to Pittsfield and Skene's pistols had been placed on board his appropriated sloop, which had been renamed *Liberty*.

Schuyler must have imagined that his Saratoga plantation might just as easily have been sacked "in the name of the Continental Congress." To the new commander of the Continental Army in the North, it seemed as if the Green Mountain Boys were out to exploit the war for their own advantage.

In Philadelphia the Continental Congress responded negatively to the capture of the forts, feeling that the unauthorized use of its name and the capture of the posts escalated the possibility of British military reprisals, and it was suggested that the forts be abandoned. On May 29 Ethan Allen wrote to Congress in opposition because "the consequence of [such action] must ruin the frontier settlements which are extended at least one hundred miles to the northward from that place." If the south end of Lake George was the line of defense, the settlers would be exposed to invasion from Canada and "should after all their good service in behalf of the country . . . be neglected, . . . they will be of all men most consummately miserable."[23] Allen was already opposing any movement of the frontier southward because of his family's interest in the Lake Champlain area. He went on to claim that if the forts were abandoned "Indians and Canadians will be much more inclined to join [the British] and make incursions into the heart of our country." Here Allen foresaw the situation that Vermont would later face after Burgoyne captured Ticonderoga in 1777.

Congress was far away and it vacillated on what to do with the forts. Faced with these headaches, Allen decided to quit Fort Ticonderoga and make a reckless attempt against St. Johns on the Richelieu River. By the end of the month he had left the problems of Ticonderoga to others and moved to northern Lake Champlain, apparently to create his own invasion of Canada—although he lacked authority to do it.[24]

ETHAN ALLEN AND THE BENNINGTON CONSERVATIVES

Only two months after the capture of Fort Ticonderoga, the Grants Committees of Safety, led by the committee from Bennington, convened at Dorset, north of Arlington, to vote for officers for a Continental regiment. The regiment belonged to New York, which had approved the Dorset meeting, although the election of officers was not a procedure the state favored.[25] Pastor Nathan Clark was chair and Deacon

John Fassett, Sr., was the clerk, representing the continuing influence of Bennington Separatists. They were determined to wrest control of the Grants military forces from Ethan Allen. Earlier, he had drawn up a list of Green Mountain Boys to serve as captains, with himself, of course, as lieutenant colonel and commandant of the new regiment.

Instead of Allen's slate, the Dorset committees named steady Seth Warner as lieutenant colonel and commandant and Samuel Safford as major. Warner was a Green Mountain Boy, but he had served in minor Bennington offices and was astute, making him more acceptable than Allen. Safford, eldest son of early Bennington settler Deacon Joseph Safford, served on Bennington's Committee of Safety, having been elected a selectman numerous times and having supported the effort to bring about an understanding with Governor Tryon.[26] This was only the beginning of his thirty-two-year record of military and political service to Vermont. The selection was a personal rebuke to Ethan, although his conservative brother Heman was named a captain and his brother Ira and cousin Ebenezer were named lieutenants, so the family was well represented in the regiment. None of the elected Allens had been directly involved in early Green Mountain Boy activities.

In retaliation, Ethan Allen branded the Bennington Committee of Safety as "old farmers" because they actually tilled the soil, something he had not mastered. But the committee, who remembered how Allen's violence had scuttled the truce of 1772 with New York, did not want a repeat of that.[27] Certainly some on the committee were religious men, who had come to the Grants to practice their Separatist beliefs. They saw Allen as a Godless hypocrite whose violent actions were destructive of the communal religious society that had been established in Bennington. There were more immediate reasons to oppose him as well. After capturing Ticonderoga, he had been unable to maintain military discipline at the post and had failed in his reckless attempt to take St. John's.

The rejection of Allen at Dorset did more than simply diminish his authority. It ended the reign of terror the Green Mountain Boys had fostered. As the paramilitary military group they now faded, since military authority belonged to Warner's Continentals. Many Green Mountain Boys did find an outlet by participating in the politics that led to the establishment of Vermont's independence and constitution.

As a result of the rebuff by the "old farmers," Ethan Allen began courting New York authorities, hoping to obtain a command from them. Already on June 2 he had begged the New York Congress to listen to "an impertinent proposal" to authorize him to raise "a small regiment of Rangers."[28] Even Philip Schuyler was surprised that Allen had not been chosen at Dorset to command the new regiment, but he made no effort to intervene, and he tried to find a place for the disgruntled Vermonter. Brigadier General Richard Montgomery, commander of Congress's invasion of Canada, rejected a place for Allen in his campaign, but Schuyler finally let him join the expedition against Canada as a volunteer. Schuyler also faced the problem of clearing the remains of Allen's force from the captured forts. Many of these volunteers, like Allen, continued to loiter around the forts without any regimental or militia affiliation or a place in the Canadian invasion. Schuyler ordered that they would have to join a military unit to receive a food ration, and they soon disappeared.

New York provided green uniforms faced with red and tents for Warner's new Continental regiment, with each recruit having to provide his own firearm.[29] But Warner was having difficulty obtaining the five hundred authorized recruits in the Grants and would be forced to accept New Yorkers and other New Englanders. Lieutenant Ira Allen joined Warner in recruiting men to be sent to Ticonderoga, where Montgomery was gathering the army to invade Canada, but the ranks of Warner's regiment would never come close to being filled. By late September some members of the new regiment had reached Isle aux Noix in Canada and Warner followed, but after serving about two months in the Canadian invasion, on November 20 the regiment was discharged by Montgomery because they were not clothed to withstand the rigors of a Canadian winter.

This was not the end of Warner's Continentals, as they would be reconstituted several times, serving almost to the end of the war, but their military record would be mixed. By September 26, 1776, some of them had seen action under the command of Captain Jonathan Fassett, Jr., and Lieutenant Mathew Lyon at Jericho, where they protected a blockhouse filled with wheat. As Guy Carleton's forces prepared to advance down Lake Champlain, the appearance of Indian scouting parties nearby caused the Continentals to rebel, and they could not be persuaded to remain and defend the area.[30] They crossed the Onion River with their officers in tow, rather than face the war parties. Continental Brigadier General Arthur St. Clair ordered a court-martial, which sentenced all the officers to be cashiered or dishonorably discharged. Eighty of Fassett's Continentals were imprisoned by Vermont authorities and sentenced to corporal punishment. Fassett and Lyon had been two leading Green Mountain Boys, who had now begun their Continental military career with the embarrassment of this court-martial.

At Ticonderoga over the winter of 1775–76, the goal of the Massachusetts and Connecticut men who had taken the fort was finally fulfilled when Brigadier General Henry Knox was able to haul many of the fort's cannons overland to Boston, where their appearance on Dorchester Heights helped to convince the British to evacuate.[31] The Green Mountain Boys were not involved in this crucial activity.

THE SCHUYLERS OVER THE JOHNSONS: TRIUMPHANT AT LAST

Meanwhile in New York, Schuyler sought to settle a score with the Mohawk Valley Johnsons, longtime rivals of his family, as well as potential Loyalists.[32] Although the founder of the dynasty, Sir William Johnson, had died in 1774, his son and heir, Sir John, remained at Johnson Hall, where rumors spread that he supported the crown. The basis of his power was threefold: his influence with the five hundred Scottish, Irish, and Palatine tenants on his lands; the respect of the Six Nations toward his family; and his support of the existing legal and militia systems throughout the Mohawk Valley. Sir John Johnson had written to Governor Tryon about his willingness to arm and enlist Loyalists in the king's service. Schuyler hoped Sir John would change his mind, and if not support the rebel cause, at least remain neutral.

On January 16, 1776, at the call of the Albany Committee of Correspondence, 3,000 Albany and Tryon County militiamen were sent to Schenectady for Schuyler's invasion of the Mohawk Valley. This was a time for caution, as the force was regarded as too large and Schuyler feared that the militias would get out of hand and plunder the Loyalists in the valley.[33] His objective, then, was to first try to persuade Sir John personally, rather than use his military strength. But before he met with Sir John, he had to deal with another concern, defusing Mohawk opposition to the presence of his army. In a meeting with a Mohawk delegation at Schenectady, Schuyler assured them that the army was not there to threaten them but rather the Johnsons. In turn, the Mohawks countered that they were not preparing for

war.[34] In the meeting, Abraham, one of the sachems, in the capacity
of peacemaker, sought to avoid bloodshed by suggesting that only
three or four of Schuyler's men mediate with Sir John. Schuyler
urged the Mohawks to remain neutral, as they had promised at the
Albany Treaty in 1775, and agreed to write to Sir John for an inter-
view, asking that a few Mohawks might attend to act as interpreters.
The Mohawk sachems praised Schuyler and said they would attend
his meeting.

On the evening of January 17, Schuyler met Sir John and a number
of his mostly Catholic Scottish tenants sixteen miles beyond Schenectady, where he proposed a number of necessary conditions if Sir
John were allowed to stay.[35] Sir John and his tenants would have to
surrender their arms, cannon, and military stores and agree not to
serve in the war. Furthermore, Sir John was not to leave Tryon County.
Six hostages from his Scottish tenants were to be held by Schuyler
to guarantee these conditions. Considering the past influence of Sir
William over Albany County affairs, the most humiliating condition
required that all Indian trade articles be given to Schuyler to support
rebel Indian policies. Schuyler promised that if Sir John agreed to these
terms, he and his tenants would not be molested and could remain
in the Mohawk Valley.

Sir John was given till the next evening to think it over, and in
the meantime Schuyler moved closer to Johnstown.[36] Schuyler now
employed William Duer, the New York City speculator who owned
land in the region, to carry on further direct negotiations with Sir
John. Allan McDonnell, representing the Scottish tenants, joined Sir
John in his reply to Duer. The tenants wished to keep their personal
arms but would deliver up the rest of their weapons and they would
not provide hostages because they had no military organization from
which to choose them. The reply continued contentiously: Sir John
would not be confined to Tryon County, and he had no Indian trade
goods to give Schuyler. In conclusion, it said they would rely on
Schuyler's promise of protection if they surrendered their arms.

When notified of the haughty reply, Schuyler angrily announced
that he was marching on Johnson Hall and that, to spare the willowy
Lady Johnson from danger, she should leave at once with a passport
from him.[37] At the crucial moment the Mohawks interceded, calling
on Schuyler, claiming that Sir John only wanted to defend himself
and asking Schuyler to extend the deadline. Wanting to curry favor

with the Mohawks, Schuyler agreed to the further delay. But Sir John's new conditions were only slightly more accommodating to Schuyler's demands. Schuyler agreed to let the Scots keep their personal arms if they listed them, that Sir John Johnson could travel outside the county but not to seaport towns, and that six tenants would be held prisoner—their fate in the hands of Congress. The patrician general concluded that all the Scots must surrender their arms at noon on January 20, 1776. The agreement was signed, and Schuyler entered Johnstown on the 19th, announcing that the Scots should comply with their arms the next day, which they did, though not with their personal broadswords and dirks.

A new circumstance, an election of candidates from Albany to the New York Assembly intervened, and Schuyler was forced to leave the confrontation with Sir John and return quickly to Albany. The rebel militia had the franchise, and their votes were needed to nominate pro-rebel candidates for the Assembly, as Loyalists were numerous enough to win contests. In the meantime, Schuyler was complimented by President John Hancock for his prudence in disarming Sir John and his retainers.[38] The entire incident seemed to show that gentlemen could come to peaceable agreement, even in the midst of growing conflict.

While Sir John appeared satisfied to Schuyler, in fact he was not. Schuyler was also having difficulty in keeping the Mohawks neutral because he lacked the trade goods he thought he could secure from Sir John. In May 1776, when rumors accused Sir John of being in contact with the British post at Niagara and favoring the crown, Schuyler finally decided to arrest Sir John and hold him under close confinement.[39] Colonel Elias Dayton and three hundred Continentals were ordered to take him in secret from Johnson Hall to Albany and eventually to imprisonment at Washington's headquarters down the Hudson. Schuyler wrote again to Lady Johnson, offering her protection, and he also tried to get the McDonnells to join their elders held as prisoners. Sir John's factor in Schenectady, the Loyalist Daniel Campbell, warned him that Dayton's Continentals were coming for him.

Before Dayton's Continentals arrived, Sir John acted. On May 19 he and 170 to 250 tenants and friends escaped from Johnson Hall and traveled through the Adirondack Mountains, guided by Mohawks— John Deserontyon, the Hill brothers, Aaron Kanonraron and Isaac Onoghsokte. They suffered from hunger during a ten-day march, until they were rescued by Akwesasne Indians.[40] Sir John came to Montreal Island on June 19, hearing that the rebels had evacuated the city as they fled from Canada.

In the Mohawk Valley, Dayton's Continentals looted Johnson Hall, much as Herrick's men had done at Skenesborough.[41] Most of the wives and children of the tenants, as well as Lady Johnson, had been left behind. She was taken as a prisoner to Albany, where she gave birth to a son, John, in October, and then the Albany Committee gave her a pass to travel south toward New York City. With the help of Loyalists, she escaped and met Sir John, who conveyed her to British-held New York City.

In Canada Sir John's tenants became the basis of the King's Royal Regiment of New York, established only a month after he left Johnson Hall. Sir John was lieutenant colonel, and James Gray major, of the new regiment, and when Sir John went to New York in the winter of 1776–77, Gray commanded it.[42] This early Loyalist regiment would often return to the Mohawk Valley to retaliate and bring Loyalist families to Canada. This was not at all the way that Schuyler had hoped his negotiations would turn out.

Ethan Allen was by no means the first to suggest the need to take Fort Ticonderoga, and the group of conspirators that gathered at Castleton had leaders, men, and limited funds and supplies from Connecticut, Massachusetts and New York, as well as the Grants. The main concern of the Connecticut and Massachusetts men, including Benedict Arnold, was to obtain cannon from the fort, which could be used for the siege of Boston. Ethan Allen had to blend his interest in the independence of the Grants with those of the emerging War of Independence. He led the force that easily captured Fort Ticonderoga from its surprised British garrison, but despite his claim, Allen had no authority from either the Great Jehovah or the Continental Congress to seize the fort. Besides, once he captured the fort, he proved to be incompetent at garrisoning it. Allen was too violent a pagan for the leaders of Bennington, who chose Seth Warner rather than Allen to command the Continental regiment to be raised in the Grants. By 1776 Allen and the Green Mountain Boys would lose military authority and be relegated to a political role in the development of Vermont.

The capture of Ticonderoga and the sack of Skenesborough brought the region suddenly to the forefront of the independence movement. Neither of these events was enthusiastically received by Congress or the Continental Army commander, General Philip Schuyler. To them, the possibility of replacing the misguided North ministry in London and reconciling with the mother country was still very real. Congress seriously considered returning Ticonderoga to the British, while Ethan Allen opposed such action, as he felt it would force the abandonment of the northern frontier as well as his family's land investments near Lake Champlain. The sack of Skenesborough was viewed by Connecticut authorities, Benedict Arnold, and Schuyler as an act of vandalism, and it continued the reign of terror that the Green Mountain Boys had unleashed against New York titles. Schuyler had the ruined property returned to the Skene family. Despite Schuyler's inclination toward reconciliation and careful diplomacy, the Johnsons and their tenants would leave the Mohawk Valley and settle in Canada. The possibility of reconciliation in the region seemed dim.

4

GUY CARLETON AND THE REBEL RETREAT FROM CANADA

Congress imagined that Canada would make an ideal fourteenth colony in support of the American effort to topple Lord North's ministry and limit the powers of Parliament. At the time, few realized that the ultimate failure by the rebels to bring Canada under their control in 1776 would leave them open to continuous invasion for the next six years from that northern British-held bastion.

It fell on the shoulders of Major General Philip Schuyler, as commander of the Northern Department, to organize the invasion of Canada. He went to Ticonderoga to plan for it, arriving on July 18, 1775—about two months since Ethan Allen had captured the fort. Despite a garrison of six hundred, the place was found in such a sorry state that Schuyler was able to approach the guards at the Lake George landing without being challenged, most of them being asleep. He commented, "With a pen-knife only I could have cut off both guards and then have set fire to the block house, destroyed the stores and starved the people there."[1] Food and ammunition were lacking, though rum was plentiful. The stores, Schuyler found, were subject to "very considerable waste or embezzlement," and he fumed that the army was rife with corruption. While Ethan Allen was gone and the bulk of the garrison was now under the command of Colonel Benjamin Hillman of Connecticut, the men were notorious for treating their officers with contempt and insubordination.

It would take all of Schuyler's skill to change this situation at Ticonderoga. By the end of the year, Hillman had seen the light and resigned his Continental commission and returned to the militia. After bestowing the command of the Canadian expedition on a fellow Yorker, Brigadier General Richard Montgomery, Schuyler would designate 1,300 men for the invasion. By August, troops had been gathered north of Albany from Connecticut, New York, and New Hampshire.

Through fall, winter, and into spring, Schuyler attempted to supply the rebel army in Canada with fresh reinforcements, food, and powder. His chief staging area above Albany became Fort George, at the head of Lake George, from which supplies could be portaged at Ticonderoga and loaded on vessels to sail up Lake Champlain.[2] When Seth Warner recruited his second Continental regiment for the relief of Canada, Schuyler provided bounties for 736 recruits—yet when they arrived in Canada, Warner's men numbered only 417. Warner was not the first rebel officer who kept men in his accounts even though they had disappeared from his ranks. Despite this problem, the invasion of Canada was now fully supported.

Guy Carleton

Meanwhile in Canada, the British forces were led by Governor Guy Carleton, a military man who would display hidden talent in dealing with civilian matters. Carleton was born in 1724 in Sabine, County Tyrone, Ireland.[3] His military career began at the age of eighteen, when he was commissioned an ensign in the 25th Regiment. Nine years later he joined the First Foot Guards, and by 1757 he had risen to the rank of lieutenant colonel. A year later he held the same rank in the newly formed 72nd Regiment. Carleton first saw service in Canada during the Seven Years' War, where he was a protégé of the brilliant James Wolfe. For the Louisbourg expedition of 1758 and the siege of Quebec a year later, Wolfe chose Carleton as respectively his aide and quartermaster general—even though George II had rejected Carleton for both positions. Carleton was able to gain the Quebec appointment only after direct intervention with the king. The German king's animosity may have come from the fact that Carleton had criticized the ability of Hessian soldiers. During Wolfe's siege of Quebec, Carleton provisioned the army and acted as an engineer, supervising the placement of cannon. He was wounded in the head, and after Quebec's fall in October 1759, he returned to recuperate in England. Two years later he was designated commander of the 72nd Regiment in an attack on Belle-Ile-en-Mar, an island off the French coast. While the island was taken, Carleton was again wounded, this time seriously. Still, a year later he was a colonel in the British expedition against Havana, where he must have met Philip Skene. In Cuba he was again wounded, and he retired from active service as the war came to an end.

Since Carleton was deservedly retired and had no administrative experience, it was a surprise in April 1766 when he was named acting lieutenant governor of Quebec.[4] Connections explain his appointment: the Duke of Richmond, the new secretary of state for the North American colonies, had been his tutor and was also colonel of the former 72nd Regiment in which Carleton had served. Carleton's appointment included the title of commander of all troops stationed in Quebec. However, he was only to assist the governor of Canada, James Murray—the veteran brigadier of the 1759 Quebec campaign—with whom he was soon at loggerheads. All Quebec officials, from the governor down, were unsalaried, forcing them to seek income from what they charged for the prerogatives of office. The system naturally led to corruption, and Carleton sought to reform it by introducing salaries for officials. Upset, Murray resigned in 1768 and Carleton replaced him, becoming captain-general and governor-in-chief of Canada.

In 1770 Carleton returned to England, where he married Maria Howard, daughter of the second Earl of Effingham. He was forty-eight, she only nineteen, certainly a marriage based on an alliance of property and influence. Promotion to major general followed only three days later, and it was then that he drafted his thoughts on Canada, which became the basis for the Quebec Act. He carried this document with him on his return to Quebec in September 1774.

His Quebec Act was greeted by French Canadians with favor, but English Canadians were less pleased, and the Sons of Liberty in the colonies thought it an abomination. The act maintained French Canadian law and the authority of the Catholic Church in Canada.[5] The rebel propagandist Thomas Paine raged, "It was once the glory of Englishmen to draw the sword only in defense of liberty and the Protestant religion, or to extend the blessings of both to their unhappy neighbors" and now "popery and French laws in Canada are but a part of that system of despotism, which has been prepared for the colonies" by the Parliament. The Quebec Act established Carleton as a force in Canadian affairs who was tolerant of French Canadians, but also as a foe of Protestant leadership in the colonies, especially the ministers of the Congregational Church.

Invasion and Retreat of the Rebel Army

In May 1775 Carleton had just gotten word of the Battles of Lexington and Concord when he was informed that Ticonderoga and Crown Point had been taken. He had previously sent two regiments to help General Gage in Boston, leaving him with only eight hundred regulars in all, most of them dispersed in garrisoning forts in the Great Lakes.[6] While mission Indians might support his forces, Carleton was reluctant to use them. He believed that Indian support for the British would be a boon to rebels because Indians could not fight without committing atrocities. The French Canadians, whom he courted in the Quebec Act, failed to rally to the militia drum beat and he learned early in the hostilities not to depend on them.

The aggressive rebel army led by former British officer Richard Montgomery appeared in Canada beginning in September 1775 and carried all before it. St. Johns fell after a siege, then Montreal was bloodlessly taken, and Carleton barely escaped down the St. Lawrence River to defend Quebec. There he was besieged by Montgomery, now joined by another rebel force of eight hundred under Benedict Arnold that had marched to Quebec by way of Maine. The rebels were finally defeated in an attack upon the city in a snowstorm on December 30. Montgomery was killed making an attempt on the Upper Town's defenses, while Arnold was wounded in the streets of Lower Town.[7] The command of the remaining army was left to a group of officers of whom Captain Daniel Morgan was most conspicuous. While the rebels were able to capture some street barriers, British troops soon surrounded them and fired cannon into their hiding places. With their firearms too wet to discharge, the rebels surrendered, though Morgan in tears of rage refused to give them his sword and would have been killed had he not handed it to a priest, who was a bystander in the crowd.

At the beginning of 1776, Arnold held on stubbornly to the siege of Quebec and Carleton still had only a few regulars, sailors, and untrustworthy city militiamen to oppose him. Carleton did not receive his first reinforcements to break the siege until April, and more substantial relief came only in the following months, including generals John

Burgoyne, Simon Fraser, William Phillips, and Friedrich von Riedesel.[8] With 10,000 troops now in Quebec, Carleton moved quickly with the help of the relief fleet and took back Trois-Rivières and Montreal, though he failed to bag the main rebel army, which escaped by way of St. Johns to Lake Champlain. It was at this time that Sir John Johnson joined Carleton with his first Loyalist force, swollen beyond his tenants with Canadian Indians and militia to nearly 500 men.

As the rebel army retreated down Lake Champlain, it disintegrated. Continental Army doctor Lewis Bebee explained the disaster in these terms: "God seems to be greatly angry with us, he appears to be incensed against us, for our abominable wickedness."[9] When the retreating army arrived at Ticonderoga at the beginning of July, an epidemic of smallpox was raging, and British Indian allies were nipping at their heels. It was no wonder that Jeptha Hawley's son, Ichabod, who had joined the rebel invasion of Canada, probably in one of Warner's regiments, decided not to reenlist in the faltering army.

The Building of Schuyler's Lake Champlain Fleet"

With Canada lost, the control of Lake Champlain now became crucial in the effort to stop what became Carleton's invasion. On July 23, 1776, Congress gave orders to recruit marines and seamen for a Lake Champlain fleet. To attract more noncommissioned officers, Congress also offered additional monthly pay.[10] Some of the seamen came from John Philip de Haas's First Pennsylvania Battalion, which was already at Ticonderoga. Others, like Captain Samuel Van Vechten, commanded a company of Albany County militia from the Coxsakie and Great Imboght (Catskill) districts, on the lower Hudson. They gathered in camps at Skenesborough, which were unsanitary and lacked medical organization. On September 23 Van Vechten wrote of "the disagreeable distemper" he had acquired while working on the construction of the fleet.

The overall responsibility for building the fleet lay with Philip Schuyler, who was masterful at supervision of a project from a distance, managing his subordinates through letters and occasional appearances. The great difficulty was that Skenesborough had been sacked the year before and thus had little on hand to prepare a fleet. Naval supplies had to come all the way from Albany.

Schuyler's supply system would depend upon his connections with merchant patricians like Killian Van Rensselaer's second son,

Philip. He belonged to a branch of the Van Rensselaer family that worked for a living as merchants. He was heavily involved in the export of wheat and flour and the import of textiles. During the war, Philip and his wife Maria lived at their farm in the town of Bethlehem, because he had turned their steeply gabled Pearl Street town house in Albany into a supply depot for the Northern Department.[11] He served on the Albany Committee of Correspondence, and Schuyler named him Albany's public storekeeper. To meet Schuyler's needs at Skenesborough and Ticonderoga, he gathered and provided provisions, powder and lead for musket balls, and even cable and anchors from Albany sloops like his own.

Historians have called the naval force building at Skenesborough Benedict Arnold's Navy.[12] This conception is clearly much exaggerated. Schuyler and Arnold worked as a team, a relationship that was unusual for Arnold, who always strained for independent action. Arnold was conspicuous in building the fleet at Skenesborough and Ticonderoga, but more crucially he was prepared to take the finished ships for maneuvers on Lake Champlain. He would command the force that ultimately met Carleton's fleet. In this project he worked with rather than against Schuyler.

To cultivate Arnold, Schuyler would settle a dispute in Arnold's favor that involved another patrician family, the Wynkoops. Of a Hudson River Valley dynasty, Jacobus Wynkoop had been made conditional commodore of the Lake Champlain fleet by the New York Provincial Congress in March 1776.[13] In August, when Arnold sent out a naval force, Wynkoop ended up firing a warning shot at Arnold's ships because he felt the ships should be under his command. In a heated discussion that ensued over who had command of the fleet, Arnold threatened to arrest Wynkoop. Schuyler was impressed by Arnold and wanted to maintain a good relationship with him, so he put his patrician connections aside and recalled Wynkoop to Albany, ending his appointment as commodore.

Beyond the fleet, the defenses of Ticonderoga had to be prepared to meet Carleton. In the first week of July, Schuyler, Arnold, and a new major general, Horatio Gates, conferred at Ticonderoga and decided that it was here that the retreating army of the Northern Department would make a stand. To the north, they agreed, Crown Point was indefensible and had to be evacuated.[14] Their first action was to remove the festering smallpox hospital from Ticonderoga to the south end of Lake George, so that the sick would be separated from the well—a task that was only partially accomplished. Schuyler, Gates, Jonathan Trumbull, Jr., the paymaster, and the Northern Department's chief engineer, Jeduthan Baldwin, then inspected and mapped the entire Ticonderoga area as the basis for decision making. This accomplished, Schuyler returned to Albany, leaving Gates in immediate charge of the fortifications.

While Schuyler focused on building ships at Skenesborough and sending them to be outfitted at Ticonderoga, Horatio Gates extended Ticonderoga's defenses far beyond the crumbling fort that Ethan Allen had taken.[15] Realizing that the fort alone could not withstand a formal siege, Gates employed Thaddeus Kosciuszko, the Polish engineer, to strengthen the strategic area. The old French lines, a rotting log barrier about half a mile from the fort, where the French had repulsed Abercromby in 1758, were refurbished to protect the fort from the south. Across the lake from the fort was a peninsula of modest elevation, but with steep banks, on which Lieutenant Colonel Jeduthan Baldwin constructed two major fortifications: a star-shaped fort in the center and a horseshoe battery above the lake along the point. Additionally, he had wells dug, roads constructed, a crane erected, and barracks, storage buildings, hospitals, and palisades built. Dubbed Mount Independence, Baldwin's works and the others were too extensive to be finished by the end of the year. Gates even planned to fortify Sugarloaf Mountain, which commanded the fort; however, while it was the suggestion of many, this was never accomplished.

As for a garrison, Gates had the remains of the Continental Army that had invaded Canada, which, on account of Schuyler's reinforcements, was considerable. However, it was still infected with smallpox. Gates not only moved 3,000 sick soldiers to the south end of Lake George, but he also made the decision to forbid inoculation.[16] It was not that Gates was skeptical about the effectiveness of inoculation as a prevention, but that the process of doing it was impractical for the thousands of healthy soldiers in his army. Inoculation required at least a month of quarantine, in which soldiers were inactive and during which time healthy soldiers risked being exposed by the inoculated to the disease. At first inoculated reinforcements were quarantined at Skenesborough, but then Gates asked that his reinforcements not be inoculated. This was opposed by many local doctors who felt that inoculation was a procedure equal in importance to the arming or clothing of militia. It was impossible to prevent militiamen from being inoculated, and because of their short enlistments, militiamen that spent time in quarantine often never arrived at their post.

The upshot was that while on paper Gates had 12,563 men at Ticonderoga by the end of September, considering the sick, those in quarantine, the troops at other posts and in transit, he really had only 6,500 effectives. Many of the militiamen, like private Lemuel Haynes of Massachusetts's Hampshire County militia, were inexperienced, having never seen combat.[17] Still it was a notable effort because Carleton's army numbered only half that figure. This would be Gates's first effort to strengthen the rebel army in the region, and he worked closely if not exactly harmoniously with Schuyler and Arnold to do it.

CARLETON'S ADVANCE ON LAKE CHAMPLAIN

Carleton saw the necessity of building a fleet to dominate Lake Champlain, although he may not have realized how lasting this achievement would be. While the transports for his troops were ready in September, the war vessels were not completed until the beginning of October. With no British navy on Lake Champlain, this fleet would be built from almost nothing. In contrast to the rebels' numerous ships, Carleton's fleet would be better armed with heavier guns and manned by experienced English sailors. His modest invading army consisted of John Burgoyne's and Simon Fraser's brigades of light infantry, grenadiers, and the 24th, 9th, 21st, 31st, and 47th Regiments, at best 3,000 British regulars.[18] To this were added 400 Indians, 100 Canadians, and the Hanau artillery, all told a bit more than 3,500. Most of Carleton's reinforcements from Europe, especially the Germans, plus Sir John Johnson's and Allan Maclean's new Loyalist regiments, remained in Canada, and it was evident that the invading force was not large enough to conduct a full-scale siege of Ticonderoga.

Carleton had begun the transformation of his British army in Canada at the recommendation of his new generals, Fraser and Burgoyne. On August 30, 1776, Fraser sent Carleton a memorandum relative to the establishment of a "Company of Marksmen."[19] A total of 100 men were to be raised by a contribution from each British infantry battalion, "chosen for their strength, activity and being expert at firing ball." Along with Canadian volunteers and Indians, the marksmen were to serve on the flanks of an army's advanced corps. Fraser concluded "a corps of this kind . . . would fatigue the enemy exceedingly by constant alarms." Carleton endorsed the proposal and within a week offered the command to versatile Captain-Lieutenant Alexander Fraser. Fraser began recruiting marksmen from the regiments, who were "to be provided with a very good firelock." He organized the company at St. Johns and left on September 10 on his first scout with marksmen and 150 Indians. His marksmen would serve as the central unit in several scouts aimed at keeping the rebels off balance.

Alexander Fraser was the type of British officer who would be in great demand as the war continued. He proved himself to be an experienced independent commander, with expertise in leading mixed parties of troops in irregular warfare. A native of Scotland, he happened to be a nephew of Brigadier Simon Fraser.[20] During the Seven Years' War, he had served in Canada with Fraser's Highlanders, the 78th Regiment. A lieutenant, after the war he stayed in Canada on half pay, and though he failed to obtain the position of superintendent of Canadian Indian Affairs that he wanted, he was given a junior position and sent twice to the Illinois country, where he attempted to negotiate a peace with the still French-influenced Indians. Stationed in Ireland by April 1776, he returned to Canada with Burgoyne's reinforcements. He was assigned independently to help Burgoyne assemble Indians to work with the British forces. His scouts against the rebels on Lake Champlain would use volunteer forces of Indians, Canadians, and British light infantry. His example shows that Carleton, Fraser, and Burgoyne favored officers and troops who could cope with North American conditions.

THE BATTLE OF LAKE CHAMPLAIN

Carleton's fleet, without his most heavily armed ship, the *Inflexible*, but including the transport for the army, was underway on October 5, 1776. Five days later the *Inflexible* arrived on Lake Champlain. An engagement with the rebel fleet would commence behind Valcour Island, where Benedict Arnold had placed his ships. The action developed in three phases: on October 11 at Valcour Island; on the next day as the rebel ships fled toward Crown Point; and finally at Ferris Bay, where Arnold burned the *Congress*. Arnold's fleet consisted of the *Royal Savage*, *Revenge*, and *Enterprise* (maneuverable schooners and a sloop); the *Congress*, *Trumbull*, *Washington*, *Lee* (row galleys); and the gunboats

Philadelphia, Spitfire, Boston, New Haven, Providence, New York, Connecticut, and *New Jersey*—in all fifteen vessels with eight hundred effective sailors and soldiers.[21] Carleton's fleet, with Captain Thomas Pringle of the Royal Navy commanding, consisted of the ship *Inflexible* of eighteen guns; schooners *Maria* (the flag ship with Carleton and Pringle on board) and *Carleton* of fourteen and twelve guns respectively; a *radeau,* a flat-bottomed, bargelike vessel with two masts, of heavy guns (the *Thunderer*); a gondola (the *Loyal Convert*); and twenty gunboats.

Arnold's fleet hid behind Valcour Island, so that Carleton's ships went by them and had to tack back against the wind to cover the mouth of the bay, having difficulty in coming close enough to fire on Arnold. However, as General David Waterbury had warned Arnold, the rebel vessels were quickly boxed in within the bay by Carleton's fleet. The action commenced at 11 A.M. The first casualty was the *Royal Savage,* which came out to fight and was mauled by the *Carleton* and *Inflexible.* The rebel ship ran aground, her crew abandoned her, and the British boarded and turned her guns on Arnold's ships, but eventually she was burned and blew up.[22] Later, the *Philadelphia* began to sink. Both the *Congress* and *Washington* suffered from the fire power of the British guns. The only chance for Arnold was when the *Carleton* was blown by the wind into the American center and hit, but then British gunboats pulled her out of harm's way. By 5 P.M. the fire had slackened, and Carleton created a line to block Arnold's battered fleet from escaping at night, assuming they would finish them off in the morning. However, in the dark of night Arnold's fleet— minus the *Royal Savage* and *Philadelphia*—escaped. They made for Crown Point, but the vessels were so damaged and unseaworthy, with the wind against them, that they scarcely sailed, only reaching Schuyler's Island about ten miles from Valcour by 7 A.M.

Upset the rebels had escaped, the British fleet tied to close on them on the 12th, but the wind was contrary and both fleets were forced to row, so that they remained in sight of each other but made no progress. The British did capture the rebel cutter *Lee.* The next day, the 13th, the wind changed and the chase, in which the British caught Arnold's ships, renewed. The *Maria* was fresh, having scarcely been involved at Valcour and moved to the front of the British fleet.[23] The *Inflexible* caught the *Washington* with General Waterbury near the Island of the Four Winds and forced it to strike its colors. The

New Jersey, Boston, Providence, New Haven, Connecticut, and *Spit-fire* were also abandoned by the rebels. Soon the *Congress* and four gunboats were all that could be found of the rebel fleet. Three British ships caught the *Congress* and knocked its main mast off, and Arnold was forced to scuttle and burn it in Ferris's Bay. Arnold and his crew made their way by land to Ticonderoga. Of the original fifteen ships in the rebel fleet only the *Trumbull, Revenge, Enterprise,* and *New York,* the last being the lone survivor of the gunboats, were left. The rebel fleet had lost over 80 sailors and soldiers killed or wounded, and a further 110 were captured. Most of these prisoners were sent by Carleton to Ticonderoga on October 15 under a flag of truce for exchange. They, including Waterbury, were paroled as long as they returned to their homes and did not take up arms against the British for the rest of the war. In offering these liberal terms, Carleton was fostering a policy of accommodation with the rebels. The British losses were insignificant; the British would refit and use several of Arnold's ships against the rebels.

A German officer, who was not present but analyzed the result from Canada, concluded: "Thus, Lake Champlain was free again as most of the enemy fleet had been transformed into nothing."[24] Crown Point was also among the spoils of the Battle of Lake Champlain, as the rebels had "set fire to and demolished everything." The post was now more of a settlement than a fort, and the inhabitants fled into the woods, leaving their household goods to the flames. Carleton took possession of Crown Point's charred ruins, attempting to use it as a base for an attack on the Ticonderoga defenses. However, the lake began to freeze over in November, and Carleton decided that with the lateness of the season, it was prudent for his small army to retire to St. Johns. At first, it was proposed that General Fraser's corps remain at Crown Point over the winter, but the post was ruined, offering no shelter from the elements. Burgoyne, who was with Carleton, agreed that the army should retreat. Lieutenant Darcy was sent as Carleton's envoy to Quebec and then London with his account of the naval victory.

Carleton had enemies both in Quebec and the British Isles. He was criticized for his conduct of the entire campaign, regardless of the fact that he had driven the rebels out of Canada and won control of Lake Champlain.[25] Previously he had prevented Lieutenant Colonel Gabriel Christie from obtaining a post, resulting in Christie venting his spleen against him and charging him with three faults: failure to catch and destroy the rebel army as it retreated toward Montreal and the Richelieu, the excessively large fleet he had built for Lake Champlain that prevented it from reaching Ticonderoga during campaign season, and the general lack of supplies in Canada. Such ammunition was valuable to Carleton's enemies, who in London included Lord George Germain, the minister for the American colonies.

In fact, Carleton had done an excellent, if not spectacular, job in expelling the war from Canada and pushing it into the Hudson-Champlain valley. When one remembers that the siege of Quebec was only broken by the appearance of token reinforcement in April and that by October Carleton occupied Crown Point and controlled Lake Champlain, the critics' charges seem unfounded. In terms of supply, while Quebec had a surplus of foodstuffs in good years, it was never enough to cover a newly arrived British army with Canadian militia and Indian dependents.[26] No means of gathering supplies from the countryside existed, and cities like Quebec and Montreal claimed priority over the army for such produce. Carleton was thus most dependent on the erratic delivery of supplies from the distant British Isles. Even with his victory on Lake Champlain, he still had no reserve of supplies, and even his base at St. Johns had not as yet been rebuilt from the damage done when it was besieged by the rebels. In fact, by not occupying Crown Point, the British army in the spring of 1777 was rested and healthy because it had wintered in the relative comfort of Canada. Carleton wisely chose to return to St. Johns and prepare for a spring offensive without the burden of defending Crown Point over the winter.

LOYALISTS AT CROWN POINT

While Carleton did not besiege Ticonderoga, it should not be assumed that the countryside north of Albany was quiet. The early restraint shown by Loyalists had disappeared by October 11, when they began to join Carleton's army at Crown Point. They had been waiting for the invasion, and as his encampment at the narrows of Lake Champlain was close enough for them to reach, they flocked to him. Their appearance was spontaneous, for Carleton had made no effort to contact them.[27] But now, while it not been part of his plans, at Crown Point Carleton began to lay the groundwork for supporting Loyalism in the region.

Loyalism was strong in the region because of family influence, like that of the Johnsons, and the leadership of many retired British and Provincial officers who had given up their homes in Ireland, Scotland, or elsewhere to settle there in the 1760s and 1770s. Reduced officers of the Royal American Regiment, like Daniel McAlpin and Francis Pfister, had an advantage because the men of that regiment had been drawn from the colonies and could readily be contacted by their old captain. [28] They secretly organized Loyalist corps on the basis of male kinship and neighborhood relationships, a situation that would continue even when Canadian authorities tried to organize them. Such units already had the discipline to penetrate rebel defensives and reach Crown Point.

The Loyalists who arrived at Crown Point came from several directions. From Shaftsbury, Arlington, and New Haven in the Grants, Justus Sherwood appeared with forty recruits. Sherwood had been a friend of Ethan Allen and a Green Mountain Boy.[29] In the spring of 1776, however, while he was visiting Bennington, rebels brought him before a judge, who sentenced him to a public flogging for speaking in support of Britain. In New Haven rebels broke into his home and looted it, as his wife, Sarah, and the children stood by helplessly. While they found nothing incriminating, they still arrested him. He was released on bail and returned home, but that very night he was again attacked and taken away. A conspiracy committee banished him to the notorious Simsbury Mines in Connecticut. Miraculously, he was able escape from the prison.

Meanwhile, Sarah had left New Haven for her father's house in Shaftsbury, bringing the children and some of their slaves with her. Her brother, Simon Bothum, was sent to New Haven to take over the farm and the remaining slaves.[30] Justus visited the Bothums' house as he moved north, recruiting followers from Shaftsbury, Arlington, and eventually New Haven, including Sarah's brother, Elijah. Justus also signed over his New Haven farm to Sarah's father to avoid confiscation. At her father's house, Sarah gave birth to a daughter, Diana, and by spring she had joined Simon at New Haven.

On November 4 another party arrived at Crown Point from Arlington, consisting of Jehiel Hawley's favorite son, Jeptha, another son, Ichabod, and their neighbor, Philo Hurlbert.[31] They had modest military experience but a respect for the crown. During the Seven Years' War, eighteen-year-old Jeptha had served in the Connecticut militia company of Captain Joseph Canfield, although he had not marched to the lakes area. Ichabod was a deserter from the rebel army, who faced severe retribution if he were captured. The Arlington men may have been recruited by Sherwood.

Also in November, from the direction of Albany, came another group, this one of ninety men, led by the Jessup brothers, Edward, Ebenezer, and Joseph.[32] They had begun organizing in January 1776 under Governor Tryon's authority, creating a battalion that would oppose the rebels in their Albany stronghold. They had made preparations, transporting provisions, including pork, beef, flour, brass kettles, and even eight cattle on the hoof, into the woods outside the city. Three companies were formed, one each commanded by Edward and Ebenezer, and one commanded by Jonathan Jones of Kingsbury. Many of the Jessups' recruits were from the Rensselaerswyck Manor, hostile to their landlord's agent, Abraham Ten Broeck, who had become a leading rebel. Solomon Jones, who happened to be studying medicine in Albany, was the surgeon's mate of his brother Jonathan's company. Their brother, David Jones, along with Joseph Jessup were both lieutenants in Ebenezer's company. Here was the beginning of the military career of these important Loyalist officers.

The home of widow Sarah Dunham Jones's seven sons, Kingsbury, north of Fort Edward, was the source of several of Jessups' officers. Jonathan and David had used a ruse to fool the rebels and join the Jessups and Carleton. In the fall they had raised a company of fifty men from Kingsbury and Fort Edward, saying that they were going to join the rebel garrison at Ticonderoga.[33] The company set out for Ticonderoga, but instead it passed through the woods around the fort and joined Carleton at Crown Point, where it would integrate with the Jessups' unit. David Jones would go back to Kingsbury to recruit and early in 1777 he returned to Isle aux Noix with thirty more volunteers.

From the Hoosic River valley came men raised by former British officer and engineer Francis Pfister. Schuyler had thought that Pfister's talents would be useful to the rebels, but it soon became clear that he would be a Loyalist. With permission to raise a Loyalist battalion from Governor Tryon, over the summer of 1776, Pfister, Robert Leake, and Edward Carscallen had recruited 650 men in the Hoosic and Camden Valleys and in the Rensselaerswyck and Livingston Manors.[34] Most of them, including Pfister, remained there, ready for action in the spring of 1777, but some went to Crown Point. After hiding in the

Hoosic Valley area and avoiding rebel confinement, in October at Crown Point Leake brought in about 30 volunteers, while Edward and John Carscallen claimed responsibility for bringing 42 of their own friends. They were mostly Palatine Germans and Scots-Irish, who had lived in Ireland and immigrated together.

CARLETON AND THE NEW LOYALISTS

In October the only Loyalist troops from New York in Canada were those of Sir John Johnson's King's Royal Regiment of New York.[35] Carleton had made them part of his Northern Department, to be recruited on the Quebec borderland. In recruiting, Sir John had the immediate advantage of enlisting his tenants, who had come with him from Johnson Hall, although some Canadians also joined. He could afford to purchase his tenants' arms and equipment from his own purse. But it was made clear by Burgoyne, acting for Carleton, that even Sir John's regiment was a local creation and would not be made part of the regular establishment—such as would happen with another, more favored Loyalist regiment then recruiting, Allan Maclean's Royal Highland Emigrants.

Sir John's second-in-command, Major James Gray, was at Crown Point in October and November recruiting from the newly arrived Loyalist refugees. In November, when the King's Royal Regiment went into winter quarters at Lachine, Pointe Claire, and Saint Anne, some of the Loyalist refugees went with it.[36] However, since the Loyalists had been organized by their own experienced officers with their own thirst for command, most Crown Point refugees stayed with their original leaders—evidence of the beginnings of recruiting rivalry amongst the Loyalist commanders.

Carleton was hesitant to go further with the hundred-plus Crown Point refugees, even though they had demonstrated that they were anxious to serve as soldiers. He was ambivalent to Loyalists being formed into military units because he saw them as being costly, similar to Indians.[37] Without detailed instructions from the ministry, he would be forced to develop a policy toward them. He lacked resources to treat the refugees as members of regular regiments, and they lacked the wealth and influence of Sir John, who could afford to recruit a full battalion.

Still, when John Peters arrived from the Grants late in 1776 with a small following that probably included the French brothers, Jeremiah and Gershom, Carleton did not turn a deaf ear. Peters offered to recruit a Loyalist unit in the Grants. But while Carleton was clothing and paying the Loyalists now in Canada as refugees, providing them with "an asylum till they can do better for themselves,"[38] it was not till May 1777 that Carleton allowed Peters to form the Queen's Loyal Rangers. Not till he was with Burgoyne, on June 22, was Peters appointed lieutenant colonel of the Queen's Rangers, and this rank was not to last. Thus, Loyalists who came to Canada had to be patient if they were anxious to form military units.

Already Carleton found his Loyalist refugees difficult to manage. In January 1777 the Jessups suggested they elect their own officers, a proposal that British officers considered ridiculous. Carleton tried to place the refugees under an existing authority, suggesting that Governor Tryon might want them back. The Jessup brothers, Peters, and Samuel Adams of Arlington opposed the loss of their autonomy, leading Carleton to put them under the command of Edward Jessup's friend, Major James Gray of Johnson's regiment, where they retained their companies. In these units, they could be clothed, fed, and housed. This command was extended to include "boys of 15 or younger and old men."[39] The men and boys were to stay in designated barracks, rather than being spread among homes in the countryside.

No policy of encouraging Loyalist families to immigrate to Canada existed. Carleton drew the line at supporting women and children as refugees, even for the wives of Loyalist officers. While they were provided with aid when they first arrived, women and children were encouraged to find relatives or friends to live with. Despite this obstacle, some came. Early in 1777 John Peters's wife and seven sons—the eldest only fourteen years old—were taken to Ticonderoga and then sent to Canada by the orders and gallantry of Brigadier General Anthony Wayne. They arrived in St. Johns on May 4, much the worse for wear.[40] Also in May fifteen Grants Loyalists were captured at Otter Creek, preventing them from reaching their destination.

Carleton had driven the war front from Canada and pushed it into the Hudson-Champlain valley. By November he was victorious over the rebel fleet and occupied Crown Point, controlling Lake Champlain. He had also established himself as a presence in Canadian affairs for the next two decades.

Despite difficulty in finding a definite place for them, Carleton's experience with the Crown Point refugee Loyalists led him to believe that the inhabitants of the Saratoga and Albany area were supportive of the king and would be ready to take up arms to assist a British invasion from Canada. His view was obviously crucial in encouraging Lord North's ministry in London to emphasize the value of Loyalists in future campaigns. What Carleton did not realize is that by supporting the Loyalists even moderately, he was escalating the existing regional civil war.

5

PROMOTING LOYALISM AMONG NATIVE AMERICANS

In Britain, a wide range of opinion existed on the value of Native Americans in warfare. The crown's chief adviser, Lord Jeffery Amherst, a veteran of the Seven Years' War in the region, thought Indians to be a nuisance. Commander-in-chief of the forces and a Cabinet member from 1778, Amherst harbored views that influenced both Carleton and Burgoyne. He agreed with the ministry's opposition in Parliament that Indians were barbarians, which made them uncontrollable in warfare, and he condemned the development of all American auxiliaries.[1] He felt the War of Independence was to be won by disciplined regulars, fighting in the style of a European conflict, including sieges and formal battles. Moreover, the special relationships that the French had established with the Indians were an expensive frill, which failed to justify continuing the presents and Indian Affairs Departments that spoiled them. It was hard to ignore the opinion of the experienced commander-in-chief when he asserted that it was best to avoid the use of auxiliaries, and his perspective was unfortunately a beginning point for many British officers.

Despite Amherst's opinion, George III and his ministers, Lords North and Germain, wanted to use Native Americans to help subdue the rebels. Vocal opposition to the war was based in Parliament and the critics of Lord North's ministry found the use of Native Americans an irresistible issue.[2] George III and his ministers had to contend with this Whig opposition if they were to manage Parliament to obtain financial support to conduct the war. The Whigs would use any setback or indiscretion to bring the ministry down. Hence the monarch and his ministers chose to tread lightly in discussing the use of Indians while in Parliament, while urging their generals in America to use them. This was not so much because of the effect it would have on American public opinion, which knew what to expect from Indian warfare, as British opinion at home, which had a direct effect on issues in Parliament. At this time, Burgoyne would side with the king and his ministers in making Native Americans part of his army.

NATIVE AMERICAN SOURCES FOR BURGOYNE

For the Saratoga Campaign, Native Americans would come from four regions: the Iroquois League of Six Nations, the Canadian mission Indians, the distant Great Lakes peoples, and the natives of the Stockbridge Indian mission in western Massachusetts. All of them had participated in the Seven Years' War and some had claims to portions of the Hudson-Champlain region as hunting and fishing grounds.

Among the Iroquois, the Mohawks were the most acculturated and, because of the Johnsons, the most consistently loyal to the king. The Mohawks had a special relationship with the Saratoga area. They had triumphed in late seventeenth-century combat with New England Indians and gained control of the Hoosic Valley, which was then an important east-west trade route.[3] To reach the Hoosic, the Mohawks had to travel through the Saratoga area, and they claimed it as hunting and fishing ground, a crucial part of their food supply beyond their cultivated fields in the Mohawk Valley. In the 1740s William Johnson, speaking for the Mohawks, had condemned the earlier, ridiculously expansive Kayaderosseras Patent as encroaching upon their fishing and hunting territory. The Mohawks knew the Kayaderosseras as a wandering creek, feeding into Saratoga Lake, where the fishing was excellent and to the north of which the Bear Swamp provided game. They had accessed the area before contact with whites and the Mohawks of Fort Hunter and Canajoharie still used it. The Fort Hunter Mohawks were hunting there in the winter of 1776–77, when they offered protection to Loyalist Daniel McAlpin, showing that they considered it their territory.

The other five peoples of the Iroquois—the Oneidas, Onondagas, Cayugas, Senecas, and Tuscaroras—supposedly united around the council fire at Onondaga, the most central location near present-day Syracuse, and hammered out policy and tried to maintain the diplomatic relationship of the Covenant Chain.[4] This alliance between the Iroquois and other villages stretched to the Ohio country. As the special ally of the Iroquois, the British had taken advantage of this web of relationships in the Seven Years' War. By the time of the War of Independence, however, both the covenant and the Iroquois League were beginning to come apart. Instead of unity in the League, there was division at the beginning of the war, as only the Mohawks could be depended on as British allies, and the other five peoples favored neutrality. At the time the neutral policy made sense for it allowed them to conserve their resources as they watched the emerging war from the sidelines. British and rebel efforts would undermine this neutral position and the Mohawks were joined by Senecas and Cayugas and finally Onondagas in support of the British, while the Tuscaroras and Oneidas clung to the neutral position. Only the Oneidas would openly support the rebels.

Another source of Native Americans for Burgoyne would be the Canadian missions, first established by Jesuits and Sulpicians in the seventeenth century, which became Catholic refugee centers, inhabited by so-called praying Indians.[5] Kahnawake, Kanesetake, Akwesasne, Oswegatchie, Odanak, Becancour, and Lorette had been located near, but not in, Canadian population centers so that the Indians could avoid the evil effects of European civilization—such as the consumption of liquor. These missions had the advantage of being subsidized under the French government, and after the conquest the subsidies were continued by the British. In the Seven Years' War the mission Indians had scouted and raided the English borderlands, an activity that had become commonplace to them. While they had to be treated by British authorities as independent allies, of all Indian peoples, because of their geographical proximity to Montreal, the missions could most easily be coaxed into war. At the beginning of the War of Independence, the paternal role of the French was what the British authorities, like Governor Carleton, hoped to duplicate, making mission Indians their most consistent source of support. However, because they were such an amalgam of peoples, the missions were full of factions, and a decision to support any side always had its opposition. Thus it was true that the rebels, when they invaded and occupied Canada briefly, made an effort to cultivate them and found some support among the mission Indians.

Guerrier Iroquois

"Iroquois Warrior" by Jacques Grasset de Saint-Sauveur, from his *Travelling encyclopedia* (Paris, 1796). Reproduction, Library and Archives Canada/Bibliothèque et Archives Canada, Ottawa.

Elsewhere, the Great Lakes Indians were the most distant from the scene in the "pays d'en haut," where they experienced only glimpses of white civilization. Present with Burgoyne would be the Foxes, who resided north of Green Bay, and the Mississaugas, who lived on Georgian Bay in Lake Huron.[6] Also with Burgoyne were the Chippewas, who had earlier joined the Ottawas in Pontiac's uprising. The original homeland of the Ottawas, who would play a most significant role in the Burgoyne Campaign, had been the Ottawa River between Montreal and Lake Huron. In the seventeenth century the Iroquois drove them west, and in the mid-eighteenth century their villages were concentrated at the west end of Lake Erie, at strategic Michilimackinac, and at Green Bay on Lake Michigan. Pontiac, who led the Indian uprising of 1763, was an Ottawa, and for this reason the English thought of his followers as the least acculturated, most pagan, and most brutal warriors. In fact, they had the same experiences as their more eastern neighbors, assimilating white captives into their society. Many lived at or near British forts and were disappointed at the inability of the commanding officers to provide the support that had been offered in the days of New France. The Ottawas had to be coaxed by veteran French Canadian officers, who were now serving in the British Indian Departments, to get them to come the distance of a thousand miles or more by canoe. Actually, they knew the Ottawa River route well because the fur trade often brought them to Montreal.

Lastly, after the Seven Years' War, a handful of Mahicans and New England refugees remained in the Town of Stockbridge in the Berkshires, where by the 1770s they had formed the largest remaining praying Indian mission in Massachusetts. Originally conceived of by the General Court and Protestant missionaries, the mission and town of Stockbridge had been established in 1740 and settled by refugee peoples of the New York–Massachusetts borderland, that is, the remains of the Mahicans, Housatonics, and Wappingers.[7] To provide a civilizing influence on these Indians, prominent white families were also invited by the General Court to join the missionaries and settle. The whites grew in numbers, gained the best land, and quickly took control of town government.

The marginalized Stockbridge Indians remained on their shrinking land. Despite the abuse of neighboring whites, they became accustomed to seeking their advice in town relations, and by the 1770s they were also in debt to them and were now totally surrounded and outnumbered by them—making it difficult for them to follow an independent course of action. Reduced to a population that never exceeded two hundred, the abused Stockbridges would follow their white neighbors and consistently support the rebels and join their armies.

Native American Warfare

Native Americans had developed their own type of warfare as result of conditions that were introduced by Europeans in the seventeenth century. With the appearance of European firearms, Indians needed to avoid frontal confrontations and the heavy casualties that resulted.[8] The ambush became their forte, and they preferred to hide behind trees and make every effort to lure their enemies on to unfavorable ground, rather than meeting them head on with a war club, a skill that they increasingly regarded as ineffective. They were not about to stand up in lines as European armies did and suffer heavy casualties to win conflicts.

Indian emphasis on preservation of life in warfare, rather than fighting to the death, was also a result of demographic decline. In the eighteenth century all Indian peoples exposed to white diseases had high death rates, but those that were closer to white settlements—like the Mohawks to Albany and Schenectady—suffered more than most Iroquois. This is why most Indian villages were smaller than they had been at the beginning of the eighteenth century and typically numbered only one to two hundred inhabitants. Native Americans were unable to cope with viruses like smallpox, which their medicine men found impossible to stop. European officers noted how they tried to deal with disease: "savages . . . often change their dwellings, particularly when the smallpox appear among them; then they move on and let those inflicted with the pox lie until they are well again or have died. Since they allow old people, women and children to shift for themselves, the pox are wont to cause great devastation among them."[9] This way of coping may seem heartless, but given the state of their medicine, it was the only way for a village to survive.

European firearms and diseases led to an intensification of warfare, especially among the Iroquois, to replenish their villages' populations through fresh captives. This need was integrated with their ritual of mourning, in which they sought a captive from outside of their village to replace a deceased person.[10] When warriors returned with precious captives, the elder women chose to adopt or execute them. Children and younger adults were favored for adoption because they were more easily molded to Indian ways, and adoptions usually outnumbered executions. Once adopted, former captives were loved and treated as well as any member of the village. Execution was also a ritual, another form of adoption, for the captive was given a death feast at which he might recite his exploits. On an appointed day, the captive was tied to a stake and slowly burned and tortured to death, his remains being cooked for a village-wide feast. Europeans saw only the burning and eating of flesh, not the spiritual meaning behind the ritual.

By the time of the War of Independence, the captive situation had been modified by the intervention of whites, who were supposedly motivated by sympathy for captives. Although captives were still adopted into Indian villages, if it appeared that they were not fitting into the village community, they could be sold to the government or private families.[11] This usually took place in the great center of Indian trade, Montreal. Other captives were actually purchased by officers as they were rounded up after battle. Government purchase meant that captives were treated as war prisoners and might be exchanged to return home. It was a popular alternative among captives because it theoretically prepared them to go home. However, this ignored the fact that prisoner exchanges often took years and that during that time, prisoners were incarcerated, their treatment varying seasonally, from decent in the summer to abominable in the winter. In the private family alternative, which chiefly involved residents of the Montreal area, treatment was regarded by many as the best, for the captive lived in white society. However, most captives were purchased to be servants, an occupation for which few had an inclination, and their efforts to run away were considered betrayals and punished harshly. With hindsight, captives who chose between these alternatives must have wondered if they might not have fared better in an Indian village, where they were treated as well as any member of the community.

The War of Independence did renew the influence of Native Americans by creating a new expansionist North American state, which they could play off against the British imperial state.[12] Early in the independence conflict, Native American political middle ground and neutrality led them to be courted by both sides. Ultimately, their dependence on the two governments for ammunition, goods, and sustenance forced most peoples to favor the more generous of the two—undoubtedly the British Department of Indian Affairs.

CONTINUATION OF THE MOHAWK DIASPORA TO CANADA

Early in the War of Independence, when the Johnson family and their friends began to leave the Mohawk Valley, many Mohawks came with them to Canada. This had the effect of further depopulating their two major villages at Canajoharie and Fort Hunter.[13] By the time of the Saratoga Campaign, most of the Mohawks had left because of rebel pressure and were concentrated around Montreal, at Fort Niagara, or to the south at Oquaga. This emigration was not new because earlier the Mohawks already had populated the Canadian missions at Kahnawake, Kanesetake, and Akwesasne, finding a place of refuge among their brothers.

Under surveillance of the Albany Committee of Correspondence in 1775, Guy Johnson, now superintendent for Indian Affairs, chiefly serving the Iroquois, was the first of the Johnson clan to go to Canada. He gathered 150 friends in mid-June, and after holding an Indian conference at Oswego, they traveled by way of Lake Ontario to Montreal. The refugees included Daniel Claus, Joseph Brant, John Deserontyon, Gilbert Tice, and Sir William's half-blood sons, William of Canajoharie and Peter Johnson.[14]

An early sign of Indian loyalty to the British came about a month later, when, with Governor Carleton's blessing, Guy Johnson held a great council outside Montreal.[15] The superintendent of Indian Affairs invited Canadian Indians from both the missions and the Great Lakes, as well as the Mohawks, who were now, thanks to Johnson, numerous in Canada. Guy Johnson reported that 1,700 Indians attended, including some Mississaugas from Lake Ontario. Much like the French Canadians, the mission Indians had declared neutrality and were wavering in their support for the British. To bolster their support, Guy emphasized the rebels' greed for land and the inability of "the Bostonians" to provide trade goods. The Mohawks were told that the land they left behind should be retaken by driving the rebels out. Guy claimed that those assembled agreed to join the British, but it is known that some of them were treating with the rebels at the same time, still following a policy of neutrality, for playing off the rebels against the British remained advantageous.

Discord within the Departments of Indian Affairs

In moving Native Americans into the British camp, the consistently financed Departments of Indian Affairs played an important role.[16] By holding councils, providing presents, and honoring the rituals of their villages, the departments were ultimately successful in keeping most Indians loyal. At least the departments had a budget, although it was constantly in red ink because of the many demands upon it. Appointed in London, the superintendents were responsible for designating and paying their own subordinates in America and providing the presents that were so crucial to Indian diplomacy. Active departments actually financed their own rangers and warriors and conducted their own raids.

Guy Johnson's department had been established during the Seven Years' War by the great patron of Indians, Sir William Johnson. Now Guy Johnson had subordinates like Daniel Claus as deputy superintendent of Canadian Indians, Joseph Brant as his secretary, and soldiers like Captain Gilbert Tice. Claus was a German immigrant who had come to the Mohawk Valley and lived with the Brants and then Sir William Johnson. While working in the Indian service, he married Sir William's daughter Ann and befriended and educated young Joseph Brant. As the brother of Sir William's Mohawk wife, Molly, Joseph was better educated than most white men, so that he and Claus tied the Mohawks to the Anglican Church by translating the Anglican Book of Common Prayer into Mohawk. Captain Tice, a Johnstown tavern keeper with military experience in the Seven Years' War, would raise rangers for Guy Johnson's department and in 1777 serve under Barry St. Leger at Oriskany and later at Ticonderoga.[17]

While Carleton needed Indians to defend Canada, he was not a friend of the Johnsons, whom he saw as challenging his authority over Quebec's Indian affairs. Established in 1773, the Quebec Department's authority stretched all the way to Michilimackinac in the Great Lakes. For this vast territory, Carleton made a stipulation about the use of his Indians that made it difficult for Guy Johnson to work with his department. He would not allow his Indians to fight outside the boundaries of Canada, that is, below St. Johns.[18]

After Guy Johnson and Daniel Claus arrived in Canada, Carleton eliminated Claus's job and much of Johnson's authority, bolstering his own Quebec Indian Department. Thus, Carleton would not support an expedition into New York as outlined by Guy at the July conference. Carleton wanted to keep control of Canadian Indian affairs so as to gain the support of Montreal fur traders for the defense of Canada, and he also felt that Guy was escalating the conflict, which he hoped might still be settled by compromise.[19]

Carleton's choice as superintendent of the Quebec Department was a Scot, John Campbell, a veteran of the 42nd Royal Highland Regiment, who had been wounded at Ticonderoga in 1758 and had served with Amherst in the conquest of Canada.[20] After a visit to Britain, in 1765 he became commandant of Detroit, where he gained experience dealing with Great Lakes Indians. Campbell also cemented alliances with French Canadians by marrying Marie-Anne, the daughter of Luc de La Corne, the Sieur de St. Luc, the veteran Canadian leader of French Indian auxiliaries. The Quebec Department was staffed by the extended families of La Corne and Campbell. Carleton also would seek to place officers like Captain Alexander Fraser in each of the Canadian mission villages. These well-born Britons would adopt Indian dress and become partially acculturated to better influence the village.

In his role as superintendent, Campbell encouraged some of the nearby mission Indians to resist the rebel invasion of 1775. Mission Indians shared responsibility for the defeat on September 6 of Ethan Allen's clandestine force on Montreal Island.[21] In this fray, Peter Johnson, sixteen-year-old son of Molly Brant and a member of the Iroquois Indian Department, looked most like a gentleman, so Allen, in surrendering, presented his sword to him. It was possible to be both an Indian and a gentleman while serving in the Indian Departments.

However, Superintendent Campbell was soon captured by the rebels and sent to New York, not to be exchanged until 1777, when he would be in charge of most of Burgoyne's Indians.[22] He and his father-in-law would attract a force of Great Lakes Indians for the Saratoga Campaign, before they had a falling out that caused a duel between them. Campbell genuinely took to Indian affairs, and when he died in Montreal in 1795, his funeral was attended by numerous citizens of all ranks, including a large body of Native Americans.

To counteract Carleton's hostility to their influence over Indians and his reticence in using them, Guy Johnson, Joseph Brant, John Hill Oteronyente, Daniel Claus, and others of Guy's department left Quebec on November 11, 1775, and sailed for Britain.[23] They hoped that British authorities would modify Carleton's influence over Native American policy and sought assurance from the crown as to the extent of their role in Indian affairs. Claus was especially anxious, because Carleton had refused to recognize his skills with Canadian Indians, leaving him without a position. In Britain the Johnson party successfully gained recognition, especially impressing Lord George Germain, the minister for America, who would remain supportive of the extensive use of Indians for the rest of the war. As a result of the visit, the Johnson party would obtain most of the assurances they sought; however, Claus still failed to obtain a position, forcing him to remain in Britain to plead his case.

To enhance the popularity of the Johnson party in Britain and to show that the Indians were not barbarians, three portraits were painted of the Iroquois visitors by Britain's leading artists. Benjamin West portrayed Guy Johnson with an unidentified Indian, while George Romney did Joseph Brant at the request of the Earl of Warwick, and Mrs. Richardson—at the cost of the British government—did John Oteronyente.[24] The portraits were definitely propaganda pieces for home consumption. Guy Johnson was shown in an English uniform, but with Indian decorative beadwork on his hat, his braid, and his sash. Conversely, Brant and Oteronyente, while plumed, showed acculturation to British ways in that they had the elegant linen shirts and silver gorgets of the typical British officer. Crucially, the Indians were portrayed as tranquil and handsome, without any of the trappings of savage passion. To the British, the Johnsons and their allies appeared to be the very ideal of a noble savage.

DEVELOPING BRITISH POLICY TOWARD NATIVE AMERICANS

In contrast to what was being portrayed in Britain, the opinions held by most British officers in Canada showed they lacked an understanding of Indian culture. Many officers were blind to the Indian perspective of warfare, belittling their motivations for participating in conflict. A British general in Burgoyne's army complained, "There is no dependence upon even those Indians who are declared in our favor, and there are a number in that country our avowed enemies . . . there has not been a single instance where the Indians have fulfilled their engagements but are influenced by caprice, a dream or a desire of protracting the war, to obtain presents, and have dispersed and deserted the troops."[25]

The officers did not realize that Indians took so much booty because it was one of the few sources of manufactured goods necessary to sustain their villages. They did not see that the Indians could only support themselves in the field for a limited time and that, while many left, many also returned. A gulf of misunderstanding was fostered.

Carleton would use Indians sparingly in order to maintain control over them and to prevent their depredations.[26] No wonder both he and later Burgoyne made the exaggerated claim that the only reason they cultivated Indians was to prevent them from going over to the rebels. Carleton was no Amherst, however; he would work with Native Americans and ally with them when an occasion demanded it.

Making Allies for the Campaign of 1776

By the summer of 1776, Carleton would put aside his fears about Indians and urge them to join his expedition against the rebels on Lake Champlain. He recognized that Indian tactics allowed them to undermine a local population's ability to defend itself. He needed Indians to serve as scouts and to put fear into rebel armies because they could not cope with their marauding method of warfare. He spent more time than Burgoyne would for his expedition on gathering about four hundred Indians for the invasion of Lake Champlain.[27]

To do this, he held several conferences around Montreal in June and July 1776 with the Iroquois, the mission Indians, and the Great Lake Indians. At the first, on June 23, Carleton greeted representatives of the Iroquois and their related Canadian missions assembled in the former Jesuit church at Montreal. It had been prepared for the ceremony so that "about 300 [Indians] were present from the nations; these were sitting on benches around the church smoking tobacco."[28] At the conference, Carleton was aided by Captain Christopher Carleton, his nephew and secretary, who would act as his uncle's Indian liaison in the expedition to Lake Champlain.

Having completed pleasantries with the Indian audience, Guy Carleton then reproached the Kahnawakes, whose mission was only a few miles from Montreal, for having been neutral and failing to join the king at the beginning of the war. The Kahnawakes alleged that it had been the fault of their oldest leader, who at the age of eighty was not present. Whereupon the assembled Indians were taken into the service of the king for one year, although they would have to wait for further directions as to where they would serve. Carleton was suspicious. "One of the leaders of this nation wore on this occasion the coat of General [Edward] Braddock whom he had killed in the [Seven Years' War]; his little son of nine years wore the vest belonging to it."[29]

Nine days later, Carleton and his officers went to the Kahnawake mission itself, where the residents turned out with flags and formed two lines, between which he and his staff passed while they were saluted with a discharge of small cannon and firearms. They inspected the church, presided over by a Jesuit, and its silver utensils, and they entered the Indian cabins, which were mostly in rundown and dirty condition. As to their foodways it was observed, "The Indians raised nothing but corn, which they prepare in different ways for food and they were deeply involved in raising cattle, to replace declining hunting and fishing resources."[30] The conference was part of a long-term effort to win over the Kahnawakes. Not until September were they finally allied to the British.

The Kahnawakes would scout Crown Point for Carleton's invading army, where they took five retreating rebels prisoner, bringing them to St. Johns.[31] Since Carleton had placed a British officer and several Canadians with the Kahnawakes, they were prevented from taking scalps. However promising they were, Carleton did not get to test his Indian allies further because, as seen, he decided to abandon Crown Point.

Earlier on July 18, 1776, Carleton held a conference with Native Americans at Montreal with deputations from distant nations living between and near Lakes Ontario and Erie. They numbered about 180 "good looking and well built men." They offered their grandfather, the King of England, and their father, General Carleton, their services against "the Bostonians." Carleton received them in a friendly manner, since they had come a long distance and in the past they had aided the French. He did not, however, accept their services at this time but requested they keep themselves in readiness until needed, in the meantime protecting the Great Lakes territory. He knew they had a reputation for being uncontrollable, and he still followed a policy of restraint in using Indians. They reacted to him positively, with these words: "Since the rebels have revolted against the English nation, we have come to offer the King our services and will love and obey Gen. Carleton, who has been quashing the enemy's assaults."[32]

Before Carleton's expedition set out for Lake Champlain, Joseph Brant and Guy Johnson returned from Britain, arriving in Staten Island and observing General William Howe's conquest of New York City. Afterward, Brant, with Gilbert Tice, went on to Oquaga and Fort Niagara rather than return to Montreal. Late in December 1776 he was thinking of a new offensive, as he wrote to urge the mission Mohawks at Kanesetake to support the British and join him in a raid in the Mohawk Valley "to deliver my brothers the Mohawks, who I imagine are [rebel] prisoners." [33] Brant went on, "I do not think it right to let my brothers go to war under the command of General Carleton as [he] expects and tries to have Indians under the same command as the regular troops, but it will be the best method for us to make war our own way." Brant was already showing himself to be an independent Indian leader, who emphasized the Indians' method of warfare rather than allowing them to be placed under the restrictive control of a general like Carleton.

By now it was evident that Carleton's restrictions on the use of Indians could not last. Despite their early wavering, the Six Nations, the mission Indians, and the Great Lakes Indians would become more directly involved in the emerging conflict. The rebels, furthermore, were not about to sit by and let most Native Americans become British allies.

SCHUYLER'S DIFFICULTY WITH NATIVE AMERICANS

In 1775 Congress created three committees of Indian Commissioners, with Philip Schuyler as president of the Northern Department Commissioners.[34] He would keep this position throughout the war, even after he resigned as a major general of the Continental Army. As we have seen, the Schuyler family had been involved in Indian affairs since the seventeenth century by chairing and sitting on the board of colonial Albany's Indian Commissioners. They had lost power to Sir William Johnson, the superintendent of Indian Affairs, but with the expulsion of the Johnsons from the Mohawk Valley, they saw a chance to regain their influence. Following family tradition, Philip Schuyler was an old hand in calling Indian councils, making presentations, and providing the crucial gifts that sealed any diplomatic bargain.

Schuyler held the first Northern Department Indian conference at Albany late in August 1775. He followed the congressional representatives at the conference in promoting a neutral policy for Native

Americans, unless they were actually found to be serving the British in hostile activities.[35] At this early stage of the war, the neutral policy suited not only the rebels but most of the Iroquois League and many of the Canadian missions. However, only the Oneidas, under the influence of their rebel missionary, the Reverend Samuel Kirkland, and their dependents, the Tuscaroras and the new Stockbridge villages that had relocated near the Oneidas, took Schuyler's call for the conference seriously and attended. Kirkland's missionary work had New England backers, and his hostility to the Johnson family's influence over the Six Nations dated from before the death of Sir William in 1774. Schuyler did make an effort to placate the Mohawks of Fort Hunter, by allowing their Anglican missionary, the Reverend John Stuart, to stay, but the diplomatic gesture actually firmed the alliance between the Mohawks and the British.

The one subject that Schuyler refused to discuss was the issue foremost on Indian minds: land claims. The aggressive seizure of their lands by whites was of far greater importance to them than Congress's quarrel with Britain. Instead, the attendees were entertained by bull-baiting and a foot race in the streets of Albany, and the Oneida and Stockbridge women sang twice to the gathering. To seal Congress's peace initiative, presents were distributed to the Oneidas and Tuscaroras, which the hosts helped them carry as far as Schenectady. While neutrality was accepted by those Indians who attended, land issues remained unsettled, and the conference was not an indication of what the majority of the Iroquois felt.

Ultimately, however, Schuyler and his commissioners could not afford to maintain an organization like the British Indian Departments. Schuyler did not have the resources to support the congressional peace policy, as he was bombarded by Indian requests for hunting ammunition, clothes, and manufactured goods. At this time, he sidestepped the issue of using Stockbridge Indians because he could not supply them, and he passed their request to serve on to Congress.[36]

After Sir John Johnson left the Mohawk Valley for Canada, Schuyler finally called an Indian council at German Flats in early August 1776 to reassess his position with the Six Nations.[37] He had delayed the council to get as good a turnout as possible, but attending were only 150 chiefs and warriors, mainly from the Oneidas and Tuscaroras, so that support was identical to the previous year. A treaty was draw up at German Flats, but it meant little because so few Indians attended.

Kirkland and his Oneidas were now isolated, surrounded by hostile members of the Six Nations. Schuyler did place Elias Dayton's New Jersey Continentals as a permanent garrison in the Mohawk Valley to support the Oneidas.

By June 1776 Congress was no longer upholding its earlier peace policy, instead forcing Indians to choose one side or the other. The rebel defeat in Canada led the Kahnawakes to observe that the rebels seemed "too weak to protect them against the severity of the English."[38] As we have seen, the Kahnawakes would not risk committing themselves until they knew the British would be victorious. Although rebel-inspired parties existed in many of the missions, after the retreat of the Continental Army from Canada in early 1776 they declined in influence, and most of the missions came to support the British.

While Schuyler failed to detach the mission Indians and most Iroquois from the British, the rebels found a sympathetic ear in the town of Stockbridge, Massachusetts. When the War of Independence broke out, seventeen Stockbridges enlisted in the Provincial army and traveled with their families to serve under Washington at the siege of Boston.[39] As yet they fought in Indian style, rather than mustering with the Massachusetts militia. They asked that no liquor be provided for them as it rendered them unfit to fight. Later in the year, Stockbridge Indians, headed by Captain Abraham Ninham, who had attended the Stockbridge Indian School, and Winthrop Hoit, who served as translator, helped the rebels who had invaded Canada to contact the mission Indians.

After the rebels' early peace policy was set aside, the numbers of their actual Indian allies were limited. Only the Stockbridges served with the rebels. The Oneidas showed interest in supporting the rebels and some would eventually join Gates at Bemis Heights. Schuyler was a master of supply, but his first priority was the Continental Army and rebel militia, and only crumbs were left for the Indian commissioners. Within these limits, however, he made every effort to cultivate Native Americans, never doubting that they could be valuable allies.

Despite their concerns about Indian conduct, North American British generals also saw them as important allies to be cultivated. The British Indian Departments guaranteed the presence of Indians in their expeditions, once the rebels were driven from Canada. Most British officers had to remember, however, that Indian peoples had their own specific goals, be it the replenishment of their population through obtaining captives or the seizure of booty that might be their only source of white manufactured goods. The early aloofness of Carleton would disappear when he weighed it against how effectively Indians could scout, raid, and put fear into rebel soldiers. Like Carleton, Burgoyne would have to use infinite patience in dealing with them so as to garner their support.

Schuyler's efforts to replace the Johnsons by holding Indian councils in the Albany region displayed the weakness of the rebels in relations with Native Americans. The resources of Schuyler's Indian commissioners remained limited, not just in terms of council gifts, but of the continued sustenance that Indians expected as allies. Only the Oneidas, Tuscaroras, and Stockbridges would appear at Saratoga as allies of the rebels.

PART III

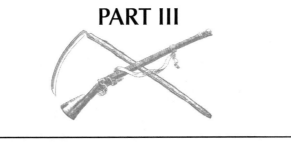

THE SARATOGA CAMPAIGN

6

BRITISH SUCCESS
Ticonderoga, Hubbardton,
Skenesborough, Fort Ann

By the spring of 1777, efforts at reconciliation between the colonies and the mother country had come to a standstill because the previous year's Declaration of Independence had, as far as Congress was concerned, removed the issue of independence from negotiations. Among Burgoyne's officers it was evident that the rebels were now responsible for continuing a violent war. British volunteer and ensign Thomas Anburey concluded, "The [rebels], when they drew the sword, must have foreseen a bloody contest, and expected all the horrors of a war, carried on as it were in their own bosoms, laying waste their fields of harvest, destroying every comfort, and introducing every misery mankind is capable of devising."[1] Now that the rebels had brought the war on themselves, he felt, they were to reap the consequences of a professional army conquering their territory. This attitude assumed that the British army would have to destroy all that was in their path, without discriminating between friend and foe—a far too simplistic view of what would happen, and not one favored by Burgoyne.

To invade a second time from Canada, Burgoyne had 8,500 men, a considerably larger force than Carleton's of the previous year. Of the 7,500 regulars the British slightly outnumbered the Germans.[2] At this time the auxiliaries—Loyalists, Indians, Canadian militia, and teamsters—made up fewer than one in nine of Burgoyne's invading force. However, these numbers would fluctuate during the campaign as men came, were organized, went to garrison duty, or returned to Canada and beyond.

As noted, Burgoyne had his own plan for invading the region from Canada in the spring of 1777. He felt his background had prepared him for command of this army. He was born in London in 1723 and educated at Westminster School, which was popular with military families.[3] At the age of fifteen, he entered the British army. Burgoyne saw active service in the Seven Years' War, but in Portugal not America, where he won an important victory at Prato Rio in 1762. After the war, he was elected to Parliament and became a leading figure in London social circles. Promoted to major general in 1772, Burgoyne came to Boston three years later, just after the confrontation at Lexington and Concord. He was present, but without field command, at the Battle of Bunker Hill. After this costly victory, he went back to England to use his political influence to gain an independent command. He was sent to Canada in 1776, as second-in-command to Guy Carleton, so he still longed for his own command. Back in London for the winter, he maneuvered to gain the top position of the proposed expedition against Albany in 1777, while leaving Carleton as governor of Canada. Burgoyne never directly criticized Carleton, but he knew Germain disliked him, and he presented a plan for the expedition as his own idea. When Carleton found out in Quebec that he had lost the command, he was angered by what had gone on in England and resigned, although it took a year to replace him. After his defeat at Saratoga, Burgoyne defended himself before Parliament in 1779, claiming he had not maneuvered for the command. Thus a plethora of documentation on Burgoyne's effort to get the command exists, but all of it is biased.

Because of his service in America, especially at Bunker Hill, Burgoyne knew how fatal a frontal attack by British soldiers could be. He commented on how rebel soldiers turned "every tree or bush into a . . . temporary fortress," from which they could only be dislodged by "either cannon or by the resolute attack of light infantry."[4] He was aware of the need to reform his army to reflect American conditions and yet retain the advantages of superior military organization and cohesion. What he desired was more units of British light infantry and German Jaegers and to train all British troops like them. Light infantry and grenadier companies had existed for each British regiment to meet both European and American conditions in the

Seven Years' War. After that war, however, the light infantry had fallen out of favor and only been reemphasized in 1773, two years before hostilities broke out. Burgoyne wanted the light infantry back in the limelight of North American armies and to be more numerous than the current one company per regiment.

What impressed a cavalryman like Burgoyne was the speed of light infantry.[5] They moved at a trot rather than walking, and their favorite place in the line was on the flanks, where they could get behind the enemy. They were masters at skirmishing, dividing in small groups, exposing themselves only long enough to fire at the enemy. From the beginning, their uniform was lighter than that of the regulars, with coattails cut off and tricornered hat cut down. In the field, they discarded the heavy drums that regulars used for signals and adopted the German Jaegers' loud hunting horn. Nicknamed the Light Bobs, they compared their work in seeking rebels to fox hunting. The light infantry was also known as the place to serve for energetic officers who wanted a promotion, since light infantry companies were most watched and measured by generals. The Germans had similar special units of Jaegers, light infantry, and grenadiers, but their other troops were not trained in these tactics, which may explain the slowness associated with them.

To cope with the rebels, Burgoyne's top officers were a talented lot: Simon Fraser, William Phillips, James Hamilton, and the Germans Friedrich Adolph von Riedesel, W. R. von Gall, and Johann Friedrich von Specht. All had been in Canada since 1776, and the British officers had served under Carleton in the invasion of Lake Champlain. Several were Scots, reflecting the increasing role that nation was playing in the British military since the union of England and Scotland at the beginning of the eighteenth century.

Simon Fraser was as Scottish as the original Argyle patentees when he came to North America in 1755 as a lieutenant to serve in the newly organized 60th Royal American Regiment. Born in 1729 at the Fraser ancestral estate of Bainain in the Highlands, he was the second youngest son of Alexander Fraser.[6] The family suffered heavily for supporting Prince Charles at Culloden in 1746, and their house was destroyed and estates confiscated. At the age of eighteen, Simon entered the Dutch service and was wounded during the siege of Bergen-op-Zoom. He continued to serve in Holland as a member of the Scots Brigade. He then went to North America, making him the only one of Burgoyne's generals who had experience there during the Seven Years' War. After service in the 60th Regiment, in 1757 he was transferred to Fraser's Highlanders. As a lieutenant and then captain, he was present at the capture of Louisbourg and the fall of Quebec. Wolfe used him for intelligence gathering during the siege of Quebec because he spoke French.

With the Seven Years' War ended, Fraser was transferred to Germany and served on the staff of Ferdinand of Brunswick, who would supply most of the German troops for the Burgoyne expedition. Commissioned major of the 24th Regiment, in 1768 he became its lieutenant colonel. He served at Gibraltar and then in Ireland, where he met his future comrades, John Burgoyne and William Phillips. He came back to Quebec with the relief force in the spring of 1776. In June, after reorganizing the Canadian army, Carleton named him brigadier of his advanced corps, and he was with him at Crown Point. While Fraser's commission as brigadier only held in North America, he was tapped by Burgoyne the next year for the same position when he was forming his army. While older than most of Burgoyne's generals, Fraser was still six years Burgoyne's junior. He was a brave leader of men in the field, and that alone made him Burgoyne's most indispensable general.

Fraser had met the prominent artillery officer William Phillips in Ireland. Born in Wales in 1731, the son of a British military family, Phillips was slightly younger than Fraser.[7] At sixteen he had enrolled in the Royal Artillery Academy at Woolwich as a gentleman cadet. This was the only school of military studies in Britain, showing that artillery and engineering were fields that required brains as much as bravery. Philips excelled in every facet of gunnery and artillery warfare. When the Seven Years' War broke out, he was sent as a captain to Germany with the British Expeditionary Force. During the battle of Warburg, Phillips executed a new maneuver by sending his heaviest guns into battle, cutting off and entrapping a French army with these guns. By the end of the war, he was a lieutenant colonel and had established the musical group that became the Royal Artillery Band.

After the Seven Years' War, Phillips continued to be active as inspector general of the artillery in the Mediterranean and then commander of artillery at Woolwich. In 1772 he was named lieutenant governor of Windsor Castle, and two years later he was promoted to brigadier.[8] Like Burgoyne, he pursued a political career, and in 1774 he was elected to Parliament from Boroughbridge in Yorkshire. With the upheaval in the colonies, Phillips was named a major general and sent to Quebec in the spring of 1776. Carleton ordered him on to St. Johns, where he was responsible for outfitting the new British fleet that swept the rebel fleet from Lake Champlain. It would be difficult to imagine a brighter and more dedicated artillery officer.

Another Scot, James Hamilton was only thirty-one years old, by far the youngest general in Burgoyne's army. From his father he would eventually inherit the title of Laird of Murdostown.[9] Like Fraser, his brigadier rank was limited to North America. He commanded at Ticonderoga after its capture but itched to see action and was replaced by Brigadier Henry Powell in early August. He led the 21st Regiment and would serve with distinction at the Battle of Freeman's Farm.

Considering Burgoyne's emphasis on speed, a key officer had to be the commander of the British light infantry: Alexander Lindsey, Earl of Balcarres. Another Scot, Lindsey was only a youth of twenty-four at the time of the Saratoga Campaign.[10] He had been commissioned an ensign in the 55th Regiment ten years before, and four years later he advanced to captain of the 42nd Foot. In between he served at Gibraltar and studied at Göttingen University in Germany, which had been founded by King George II. At the end of 1775 he purchased the rank of major in the 53rd Regiment. When he arrived in Canada in 1776, Carleton chose him, despite his inexperience, to be commander of the light infantry, and Burgoyne continued him in this position.

Below these key positions, about twenty-five officers provided the chain of command for each British regiment. A good example of a career officer is Lieutenant William Digby of the 53rd Regiment. He joined that regiment as an ensign in Ireland in 1770.[11] Three years later he was promoted to lieutenant and joined one of the flank companies, the grenadiers. He seemed on track to further promotion, and in 1776 he embarked from Ireland with Carleton's reinforcements. He was in Carleton's invasion force, and upon its return to Canada, he wintered at Chambly on the Richelieu River. In Burgoyne's campaign of 1777, his was among the two flank companies of the 53rd chosen to go, while the other eight companies were left to protect Canada. In July the remaining companies of the 53rd were sent south to garrison Ticonderoga, so the full regiment was involved in the campaign after all. Digby kept a journal of the Burgoyne expedition that is an important source of the British perspective.

What motivated these experienced officers to come to Canada and serve under Burgoyne? Promotion was one answer. For officers in the British army, promotion was a multifaceted process combining money with patronage and occasionally merit that was measured by distinction on the battlefield. In Protestant Ireland—as fertile a ground for army officers as Scotland—"placement in the forces was a last resort," for family patriarchs with many sons, who had failed to obtain places for them in the clergy, the law or the government.[12] Those who succeeded in purchasing a commission hoped to prosper, but they could find themselves stuck in ranks after ten or even twenty years' service because they lacked further money to purchase the next rank above them. This was a reason why Horatio Gates had left the British army and was now a Continental general. Others lacked connections, especially with the general staff or among the peerage. While money and patronage were important, brilliance on the battlefield and its recognition by superior officers could cut through these two barriers. Some regimental lieutenant colonels shepherded their favorites into higher rank. Thus combat was desired by younger officers, who saw it as a chance to prove their mettle and gain promotion.

Older officers, however, were less keen and sought staff positions that provided more pay and less demanding physical exertion. Efforts by the Hanoverian monarchs and their commanders to end purchase and instill greater professionalism in the army inevitably failed. The system was not as corrupt as it sounds, for the purchase of commissions allowed aged officers to sell their commission and obtain a sum of money for retirement.

The Germans

The leader of the German contingent, Baron Friedrich Adolph von Riedesel, proved to be a major asset to Burgoyne, although as a German, he felt he was treated as an outsider. At thirty-nine years old, he was the second youngest of Burgoyne's generals and was fifteen years Burgoyne's junior. Of a noble Hessian family, Riedesel's father sent him to Marburg University at the age of fifteen to study law.[13] He was an inferior student, and he spent much time admiring the parades of the Hessian infantry quartered in the city. He was recruited by a Hessian officer, who claimed that he had his father's consent to enter a Hessian regiment. The youngster joined the regiment, but when he wrote to his father, he found the officer's claim was a hoax, and his father was angry, cutting him off from all financial assistance. He was left to make the best of his new military life.

His Hessian regiment was hired by the British and he went to England, where he learned English, although imperfectly.[14] He was then sent back to Germany to participate in the Seven Years' War. Becoming a favorite of Prince Ferdinand of Brunswick, he left the Hessian army to serve him. By the time the American War of Independence broke out, he was a colonel in the Brunswick army and was given an important promotion to major general and commander of the troops hired by the British ministry from Prince Ferdinand. He claimed serving the British was no problem, for he felt, in military matters, he knew no duty but his orders. He also possessed a family, for in 1762 he had married a seventeen-year-old girl from Brandenburg, Prussia, Friederike Charlotte Louise von Massow. By 1776 they had three daughters.

His first duty in February 1776 was to march his 2,282 men and their 77 wives to Stade on the Elbe River, where they embarked for Portsmouth, one of Britain's chief naval bases.[15] In all, 4,300 Brunswickers and 668 Hessians would be gathered at Portsmouth. The British were critical of Riedesel's recruits; they felt they were either too young or too old and that many were not properly outfitted, as there was a lack of overcoats for the Canadian winter. The fleet of thirty vessels finally sailed from Portsmouth on April 4 and arrived at Quebec as part of a relief force on June 1. Riedesel adapted easily to Canada, noticing that he was able to get meat and milk in profusion, but that the country lacked vegetables and fruit. Carleton gave him a mixed command of one English and two German battalions, plus Canadians and Indians, to do mop-up operations between Quebec and Montreal as the rebels fled from Canada. However, his German regiments did not follow Carleton in the invasion of Lake Champlain, as they were held back to defend Canada.

Riedesel was supported by two German generals whose role in the Saratoga Campaign has been as neglected almost as much as the excellent service of his Brunswick and Hessian soldiers. W. R. von Gall arrived in Canada with Riedesel in June 1776, where he held the local position of brigadier general.[16] He was the only Hessian general officer in Burgoyne's army and commanded the brigade consisting of the Erbprintz Hesse-Hanau Regiment and Prinz Friedrich's Brunswick Regiment. He was to show the competence of an experienced professional at Saratoga. The other German brigadier was Johann Friedrich von Specht, a Brunswicker, who also held the local position of brigadier general. He led the brigade consisting of the Rhetz, Specht, and Riedesel Regiments, the Rhetz being a Braunschweig Musketeer regiment under the command of Major Balthasar von Lucke. Also a complete professional, von Specht kept a journal that shows the German perspective of the Burgoyne Campaign.

British officers were almost as disdainful of their German associates as they were of the rebel command. After Burgoyne reached Skenesborough, on July 16 a disturbance broke out between British and German soldiers, fueled by liquor. Burgoyne responded that "any conduct . . . whether of British or German, that shall tend to obstruct the harmony, which has hitherto so happily reigned between the two nations . . . will be punished as a crime the most fatal to the success and honor of the Campaign."[17] He saw that if he could not maintain order within his two contingents, he certainly could not confront his enemy with a unified force. The division between the two forces would continue to smolder, as time and again the Germans proved themselves competent professional soldiers.

Even the most rapidly moving units in Burgoyne's army were slowed down by their camp followers. The British army allowed six women per company to do the laundry and attend in the hospital. They had to be married to one of the soldiers, although they did not cook for their husband. Each woman was issued half the ration of a man by turning out on morning parade to be counted, thus they were referred to as "women on ration."[18] If their husbands died, the women had ten days to marry another man from the regiment or be turned out. Other women were more loosely attached to the army, but they were not regarded as proper. Regimental commanders constantly ordered these women to leave, but the continued repetition of this order shows that they remained an integral part of the British army.

Besides the women, the army was also accompanied by sutlers, who were issued permits. From Burgoyne's headquarters at Skenesborough in mid-July, it was ordered that "all persons desirous of establishing huts or tents in the rear of the army, for the sale of useful commodities, are to apply to the Adjutant Generals in order that the nature of their traffic may be inquired into."[19] Among the permit stipulations was prohibition of the sale of liquor to soldiers or Indians.

Burgoyne's Canadians

When he was planning his campaign in London, Burgoyne placed emphasis on Canadians as the chief source of his auxiliaries. They were to number 500, perhaps more; in contrast he expected almost nothing from the Loyalist refugees. He may have been thinking of the Canadian militia's proud service record during and before the Seven Years' War against the British.[20] In 1757 the Marquis de Montcalm had gathered nearly 3,000 unpaid Canadian militiamen for the destruction of Fort William Henry, although his effort was restricted in duration so the militia could return for the harvest. Anyone, however, who had been in Canada in 1776 knew that this was no longer the case. Carleton had experienced only the lethargy of his Canadian units in the defense of Quebec, and he correctly put little stock in them. The habitants did not even want to serve as defensive militia, let alone in an expedition against the rebels. Carleton had devised a system by which Canadians were to be recruited by French-Canadian officials so they would have their own officers. Carleton hoped to attract French-Canadian aristocrats to these leadership positions. As an example, Charles-Louis Tarieu de Lanaudière, the heir of an important French-Canadian family, had returned to Canada in 1767 to look after his family's land holdings, and in the process he became a supporter of the British regime. He was one of the few officers with Carleton when he escaped the rebels at Sorel and went to Quebec. However, when Lanaudière tried to recruit militia for Carleton in 1775, he failed miserably. At Berthierville, on the St. Lawrence between Montreal and Trois-Rivières, the unarmed recruits he had gathered were attacked by the habitants and he was humiliatingly taken prisoner, though eventually he was released.

Other examples of French Canadians who supported the British are René-Ovide Hertel de Rouville and his brother, Captain Jean-Baptiste Hertel de Rouville. The former was a beneficiary of the Quebec Act as one of the first two French-Canadian judges appointed under its provisions, while the latter was a captain of the Quebec militia, who would serve with St. Leger in the Mohawk Valley. The brothers were thus tied to the British regime. But their fellow French Canadians accused them of being sycophants and refused to cooperate with their recruiting efforts.[21] The habitants supported neither the British nor the rebels during their brief occupation. This neutrality was far from a

Quaker's pacifism, rather it stemmed from deeply conservative Catholic religious values and mistrust of capitalistic British Americans.

After the Canadian winter of 1776–77, Burgoyne stubbornly made an effort to raise three companies of volunteers from Quebec, Rivière-du-Loup, and Montreal. They were to be enrolled for the entire year. Selected as company captains were Samuel McKay, René de Boucherville, and David Monin, all experienced from Carleton's previous campaign. McKay declined the rank and would serve in other capacities. He was replaced by Jean-Baptiste Hertel de Rouville. Boucherville's and Monin's Montreal area militia left Ticonderoga on July 26 to join Burgoyne's army, but they were not conspicuous at the Battles of Freeman's Farm and Bemis Heights.[22] By September 14 the remaining Canadians of Boucherville and Monin were viewed by British officers as untrustworthy—although the Canadians may have seen themselves as perceptive. However, because Monin was killed at Freeman's Farm on September 19, he did become a hero to British officers.

It is impossible to judge how many Canadians ended up with Burgoyne's army. Many served as artificers and teamsters along Lake Champlain, especially at Ticonderoga. However, from the beginning of Burgoyne's campaign they tended to desert.[23] Burgoyne made a point in the Convention of October 17, 1777, to gain permission from Gates to allow them to return to Canada, concerned as he was that they should not be mistaken for regulars in his army. Certainly they did not play the part in Burgoyne's expedition that he had hoped.

St. Leger's Expedition

A diversion in the Mohawk Valley had always been part of Burgoyne's plan, although Lieutenant Colonel Barry St. Leger's diversion drew off men from Burgoyne, especially Native Americans and Loyalists, that might have bolstered him. St. Leger had 100 men from his own regiment, the 34th, 246 from Johnson's Royal Regiment of New York, 100 from the 8th Regiment of regulars, 50 Hanau Chasseurs, 50 Canadians under Captain Jean-Baptiste Hertel de Rouville, 105 of Butler's Indian Department rangers, and a large number of Mississauga and Mohawk Indians, perhaps 1,000 in all.[24] Burgoyne's plan envisioned that this diversion would take pressure off his army because the rebels would need to send men from Albany to confront St. Leger in the Mohawk

Valley. St. Leger's expedition has been extensively covered elsewhere and will not be part of this account.

In comparison to Howe's force of about 25,000 in the New York City area, Burgoyne's army was a very modest force. It did have able officers, the best of their profession, who were concerned to gain promotion not just though the usual channels but by bravery on the battlefield. As a result of their conquests in the Seven Years' War, British officers felt that they and their men had esprit de corps, based on their superior record of victories over other nations. This grated on the Germans, who remained apart, even though they made up almost half of the army. By this time, many British officers were also disrespectful of all colonials, not just rebels but also their own allied Indians, Canadians, and Loyalists. From the beginning the army would need more Indians and Loyalists for scouts, intelligence gathering, skirmishing, and fighting on the battlefield. The army's weakness was in its lack of such auxiliaries.

TICONDEROGA, "GIBRALTAR OF THE NORTH"

After Carleton had left Crown Point on November 4, 1776 there was a rapid retreat of rebel officers from Ticonderoga, including Gates, Arthur St. Clair, and James Wilkinson, to winter in more hospitable surroundings. Gates claimed to be reinforcing Washington's army, but once he arrived in the Philadelphia area, he was far more interested in lobbying Congress for command of the Northern Department.[25] He played no part in Washington's brilliant forays against Howe's outposts at Trenton and Princeton, instead following Congress all the way to Baltimore, where they had fled fearing that the British would take Philadelphia. He perceptively saw that Congress, not Washington or Schuyler, was in reality his commander and that an end run to Baltimore would be profitable. By winning the sympathy of congressional politicians, he hoped to replace Schuyler.

Most of the defending army at Ticonderoga also left in the middle of November, enlistments having expired and, anyway, it being impossible to maintain so large a force over winter. That left Colonel Anthony Wayne in charge of a garrison of 2,500 men, half of whom were on the sick rolls. This number would be further reduced as winter wore on. It was so cold in these months that Wayne claimed, "I was not half thawed until I put one bottle of wine under my sword belt at dinner . . . for by the time one side is warm [in front of the fire] the other froze."[26] He struggled to maintain discipline, while constructing the piers for the bridge of boats across Lake Champlain to Mount Independence that was meant to hold the sprawling fortifications together.

Ticonderoga was a wind-blown and isolated place. Garrisons had all they could do to survive over the winter. Engineer Jeduthan Baldwin wrote that it "was so cold we could not work at the bridge" across Lake Champlain. Insubordination as a result of jealousy between the garrison's Massachusetts and Pennsylvania regiments was common. The garrison continued to contract, as Continentals went to Washington's army and were replaced by militia.[27] It was clear the garrison was growing weaker, but when New Hampshire legislator Josiah Bartlett tried to send Long's Continental Regiment to reinforce it, the excuses were legion: not enough commissioned officers, not enough money to pay them, no winter clothing. By March 2, 1777, the garrison had only a bit over 1,000 effectives, and 850 of these were New York militiamen.

By early June conditions at Ticonderoga had improved. Continental colonel Nathan Hale of New Hampshire thought the war would not last. He speculated to his wife, Abigail: "Should the war continue; which I hope will not be the case, should we be able to maintain our ground this campaign, I think we have the greatest reason to expect [the war] will soon be over."[28] Though, he added, the "overruling hand of Providence" might change this. Hale had been a merchant in Rindge, New Hampshire, where his wife was now in charge of family affairs, including the collection of rent revenue from his tenants. He clearly wanted to return home to again take charge of his business affairs.

The command situation for the Northern Department was confusing as Gates returned from Baltimore. Congress had ordered Gates to take command of Ticonderoga again, but in the spring of 1777 he had never gotten farther than Albany, hoping that Congress had meant that he, rather than Schuyler, was now in command of the Northern Department. However, Congress confirmed that Schuyler was still in command, making Gates subordinate to him, so he left Albany in early June, not for Ticonderoga, but again southward to lobby Congress for the prize he sought.[29] As confusion grew, Congress knew it needed a commander for Ticonderoga, and in April it promoted Arthur St.

Clair to major general and named him commander of the vast works that had been initiated by Gates. St. Clair arrived at Ticonderoga at the same time Gates was leaving Albany for Congress.

Like many former British officers, St. Clair was a Scot. He had come to the colonies in 1757 as an ensign of the Royal American Regiment, in which he served at the capture of Louisbourg and on the Plains of Abraham outside Quebec. Born in 1736, he was the son of a merchant of Thurso, the northernmost point in mainland Britain. He studied medicine at the University of Edinburgh and interned as a doctor in London.[30] When the Seven Years' War ended in 1762, St. Clair bought 4,000 acres in western Pennsylvania and became a local squire. In 1775 Congress made him a Continental colonel, and he served with Washington in the Trenton and Princeton Campaign. Clearly, the command of Ticonderoga was a promotion, his first position of independent responsibility.

St. Clair found the fortifications at Ticonderoga much weaker than they had been in the fall of 1776 because the garrison had used the abatis and other structures as firewood during the winter. He had barely 2,000 troops fit for duty and only 300 artillerymen to service the numerous guns.[31] The bridge across the lake was unfinished, as were the Mount Independence defenses on the east side of the lake. St. Clair was hesitant to call up more militia because he did not have enough supplies to feed them. Schuyler sent reinforcements, building St. Clair's garrison to 3,500 men.

The arrival of 800 reinforcements under Lieutenant Colonel Seth Warner on July 5 bolstered the garrison to about half the size of Burgoyne's army. Warner had recruited his reinforcements from several states. Under orders from St. Clair, he went to the Rutland area, and by July 1 he was gathering militia from the Grants, Massachusetts, and New Hampshire to add to the Ticonderoga garrison. In convincing the militia to leave their farms, he colorfully exclaimed, "I should be glad if a few hills of corn unhoed should not be a motive sufficient to detain men at home."[32] He soon had Colonel William Williams of the eastern Grants and Colonel Samuel Robinson, Jr., of Bennington at Hubbardton, and he expected Colonel Benjamin Bellows's New Hampshire regiment to join them. Already, Warner was finding it necessary to depend on states like New Hampshire or Massachusetts to supplement the Grants' limited resources. He did ask the Grants convention at Windsor for beef cattle for the expected long siege of

Ticonderoga. With this force, Warner was able to reinforce St. Clair just before Burgoyne surrounded the fortifications.

ANTICIPATING THE ARRIVAL OF THE BRITISH

Before Burgoyne set out, Loyalists staged premature uprisings, based on the news that his army was coming. South and east of Albany, in the Van Rensselaer and Livingston manors, discontent over land titles had existed since an uprising eleven years before. When the Van Rensselaers and Livingstons chose to become rebels at the beginning of the war, their tenants reacted with hostility and begun awaiting the arrival of an invading British army that would "come to the Kings people" and support modification of their leases.[33] The landlords of the two manors had sought to organize their tenants for the cause of independence, but the tenants refused to take an oath to support the rebel committees, to join the rebel militia, to supply teams for the defense effort, or to vote in elections the way their landlord directed. The tenants argued that they had to stay out of the conflict because if they were killed in the war, their short-term leases meant that families would be on their own and destitute. To remedy this situation, they wanted long-term leases, certainly for a lifetime. It has already been noted that some of these tenants joined Carleton at Crown Point in October 1776.

The unrest at the Van Rensselaer and Livingston manors continued into 1777, making the tenants potential Loyalists for Burgoyne, especially if he were able to reach Albany. Matters came to a head in May, when five hundred tenants organized for an uprising—too early, for Burgoyne was then only preparing to leave St. Johns.[34] Among the discontented were Nobletown tenants, who had come from Hanover, Germany, as well as New Englanders, who had a history of confronting the landlord. To overawe the tenants before the uprising could begin, Robert Van Rensselaer and John R. Livingston mustered a hundred Claverack and two hundred Dutchess County militia. The tenants failed to organize and three hundred were jailed by the militia. A month later, with the tenants staying away from the polls in the first election for New York governor, Philip Schuyler, the favorite of the landlords, lost to George Clinton. Schuyler's majority from the manors was lower than assumed because the tenants boycotted the election rather than support their landlords' ticket. After the confrontation, the tenants remained unbowed and determined to make a rendezvous with the king's troops coming from either Canada or New York City.

Following this abortive uprising, the manors were not peaceful, as Burgoyne's expedition captured Ticonderoga and moved southward. On August 7, 1777, the Albany Committee of Correspondence ordered Captain William Price to go to the eastern part of Rensselaerswyck "with the greatest silence and dispatch" and "destroy and secure all such persons, as you shall find in arms against the State."[35] They offered a reward for taking the two Loyalist ringleaders, Andrew Palmetier and Gershom French, French having returned to raise the king's standard in Rensselaerswyck after joining Carleton at Crown Point in 1776. The committee also ordered Price to move families and their possessions "to a place of Safety." Evidently, Price could not raise a force fast enough, and a week later Lieutenant Colonel Ten Broeck was ordered to place a hundred Albany County militiamen for Rensselaerswyck at the disposal of the Albany Committee. However, by September 30 Price had arrived and rounded up Loyalists, but while the committee doubtless hoped that Price had stopped the flow of recruits to Burgoyne, he in fact had not. The core of Francis Pfister's Loyalist band that would join Lieutenant Colonel Friedrich Baum's foray in mid-August would come from Rensselaerswyck's East Manor. Tenant discontent would produce many Loyalist recruits for Burgoyne's expedition.

Burgoyne's Advance against Ticonderoga

Burgoyne was anxious to begin the campaign, and his larger vessels sailed from St. Johns on May 28, well before his army had been gathered. It was not until almost a month later that the army left winter quarters and moved southward to Lake Champlain. The vanguard was commanded by Brigadier Simon Fraser; in addition to the light infantry it included grenadiers, the 24th Regiment, Captain Fraser's company of marksmen, and for scouting, Indians and Loyalists. On Lake Champlain, a camp was established at the mouth of the River Bouquet, and Fraser's Advanced Corps was placed at Gilliland's mill and farm.[36] Lieutenant Richard Houghton was there on June 17 with 230 mission Indians, ready to become Burgoyne's "eyes and ears." Late in June Alexander Fraser's marksmen and Indians scouted from Otter Creek as far south as the Skenesborough area and then returned by way of

Ticonderoga, reporting that Fraser had taken nine prisoners and disarmed all the inhabitants of the county covered by the scout. By July 1 Brigadier Fraser's vanguard was within sight of Ticonderoga.

The rebels made no effort to defend Crown Point, as the extensive fortifications built by Amherst in 1759 were now a charred ruin.[37] As with Carleton in October 1776, Burgoyne was able to land there unopposed and then move by land and water south toward Ticonderoga. He wanted to make sure that the rebel garrison could not escape by either the La Chute River connection to Lake George or into the Grants by way of Mount Independence and Lake Champlain's South Bay. Charged with closing down the Lake George route, Brigadier Fraser did this quickly by capturing the key defensive post, Fort Mount Hope. He then sent Fraser's vanguard of marksmen, Jessup's rangers—their first appearance in combat—and mission Indians to cut off the rebels retreating before them to Ticonderoga's French lines. The Indians followed too closely and were warmly received by the rebel defenders at the French lines. On the east side, Riedesel had more difficulty in reaching Mount Independence, as the way was obstructed by swamp.

Meanwhile, Burgoyne looked for positions to place his cannon for the expected siege. His chief engineer, Lieutenant William Twiss, scaled Sugarloaf Mountain, which commanded both Ticonderoga and Mount Independence.[38] Its strategic location, overlooking the lake, had been discussed often by Gates, Schuyler, Kosciuszko, and Colonel Jonathan Trumbull, Jr., but no one had gotten to the point of fortifying it, some assuming it was too steep and wooded to allow guns to be drawn to its summit. But now British light infantry occupied the mountain, and Twiss had guns dragged up to the top and pointed at Fort Ticonderoga.

When St. Clair saw the glint of the gun barrels, he knew his defenses were exposed. On July 5 a council of war was hastily called and his generals unanimously voted to abandon the extensive works and retreat. It was to be a nighttime evacuation, involving all his troops. St. Clair was lucky, for Riedesel still was not in position to effectively block the route to the Grants and Skenesborough, and that was the route the rebels chose to take. Burgoyne entered Fort Ticonderoga the next day, appropriating all the public stores, ammunition, and heavy baggage the rebels had stored for a siege that never happened. Thus the elaborate works at Ticonderoga were taken, in the words

A view of Ticonderoga from the middle of the channel in Lake Champlain, at the approach of Burgoyne, 1777, by James Hunter. Reproduction, Library and Archives Canada/Bibliothèque et Archives Canada (R9266-3492), Peter Winkworth Collection of Canadiana/e002139843, Ottawa.

of a British officer, "by the mere countenance and activity of [Burgoyne's] army."

The Rebel Retreat to Hubbardton and Skenesborough

St. Clair's retreating army split in two, part going by water down Lake Champlain's South Bay, while the bulk went with St. Clair by land toward Castleton. The part of the army with St. Clair arrived exhausted at Hubbardton on July 6 and after a few hours of rest moved on to Castleton. Warner was with St. Clair, back in the area he had started from only a few days before.[39] He knew Hubbardton, for he had established it as a rendezvous for local militia forces and his Continental regiment.

As St. Clair retreated further from Hubbardton, he left Colonel Ebenezer Francis, the senior officer, and Warner in charge of the rear guard. They had two companies of Francis's 11th Massachusetts Continental Regiment, Warner's depleted Continental regiment, and Colonel Nathan Hale's 2nd New Hampshire Continentals, perhaps 835 men in all.[40] In addition to the Continentals, Warner had gathered 100 militiamen earlier from the Grants. As the rear guard, also present were 300 burdensome stragglers and invalids. In all, the force consisted of over 1,200 rebels—perhaps a third of St. Clair's retreating force. Warner had orders from St. Clair to "move on moderately." However, with most of his command fatigued, he and Francis decided to spend the night in Hubbardton and leave early in the morning.

Unbeknownst to Warner and Francis, Simon Fraser's pursuing troops had caught up and were only three miles from Hubbardton. During the night, Fraser's vanguard of Loyalists and Indians scouted the rebel position and took prisoners.[41] Hubbardton would be the second action of the rangers under Ebenezer Jessup, his company numbering 57 men. John Peters's corps was also there and so was Samuel McKay, but without a command. Fraser had the 24th Regiment and the light infantry and grenadiers under the Earl of Balcarres, as well as the Brunswick troops under Riedesel—although they were behind the rest. Fully informed, Fraser had 750 men up at three a.m., and after less than two hours' march, they discovered Warner's men making breakfast.

Hubbardton would be the most forested site of any action in Burgoyne's campaign. Yet it was a crossroads, where the road from Mount Independence met the Crown Point Road and carried on to the south toward Castleton and Skenesborough. At the meeting of the two roads was a clearing containing a cabin, built by John Selleck. On July 7 the British advanced down the Mount Independence road until they met rebel fire at Sucker Brook, an encounter in which Major Robert Grant of the 24th Regiment and several Loyalists were killed.[42] The rebels retreated from the limited protection of the brook to a nearby forested hill, where the height gave them an advantage. Not all made it to this position, as most of Hale's New Hampshire Continentals fled in disorder and were taken prisoner by Fraser's men. Colonel Hale was taken prisoner as well, certainly dashing his hopes that the war would soon be over. Some of Hale's men under Major Benjamin Titcomb did get up the hill, Francis and Warner putting together a volley that allowed them to hold their ground. In five hours of fighting, both sides sustained heavy losses, as the British light infantry moved around the hill, cutting off the possibility of the rebels escaping to Castleton. The rebels continued to hold their advantageous position on the hilltop, while Fraser, outnumbered from the beginning, was about to order a desperate bayonet charge.

The day was saved for Fraser by the timely appearance of Riedesel with his Jaeger company, grenadiers and light infantry advancing with fixed bayonets, and his regimental band playing, making it seem as if it was his full force.[43] This contingent of 130 Brunswickers was enough to turn the tide. They moved to the other side of the hill in an effort to prevent the rebels escaping to the north, and Fraser's bayonet charge came on. The rebels left their strong position on the hill, defending themselves against the light infantry on a further ridge, and while almost surrounded they were able to get away on the Crown Point road or through the woods. Warner told the remains of his Continental regiment to scatter and meet him at Manchester. Colonel Francis was killed, and Hale and his men made up the bulk of the 234 prisoners the British took. It is assumed that the sick and wounded with Hale's command were also taken. In the bloody affair, the British had 198 officers and men killed or wounded, while the rebels had lost 90—not including prisoners.

Nearby, St. Clair heard the sound of the battle and knew that two New Hampshire militia regiments under Colonel Benjamin Bellows were only two miles from Hubbardton. He sent orders for them to join Warner and Francis, but as an example of how far militia could be trusted, they refused and hurriedly retreated to Castleton.[44] The British stayed and buried the dead and treated the wounded, establishing a temporary hospital around the Selleck cabin that would eventually be moved to Ticonderoga. Francis was buried on the battlefield, under the supervision of Riedesel. When Fraser and Riedesel moved off toward Skenesborough on July 9, local residents stripped the dead, and two months later the Vermont Council of Safety offered to pay for the return of the arms and accoutrements that were taken.

This was the first test for British regulars in the Grants, and on the whole their officers felt they did well. Volunteer Anburey experienced the novelty of fighting as light infantry: "In this action, I found all manual exercise is but an ornament, and the only object of importance . . . was that of loading, firing and charging with bayonets; . . . whether it proceeded from an idea of self-preservation, or natural instinct, but the soldiers greatly improved the mode they were taught in."[45] After the battle, an ensign in the 53rd Regiment, Thomas Hughes, summed up the British perspective: "This engagement did our troops the greatest honor, as the enemy was vastly superior in numbers, and it was perform'd in a thick wood, in the very style that the Americans think themselves superior to regular troops." The British observers admitted the rebels fought well, but felt they had matched them in the terrain that was thought to be most advantageous for them.

After leaving Warner and Francis at Hubbardton on July 6, St. Clair's army had retreated to Castleton. On the evening of the next day, Lieutenant Mathew Lyon appeared there to offer his services as a guide for St. Clair's army. In the effort to reach Schuyler's army on the Hudson River, Lyon led them to Pawlet and Manchester, and then west, following the Batten Kill to the Hudson.[46] St. Clair's army of 1,700 men then turned northward to Fort Miller, where Schuyler awaited them, treating them as needed reinforcements when they arrived on July 12. He had worried that St. Clair might have strayed as far south as Bennington. Overall, St. Clair had lost half his Ticonderoga force; a few had come to Schuyler by way of Skenesborough and some remained in the Grants, but many militiamen had simply gone home. The loss of over 300 men at Hubbardton had been heavy, and the militiamen continued to melt away when their enlistments were up. Of the rebel prisoners taken at Hubbardton, by the end of July some were enrolled in "the King's Service" at Ticonderoga.

After Hubbardton, the Vermont Council of Safety asked Warner to remain at Manchester, coordinating his Continentals with Colonel Herrick's newly raised rangers to defend the territory against Riedesel's Germans, who had returned to Castleton to implement Burgoyne's pacification.[47] Schuyler included Warner's Continentals in St. Clair's command and ordered Warner to Saratoga, putting him on the spot between the two conflicting authorities. However, when pleas came from the Grants to allow Warner's command of 250 to remain in Manchester and watch the Germans, Schuyler agreed. From the perspective of Ira Allen, Manchester was now the northern defensive line of the Grants. Holding this line would be the Vermont Council of Safety's chief defensive strategy.

Skenesborough

As previously mentioned, when St. Clair evacuated Ticonderoga on July 6, five hundred of his men retreated by way of South Bay to

Skenesborough, traveling leisurely down the lake on the remains of the fleet, confident that the iron-chain-and-log floating bridge in front of the fort would prevent the British from pursuing them.[48] British gunboats came up, however, and with a few well-directed cannon shots broke the chain and then cut through the floating bridge. With a northerly wind, the British were only about two hours behind the retreating rebels. Before South Bay ended, Wood Creek cut to the east and the rebel flotilla traveled on it past rocky heights toward Skenesborough, the terminus of water transportation. When Burgoyne's flotilla reached the mouth of Wood Creek, he disembarked the 9th, 20th, and 21st Regiments, with orders to proceed over land to gain the Fort Ann road, cutting off the rebels' only means of escape to the south.

Then Burgoyne's ships and gunboats followed Wood Creek to Skenesborough harbor, which he seized from the evacuating rebels, capturing all but two of the vessels that remained from Arnold's navy. New Hampshire Continentals under Colonel Pierce Long sent their invalids and women south on Wood Creek and set about burning the fort, barracks, outbuildings, and stores that had been erected and refurbished to build the rebel navy. The mission Indians and sailors with Burgoyne did their best to extinguish the flames and save the stores. The next day a "kind of county fair" was held to distribute the booty, including half roasted beef and pork, corn, wheat, and fruit.[49] The three British regiments that had been landed earlier had tough going in the terrain and were unable to trap Colonel Long's 150 men fleeing south on the road to Fort Ann. Skene's home became Burgoyne's headquarters and when Skene himself arrived, they began to organize a pacification program in the Castleton-Manchester area.

CONFRONTATION AT FORT ANN

At Skenesborough, Burgoyne also ordered Lieutenant Colonel John Hill with part of the 9th Regiment to pursue the 150 retreating rebels and baggage under Long, who had stopped to occupy Fort Ann, about ten miles to the south on Wood Creek.[50] By evening, when Hill camped next to Wood Creek, he was a mile north of the fort, but his force numbered only 190, so he sent to Burgoyne for reinforcements. The next day, July 8, he moved against Long, who had been reinforced by 400 Albany County militiamen from Rensselaerswyck, commanded by Commissary Philip Van Rensselaer's brother, Colonel Henry K.

Van Rensselaer. Hill was now outnumbered almost three to one. After initial contact, fighting continued, as Hill fell back to his encampment at the bottom of a ravine and then was forced to send his men up the steep ravine to a hill that was a better defensive position. He held the ridge for two hours against the hot fire of the rebels.

Hill was in trouble, running low on ammunition, when he heard a war whoop, to which his troops replied with three cheers, assuming they were reinforcements arriving from Skenesborough. In fact it was only a fellow officer, Captain John Money, who had run ahead of his wavering Indian party, but it was enough for Van Rensselaer, who was also running low on powder, and he drew back. Despite rebel determination and orders from Schuyler to hold the post, Long burned Fort Ann and retreated south to Fort Edward. Badly wounded in the thigh, Van Rensselaer was sent to his father Killian's house at Greenbush to recover and maintain the family honor as supporters of Congress and officers of the Albany County militia. The British captured two of Long's Second New Hampshire regimental flags. Reinforcements from Skenesborough of the 53rd and 47th Regiments did arrive well after the action and brought off Hill's soldiers.

At Fort Edward, Schuyler attempted to gather enough men to make a stand. As mentioned earlier, the British had abandoned the fort in 1766, and it was in such bad condition that Schuyler could jump his horse over the curtain walls. The countryside was in full alarm, but no one wanted to join his army, looking rather to their own defense. From Colonel John Williams at Salem, the commander of New York's Charlotte County militia, came a request for militia provisions, to which Schuyler answered that he would have to get them "in the best manner you can." To Schuyler, Salem was not a likely target for Burgoyne, and "it would be the height of imprudence to disperse my army into different quarters, unless there is the most evident necessity."[51] In the month of July, Schuyler's Northern Department had suffered four reverses at the hands of Burgoyne, leaving Schuyler struggling to maintain an army.

At Skenesborough, Burgoyne was again celebrating. On July 10 he ordered that "Divine Service will be performed on Sunday morning next at the head of the line at the head of the advanced corps and at Sunset on the same day a *feu de joye* will be fired with cannon and small arms" throughout the various posts.[52] This was a high moment for Burgoyne, when he was clearly making a name for himself, based

on the assumed superiority of his army, which seemed to defeat any
enemy it faced.

Thus the first phase of the Saratoga Campaign ended on a high note
for Burgoyne's army. Experienced the year before with Carleton's invasion and well rested over the Canadian winter, Burgoyne's British
troops had been encouraged to use light infantry tactics. His invading
army had the ability to move quickly and surprise the rebels, who
actually outnumbered them in the confrontations at Hubbardton and
Fort Ann. His artillery went up Mount Defiance to the surprise of
St. Clair, and his experienced bateau men plied the lakes and the creeks
and rivers as effective transport routes. He had motivated his army
to adapt to the terrain and use it to their advantage. Overall, the
invading army appeared to be invincible. This was a perfect position
from which to initiate efforts to win the hearts and minds of the
region's people.

7

Degrees of Loyalism

When Burgoyne was defending himself before Parliament in 1779, he made Loyalists like Philip Skene the chief scapegoats for his defeat. Skene had said that the countryside would rise to support Burgoyne when, in the general's opinion, it had not. Burgoyne was also critical of his Loyalist officers, for they had worked so diligently on recruiting that they had neglected what their corps were best at, namely, "searching for cattle, ascertaining the practicability of routes, clearing roads, and guiding detachments or columns upon the march."[1] By then his views were jaded because he was politically motivated, having joined the opposition to the government of Lords Germain and North, who had fostered a policy of using Loyalists. Burgoyne had formulated his view in England to vindicate himself after his surrender, and it did not reflect the reality of his previous dealings with Loyalists in North America.

Did Burgoyne find "a population openly hostile and the countryside stripped in his path," as some historians have contended?[2] This makes his relationship with Loyalists crucial, because if they did not respond and were unwilling to supply him, the closer he got to Albany the more he would be surrounded by a militia of hostile Yorkers and Grants men.

In fact, Burgoyne's view of the use of Loyalists in 1777 was not fixed; it evolved over the length of his campaign. In planning the campaign, he had never conceived that Loyalists would play an important military role.[3] This contrasted with General William Howe, who in late 1776 and early 1777 had been more conspicuous in organizing permanent Loyalist regiments with definite combat possibilities in the New York City area. Howe was able to take three Loyalist regiments on his expedition against Philadelphia, and upon occupying the city he set out to recruit more. In fact, he took the rank of colonel of the 1st Battalion, Pennsylvania Loyalists, an unprecedented act among British generals, for it meant that he was the patron of the regiment. In contrast, Burgoyne was not sure he wanted Loyalists as soldiers.

ATTRACTING LOYALISTS DURING BURGOYNE'S INVASION

When Burgoyne invaded the Champlain Valley in June 1777, his Loyalist forces were small, numbering only 83, against 7,500 regulars, 500 Native Americans, and 300 Canadians.[4] His emphasis with axillaries was to recruit Canadian militia, a path that ignored the Loyalist turnout that greeted Carleton at Crown Point in October 1776 as well as the dismal record of the Canadian militia in the defense of Canada. As Burgoyne's campaign developed, the number of Loyalists serving in a military capacity increased, reaching a peak of about 800, almost ten times those who had left Canada with his army. Between June and October, Loyalists officers made great strides in filling the ranks of their units, a situation that made them increasingly valuable, as Burgoyne's regulars shrank in numbers. None of these figures touch on the number of Loyalist families who favored Burgoyne's army or attended his pacification gatherings, the group that originally most interested him. For them, we have only impressionistic figures. For instance, 400 inhabitants appeared to take an oath to the king at Castleton, while the Argyle Protectionists numbered about 500. By the region's standards, these were substantial numbers. Analysis of Loyalist claims after the war shows that more future Canadian Loyalists joined the British during Burgoyne's Campaign than at any other time in the war.[39]

Burgoyne was no hard-liner who favored violence and destruction in dealing with rebels; rather, like Carleton, he was closer to a conciliatory position. Instead of slash and burn, Burgoyne pursued the ideal of winning the hearts and minds of the inhabitants of the Hudson-Champlain region. This is outlined in his early proclamation of June 23, 1777, announced at the mouth of the Bouquet River on Lake Champlain. He offered protection and security, but not arms, to His Majesty's loyal subjects. His expedition was to restore "the rights of the [British] constitution and duty to their sovereign" and to prevent the rebel assemblies and committees from "arbitrary imprisonments, confiscation of property, persecution and torture," which he claimed "was unprecedented [even] in the inquisitions of the Romish Church."[5] He also invited "all persons in all places where the progress of this army may point . . . to maintain such a conduct as may justify me in protecting their lands, habitations and families." Thus, for the region's inhabitants he was restoring security against unchecked rebel intimidation and the legal basis of government as it had been under the crown. All he wanted of them was that they "remain quietly at their houses, that they do not suffer their cattle to be removed, or their corn and forage be secreted or destroyed." Burgoyne asked them to sell supplies to his army and promised that all provisions they brought to his camp would be paid for "in solid coin." This was Burgoyne's view of how the countryside would be restored to the king, a role in which his army would protect Loyalist families from rebel militia and reestablish the king's courts—if the populace would remain in the countryside. This document was printed and would circulate in the areas Burgoyne's army traveled through and beyond, as far as the Connecticut River valley.

Early on, Burgoyne used his Loyalist soldiers in the same way he did his Canadians, that is, for maintaining transportation and supply lines, distant from any possibility of combat. In July 1777 Jessup's men were involved in escorting horses from Canada to Crown Point.[6] They were not yet formed into corps, for to Burgoyne they were not yet soldiers, despite their name, the King's Loyal Americans. He had no real instructions as to what to do with them, anyway. Lord Germain in London had only said he needed to have Loyalists but had been vague on the specifics of how to organize them. While Burgoyne knew he was to cultivate them, at first he also drew the line at allowing them to recruit in the areas his army passed through—even though many of the Loyalists who joined Carleton in October 1776 had been eager to do this.

LOYALISTS AND THE REBEL "INQUISITION"

Loyalism did not grow in a vacuum; it reacted to the pressures of rebel militias that, Burgoyne claimed, used the tactics of an "inquisition."

The rebels could not practice pacification like Burgoyne, because their ideal was a citizen army in which almost every male was required to serve in some capacity, so that those who failed to were automatically the enemy. Thus the rebels had to prevent Loyalists from participating in the war. Rebel militias were ordered to carry out a watchful policy of house visits, under the cover of darkness, to undermine Loyalist efforts to organize military units or reach the safety of Burgoyne's army and Canada. These policies were developed by General Schuyler as he retreated, by Ira Allen in Manchester, Vermont, by the Albany Committee of Correspondence, and by other rebel committees. They referred to local Loyalists as "disaffected people" and their activities as "skulking," with the implication that Loyalists were underhanded and sneaky.[7]

Typically, early in 1777 the Albany Committee of Correspondence received information that there were forty-six Loyalists with a barrel of powder concealed in woods only three miles from the city.[8] The Loyalists were still there in June, at the beginning of Burgoyne's invasion, when it was claimed that some of the ringleaders of this insurrection were hiding in the woods and up to no good. They must have joined Burgoyne, for there is no record they were ever caught.

North of Albany, fear existed of Loyalist uprisings in places like Saratoga. As Burgoyne advanced, the Albany Committee of Correspondence announced that "the present situation . . . requires our most serious attention on every quarter in the northern part of the county, we are overwhelmed by the influence of our enemies on the well affected part of our militia." The Loyalists were "daily collecting strength to oppose us in every peaceable measure we have hitherto adopted . . . and are now endeavoring to collect a large body at Saratoga to perpetuate some inhuman deed."[9] Attempting to join Burgoyne or leave for Canada was now regarded by the rebels as an act of insurrection.

Faced with the uprising of Loyalist bands, it was evident that special militia units, separate from Schuyler's army, would have to be created to specifically oppose Loyalists. The commander of the Albany County militia, Abraham Ten Broeck, announced a levy of every tenth man on his militia rolls to form a force for "quelling insurrections or any disorder that might happen." By mid-August the Albany Committee had recruited two companies of rangers to serve within the county, "considering the robberies committed, and the [Loyalists] in different parts of the county gathering under arms against the good people of the state."[10] These special militiamen

The Albany City Hall, Courthouse, and Jail, erected in 1740. Here Loyalists were confined and the Albany Committee of Correspondence met, as did the Albany County sessions of the Commissioners for Detecting and Defeating Conspiracies. From Codman Hislop, *Albany: Dutch, English, and American* (Albany, N.Y., 1936).

were not about to allow Loyalists to organize in their midst in preparation for the arrival of Burgoyne.

Removing People from Burgoyne's Path

In 1776, for the first time since the Seven Years' War, the Hudson-Champlain region had faced an invasion by professional soldiers, namely

Governor Guy Carleton's British regulars. Philip Schuyler had wondered how best to defend the countryside from that invasion. He urged settlers to retreat back from the borderland, which now stretched to Lake Champlain. He felt that they should not be present to be seduced by the enemy and that defense could be coordinated more easily on a shorter perimeter. Underlying his view was the conviction that borderland farmers made reluctant soldiers.[11]

In contrast, the Grants' Ira Allen took the position that borderland farmers were a potential defensive force, urging the settlers in Carleton's path to remain. He wrote in July 1776 to the citizens of Poultney, "[I] advise you to look sharp and keep scouts out. But not to move except some families much remote from the Main inhabitants."[12] A year later, he was of the same mind, urging the inhabitants of northwestern Vermont to return to their homes "and assist in defending this and the United States of America from the ravages of the enemy." With the fall of Ticonderoga the controversy reemerged.

As Schuyler retreated from Fort Edward before Burgoyne's advancing army, he found that there was no way he could allow people to stay; he had to force them to move and abandon their farms. His army was too small and disorganized to face Burgoyne, so as it retreated, a scorched earth policy was enforced, destroying bridges, blocking roads, diverting streams, confiscating cattle and foodstuffs, so that the enemy would be delayed and have no sustenance.[13]

Schuyler's policy also included his crucial order—the equivalent of Burgoyne's proclamation—that settlers not participate in Burgoyne's pacification activities and that those who did would be "dealt with as traitors to the said states."[14] Schuyler wanted settlers to leave their farms and take their families farther south. He advised Ira Allen in Vermont to follow his example and avoid the settlers' temptation of "going to the enemy for protection." He would also not allow settlers within his camp for fear they were spies.

Schuyler's policy was far from popular in New York, and at the Charlotte County Committee meeting at Salem on July 25, a committee of appraisers was appointed to estimate the value of inhabitants' crops and buildings.[15] They hoped to obtain recompense in case they lost their property because of Schuyler's order to leave. His policies seemed harsh, but no one knew the inhabitants' inclinations better than the landlord of Saratoga.

Following Schuyler's directive, refugee families from the countryside did arrive in Albany by August 4, although some came from the

Mohawk Valley, not just the region north of Albany. The motives of the refugees are unclear; they may simply have come to protect themselves from the depredations of either army, especially their Indian allies. When they came, they brought their milk cows with them, but found there was no pasture. Suitably, the Albany Committee solved this need by confiscating pasture near the city belonging to Edward and Ebenezer Jessup.[16] About two weeks later, more pasture was purchased for the refugees. The rebels themselves had confiscated cattle from abandoned farms and had driven them into a large herd with Schuyler's army. On August 21 the deputy quartermaster general, Lieutenant Colonel Udny Hay, requested that the Albany Committee find pasture for this army herd. In fact, because so much livestock had arrived, the need for pasture around Albany became acute.

How effective Schuyler's policy was in combating the rise of Loyalism is hard to gauge; the momentary vacancy of a farm did not mean it was abandoned or that its owner was of rebel sentiment. While Burgoyne's army found many farms unoccupied, they were not abandoned but were being well maintained, even to the daily gathering of cattle to be milked. Many farmers simply took to the woods near their farms and returned when parties from either Schuyler's or Burgoyne's army were gone. Certainly, Schuyler's policy was meant to thwart Burgoyne's efforts to bring Loyalists to his army, but it is questionable as to how many settlers even knew about the policy. In late November 1777, after Burgoyne surrendered, Duncan Shaw petitioned the Albany Committee for forgiveness for remaining at his farm near Fort Edward and asked to "be enrolled as a Subject of the State."[17] Shaw's motivation is anyone's guess, but he was one of a very few who admitted he violated Schuyler's order, and he did this only after Burgoyne surrendered.

The Continuation of Loyalism in Charlotte County

Burgoyne must have been heartened by the strong showing of Loyalism at Skenesborough in Charlotte County. It was Loyalists from there who would be the first to rebuild the bridges and roads for Burgoyne that Schuyler had destroyed in his retreat.[18] They also began to shadow and snipe at Schuyler's army from the east side of the Hudson River as the rebels descended on the west side by stages, below Fort Edward to Stillwater. Some of Schuyler's own tenants were Loyalists, and they were pleased to see him and his wife, Catherine, evacuate his Saratoga plantation in the face of Burgoyne's advance.

In early August, Burgoyne's proclamation in support of the king appeared nailed to many doors on the east side of the Hudson River, between Kingsbury and Fort Miller. The Loyal inhabitants had been asked "to wear a signal in their hats, and put signals before their doors, and also on their cattle's horns, that they were friends to the king and had stayed on their farms."[19] In Charlotte County, the mere possession of Burgoyne's manifesto, along with knowledge of Loyalist gatherings at Monroe's Meadows in Hebron, was enough for militia captain Joseph McCracken of Salem to arrest and imprison the miller, William Reid. After taking a rebel oath, Reid would be released, but not until after Burgoyne's surrender. In Burgoyne's army, Lieutenant William Digby reported on July 30 that "many country people came to us for protection. Those are styled by the enemy Royalists, and greatly persecuted if taken after fighting against them."[20]

Salem and Hebron were east of the Hudson, away from the chief route of Burgoyne's army, and known as strong centers of rebel sentiment. Yet neither town was without its Loyalists. Salem's Pelham Presbyterians, true to their Massachusetts roots, favored the rebels. However, they were countered by the over three hundred Scots-Irish settlers from Ballibay, Northern Ireland, brought by Reverend Dr. Thomas Clark to Salem in 1764. Referred to as those from "the Old Country," some favored the rebels because, as Presbyterians, they had been discriminated against by the established Anglican Church.[21] But some, including Clark himself, remained neutral in their loyalty. They were grateful to the crown for letting them leave Ireland and settle in Salem. The Telford, Blake, and Bell families were Loyalists, and as a result of the friction this caused, in 1777 Margaret Telford was accused of being a witch. The Bells ultimately went to Canada, but the other two families were able to remain and continued in Dr. Clark's church. He investigated the accusation of witchcraft against Margaret Telford and found "nothing tangible . . . for the church to take a hold of." No official ruling was made on the accusation, and the whole issue was dropped by 1782. Certainly, Salem's division between rebels and Loyalists caused nasty accusations.

Another incident showing the political division in Salem concerned Captain John Armstrong of the Charlotte County militia. Armstrong was not only "a violent Whig," but a capitalist who owned a store, which he felt needed business from the nearby Camden Valley, the center of Methodism and Loyalism. To attract Camden Valley Loyalists like Thomas Ashton as customers, he decided to hire someone from there to work in his store.[22] His choice was eighteen-year-old John Bininger. However, Armstrong's rebel neighbors were upset by the hiring, which they felt was a compromise of his Whig principles. In the spring of 1776, when Armstrong was away, rebels seized Bininger, carried him away, whipped him, and told him never to come back. Later, John Bininger took this to heart and had no hesitation in joining a Loyalist corps.

One place that Salem's Colonel John Williams, commander of the Charlotte County militia, monitored as a nest of Loyalists was Munro's Meadows, a settlement established by Henry Munro, to the north in Hebron. An educated Scot, in the Seven Years' War Munro had been a Presbyterian chaplain to the 77th Regiment, Montgomery's Highlanders, and when discharged he received this grant of 2,000 acres. After the war he went to England, where he was ordained an Anglican missionary and sent back to America to become rector of Albany's St. Peter's Church. He also preached to Mohawks at Fort Hunter and to black slaves allowed by their Albany masters to attend his Friday and Sunday evening class. Meanwhile, in 1765 he advanced his influence by marrying Eve Jay, sister of the famous New York jurist and future rebel, John.

Munro, whose permanent home was Albany, occupied his Hebron land in the summer, draining much of the swamp to create lush green meadows, where he built a seasonal cabin.[23] He persuaded six families of Scottish Highlanders discharged from the army to move there and leased them a hundred acres each for twenty-one years at a modest rent of one shilling per acre. All the tenants of Munro's Meadows as well as Munro himself would become Loyalists.

Munro's seventeen-year-old daughter, Betsey, chose to move to Munro's Meadows from Albany in 1774 because she did not get along with her stepmother. Residing among the Scottish families, she would be a Loyalist woman on her own, a fact that fit with her very independent and even reckless character. In 1776, after she rejected the marriage proposal from Schenectady Loyalist Alexander Campbell, she reluctantly agreed to marry Donald Fisher, a former sergeant of her father's 77th regiment. Fisher had bought land in Hebron, Granville, and Pawlet from his army comrades and moved into a home at Munro's Meadows. When Burgoyne arrived in the area, Colonel John Williams asked Fisher to contact Burgoyne or Philip Skene to obtain "a protection for him and all the committee in Salem." Instead of carrying out Williams's mission, Fisher and his half brothers showed their true colors and joined one of Burgoyne's Loyalist corps.[24] In retaliation, Williams had neighboring rebels remove and sell the contents of Fisher's house and then, as Betsey watched, burn it to the ground. Betsey and her infant were forced to walk to Burgoyne's army at Fort Edward, where she and her husband were reunited. Before Betsey left she gave her husband's papers, surprisingly, to Williams for safekeeping. Such contacts fed suspicions that Williams was becoming a Loyalist. Incidents like this show that, despite the Salem area's reputation for supporting the rebels, it was far from unified in these sentiments.

Loyalist by Accusation: Protectionists and Other Neutrals

Loyalists and neutrals blended with each other as Burgoyne proceeded. He was almost as frustrated by their qualified allegiance as he was by the rebels. In the summer, some Scots-Irish in the Salem and Cambridge area claimed the status of "protectioner." This is evident because after Burgoyne's surrender twenty-two immigrants, who probably came with Dr. Clark from Northern Ireland, petitioned the New York Council for mercy.[25] They claimed to have served with the rebels at Ticonderoga until it fell and then returned to Salem, where they were involved in the building of Fort Williams, a post that General Schuyler had requested. However, when Burgoyne sent out his manifesto, demanding that all come to him for protection, they fled to the rear of his army near Fort Edward. There they lived on their own provisions and claimed they did not take up arms against the rebels, confessing now to be "protectioners." As a result of their petition, the New York Council and Assembly ordered that they be allowed to remain on their farms and shielded from retribution, but some Cambridge rebels wanted revenge and tried to intimidate and flog them.

Also after Burgoyne surrendered, another group of four Salem citizens were accused of protectionism during the invasion. They were ordered before the Albany commissioners in April 1778 "for having remained on their habitations, and going to the enemy . . . and that their only inducement was to save their families from being scalped by the Indians."[26] They were allowed to return to their habitations subject to their being faithful citizens and making a monthly appearance before a commissioner.

The Argyle Protectionists

By far the largest group of protectionists would come to Burgoyne from Charlotte County's Argyle Patent near the Hudson River. On July 20 Argyle horsemen, including James and Alexander Campbell, Alexander McNaughton, Jr., and Robert Blake, rode into Burgoyne's camp at Hudson Falls to see what his army was like. Five days later, the key event in creating the Argyle protectionists took place: the John Allen family massacre. As previously described, a party of eight Iroquois allied to Burgoyne, while raiding in the area north of Albany, killed the five members of the Allen family and killed or carried off their slaves. The Allen massacre "created a great alarm among the [Loyalists] of Argyle, and they flocked in great numbers to [Hudson Falls] to solicit Burgoyne's protection against the marauding savages."[27]

Argyle patentees joined Burgoyne's army with their families and cattle as protectionists. On July 31 J. F. Wasmus reported that in the past days, "several inhabitants came out of the woods with women and children and had a great number of cattle with them. One farmer alone had more than 60 head of horned cattle."[28] The next day a British officer reported, "an entire company of [Loyalists] had crossed over to our army with their officers and even their flag. They had brought along a note, signed by several [Loyalist] officers, according to which they were to expect more than 500 [Loyalists] in the next few days." The figure seems accurate because there were that many Argyle patentees. While Burgoyne offered protection and limited rations, he could not provide them with housing. Although it was summer, the Argyle protectionists were so numerous that they did not have an easy time finding shelter and living on the edge of Burgoyne's army.

The Argyle patentees gradually defined themselves as protectionists. A British officer noted that "these [Loyalists] did not show any strong desire to serve in our army but were most anxious to return home, especially since the harvest was about to begin."[29] They certainly sold cattle to the British, as Burgoyne wished Loyalists to do, but they were not about to leave their families to become soldiers.

In fact, to keep both sides informed, in October, 1777 the Argyle protectionists, in a town meeting, instructed John Johnston to write a letter to the commander of the Charlotte County militia, John Williams, explaining why they had not answered his call to arms. They claimed they lacked arms and were constrained by the savagery of the Indians to come under an "Oath of Neutrality" to Burgoyne. They flattered Williams as a "gentleman of generosity and honor" to be forgiving and claimed that they would be useful to the state in the future.[30] Again, Williams found himself dealing with a considerable number of presumed Loyalists and was forced to accept their reasoning.

While the rebels may have felt that the patentees joining Burgoyne were Loyalists, the Argyle settlers wanted to remain where they were and keep their land. Legalistically, they later explained their action to the New York legislature and asked to return to their jurisdiction, claiming to have been under "a tie of neutrality to the British King" and that they had only fled to the British for protection against Indians.[31]

The local rebels were naturally suspicious and labeled "protectioners" disparagingly. The Commissioners for Detecting and Defeating Conspiracies were called to investigate the Argyle patentees' relationship with Burgoyne. However, on May 15, 1778, the commissioners concluded "that [the patentees] numbers are too large to be removed or dealt with in a vigorous manner."[32] They decided to offer them reinstatement as citizens if they confessed to having taken up arms against the rebels and were willing to take an oath of neutrality whereby they were required to aid the state, except for bearing arms. Such compromises were typical of New Yorkers in the aftermath of Burgoyne's defeat, but the rebels were not to remain conciliatory for long, as later, New York's Governor Clinton became more vindictive.

The patentees did agree among themselves not to participate in local politics. The Argyle settlers remained a clan, true to their Scottish roots, and they did not vote in the first Charlotte County election under the New York State constitution, which was held in September 8, 1778.[33] The rebels were actually relieved. Since only 198 votes were cast, largely from Salem, had the patentees voted, as the largest bloc of votes they could have easily swung the election in favor of a neutral or even Loyalist candidate.

Rebel suspicion remained. An Argyle patentee wrote: "Some fiery men openly declare that they will drive off the Scots and Irish, as [Loyalists], from Argyle and Salem, so that unless the good legislature interpose and help us, then Canada and the depths" will be our fate.[34] Despite such warnings, by following their protectionist position the Scots survived the war with most of their land intact and did not have to move to Canada. Only one property, that of Alexander Campbell, was later confiscated by New York State, a great contrast with the fifteen parcels taken in Kingsbury. Of course, Burgoyne was not aware of the protectionist aftermath in early 1778. Had he been, he would have better understood their perspective on Loyalism.

The Quakers

Quakers were more comprehensible to Burgoyne than the protectionists. The Quaker sect had been founded in seventeenth-century England and been involved in the settlement of North America, and in many colonies the Quakers' pacifism had been legally recognized in the colonial wars. New York laws had exempted them from military service, and because Quakers refused to take oaths, in 1734 the New York Assembly passed a bill giving New York Friends the same status as English Quakers, in which a simple affirmation could be substituted for an oath.[35]

During the War of Independence, Quakers were caught in the middle of the civil conflict, in which the rebels did not tolerate neutrals who refused to bear arms or who would not swear an oath to anyone—let alone Congress. In Easton, on the east side of the Hudson River opposite the site of the Battles of Saratoga, Quakers were numerous and described as "peace-loving." [36] Their religious meetings were centers of quiet devotion; the Easton Quakers claimed that when Burgoyne's marauding Indians broke into one of their meetings, their calm and silent countenances impressed the warriors so much that they ordered the place spared from impending destruction.

To the north, the Queensbury and Wing's Falls Quakers tried to remain neutral when the War of Independence broke out but were forced by rebel bands to provide them with cattle. Their leader, Abraham Wing, had operated a tavern that had been frequented by Loyalists like the Jessup brothers.[37] The Quakers were also unable to gain the respect of the British invaders, who twice—1777 and 1780—burned them out of their homes, after which they decided to retire to Dutchess County. Four years later the Quakers returned and petitioned Congress to replace their losses, which included mill equipment, cattle, horses, potatoes, grain, and hay. However, they got no help from that authority.

Loyalists were a varied lot. Some like Protectionists and Quakers were not about to bear arms for the king, and Burgoyne hesitated to organize Loyalists into military units. Rebel policies influenced Loyalism, opposing the effort of Loyalists to maintain their farms, gather together, or join Burgoyne. As Philip Schuyler's army retreated, he ordered all inhabitants to abandon their farms because he saw the populace as of no defensive value and feared they would go over to the enemy or at least offer to sell them supplies. While some families ended up in Albany, his policy was far from popular and many stayed on their farms, disappearing into the woods when it was convenient. The Albany Committee aided him by raising militias and rangers to confront what they felt were skulking Loyalists. With the Vermont Council of Safety, Ira Allen directed families to stay on their farms and maintain a defensive border. At Skenesborough and then Fort Edward, Burgoyne opened his camp to many Loyalists. However, a substantial number were protectionists, who viewed themselves as neutrals and stayed with him only temporarily. They sought his army because they feared the depredations of his Indians. This left Burgoyne with the suspicion that they could not be depended upon and were even possibly rebel spies.

8

In Vermont, Taking an Oath of Allegiance to the King

A t his headquarters in Skenesborough on July 11, Burgoyne wrote a letter to Lord Germain for instructions on how to use his Loyalists, as if he were already trying to protect himself politically, for he knew very well he could not expect an answer before his campaign was over. The day after he wrote to Germain, he put Philip Skene in charge of "an office . . . established . . . to regulate all such matters which concerned the local inhabitants, the deserters of Rebels, the recruitment, commerce and sale of horses and cattle; [and] all those that were looking for guarding."[1] He gave Skene a commission, but not a rank, so that local inhabitants were now under his authority in civil if not military concerns. Skene would not be involved in raising a Loyalist corps, the activity that concerned most Loyalist leaders. He would, however, convince Burgoyne that Loyalist sentiment was strong in the Hudson-Champlain valley, leading the general to expect Loyalist support. At the time, Burgoyne was convinced that Skene was the best man to implement a pacification policy.

Remember that Skene's estate had been ransacked by Herrick's band, and it would take him a year to catch up to Burgoyne's army at Crown Point. The delay was caused by Skene's return from England, he having unknowingly landed at Philadelphia, been imprisoned as a Loyalist, and then sent to Connecticut, where he remained until he was exchanged early in 1777.[2] He had left New York and gone back to England, but decided to return to Quebec with his son, who also had been imprisoned and released.

As the developer of Skenesborough, Skene had knowledge of the region. He had traded livestock throughout the area and knew where the animals could be found. Immediately to the south in Schaghticoke, he had a number of cattle collected and driven to Burgoyne's army. He was able to write David Remington of Castleton and Roger Stevens of Pittsfield, in Vermont, requesting carriages and horses for Burgoyne's German dragoons and also promising that Burgoyne's Indians would not harm the Remington family.[3] Remington responded with three yokes and teams of oxen, joining Burgoyne's army and serving as conductor of teams. In November 1777 his property would be confiscated and he would be banished from Vermont by the council.

Still, there was a lack of reality to some of Skene's expectations— after all, he had not been in the area in the past three years. On July 19 he wrote to Philip Schuyler, asking to discuss the current political situation with him, with an aim toward a peaceful solution to the now raging war.[4] Needless to say, Schuyler deflected him with the excuse that only Burgoyne could propose such a discussion. Sentiments had gone far beyond those of 1775, when Schuyler tried to protect and restore Skene's property.

Loyalists would go to either Burgoyne's army or to pacification gatherings, where they were asked to take an oath of allegiance to the king and sell cattle and flour to the army. While conferring with Skene, Burgoyne decided to call his first pacification meeting of the inhabitants, where Loyalists would be encouraged to show themselves and offer their support—though not necessarily take up arms. The goal was to win support for the king, not just of open Loyalists, but the entire population of an area. Burgoyne issued a proclamation calling this meeting for July 15 at Castleton, where deputies from the Vermont and New York towns of Hubbardton, Rutland, Tinmouth, Pawlet, Wells, Granville, Salem, the Camden Valley, and Cambridge could swear allegiance to the king and be guaranteed protection of their property. Skene was to conduct the meeting that would "not only give further encouragement to those who complied with the terms of [the June] manifesto, but also communicate conditions upon which the persons and properties of the disobedient [rebels] may yet be spared."[5] Thus, even rebels were encouraged to come, change their ways, and swear allegiance to the king.

On the appointed date, four hundred turned out in Castleton, chiefly from the nearby Vermont towns of Manchester, Rutland, Poultney, Clarendon, and Granville, New York.[6] Skene presided, ably seconded by Jehiel Hawley, who had been named president of the Board of Examiners, established to separate the true Loyalists among those gathered. Hawley performed this duty judiciously, without a sign of vindictiveness. Skene administered the loyalty oath and some took it, but many declared that they simply wanted to observe complete neutrality and hoped that Burgoyne would respect their views. A few days later Germans troops were in Granville, where the farmers were being induced to go to Skenesborough with their oxen teams.

The Castleton meeting turned out to be very disturbing to rebel leaders because it showed that support for their cause was soft. At Fort Edward, Schuyler and New York congressman Gouverneur Morris were afraid that settlers in Vermont would be attracted by Burgoyne's Castleton pledge. Morris noted on July 21 that "Skene is courting [Vermont] with golden offers. He has already gained many, and many more are compelled to submission. There are not a few advocates of the British government among them. . . . Skene is at hand to flatter them with being a separate province and . . . to give them assurance of being confirmed in their titles, however acquired."[7] To Morris, Skene was already tailoring the British approach to the desires of unlawful Vermont.

New Yorkers also were suspicious of Seth Warner. Remember that Schuyler had allowed him to stay at Manchester, where he chiefly commanded the third of the Continental regiments he had raised. As Congress had ordered, it had been recruited from veterans of the Canadian campaign of 1775–76, without any state affiliation.[8] Some New York representatives, however, had tried to have Warner removed from command of this Continental regiment because of his previous violence, when he was a Green Mountain Boy. However, Schuyler and Morris were more conciliatory because they feared that, if Warner were not continued as commander of his regiment at Manchester, he might carry Vermont into the hands of the British. The implication of going over to the enemy does not fit Warner's character, but it was happening in the case of several important Vermont families.

Following the Castleton meeting, a number of Vermont leaders defected, among them Benjamin Spencer, a 1767 settler of Clarendon, south of Rutland. As a resident of New York's Charlotte County, he accepted New York appointments as justice of the peace and assistant judge of the Common Pleas Court.[9] Six years after he settled, he and other New York grant settlers had been threatened by the Green Mountain Boys, who burned the roof of Spencer's house and vandalized other homes. It was then that Ethan Allen offered Spencer the services of Jehiel Hawley in purchasing a New Hampshire title. Spencer did not buy a New Hampshire title since he had one from New York, but because he was respected by his constituents, he was elected to the Provisional Convention of 1777, which wrote the first Vermont constitution. Over the opposition of Ira Allen, he was even named to the Council of Safety, which ran Vermont before the constitution was in effect. Spencer, however, never met with the council; instead, he and his twenty-year-old son Hazelton left Clarendon in July to join Burgoyne's army. Benjamin would die while serving with Burgoyne.

Another defection after the Castleton meeting was William Marsh—an especially galling event to the Allens, for he had been a Green Mountain Boy. Settling in Manchester, Marsh had become a major landholder, and in 1769 he built and began to run a tavern. During Burgoyne's invasion, the Council of Safety actually met in his tavern, and Arthur St. Clair stayed there during his retreat from Ticonderoga. Marsh was one of the few who had supported Ethan Allen's candidacy in 1775 as colonel of the Grants Continental regiment, claiming that Allen had been rejected because the Dorset leaders had not consulted many communities.[10] He did represent Charlotte County, along with John Williams, at the New York Provincial Congress on May 22, 1775, and he was active for the Grants in 1776 by encouraging the eastern townships into a union with those in the west and aimed to make the Grants independent of New York. However, after the defeat at Hubbardton, Marsh urged settlers to remain north of Manchester, a policy that Ira Allen claimed he used to lure settlers to the British. Marsh went to Skene's Castleton meeting in mid-July and then moved his family to Dorset, and from there he joined Burgoyne.

A further defection was Jeremiah French, who joined Burgoyne on July 5 and was named a captain in John Peters's Queens Loyal Rangers. Arriving in Manchester in 1764, Jeremiah became a leading landholder, town clerk, selectman, and constable, whose sister Sarah married William Marsh.[11] French had actually gone to Canada in late 1776 or early 1777 and then returned to settle his affairs and bring his family to Canada. In April 1777 he was caught on suspicion of being a Loyalist and imprisoned at Ticonderoga, from whence he escaped, leading the fort's commander to offer $30 reward for his return. French was again taken prisoner and was not exchanged until 1779, when his friend Justus Sherwood arranged it. He continued to serve in the Queens Loyal Rangers, along with his brother Gershom, a lieutenant. Spencer, Marsh, and French were all motivated by the pacification offer that had been spread from the Castleton meeting.

Riedesel and the Pacification of the Castleton-Manchester Area

Some British officers, with the benefit of hindsight, later complained about the results of the manifesto and the Castleton meeting. Volunteer Thomas Anburey commented, "General [Burgoyne's] manifesto has not had the desired effect, as intelligence is brought in that the [rebel] committees are using their utmost endeavors to counteract it, by watching and imprisoning all persons they suspect, compelling the people to take arms, to drive their cattle and burn their corn under the penalty of immediate death; and sorry am I to add that numbers of [persons well disposed] to the success of our arms have already undergone that fate!"[12] On the spot at Castleton, Friedrich Riedesel was more specific, expressing the concern that the meeting attendees "only came that they might find out the names of those who were truly loyal and afterwards betray them. . . . No sooner had Colonel Warner heard the report of these spies, than he at once advanced, plundered the loyalists, took away their cattle and even carried off the men themselves." It appears that the Castleton attendees were now in the open to reprisals by Warner's men. Certainly, the rebels were making an effort to counteract the manifesto and Castleton meeting.

Part of the problem with the Castleton meeting was that many settlers had taken Burgoyne's offer of protection literally: they had come into his camp to avoid the depredations of war, and they saw themselves as neutral when it came to taking arms for either side. This was the first but not the last time that Riedesel and Burgoyne would run into "protectionists," who simply wanted the safety that Burgoyne promised. Castleton's protectionists were willing to supply Riedesel's army of occupation with "large quantities of fresh provisions."[13] They believed that Vermont would be conquered by Burgoyne and sought protection while remaining on their farms. They were not necessarily ready to take up arms for the king, and Burgoyne had not asked them to do that anyway.

Various towns reacted differently to the pacification policy introduced at Castleton. It was estimated by a German soldier that Poultney was dominated by rebels, while Castleton was one-third Loyalist and Clarendon was overrun by neutrals.[14] One way of identifying Loyalists in the Castleton area was that they attached a placard of Burgoyne's manifesto or the call for the Castleton meeting to their houses. Later, Clarendon would have more individuals banished as Loyalists by the Vermont Assembly than any other town—even more than Arlington. Overall, about one third of the Grants were said to be Loyalist or neutral—but these are impressions, for it is impossible to find actual numbers.

The success of the German occupation of the Castleton-Manchester area must also be considered. For almost a month after the rebel defeat at Hubbardton, Riedesel's Germans were there. The presence of the Germans involved professional troops in the civil war between Loyalists and rebels. As early as July 10, Lieutenant Colonel Heinrich Breymann camped separately from German troops at Castleton to support the Loyalists. His orders included not only recruiting Loyalists, but protecting the wounded at Hubbardton—who had yet to be moved to Ticonderoga—and "to create an alarm towards the Connecticut [River]."[15] This last was Burgoyne's pet project, although it was impossible to execute, given the mountainous terrain of the Grants.

When Riedesel went to Castleton, he had up to 2,000 troops to command in July pacification operations, which were meant to please as many of the inhabitants as possible. He confronted the difficulty of discriminating between friend and foe by explaining that "there were a large number of loyal inhabitants scattered through the country, who were often taken for rebels, [and] the strictest orders had to be issued least the soldiers should treat them as such." There was to be no plundering, although the Germans found many habitations in the area deserted and took advantage of this, "by making much freer use of the garden fruits in their fields," which they felt were going to waste.[16] His Germans were probably the most disciplined troops of Burgoyne's army because they were hired professionals, uninterested in the politics of the war, without the hatred of rebels that the British army had acquired. While they must have stolen from unoccupied farms, they did not loot indiscriminately.

Riedesel's Germans had no difficulty in purchasing supplies and living off the land, even though they observed that Vermont farms were not as productive as those in New York. The day after the Castleton meeting, Breymann's officers bought horses from the inhabitants to move their personal baggage. Two weeks later, Brigadier General Specht described how "we found the abandoned houses of most of those who had been against us. To start with, we had ox-drawn wagons in a circumference of 13 miles rounded up. We did this in order to have the minimum of necessary vehicles to remove the ammunition, the provisions and items of regiments . . . in case of new movement by the army; we also were eager to have our most essential necessities."[17] Well before the Battle of Walloomsac, the German troops were involved in providing the army with wagons and food from apparently abandoned Grants farms.

To search for rebels, Riedesel sent out detachments to various towns beyond Castleton. His Wells detachment returned and reported "that those of the inhabitants who had fallen under suspicion of disloyalty, had left their houses, taking their furniture and most of their stock with them. Nevertheless, the detachment brought in a few cattle and carts with the teams belonging to them." The detachment from Tinmouth "brought with them 4 prisoners, and about 60 head of cattle." Mistakenly, it was claimed that Colonel Warner was "so alarmed at the sudden appearance of this detachment, that he immediately evacuated Manchester, and retreated to Arlington."[18] Warner did send some Continentals to Arlington, but they found the place, as might be expected, to be hostile.

The Grants Leadership and Pacification

Warner's command would try to oppose the pacification policy by harassing Riedesel's troops and Loyalists. Inhabitants were forced to move in several directions. J. F. Wasmus observed that grantees as close as five miles to the German camp, who wanted to be good Loyalists and avoid the rebels, had to fight against Warner's men, who "robbed them of all their belongings and generally treated them abominably."[19] Other grantees, like those along the Poultney River, were well disposed toward the rebels and thus had gone with their families and cattle to Warner. Droves of cattle were also confiscated from Loyalist farms by order of the Vermont Council of Safety and sent to Bennington to be sold, so that the accumulations of such items made Bennington an important center of supply. Those who would swear an oath of allegiance to the United States before the Council of Safety were discharged to return to their land.

Riedesel and his officers observed Warner carrying out Schuyler's orders concerning the rooting out of Loyalists and encouraging the abandonment of farms around Manchester. By the end of July, Specht reported that "Congress has pronounced a decree whereby all inhabitants of the region had to leave their homes and go further east taking everything they could; all the damage they would incur from leaving their non-transportable effects and ungathered harvests behind would be refunded."[20] This last, of course, was pure propaganda, but evidently Specht had it on good authority.

Despite Riedesel's restraint, bloodshed between the opposing sides was inevitable. At Tinmouth on July 27, Quaker Loyalist and farmer John Irish was killed by Lieutenant Isaac Clark and a party that included Lieutenant Ebenezer Allen and two more of his rangers. According to Irish's wife, he was assassinated as he opened the front door.[21] The murder caused an influx of refugees to seek Riedesel's protection. Irish had come from New York's Nine Partners Patent and settled in Tinmouth in 1768, before Ebenezer Allen made his home there. But Irish had gone to the Castleton meeting and taken the oath to the king, and under Warner's orders this was enough of a reason to kill him.

When Warner attempted to take Loyalist cattle, he found the task of discriminating between rebel and Loyalist to be as difficult as it had been for Riedesel. It was soon discovered that Allen's rangers and Vermont militia, including Herrick's recruits, were looting rebel farms as well as those of Loyalists. From the Council of Safety on July 28, Ira Allen ordered Vermont rangers to stop vandalizing settlers north of Manchester, until Warner could investigate the towns and distinguish those who were friend or foe. There is no evidence that Warner was able to do this. Also, Ira Allen again switched his policy, claiming the council had never wanted farmers to remain in the area. It was the fault of the "infamous William Marsh, Benjamin Spencer, Simson Jennison, John McNeil and others" who had promoted the policy of remaining and then had gone over to the enemy.[22] Confusion reigned among the Vermont and Continental authorities on how to oppose Riedesel's pacification.

After August 1 Riedesel and his troops were gradually recalled from the Manchester front to rejoin Burgoyne. They had brought a measure of protection to area Loyalists and had gained supplies and transport, and they may have obtained the respect of neutrals because of their discipline; they had certainly tied down the Grants' meager defensive forces. Warner, under Schuyler's orders and with the aid of Vermont rangers, had aggressively done all he could to counteract them. Both sides had difficulty in distinguishing friend from foe. The German pacification that began at Castleton and continued at Manchester set the scene for a larger confrontation that would take place in mid-August near the Continental depot at Bennington.

Burgoyne and Skene planned more meetings like that at Castleton. One was discussed for Fort Edward, including the calling of a Charlotte County court, but it did not take place.[23] The next pacification meeting would be hosted by Skene and Colonel Friedrich Baum and would be held in mid-August at Cambridge, New York.

MILITANT LOYALISM IN ARLINGTON

Well below the Manchester line, Arlington's Loyalists viewed Burgoyne's army as liberators. In addition to the Hawleys, Arlington was the home of the notorious Dr. Samuel Adams, a New Hampshire grantee who had come to Arlington in 1764. Like Jehiel Hawley, he became willing to replace his New Hampshire land title by purchasing one from New York. For this, in 1774, he was convicted by the Green Mountain Boys and hoisted up the Catamount Tavern signpost in Bennington, where he was humiliatingly suspended for two hours.[24] When the War of Independence came, Adams became a Loyalist, remembering what the Green Mountain Boys had done to him, and he and his sons were imprisoned in 1776. They escaped in October, evidently going to Carleton at Crown Point. In January 1777 Carleton accepted Adams as a captain to lead his own independent Loyalist company, although he had few men beyond his immediate family until he returned to Arlington. The example of Adams helped to prevent the town of Arlington from joining other communities and participating in Vermont's political development: the town failed to send representatives to the popular conventions held at Dorset in 1776, Westminster in 1777, and Windsor the same year, or to help to write the Vermont constitution. Arlington was definitely a community for rebels to avoid.

From mid-July Loyalists in Peters's and Adams's corps, like Justus Sherwood, Jeptha and Reuben Hawley, as well as Indians, were detached at Skenesborough to raid the retreating Northern army. This party advanced to Arlington, on the way breaking the windows in Cephas Kent's tavern at Dorset and cutting down the liberty pole that stood before it.[25] These raiders knew that they would be welcomed in Arlington by Loyalists who were their friends and relatives.

As mentioned, around July 20, when he was opposing Riedesel's pacification, Seth Warner sent some of his Continentals, under Sergeant Jacob Safford, to see if Arlington might be a possible place of refuge for his army.[26] Local militias under Lieutenant Simeon Lyman and Lieutenant Matthew Lyon joined the Continentals. Numbering about a hundred, they attempted to occupy Arlington and bring off cattle. But they found Arlington Loyalists ready to oppose them. Arlington Loyalists Benjamin Eastman and Phinehas Hurd had been active in nearby Sandgate, convincing the inhabitants to disarm, and Arlington Loyalists had already gathered cattle and food stuffs for Burgoyne. Captain Samuel Adams was there with his Loyalist friends, attempting to deliver the supplies to Burgoyne's army. He now had with him Jeptha Hawley as his lieutenant, Jeptha's son Gideon as his ensign, and Andrew Hawley, Zadock Hard, Nathan Canfield, and Caleb Daton— all of Arlington.

The two parties confronted each other at West Arlington, where the Continentals were unable to perform well, after the killing of a militiaman by the Loyalists disheartened Lyman's and Lyon's volunteers.[27] Having stopped the rebels, Adams was able to continue his business and lead his cattle and men to Burgoyne's camp. After Adams arrived, on August 9, Burgoyne accepted him as captain of a company of rangers, his fifth Loyalist unit, made up of recruits with his army who already been tested in Arlington. In the contest for livestock and foodstuffs, the rebels came up short in Arlington, and Warner knew he would get no support from that nest of Loyalists.

THE RECRUITING AND ARMING OF LOYALIST UNITS

The example of Arlington and Captain Samuel Adams showed that the region's Loyalists were willing to arm to drive off rebels, even if they were Continentals. At Skenesborough, only a few days after the Castleton meeting, Burgoyne finally decided to organize Loyalists into corps. While they were the most insignificant part of his army when he left Canada, his capture of Ticonderoga had raised the spirits of New York and Vermont Loyalists and encouraged them to join his expedition. On July 20 forty-six armed Loyalists arrived at Skenesborough from around Albany. Many were the descendants of German immigrants, and they told Burgoyne that the British army would be welcome in Albany.[28] Eleven days later fifty-six more arrived, several of whom spoke only German. They swore an oath of allegiance to the king and were given firearms.

The suggestion to go beyond Burgoyne's proclamation with a combat role and an organizational effort was probably made by Philip Skene. To absorb the new recruits for his campaign, Burgoyne created four corps of Loyalists, choosing as their commanders John Peters, Ebenezer Jessup, Daniel McAlpin, and Samuel McKay. However, the units were not to be permanent, and he did not provide the officers with formal commissions.[29] This treatment would be a bone of contention for the rest of the war, since Loyalist officers could not be paid without a commission. As a further humiliation to his Loyalist officers, Burgoyne originally proposed that British regular officers take charge of the Loyalist units because their officers did not know "the Art of War." When the Loyalist officers threatened mutiny, claiming they would join his Indian allies in going back to Canada, Burgoyne dropped this aspect of the proposal.

In creating his original four corps, Burgoyne ignored the regimentalization of Loyalists that Carleton had begun. His choice of the two highest-ranking Loyalist officers, Peters and Ebenezer Jessup, followed precedent, but McAlpin was questionable because he was known to be frail from exposure while hiding from rebels, and McKay had never before received a commission to raise a Loyalist regiment. While McKay had experience with Canadian troops and Indian raids, from the Loyalist standpoint he must be considered a wild card. He had no local following such as the other three, and that is why a month after his appointment he joined Baum's expedition as a volunteer without any recruits.[30]

Samuel McKay was respected by Burgoyne because of his having played several roles in the defense of Canada and because of his family's influence in the regular army. Born in Eastern Europe's Transylvania in 1737, McKay was the son of General Francis McKay, who was stationed there.[31] In the Seven Years' War, Samuel had served in the

60th Regiment with Francis Pfister, under the command of Frederick Haldimand and was on half pay when the War of Independence broke out. When St. Johns fell to the rebels in November 1776, as a member of the garrison he was made a prisoner and sent to Hartford, Connecticut, where, after four months, he and five of his men escaped from jail and after a march of twenty-nine days arrived at Crown Point, having survived by eating a dog's carcass. He was already living in St. Johns when Burgoyne's expedition was being formed. He led a successful war party at Sabbath Day Point on Lake George in April 1777, at the beginning of the Burgoyne campaign, which demonstrated his ability to command Indians. A daring individual, McKay was not as tied to property and a home as his fellow commanders.

Pfister, an officer whom Burgoyne would later praise for bravery before Parliament, was nowhere to be seen in Burgoyne's choice of Loyalist officers. Evidently neither Burgoyne or Skene was aware of his recruiting below the Hoosic Valley. Before Burgoyne decided to organize them, Loyalist officers had been authorized to raise, organize, and command units by various authorities: Pfister's papers came from New York's Governor Tryon, McAlpin's came from General William Howe in New York City, and Peters's came from Governor Carleton in Canada. McAlpin's authority showed how far Howe had gone in raising Loyalist units from New York City.[32] These diverse authorities were the source of officers' rank, though it was a moot point because none of the Loyalist corps approached being filled.

The case of John Peters is illuminating. He had been authorized by Carleton to raise a regiment in October 1776. However, his commission as a lieutenant colonel was not to be granted to him until the unit was at two-thirds of its strength, and he never received pay beyond that of captain.[33] At the beginning of the expedition, Peters had only a few more men than the twenty who had escaped from Saratoga and joined his unit in Canada in June 1777. When mustered on July 23 at Skenesborough, Peters's corps had increased to 262 men. He continued to recruit, and all told, before the Battle on the Walloomsac in mid-August, Peters claimed he had raised 643 men. These recruits would be cut to pieces at the Walloomsac, and in the aftermath rival officers would take many of his recruits, so he actually never reached the necessary two-thirds strength. While Peters would sign letters as lieutenant colonel, claiming to have been promised that rank, his superiors, Burgoyne and later Haldimand, would not recognize this rank, as his regiment had not reached the required numbers. This situation would frustrate him for the rest of his career as a Loyalist officer.

Late in July and the first week of August, Burgoyne's new corps were active. Peters, for instance, paid one of his men to carry Burgoyne's proclamation to the Connecticut River Valley. Peters's largest expense by far was the recruiting of men for his corps.[34] In July Captain McAlpin's recruits, 184 strong, calling themselves the American Volunteers, arrived. Many of them had been hiding in the Saratoga area for months, although Lieutenant Neil Robertson had escaped to Canada in April. Beyond McAlpin, the most significant officer of the American Volunteers was Hugh Munro, a Saratoga Loyalist, who would serve as commander of Burgoyne's bateaux corps. While this unit would be placed under McAlpin, in practice it operated as a completely independent company. As noted, Burgoyne would also recognize an independent company of rangers under Captain Samuel Adams of Arlington.

The Jessup brothers, Ebenezer and Edward, were also prominent Loyalist officers, Ebenezer having the same exalted title of lieutenant colonel as Peters. They faced the same ambiguity in their status as Peters had, until they were recognized at Skenesborough. While they had served with Burgoyne since May and were involved in the capture of Ticonderoga and the hot fight at Hubbardton, not until July 19 was Ebenezer made commander of the King's Loyal Americans—who previously had simply been Jessup's Rangers. Despite the combat record, the corps would be used more for intelligence gathering, scouting, and foraging, especially procuring cattle.[35] Jessup's chief responsibility was for filling his corps's ranks. He still believed he held land in New York, and he personally set aside 24,000 acres for grants to his recruits and 20,000 more acres for officers serving in his corps. This assumed, of course, that the British would win and the Jessups keep control of their New York estates.

As a result of recruiting, companies of the King's Loyal Americans were raised, to be commanded by Ebenezer's brother Edward, Jonathan Jones of Kingsbury, Joseph Jessup (another brother), James Robins, Christian Wehr, and Hugh Munro of Saratoga. In July Major Edward Jessup's company had 49 men; Captain Jonathan Jones's company, 31 men; Captain Joseph Jessup's, 60 men; and Captain Hugh Munro's, 14 men.[36] During the Burgoyne expedition, the number of the King's Loyal Americans reached at least 211 effectives.

The most renowned of the recruits for the King's Loyal Americans came from Sarah Dunham Jones's family of Kingsbury. Already in January 1777, the Jones brothers had served in the Jessups' unit, with Jonathan as captain of his own company and Solomon—a medical student in Albany—as the surgeon's mate, while David was a lieutenant in Ebenezer Jessup's company.[37] David, of course, became famous when his fiancée, Jane McCrea, attempted to join him. Sarah, Jonathan, and John would also supply Burgoyne with Indian corn, forage, and bullocks. With them the Jones brothers brought neighbors like Caleb Clossen, who by the end of the war was serving as a sergeant in the Loyal Rangers.

Yet, after creating the Loyalist units, Burgoyne claimed in Parliament in 1779 that the Loyalists did not make proper soldiers because their officers were so involved in raising their units that it detracted from their use in scouting and foraging. He questioned the motives of his Loyalists and their officers. In his words:

> I would not be understood to infer, that none of the [Loyalists] with me were sincere in their loyalty: perhaps many were so. A few were of distinguished bravery. . . . I only maintain that the interests and the passions of the revolted Americans concenter in the cause of the Congress; and those of the Loyalists break and subdivide into various pursuits, with which the cause of the King has little or nothing to do. . . . One [officer's] views went to the profit which he was to enjoy when his corps should be complete; another's, to the protection of the district in which he resided; a third was wholly intent upon revenge against his personal enemies; and all of them were repugnant even to the idea of subordination.[38]

Because there was rivalry between the officers in recruiting, there were disagreements that could only be settled by Burgoyne, and they were "a heavier tax upon time and patience." Here is a continuation of the complaints of British officers in the Seven Years' War that provincials were really as difficult to manage as Indians.

The motives which Burgoyne complained about show the Loyalists were involved in the regional civil conflict, rather than focused on their patriotism or the professional demands of the expedition. The concern of Loyalist officers for protection of their homes and neighbors and for revenge upon those who were hostile to them grated on

Burgoyne, as commander of the British army. His accusation of waiting for profit is quite unfounded, given the situation of Loyalist officers. Most had left everything behind and by 1780 would see their property confiscated.[39] The only way they could bear the expense of raising a corps was to have the ranks filled as quickly as possible and thus receive a commission and the modest payment that went with it—surely not a profit. As for their lack of subordination, this was a foregone conclusion, given the fact that they knew and had settled the region and could operate independently. It also involved the discord among Loyalist officers over recruiting, at which Burgoyne proved to be no Solomon. The only qualities that Burgoyne held up as admirable were bravery—meaning, to him, death on the battle-field—and devotion to the cause of the monarch, not qualities that counted for much in a civil war.

Burgoyne's and Riedesel's first effort to win the hearts and minds of the people at Castleton was more successful than the rebel effort to counteract it. In this sense Castleton would be a victory before Burgoyne sent his second expedition toward Vermont at the Walloomsac. However, without being required to join a Loyalist unit, Burgoyne's effort at pacification fostered protectionism, in which the inhabitants who joined him saw themselves as neutrals, simply trying to protect their families and farms from the deprivations of war. Later, he felt that he had been fooled into thinking that all those who visited Castleton were firm Loyalists. Meanwhile, Seth Warner did not tolerate such neutrals and did his best to prevent the spread of Loyalism, even if some rebels were caught in his sweeping net.

At first, Burgoyne hesitated to allow Loyalists to serve in military corps, but after mid-July he let his chosen Loyalist officers organize and recruit. He chose officers to lead four corps, ignoring some of the Loyalist units already functioning. This was still an on-the-spot deci-sion, created only for the duration of the campaign, and he felt that the recruiting activities detracted from Loyalists performing auxiliary services, at which he felt they would excel. As Burgoyne's Loyalist units developed, he also became fearful that they would be regarded as British regulars.

Frustration between Burgoyne and his Loyalists developed as to what each expected of the other. Burgoyne never lacked Loyalists—he had more than he expected—but he was confused on how to win their support. Burgoyne's successors in Canada would build on the Loyalist organizational issues that he and his predecessor, Carleton, first confronted in 1776 and 1777. Defining their motives is complicated. To this end, further Loyalist activity will be featured as this account of the Burgoyne Campaign unfolds.

9

SEEKING NATIVE AMERICAN SUPPORT

After Burgoyne's defeat, when he returned to Britain and was defending himself before Parliament, he would state that he thought his use of Native Americans "was a necessary evil," because he "had been obliged to run a race with Congress in securing an alliance of the Indians."[1] He was correct in the sense that Horatio Gates had made every effort to have Indian allies attached to his army. In his further defense, Burgoyne also argued that he "had in more instances than one controlled the Indians." He claimed that he was usually able to dominate his Indian allies, even if they tended to have their own agenda. In this contention he was mistaken.

Burgoyne needed "the necessary evil" of Indian allies to serve as scouts, to lead the vanguard of his army, and to carry the war to the countryside beyond his army. As scouts they were to provide intelligence by taking prisoners to be interrogated by British officers. Indians expected a reward for this, regardless of the quality of the information, and if this was not forthcoming, their prisoner might disappear to be treated as a captive. They were most successful in Burgoyne's vanguard. Indeed, when they were present, the rebels hardly ever dared to skirmish with the mixed vanguard of Indians, Loyalists, marksmen, and sometimes light infantry. The rebels thought of Indians as wild men, who were very cunning and had eyes and ears that were very acute.[2] As soon as Indians were reduced in numbers, the rebels were more effective in molesting Burgoyne's vanguard and outposts. Using Indians

in raiding the civilian population turned out to be much more difficult than Burgoyne claimed. In carrying the war beyond his army,
they gave him influence in an area far beyond his camp, but this
advantage was offset by the fact that they could not easily distinguish
friend from foe. Their destructive activities were among the chief
reasons that Loyalists and protectionists joined Burgoyne.

As noted, Native Americans had their own justification for warfare
and felt themselves to be independent peoples. They formed an alliance with Burgoyne only as long as it was to their benefit. They were
not in any sense European soldiers who followed an officer's orders.
In military activities they conducted what has been called parallel
war, that is, their own campaign separate from but alongside their
allies.[3] They easily subverted most of Burgoyne's efforts to restrain
them, and thus their raiding promoted further civil conflict.

By 1777, despite "their cruel and barbarous custom of scalping,"
even Guy Carleton admitted that Indians "are of essential service in
either defending or invading a country, being extremely skillful in the
art of surprising, and watching the motions of the enemy." In late April
an Indian council took place at Quebec, largely made up of representatives from the Canadian missions, who now wanted to renounce
the influence of pro-rebel Kahnawake Louis Atayataghrongthta and
instead serve under Governor Carleton. They confirmed their alliance
with Britain, and he distributed presents among them.[4] As a result,
first blood in the Saratoga Campaign—although Burgoyne did not
know it—was drawn by a party of mission Indians at Lake George
the same month. Led by the previously mentioned Samuel McKay,
they surprised thirty sleeping rebels at Sabbath Day Point, tomahawk-
ing four and taking twenty-one prisoners. While they were pursued
by Benjamin Whitcomb's rangers, they made it back to Canada safely.
Such harassing activities were a prelude to the invasion of Burgoyne's
main force and showed why both Burgoyne and Gates would need
Indian support.

Burgoyne followed Carleton's thoughts in his initial proclamation of June 23 by exaggerating his number of Indians and his ability
to control them, when he threatened to loose them on the borderland "if military necessity required."[5] As the campaign progressed,
Burgoyne became convinced that his Indians were far more effective
than his Loyalists in protecting his camp and gaining control over
an area. On September 1 he reiterated: "Our [Loyalists] were neither

careful nor agile enough, through their patrols and reconnoiterings, to give the camp the same security that the [Indians] had been able to do." Thus, Burgoyne needed allied Indians because they were his best scouts and this justified his use of them.

Indians for Burgoyne's Campaign

At the start of the campaign, Burgoyne's Indian auxiliaries numbered only 500, considerably less than the 1,700 who had gathered for the Marquis de Montcalm's invasion of Lake George, twenty years before. The early neutrality of mission Indians around Montreal had passed, and they would contribute the greatest number of his Indians. The mission Iroquois were supportive; an old Iroquois resident related that "our whole villages able to go to war are come forth against the Bostonians. The old and infirm, our infants and wives, alone remain at home."[6] The chief reason for Burgoyne's lack of Indians was that the bulk of the allied Indians—perhaps nine hundred—would be gathered with Lieutenant Colonel Barry St. Leger to attack the Mohawk Valley and Fort Stanwix.

On June 21 Burgoyne halted his advance on Lake Champlain to hold a war council with his allies at the Bouquet River, about forty miles north of Ticonderoga. This was his chance to work directly with the Kahnawakes, Kanesetakes, Akwesasne Mohawks, Abenakis of Odanak, and Algonquians gathered for the conference. Burgoyne told them: "The collective voices and hands of Indian tribes over this vast continent, are on the side of justice, of law, and the King."[7] In reference to Carleton's previous request to some that they not yet make war, he thanked them for waiting for "the King your father's call to arms." He urged them to "strike at the common enemies of your cause, [rebels who were] disturbers of public order, peace and happiness, destroyers of commerce, parricides of state."

However, Burgoyne then introduced restrictions. His allies were told that they "shall not destroy all, [that] we will regulate your passions when they overbear, to point out where it is nobler to spare than to revenge. . . . Aged men, women, children and prisoners, must be held sacred from the knife or hatchet, even in time of actual conflict." He went on to address the existence of the Loyalists: "The King has may faithful subjects dispersed in the provinces, consequently you have many brothers there, and these people are more to be pitied, that they are persecuted or imprisoned wherever they are discovered or suspected."[8] His allies were to identify the king's friends and help them. He finished with the promise that they would receive compensation for the live captives they took, but would not be paid for scalps.

Not all of Burgoyne's Native American allies were present at the Bouquet River, and thus they missed his rhetoric. The Ottawas from Michilimackinac and Green Bay were hundreds of miles from Montreal and would not appear until the middle of his campaign, when Burgoyne had reached Skenesborough. Planning for their appearance had begun earlier, when Superintendent John Campbell and his deputy Alexander Fraser had urged them to come.[9] Campbell could not speak the western Indian languages and thus had little influence in their councils, but he made up for it by using his father-in-law, the famed Luc de La Corne, who was fluent in several Indian dialects.

La Corne was a leading figure in Canadian-Indian relations, whose service bridged three conflicts: King George's War, the Seven Years' War, and the War of Independence. He was sixty-six at the time of Burgoyne's campaign.[10] A La Marine captain in the first two wars, he was always regarded by the British as "notorious for brutal inhumanity." He had operated in the Saratoga area during King George's War, and on June 23, 1747, he had attacked newly constructed Fort Clinton near Saratoga plantation and taken forty prisoners. Two months later La Corne had returned to raid toward Albany and took scalps, maintaining the pressure on Fort Clinton. In October, his goal was achieved, as the British were forced to abandon and burn the fort. In 1757, during the Seven Years' War, he served with Montcalm at the capture of Fort William Henry at the head of Lake George. In the next year, La Corne successfully led 400 Indians against a 54-wagon convoy on the road between Fort Edward and Halfway Brook, taking 60 captives, 230 oxen, and 110 scalps. This foray was meant to cut the supply line of Abercromby's still active British army and also provide La Corne's Indians with the expected captives, booty, and scalps.

In the Great Lakes region, however, even La Corne was merely another functionary of the Quebec Indian Department. Immediate leadership of the Ottawas in 1777 belonged to nearly as famous a partisan, Charles-Michel Mouet de Langlade. Langlade was born in 1729 to a French Canadian fur trader and an Ottawa mother on Mackinac Island. In 1752 he had led Ottawas in the destruction of English traders and their allies at Pickawillany in Ohio and three years later contributed to the famous ambush of General Edward Braddock.[11] He now lived in the Fort Michilimackinac area, where the straits connect Lake Superior with the other Great Lakes, and later at Green Bay on Lake Michigan, where he was a fur trader. When the War of Independence came, he put aside his earlier hostility to Britain and served as a member of the Quebec Indian Department. From the standpoint of blood and geography he was well positioned to lead Ottawa warriors from Michilimackinac and Green Bay. He would gather not only Ottawas but Chippewas and Foxes. With Langlade and La Corne, Burgoyne had masters in managing Indians for the conduct of *petite guerre*.

The Indians' Comings and Goings

Indians were independent peoples who made decision separately from Burgoyne and his army. They came and went from his army, often returning after a respite. It appears that a figure of five hundred warriors serving with Burgoyne is approximately correct, but it is also clear that the makeup of his Indian allies varied with time and place. Many were accompanied by their families, who camped separately from Burgoyne's army and were not included in his estimates. One certainty is that Indians usually had little difficulty in penetrating the rebel lines around Bemis Heights to join Burgoyne, even though their families were with them. Their superiority in making their way through the woods and their knowledge of the countryside allowed them to escape from rebel rangers.

At the council on the Bouquet River, Burgoyne had gathered Indians from Kahnawake, Akwesasne, Kanesetake, Odanak, and Becancour, that is, the domiciled mission Indians of the St. Lawrence valley. The latter two Abenaki missions provided only a small contingent, as they remained deeply divided over the matter of taking sides. By June 22 the last of the mission Indians, numbering about a hundred warriors, had arrived at the Bouquet River. Three hundred of their allies were already at Crown Point, where five days before they had surprised a scout of rebel rangers from the Ticonderoga garrison, killed or wounded ten, and captured an equal number, whom they scalped. This was a foretaste of what they could do. They were with Burgoyne when he drove the rebels from Ticonderoga, their presence most evident in the sack of the fort. Then, to the dismay of the British, many of these mission allies left, after scarcely a month of service. Using a favorite militia refrain, they said they were "nearest home" and "only begged that some part of them might be permitted to return to their harvest."[12] Burgoyne granted permission, and the next day many went away, although some remained. The mission Indians had gained the lion's share of the booty at Ticonderoga, and this news did attract other allied Indians, who now appeared to take their place and gain similar rewards.

In July, as Burgoyne occupied Skenesborough, his Indian allies carried out further raids toward Schuyler's base at Fort Edward, which showed them at their most effective. North of Fort Edward, Schuyler had placed the newly arrived men of John Nixon's Massachusetts Continental Brigade, Berkshire County militia under Brigadier General John Fellows, and some Albany County militia. Their job was the famous obstruction of Wood Creek and its road to delay Burgoyne from moving south. What is often ignored is that this work left the Massachusetts and New York troops exposed to Indian skirmishing, which caused stinging casualties. Nixon reported that Captain Daniel Lane and twenty men had been taken by Indians—though some later escaped, and on July 21 he claimed that four hundred Indians had attacked his men near Fort Ann, killing three and taking twenty captive. On July 30 and August 4, the vanguard of Burgoyne's army, consisting of Indians, Jessup's rangers, and Loyalist volunteers, drove the rebels southward, and a Loyalist commented that, in attack, "such is the natural bravery of our Indians, for they know nothing of the art of war, [that] they put their arms into a canoe, and swim over the river, pushing the canoe before them."[13] In addition to Wood Creek and the Hudson River, Burgoyne's Indians also effectively raided in the direction of Lake George, cutting off the road between there and Fort Edward.

With the rebels having retreated to Schuyler's plantation, Hampshire County militia private Simeon Alexander volunteered to go on a scout to the north. He preferred this scout to serving as a sentry because, he noted, sentries were easily picked off by Burgoyne's Indians. His scout ran into Burgoyne's vanguard and was confronted by two hundred soldiers, who fired a volley at them, forcing them into the safety of the woods. But the woods proved to be no refuge, as they were full of Indians. Alexander exclaimed, "Each man then made his escape in the best way he could, and about one-half our number were killed or taken. I escaped without a wound."[14] It was no wonder that rebel militia feared the lurking presence of Burgoyne's Indians.

The previous July, when Carleton had called the Great Lakes Indians "to go to war against the enemies of the King, our father," he had asked them not to go then, but to wait in readiness.[15] Burgoyne now wanted them, and in the spring of 1777 they gathered as soon as snow and ice permitted, not losing any time in setting out to show their willingness and loyalty. Concerned to do their part as allies, they had left their villages, wives, and children, covering as many as 1,500 miles to Lake Champlain. Some of their warriors joined St. Leger's Mohawk Valley expedition, but the rest arrived in Montreal and then traveled south. From July 17 to 19, La Corne and Langlade's Great Lakes Indians appeared in Skenesborough, and from there they skirmished southward against Nixon's force and the rebel rear guard.

La Corne and Langlade understood that Indians did not fight like the regulars, for they sought to preserve not destroy life, and they expected to be treated as independent allies. Despite La Corne's rhetoric, "Speak, and we shall obey," his force would carry on war independently of Burgoyne's direction.[16] In early August they began to complain to La Corne because of Burgoyne's reprimand and restrictions for the Jane McCrea incident. Reports of Indian losses along the Walloomsac further dampened their ardor, and they started to leave. A final congress was held on August 19, and the Ottawas, having been with Burgoyne barely a month, had their drifting made official by La Corne, who received permission from Burgoyne for them to leave. They were gone by late August—thus returning to the Great Lakes with the desired plunder and captives. What was more telling was that these warriors from Michilimackinac and Green Bay would not return to the East in 1778, for they would be forced to remain as George Rogers Clark led the first rebel invasion of the Great Lakes region.

As a result, in early August, Riedesel claimed "almost all of the Indians had left for their homes, while the army was standing still."[17] He observed that it was likely the Indians did not find the army's conditions acceptable, especially European military discipline, which was alien to them. While Riedesel may have been right about their motives, he was mistaken in thinking they were gone. Burgoyne was never abandoned by his Indian allies. In fact, more than a hundred Mohawk mission Indians, under Captains Charles-Louis Tarieu de Lanaudière and Colin Campbell, as well as Abenakis from Odanak under Lieutenant Samuel Wright, were part of Lieutenant Colonel Baum's force that left for Bennington in mid-August. Lanaudière was the son-in-law of La Corne, and Campbell was the brother of John Campbell, superintendent of the Quebec Indian Department. Some Indians were also not with Burgoyne or Baum because they used Ticonderoga or Skenesborough as a base when they marauded through the countryside. Their momentary absence may have led to Riedesel's mistaken observation.

A source of Mohawk warriors for Burgoyne were families that migrated to the Saratoga area from their homes in the Mohawk Valley, as a result of the pillaging of Canajoharie by rebels and fear that Fort Hunter, with its St. Anne's Chapel, was next. John Deserontyon, the Mohawk captain, had been wounded in the aftermath of St. Leger's retreat from Fort Stanwix, but he was able to organize the evacuation of Fort Hunter. He, Captain Aaron Kanonraron, Captain Isaac Hill Onoghsokte, and Chief Canadagia and their families numbered about 150. With 40 leading Loyalists, they fought their way through the rebels and into Burgoyne's camp. They were at his Batten Kill Camp on August 24 "with their squaws, children, cattle, horses and sheep."[18] When Burgoyne's army crossed the Hudson, the women and children went toward Canada, while the Mohawk warriors remained with him. Anburey witnessed these new allies relaxed, bathing in the Batten Kill River, unaware that the Mohawks had long regarded this river as their hunting and fishing ground—a place that might even be a new home.

Burgoyne placed the Fort Hunter Mohawks on patrol, so that the "impudent, small attacks of the Rebels will soon stop again."[19] However, only twelve days later the Mohawk warriors slipped away, joining their families on the way to Canada, where they eventually settled at Lachine, which had become an Indian refugee center, and where Daniel Claus provided for them at his own expense.

Meanwhile, on August 28 Joseph Brant led the Canajoharie Mohawks, including wives and children, to join their brethren on the Batten Kill. The Fort Hunter Mohawks went out to meet them, covering their arrival, but it took a week for the Canajoharie Mohawks to penetrate the rebel lines to join their Mohawk relatives.[20] This was after St. Leger had abandoned the siege of Fort Stanwix and retreated to Oswego. Brant and his followers, however, remained only briefly, deciding, like their Fort Hunter brethren, that Saratoga was not the place for resettlement. Brant slipped away back to the Mohawk Valley to escort Molly Brant, his sister and former consort of Sir William Johnson, and her family and relatives to reside among the Cayugas. It was becoming impossible for the Mohawks to live in their Mohawk Valley homeland—but there appeared to be better alternatives than serving with Burgoyne.

A second group of a hundred Fort Hunter Mohawks arrived at Burgoyne's camp on September 8.[21] They remained with Burgoyne longer because they were still present on October 9, and when they left five days later they were confronted by rebel militia, north of Fort Edward, and fifty-three men, women, and children were taken prisoner to Albany. Schuyler put them back in the Mohawk Valley, but in June 1778 their kin came from Akwesasne and completed their original journey by taking them to Canada. They eventually joined their fellow Mohawks at Lachine. Thus, three Mohawk parties from Fort Hunter and Canajoharie joined Burgoyne but chose to move on to Canada, where they already had many brothers.

While village identities changed, Indians allies continued to serve with Burgoyne throughout the campaign. By September 18, the day before the Battle of Freeman's Farm, sixty Indians were serving as scouts in Burgoyne's vanguard.[22] They were probably mission Indians or Fort Hunter Mohawks. Still, some Indians were serving on the east side of the Hudson or in the area from Ticonderoga down. They were still active on October 6, the day before the Battle of Bemis Heights, when sixty of them, on their own, ambushed rebels along the Hudson River, burning a farm that the rebels were using for cover. The Baroness Riedesel saw them "in war dress" at the battle the next day.

Hindsight accusations, like those Lord Harrington made in the Parliamentary inquiry in 1779, that the Indians allied to the British went over to the rebels, were merely politically motivated efforts to discredit their use.[23] There is no evidence they did; Gates's correspondence shows that his Indian recruits came exclusively from existing rebel allies, the Stockbridges, Oneidas, and possibly Tuscaroras. Gates had sought Indians and bent over backwards to obtain their good will. Indians did understand the obligations of alliances, and if they did go home, they did not join the enemy.

Controlling Indian Allies

Certainly British officers of the Indian Departments had difficulty in controlling their Indian allies. For a start, Indian warriors had a tendency to drink, not for pleasure, but in fact to become dangerously drunk. This situation was experienced by one of the best of the Canadian Indian Department's officers, Captain Alexander Fraser, Campbell's deputy superintendent. In his capacity in the Indian Department, he tried to treat allied Indians fairly and even invited them to British social occasions. This last was done with mixed results. At one such dinner, Lieutenant Anburey sniffed, "there came into the room a great number of Indians . . . who not having much ceremony, and seeing the bottles and glasses on the table, would drink with us, and began to be extremely troublesome, when Captain Fraser intervened; and, to show . . . the control he has over them, the instant he spoke they quitted the room, but not without a present, for . . . he was obliged to order his servant to give them a bottle of rum."[24] Even fair-minded officers of the Indian Departments had to offer bribes where Indians were involved in drinking.

From incidents like this, Indian Department officers were charged by their colleagues with coddling Indians. A British officer observed, "Those who have the management and conduct of [Indians] are, from interested motives, obliged to indulge them in all their caprices and humours, and, like spoiled children, [they] are more unreasonable and importunate upon every new indulgence granted them."[25] Even when members of Indian Departments did their job well, with an understanding of Indian culture, they were criticized by fellow British army officers.

Anburey—who obviously disliked Indians—warned that Indian allies could not discriminate between the King's friends and foes. To prevent them from killing indiscriminately and attacking Loyalists or neutrals, he urged a change in their ways. He claimed it was the British "task . . . to regulate [Indian] passions when they overbear, to point out where it is nobler to spare than revenge, to discriminate degrees of guilt, to suspend the uplifted stroke, to chastise and not to destroy."[26] Anburey offered a combination of religion, military discipline, and guidance from British officers to teach Indians to control their passions.

Burgoyne and his officers made efforts to prevent what they felt were the worst characteristics of Indian culture. On July 3, before Ticonderoga was taken, orders were given that "Whoever sells rum to the Savages will receive corporal punishment and be chased from the army. . . . This is very good, for when the Savages are drunk, they scalp both friend and foe." It was more than liquor that needed control. The next day, J. F. Wasmus complained enviously, "for want of horses, everything is being pulled by soldiers . . . [yet,] the savages have captured horses, oxen and cows."[27] He explained that since several of the horses that the Indians had taken as booty or stolen had previously been purchased by his regiment for transporting baggage, it was ordered that no one need buy a horse from the Indians. They were selling the same horse to their allies over and over again.

And then there were the victims of Indian raids. On July 24, 1777, Digby wrote of a common incident: "Our Indians . . . were detached in scouting parties, both in our front and on our flanks, and came to a house where [Jane McCrea] resided. . . . She fell a sacrifice to the savage passions of these blood thirsty monsters."[28] This is what a British officer thought; he was clearly more mortified by the woman's death than were the rebels. However, at Salem which was constantly alarmed over Indian raids, the rebel militia commanders actually failed to report the incident in letters to Schuyler written on July 25. Gates, on the other hand, would not let the opportunity pass and made her murder a part of his anti-British propaganda, although it is unclear as to how far he or his officers were able to spread news of the death.

On September 2, 1777, Burgoyne did write to Gates to clear himself of wrongdoing in the Jane McCrea incident. Following his policy, Burgoyne denied he had paid money for scalps, but rather that compensation was offered to Indians for captives "because it would prevent cruelty," to them.[29] Burgoyne stated that a strict accounting would be made of Indians who brought in scalps and that these should not be taken from the wounded or dying, and never from any prisoners. In Jane McCrea's case, he revealed, her death "was no premeditated barbarity, on the contrary, two chiefs who had brought her off for the purpose of security, not of violence to her person, disputed who should be her guard, and in a fit of savage passion in the one from whose hands she was snatched, the unhappy woman became the victim." While this incident may have happened, he assured Gates, "The above instance excepted, your intelligence respecting cruelties of the Indians is absolutely false."

Jane McCrea was actually a Loyalist, in that her fiancé, David Jones, was a lieutenant in Jessup's corps and a member of that Kingsbury Loyalist family. Although one theory is that she was actually mistakenly killed by rebel soldiers, at Fort Ann Burgoyne demanded that his Indian chiefs deliver McCrea's killer for punishment with death. La Corne responded that this would result in mass desertion by Indians, who would commit further crimes on their way back to Canada. The murder was thought to be the work of Wyandot Panther, a Wyandot who probably belonged to a village in the Quebec area or may have come from Ohio with the Ottawas. Punishment was left to the sachems—meaning none at all in the eyes of whites. As a result, Burgoyne stated that "he would rather lose every Indian in his army than connive at their enormities."[30] He ordered that all Indian raids in the future be accompanied by a responsible British officer.

Loyalist officer John Peters, writing with hindsight in 1779, could not see how Burgoyne could change his mind, since at the beginning of the campaign he had encouraged Indians "to fight the enemy in their own way," and now reversed himself halfway through it.[31] Apparently, the only way to deal with Indians was to set rules at the beginning of the campaign and strictly follow them. Burgoyne had been more flexible than that, but this was countered by the fact that he was surrounded by officers who did not trust their Indian allies.

GATES'S USE OF INDIANS

At the beginning of his campaign, Burgoyne had only minimal competition with the rebels in gaining Indian support. However, Horatio Gates was impressed by the scouting and harassing skill of Burgoyne's Indians, and he dropped his concern for the Jane McCrea incident quickly, as he sought to recruit his own Indian allies. Early in September 1777, Gates wrote to Timothy Bedel in New Hampshire to provide ammunition and provisions to bring all the area's Abenakis to Bemis Heights, as if they could be gathered in one place and were universally willing to ally themselves with rebels; the Abenakis did not appear.[32]

A few weeks earlier, Gates had requested that the Stockbridge Indians join his army. They responded with a group of fewer than twenty scouts, led by the sachem Mtohksin.[33] In a few cases Stockbridge

Indians had enrolled individually in Continental and militia regiments and were already serving in the Northern Department army. A few Stockbridges may have participated in the Battle of Freeman's Farm, although it is also possible they were serving with John Brown at Lake George. Mtohksin's men left Gates in late September and did not participate in the Battle of Bemis Heights, returning home for the harvest—the same reason the mission Indians had left Burgoyne. The Stockbridges tried to return in October, but they lacked clothing and were delayed, not arriving in Gates's camp until October 23, after the surrender.

More crucial were the hundred plus Oneidas and Tuscaroras who joined Gates's army on September 20.[34] To obtain them, Gates swallowed his pride and worked through Schuyler, who was still president of the Indian Commissioners. At the mid-September Indian council, Gates had requested that Schuyler call for Iroquois recruits and send them to his camp at Bemis Heights. Of those attending, only the Oneidas and a few Tuscaroras listened seriously to Schuyler's plea for support. The Oneidas had reason to be concerned, for while St. Leger had been turned back, their village of Oriska had been destroyed by the members of the Iroquois Council, who supported the British. The Oneidas thus sought revenge against the British and their Iroquois allies. Gates welcomed the Oneidas, led by Louis Atayataghrongthta, Honyery Thawengarakwen, and Peter Bread, and had them wear red woolen caps to distinguish them from enemy Indians. He also ordered his men not to crowd their camps and insult them, evidently reflecting his soldiers' true attitude toward their new allies. Gates would praise the Oneidas' service in raiding the enemy. They did scalp some of their victims, although their biggest concern was taking captives for prisoner exchange and population replenishment of their villages. Of course, Gates was pressured by rebel civilian authorities with the same complaints of barbarity as Burgoyne faced. He avoided the dilemma of taking scalps the same way Burgoyne did, by only offering bounties for live captives, not scalps.

Surprisingly, at Saratoga the Oneidas did not confront Burgoyne's Native allies. This may be because their time with Gates was less than two weeks.[35] They feared their home villages were unprotected, and they needed to hunt so they would have meat for the winter. The practice of their foodways was always stronger than devotion to any white conflict. Gates provided them with ten British prisoners, who were exchanged in Albany for Iroquois captives to be integrated into their villages. In reality, most of the Oneidas had left before either the Battle at Freeman's Farm or Bemis Heights. A few may have remained to participate in the second battle.

Despite complaints about using them, Burgoyne was never without his Indian allies. They came and left his army at will; in the case of the Mohawks, their presence actually involved looking for a new home. While he had them constantly with his army, he could not prevent their depredations, and his experience would serve as an example for later British commanders. The rebels also gained the support of the Oneidas, their one substantial Indian ally, who would suffer for their betrayal from the wrath of the other Iroquois.

Indians were effective at their type of warfare, which both Burgoyne and Gates found necessary for the success of their armies. They were excellent as scouts in the vanguard of Burgoyne's army, but unquestionably the incidents of civil conflict increased because of their marauding, which carried the war far beyond the confines of an army into the countryside. When on their own, they often were unable to distinguish between friend or foe—although militia and regulars were scarcely better at it. Moreover, they penetrated or slipped away from armies at will. Like militia they had reasons for going home, and they could only afford to spend a short time in the field. Still, as independent peoples, they had their own goals—separate from that of any army—and thus Burgoyne and Gates were frustrated in their attempts to establish control over them. Both generals had to be prepared for the bad publicity they received in Congress or Parliament when using them.

10

FORAY TO THE WALLOOMSAC

Until now, Burgoyne had been successful in achieving the goals he had outlined for his invading army, and he had begun the effort to win the hearts and minds of the people. To organize pacification of the countryside took time, and this was one reason Burgoyne did not immediately march from Skenesborough, spending about two weeks there. Here he had also to rethink his plans. Events had not gone completely as he had anticipated. Instead of an assumed long siege at Ticonderoga, he had moved quickly to take the stronghold in early July, after a very brief encounter. To corner the retreating rebels, the army moved rapidly by water to Skenesborough, and only then did it confront the logistical problem of supply for a march to Albany.

THE QUESTION OF SUPPLY

When it left Canada, Burgoyne's army was dependent on supplies brought from Britain when he arrived in Quebec in the spring of 1777. As the army was gathering, Major General William Phillips, the artillery commander, brought the problem of transport of supplies to the front by pointing out the needs of his artillery. This caused a June rush to find horses for the artillery and horse carts to carry supplies for the army. Burgoyne had assumed he could obtain a large number of carts by Canadian *corvée*, the French Canadian requirement to do free labor, but he initially got only fifty, and they were not sturdy

enough for the rigors of the roads. In July "the first transport of horses,
124 of them, had arrived at the army from Canada, and [were sent]
to Skenesborough to be used in the army for transportation of artillery, magazines and tents. [It was said] that more than 1,000 horses
are yet to come."[1] Still, the transport had been organized so late, and
Canada's resources were so limited, that the supply of horses and carts
remained a problem throughout the campaign.

After the fall of Ticonderoga, while his army was at Skenesborough,
Burgoyne decided to send his supplies and ammunition by way of
Lake George. In this way, Ticonderoga and its advanced base at Diamond Island replaced Canada as his pivotal supply source. His supply
line no longer stretched to Canada as it had at the beginning of the
campaign because ample supplies and ammunition had been abandoned by the rebels at Ticonderoga. On July 6 these stores included
flour, pork, biscuit, salt, beef, peas, and rum. Foodstuffs were still
sent from Canada, like the "rice and oatmeal and other provisions" that arrived at Ticonderoga on July 18, and were stockpiled at
the fortifications.[2]

In late July, Phillips asked Brigadier Hamilton to conduct an inventory of stores and arms throughout Ticonderoga's defenses. Acting
Commissioner John Schank of the Royal Navy and Commissary
General Assistants Louis Rousseau and Jonathan Clarke cooperated
in the accounting. Draft oxen were to be especially guarded for transport and engineering activities, while the rest were to be delivered
to the Commissary General for the troops, where they were to be
equally distributed and not hoarded by any particular regiment. In
addition, horses purchased locally and held by the garrison were to
be delivered to Hamilton's adjutant. On July 26 Major James Hughs,
contractor of horses for the army, was able to produce fifty horses
merely for an expedition to Hubbardton to remove the existing hospital
and wounded. When organized, it would be the stores and animals
being gathered at Ticonderoga that would feed and help to transport
Burgoyne's army.

The possession of Lake George by the British followed the fall of
Ticonderoga. The rebels abandoned Fort George on July 17, and a week
later Phillips at Ticonderoga ordered Lieutenant Colonel John Anstru-
ther of the 62nd Regiment and Acting Commissioner John Schank
to send out bateaux and other craft loaded with provisions from the
Lake George Landing. Canadians, raised by corvée under Lieutenant

Francis Dambourgess of the Royal Highland Emigrants, were now present to act as stevedores, transporting commodities to the landing. The commanding engineer was to follow "with entrenching tools and everything necessary to form" a post at the south end of the lake. In the following months, the Lake George landing would become Ticonderoga's most crucial dependency—one that the rebels would seek to capture to interrupt the supply line.[3]

Thus by August Burgoyne's supply came by way of Lake George, first through Fort George and then, by early September, Diamond Island, near its southern end. However, from the south end food, ammunition, and artillery had to be transported over a long-established but rough road to Fort Edward on the Hudson River. For transport, only 180 carts were available, pulled by very few animals.[4] Since the army left Ticonderoga, horses had been used for two needs, which had little to do with supply: the artillery train and the baggage of the officers. Critics of Burgoyne would charge that both these unnecessary burdens caused Burgoyne's army to stop moving. Burgoyne tried to cut down the amount of officers' baggage, but his orders were ignored, and officers were able to avoid them by purchasing their own horses in the countryside. Army wives also needed transport; Frederika Riedesel and her children arrived from Canada to join her husband, and she never lacked a carriage. The artillery seemed less important after a siege failed to materialize at Ticonderoga, but Burgoyne realized it would be needed to give him an advantage over the rebels on a battlefield.

While some historians have exclusively seen Burgoyne's logistics difficulties in terms of obtaining carts and animals, in fact, once his army completed travel from Skenesborough to the Hudson River, most of his supplies were carried, as they been on Lake Champlain and Lake George, by bateaux.[5] Wood Creek, between Skenesborough and Fort Edward, had long been a water transportation corridor, which admittedly was more of a canoe route than one for heavier bateaux. There is no question, however, that Burgoyne's bateaux arrived at the Hudson by way of Wood Creek. Once his army was on the Hudson, bridges of bateaux were regularly constructed to move the troops from one side to the other. A Loyalist corps of bateau men was eventually created to manage Burgoyne's Hudson River fleet.

Novelist Kenneth Roberts notwithstanding, Burgoyne's army was not especially delayed by rebel efforts to choke Wood Creek and destroy bridges between Skenesborough and Fort Edward. Burgoyne's army moved the distance in six days, covering about seven to eight miles a day—certainly not fast, but not slow given the fact that the road was more a trail than a thoroughfare. The army was not burdened with heavy artillery, which was transported by way of Lake George, the heaviest guns with Burgoyne being only six-pounders. As noted, Loyalist sappers were at work clearing the road and the creek before them. The Earl of Balcarres, commander of the light infantry, confirmed that it took the army less than a week to cover the distance to Fort Edward, and that "while the rebels had cut down some few trees," it "took the [Loyalists] in our army some few hours to clear."[6]

Finally, the question is to what extent Burgoyne's army could live off the land. Most historians have assumed that Burgoyne's army received very little support in the countryside. Brigadier General Specht wrote before he left Skenesborough that obtaining more "horses and vehicles turned out to be most difficult because no one would take the risk to surrender or sell the necessary vehicles or horses for the good of our army."[7] Specht may have been right about the farmers trying to save their precious carts and livestock from either army, but in reality most farms appeared to Burgoyne's army to have been abandoned—but crucially leaving most of their corps, livestock, and carts intact. There are numerous incidents of his soldiers harvesting farmers' grain and baking bread. There is also no question that protectionists and Loyalists sold livestock and grain to Burgoyne's army. Only after mid-September did the lack of local resources and supplies in general become a source of concern, largely because his army was now confined by the rebel army to a single area that over time would be picked clean by both armies.

PRIORITIES FOR THE DIVERSION

At the beginning of August, Burgoyne was south of Fort Edward, encamped at Fort Miller, using William Duer's house as his headquarters.[8] It was here that Burgoyne and Riedesel, now experienced with the conditions in the region, began to plan a diversion, separate from the main army, which would test the success of his operations in Vermont. A sortie would be sent toward the Grants, south of the Manchester area that Riedesel's men had recently occupied, closer to Arlington. The object of the expedition was "to try the affections of the country, to disconcert the councils of the enemy" and also to specifically obtain mounts for Riedesel's dragoons; provide cattle, horses, and carriages; and allow the newly created Loyalist units to recruit. It was to be a combined pacification and foraging operation, continuing the effort that Riedesel had started at Castleton in July.

Riedesel made the first plan, and he chose as its destination the Arlington area, where the dominating Loyalists would amicably receive his troops. He recommended that Lieutenant Colonel Friedrich Baum command the foray—a decision that has received much criticism from historians claiming that he was unfit for the task.[9] Much is made of the fact that Baum could not speak English, but this does not mean that his army was blind. English-speaking elements would be present in Fraser's marksmen and Peters's corps, and a considerable number of the recruited Loyalists would actually be German-speaking settlers. Historians argue that Brigadier Fraser would have been a better choice, but he was too valuable for Burgoyne to spare. Baum was not the most experienced of possible officers and made mistakes that reflected this. The officer who would be in charge of Baum's rescue, Lieutenant Colonel Heinrich Breymann, might have been a better choice, for he had participated in the pacification of the Castleton area and had experience in commanding light infantry.

Riedesel drew up the original order for Baum's raid, commanding him "To proceed from Battenkill to Arlington, and take post there, so as to secure the pass from Manchester." Then he was "to remain at Arlington till the detachment of the [Loyalists], under the command of Captain Sherwood, shall join you from the southward."[10] Justus Sherwood and Jeptha Hawley were to recruit in the area to fill the gaps in Peters's existing and Adams's newly formed Loyalist corps, to obtain horses to mount the Braunschweiger dragoons, and to forage for carriages and food for Burgoyne's main army. From Arlington the expedition was to proceed to nearby Manchester, and then through the Green Mountains to Rockingham and finally down the Connecticut River. The direction was meant to confuse the rebels into thinking that Burgoyne might join with the British army in Rhode Island. Riedesel's orders did not focus on a specific geographic target but rather, as in the pacification of the Manchester-Castleton area, allowed for a commander's on-the-spot discretion in achieving these multiple goals. If there was opposition from the enemy, it would probably come from Warner's minimal force around Manchester. When

Burgoyne reviewed the plan, he left it largely intact—but it would not remain that way.

Burgoyne's original plan had included the possible diversion to New England, and he did add detail to Riedesel's instructions. Following the pacification policy developed at Castleton, the foray was to test the affections of the local populace, to interrupt the rebel control over local government, and to protect those soldiers wounded at Hubbardton or thereabouts. In collecting horses, cattle, and carriages, receipts were to be given for them. Thus, "it may be proper to inform the country, that the means to prevent their horses being taken for the future, will be to resist the [rebels] when they shall presume to force them, and drive [the horses] voluntarily to my camp."[11] Even in this detail, no mention was made of ammunition at Bennington.

Burgoyne also asked Philip Skene to accompany Baum's expedition. Baum was directed to consult with him upon "matters of intelligence, negotiation with the inhabitants, roads, and other means depending upon a knowledge of the country, for carrying his instructions into execution."[12] Skene evidently had agents in the area acting as spies. Two years later, Blackman Browning of Cambridge, New York, was accused by the Commission for Detecting and Defeating Conspiracies of being paid by Skene for spying. The commission asked John Younglove of Cambridge to take him into custody.

Some hours before Baum marched toward Arlington, Peters's corps was to be sent forward to gain intelligence on conditions at Bennington, and afterwards they were to join Baum at Arlington.[13] Peters would not have a chance to go to Arlington, however, because the foray's destination suddenly was directed to a different place.

At the last minute, Skene convinced Burgoyne to redirect Baum's force to Bennington to seize its Continental storehouse of military supplies—sending the foray to an area that was the stronghold of Vermont rebels. This also gave the expedition the specific goal of taking Bennington, in addition to pacifying the countryside and raising Loyalists, as had been done at Castleton. John Peters protested the choice of Bennington, and later, in defending himself, Burgoyne claimed that his Loyalist officers were so negative on his change of destination that they staged a mutiny.[14] Bennington was not Arlington; pacification was not likely to work in a place known as a rebel stronghold. There may have been jealousy involved; as a native of the Grants,

Peters felt he should have held the position of influence in the expedition, an honor that belonged to Skene. Peters's protest fell on deaf ears, and therefore it was on the Walloomsac, not the Batten Kill, that Baum met hostile rather than friendly support.

The sortie began on August 11, when Baum's force moved south from Fort Miller. It consisted of 400 Germans, including Braunchweiger jagers; 50 of Fraser's marksmen—the only British troops; 80 Loyalists under Peters and Sherwood; Samuel McKay, alone without men; a detachment of 56 Canadians under Captain Colin Campbell; and 150 mission Indians under Monsieur Charles-Louis Lanaudière.[15] Two three-pounder cannon were also transported. This force would grow as local Loyalists joined along the way.

Traveling southward on the east side of the Hudson, Baum's force waded the Batten Kill River and camped the first night across the Hudson from Schuyler's Saratoga plantation. Overlooking the wheat fields and farms, his troops watched the cattle coming on their own to be milked in the evening, a chore that would not happen, as the farmers had disappeared. The foray was delayed a day in starting because of an alarm that the enemy was in the area in force.[16] On the morning of August 13, Baum finally moved southeast on a newly constructed road toward Cambridge.

From the road to Cambridge, Baum wrote to Burgoyne:

> I received intelligence of 40 or 50 rebels being left to guard some cattle. I immediately ordered 30 of the [Loyalists] and 50 [Indians] to quicken their march, in hopes of surprising them, they took 5 prisoners in arms, who declared themselves to be in the service of Congress; yet the enemy received advice of our approach and abandoned the house they were posted in. The [Loyalists] and [Indians] continued their march about a mile, when they fell in with a party of 15 men, who fired upon our people, and immediately took to the woods with the greatest precipitation. The fire was quick on our side, but I cannot learn if the enemy sustained any loss. A private of Captain Sherwood's company was the only one who was lightly wounded in the thigh.[17]

Baum thus experienced irregular warfare as he scattered parties of rebel militia on his way to Cambridge.

Baum easily occupied the dispersed village of Cambridge, camping near a large empty house that the family had just vacated. Here he remained, as the pacification policy was again applied much as it had been at Castleton a month before. Skene offered the loyalty oath to the king, and a number of inhabitants took it. More shockingly, Simeon Covel, Cambridge supervisor in 1775 and in February of that year an original signatory of the association that formed the Albany County Committee of Correspondence, proved to be a Loyalist. In July 1776 the Albany Committee of Correspondence had ordered him apprehended, but he had been cleared of Loyalist leanings and taken an oath of allegiance to the state of New York as recently as June 4, 1777. Now, however, he was placed in command of a company of Peters's Queen's Loyal Americans, chiefly made up of recruits from the Cambridge area. After Burgoyne had been defeated, the motives for becoming a Loyalist in Cambridge were described by a rebel leader: some sided with the British "through fear, some through the persuasions of artful and designing persons, others through the allurements of gain and the prospect of seeing their oppressed country in the hands of its base invaders."[18] Cambridge would prove to be more important to Burgoyne's pacification effort than Bennington, and its area appeared to be divided evenly between Loyalists and rebels.

Baum's force had bypassed Salem to the north, the hub of the Charlotte County militia under John Williams, a place he might have pacified had he gone in the original direction of Arlington. While Skene therefore could not administer oaths of loyalty in Salem, on July 13 a sermon was preached and meetings followed in which Salem's population tried to come to a consensus on how they should react to Baum's and Burgoyne's invasion.[19] As expected, the place was divided. A sermon had been preached by a visiting pastor that favored Loyalism and received Dr. Clark's endorsement. This led to accusations by the Whigs of Clark's disloyalty, and a week later the debate continued, with John Williams finally adjourning a meeting, pointing out that they had three choices: "to fight like men," to accept Burgoyne's protection, or to move off. The debate did not need to continue from the rebel standpoint, since Schuyler ordered everyone to evacuate, and Fort Williams and the Williams house were abandoned as Baum moved into the Cambridge area. Certainly Salem was as disunited as Cambridge.

From Cambridge, Baum moved further south, touching the Owl Kill as he moved toward Waite's Corners, Germans on the west side and mission Indians on the east side of the present road. They raided for supplies, and at Bloody Spring a settler was killed trying to stop them from quenching their thirst. They were close to the home of John Weir, who had established a farm and built the house in 1769. He had volunteered in the Seven Years' War, serving under Sir William Johnson as a scout until the war ended in 1763.[20] In the 1760s he married Deborah Green, the sister of his sister-in-law, and settled at Duel Hollow, southwest of Cambridge. When the war came, the Greens were open Loyalists and Weir's service with Sir William also inclined him to be a Loyalist, or at least a neutral.

Weir was, however, jolted to become a rebel on August 11, the day Baum's force left Fort Miller, realizing, he said, that Burgoyne's army could sweep all before it. He must have debated the situation and decided, regardless of his family connections, to oppose Baum. He had word sent of his decision to Cambridge militia commanders Captain Robert Gilmore, Major James Ashton, Phineas Whiteside and his sons, and their neighbor Colonel VanWert.[21] He seemed to be trying to join area rebels. As Baum moved south from Cambridge, he would miss Weir's house, where his wife and farm remained safe.

On the night of August 13 Baum was encamped at Wait's Corners. During the day, he had been joined by Francis Pfister's "army" of as many as five hundred men.[22] A year before, Pfister had sworn before the Albany Committee that he would not take up arms, and he had not gone with other Loyalists to Crown Point in October 1776. But he was not idle, even though Burgoyne had never given him command of a Loyalist corps. By early August 1777, Pfister and Robert Leake had completed recruiting this force from the nearby Hoosic valley, East Van Rensselaer Manor, Pownal in Vermont, and even western Massachusetts. Pfister's recruiting had actually split the Wait's Corners Baptist Church, as the congregation was divided between Loyalists and rebels. Almost a third of Pfister's men belonged to another church, the Gilead Lutheran Church in Rensselaerswyck, most of them being second and third generation Palatine Germans, who were urged to serve by their pastor, the Reverend Samuel Swertfeger. Pownal's Loyalists came to Pfister led by Captain Samuel Anderson. The arrival of such a force must have given Baum the impression that the countryside was with him. He had Pfister's recruits placed in Peters's corps, certainly a substantial addition to that unit.

Pfister's recruiting had the support of his wealthy father-in-law, John Macomb, who had left Albany because of the penalties the Albany

Committee had forced on him in July 1776 and was now living on his Hoosic estate, only four miles from the Walloomsac bridge.[23] After the battle at the bridge, he and Pfister's widow would be forced to hide in the woods, and as his estate was later confiscated by the rebels, he would migrate to Canada. Eventually he became paymaster of the Loyalist troops and ended up serving at Detroit.

Another Loyalist family in the Hoosic area that was poised to help Baum was that of former lieutenant Hugh Fraser. He had served in the Seven Years' War in the 78th Highland Regiment, and after the war he took up Amherst's offer of land for his veterans.[24] In 1769 he purchased a farm of two hundred acres in the Hoosic District, improving it with a house, barn, and outbuildings. When hostilities broke out in 1775 he had wanted to be neutral, and in July 1776 he had joined Pfister in swearing not to take up arms. However, the nearby Bennington Committee of Safety harassed him, forcing him to escape four months later, first to Rhode Island, where he baked bread for British troops, and then behind the British lines at New York City. He left behind on the farm his sickly wife, aged father, and four helpless children. The Fraser family thus had no fighting men, but they waited for Baum and Skene to come, holding for them two hundred bushels of wheat and two hundred bushels of Indian corn, as well as two hundred bushels more in the ground, but not harvested.[25] The harvested wheat and corn were stored at Mr. Fisher's mill, a destination for Skene as he traveled with Colonel Baum's expedition. In addition, the farm had ten oxen, twenty-five cattle, seventy sheep, and twelve hogs. It is unclear how much of this Skene obtained, but unquestionably they were ready to offer him a warm welcome.

Baum also had been collecting livestock, wagons, and supplies since he left Schuyler's Saratoga plantation, and a large herd with wagons followed his army. He reported that his force had procured a number of cattle, seventy horses, ninety tons of flour, and close to a thousand minots of grain, which the enemy had left behind in various houses. Following his instructions, he was offering receipts "to such persons as have remained in their habitations, and otherwise complied with the terms of General Burgoyne's manifesto." But he was having difficulty with his Indians, for they either destroyed or drove away what was not paid for with ready money. If he were only allowed "to purchase the horses from the savages, stipulating the price, I think they might be procured cheap, otherwise they ruin all they meet with, their officers and interpreters not having it in their power to control them."[26] Procuring horses and supplies with Indian allies required the utmost diplomacy.

When Baum occupied Cambridge, Sherwood and a few of his men went off to nearby Shaftsbury, where they visited the Bothum farm and recruited for Peters's corps. They returned to Baum with the news that the number of enemy troops to the east amounted to a surprising 1,800 men. Burgoyne had sent orders that Baum was not to take on a superior force, but he ignored them, continuing to move ahead toward the Walloomsac River. Baum was enthusiastic about his progress thus far and felt he could continue by observing "precautions necessary to fulfill both the orders and instructions of [Burgoyne]."[27] Clearly, he was taking on more than Burgoyne or Riedesel had ever imagined, and this was Baum's first mistake.

South of Waite's Corners, Baum's force arrived at the Hoosic River and then followed it to where it was joined by the Walloomsac, moving then eastward on it to Sancoick's Mills, where Little White Creek joined the Walloomsac. Here an advanced guard of 215 rebels under Colonel William Gregg was posted and preparing breakfast when Baum caught them unawares and scattered them. The owner of the gristmill, sluice, and nearby "beautiful" house, was said to be none other than the underage patroon Stephen Van Rensselaer, whose overseer had left that very morning.[28]

Skene had moved ahead of Baum, claiming "that there were many well affected inhabitants toward Bennington, who would shew themselves on the approach of troops; and that there was dejection and submission among the party attached to the congress in that country."[29] He was already at Sancoick's Mills, instructing his deputy, John Skimmings of Cambridge, to take charge of the wheat and flour at the mill and keep an account for the crown. The millers, Mr. Bull and Mr. Francis Brock, were asked to grind the grain and cask the flour as fast as possible, while Skimmings would take receipts for the flour delivered to the wagons or carts on a daily basis. The millers "left in the mill about 78 barrels of very fine flour, 1000 bushels of wheat, 20 barrels of salt, and about 1000£ worth of pearl and pot ash." As an aside, Skene was now signing his letters with the title "Lieutenant Governor of Ticonderoga and Crown Point," a pretension that would only last a few days.

Baum's force then left Sancoick's Mills, taking more horses as they marched. They arrived at the Walloomsac River bridge at noon on August 14, standing in the hamlet and before the bridge that carried the road across the river toward Bennington. Two days later—just before the Battle of Walloomsac—he reported that "100 oxen were sent to our army . . . we took possession of many other horses. All noncommissioned officers of the regt. and several dragoons . . . have horses. If this continues the regiment will soon be mounted."[30] At this point, it looked like the supply, Loyalist pacification, and recruiting goals set by Burgoyne had been met.

Defending the Grants from Outside

Earlier, while Riedesel, Skene, and Hawley were gathering Loyalists at Castleton, Ira Allen, secretary of the newly established Vermont Council, was trying to convince General Philip Schuyler, as well as New Hampshire and Massachusetts authorities, that they needed to save Vermont—as the Windsor Convention was now calling the Grants. The immediate danger was that Vermont's resistance was deteriorating because so many towns and leaders were going over to Burgoyne. Allen wrote to Schuyler about the situation, and the Continental general responded to him on the day after the Castleton meeting. As mentioned earlier, Schuyler was trying to gather troops to oppose Burgoyne's main army at Fort Edward and also prepare the country-side, including Vermont, for defense. He addressed himself to Ira's plea and confessed that he was surprised the enemy was "fortified at Castleton," urging Allen not to panic.[31] He felt that Warner's Continentals and the Massachusetts and New Hampshire militias should be able to protect southern Vermont, even without local militia. He also pointed out that Burgoyne's entire army numbered "not above 6,000" and thus Warner had enough men to defend the Manchester area from any portion of this force. Finally, he advised Allen to limit the contact the British would have with local inhabitants by ordering them to move to southern Vermont or Massachusetts.

In Manchester, monitoring the results of the Castleton meeting, Ira Allen decided to write to the New Hampshire Council of Safety, outlining Vermont's precarious predicament. He claimed that "by the surrender of the fortress Ticonderoga a communication is opened [with the British] to the defenseless inhabitants of the frontier. . . . You [New Hampshire] Gentlemen will be at once sensible that every such town as accept protection are rendered at that instant forever incapable of affording us any further assistance as some disaffected persons [Loyalists] eternally lurk in almost every town, [and] such become double fortified to injure their country."[32] Allen wanted New Hampshire to defend the Vermont borderland so New Hampshire would not find itself defending its own borders after Vermont was overrun. He continued, saying that if troops were sent quickly, then Vermont could assist them, but if there was delay, then little could be expected from its overwhelmed defenses.

Except for its nearby location, New Hampshire was not a logical source for fresh troops to oppose Burgoyne. The record of its soldiers in the previous campaign to conquer Canada was dismal. New Hampshire's John Sullivan had been a lackluster commander of the rebels' Canadian army, and he had been as responsible as anyone for the rebels being driven out of Canada.[33] In the spring of 1776, New Hampshire troops fared poorly in the retreat from Canada. Major Isaac Butterfield's New Hampshire command of four hundred was surprised at Cedars above Montreal and taken by a smaller force of British regulars and Indians, including the loss of all his provisions. Butterfield and his commander, Colonel Timothy Bedel, were court-martialed and cashiered out of the Continental Army. At Hubbardton, Colonel Nathan Hale and over two hundred New Hampshire Continentals had been taken prisoner, some, it is said, without a shot being fired.

However, the previous blemishes on New Hampshire's honor did not stop the state from responding enthusiastically to Ira Allen's plea. The speaker of the General Court, John Langdon, offered $3,000 for the relief force—the value of his silver plate and seventy hogsheads of Tobago rum.[34] He was from the Atlantic coast, a Portsmouth merchant and shipbuilder who made his money in trade between the New Hampshire port, the Caribbean, and London. He had put his business aside in 1774, when he participated in the seizure of munitions from British-held Fort William and Mary. He was directly involved in the organization of New Hampshire's Western Brigade of militia and would personally go to Vermont with his own picked company of Light Horse Volunteers.

The crucial position of commander of the Western Brigade was offered to John Stark, the renowned officer of Rogers's Rangers in the Seven Years' War, who happened to be available because he had resigned his Continental Army commission. Stark had a record of military success, serving gallantly at Bunker Hill, in Canada, and at Trenton and Princeton; yet Congress had passed over him for a promotion to brigadier general, jumping junior colonels above him, including his New Hampshire rival Enoch Poor.[35] Understandably touchy over this, Stark would accept the New Hampshire command only if he were independent of the organizations he despised, the Congress and the Continental Army—being solely responsible to the New Hampshire General Court. They accepted his terms, named him a brigadier general of New Hampshire militia, and ordered him to begin recruiting. Stark was very popular in New Hampshire, and he was able in the last two weeks of July to raise 1,492 men and officers.

On July 30 Stark marched his militia brigade from Charleston, New Hampshire, into Vermont. He moved on to Manchester, where he had his first clash over authority with the Continental Army's Northern commander, Philip Schuyler. Schuyler had assigned Massachusetts major general Benjamin Lincoln to command at Manchester, and through him he directed that Stark's force should join Schuyler's depleted army on the Hudson River.[36] Naturally, Stark refused, stating that he would move only at the orders of New Hampshire's General Court. Lincoln reported the insubordination to Congress, where a resolution was passed condemning Stark's actions and asking him to serve in the chain of command that the militia was subject to. Ever the diplomat, Lincoln made an effort to smooth matters between Stark and Schuyler.

By August 1, Stark and eight hundred of his New Hampshire militiamen had answered an appeal from Warner and joined him at Manchester, though it was now evident that the German forces at Castleton were leaving.[37] It appears that Warner respected Stark's independent position and that the two accepted an uneasy alliance, for Stark had many more soldiers under his command. Without an enemy facing them, on August 9 Stark's New Hampshire militia, Captain Ebenezer Allen's independent ranger company, a company of Herrick's Rangers, and Vermont militia raised by Warner began a march southward toward Bennington. Warner came with them, leaving his Continental regiment at Manchester to hold the line.

At Bennington, Stark received word that a party of Indians had been discovered in the vicinity of Cambridge. He had dispatched Gregg's militia, along with fifteen men from Ebenezer Allen's independent ranger company, to investigate and they occupied the aforementioned Sancoick's Mills.[38] Baum's Indian vanguard drove them out. On August 14

Stark rallied his army and marched toward Cambridge, calling out the Bennington militia. Warner denuded the Manchester line, ordering the rest of Herrick's Rangers and his Continentals under Major Safford to Bennington. Herrick's Rangers left immediately and were with Stark the next day, but many of Safford's men were on scout and had to be gathered, so Warner's Continentals were late in starting from Manchester.

As he moved toward Bennington, Stark had also been joined by about three hundred Massachusetts militiamen from Berkshire County under Colonel Benjamin Simonds. They had been ordered to Manchester, but it appears they never reached it, meeting Stark at Bennington.[39] New York militiamen appeared from Cambridge and further south from what would become Stephentown. The latter force of thirty men was commanded by Asa Douglas, captain of the 1st Company of the 17th Regiment of the Albany County militia. Douglas was sixty-four and his company was described as "Silver Grays," evidently men of considerable experience. He had already tussled with Loyalists over land claims on the border, and he knew that some of them had joined Pfister.

As Ira Allen had realized, Stark's army was not in any sense a Vermont force; the number of men under the new government was limited to Bennington's two militia companies and a majority of Herrick's Rangers. True, some of Warner's Continental regiment were also from the Grants, but all told, they numbered perhaps 300—little more than 10 percent of the force. Stark had gathered an army of over 2,000 men, the vast majority of them being militia, chiefly consisting of his own New Hampshire following.[40]

The Battle of the Walloomsac

On August 14, six miles from Cambridge along the Walloomsac River, Stark met Gregg's men retreating before the enemy, who were now only a mile behind. Stark halted and drew up his men for a confrontation, hoping to lure Baum into an attack on his superior force across the open flood plain in front of the Walloomsac bridge. Baum wisely decided to stop in the hamlet around the bridge, so Stark withdrew two miles toward Bennington. At the bridge, Baum found the Obadiah Beardsleys with oxen hooked to two wagons full of their furniture but ordered them to return to their house.[41] After some effort to occupy and fortify the hamlet, during which Beardsley threw a soldier out of his cabin, it was decided that the bridge position, central as it was, was not really defensible, and Baum looked elsewhere. Beardsley sat out the battle behind the locked door of his house, and it not clear where Hazard Wilcox and the Widow Whipple, whose houses have been described, were during the struggle.

Rather than remaining at the bridge, Baum took possession of the three hundred–foot wooded height that loomed above it and began to fortify it with the bulk of his eight hundred effectives.[42] During heavy rain, Baum mounted his two three-pounders on the height in a redoubt and placed some of his German dragoons there. Fraser's fifty marksmen were divided and placed here and in another position. Just beyond the bridge in the river flats, Baum placed more Germans and marksmen and anchored his defenses near the river by a "Tory" redoubt that held three hundred Loyalists. His Indians, supplies, and captured livestock were placed on a plateau behind the hill toward Sancoick's Mills. His men were scattered over a considerable distance in defenses and were not supportive of each other. Considering that they were outnumbered better than two to one, Baum's fortifications were his second mistake. It was from this vantage point that he awaited Stark's army.

Burgoyne, hearing from Baum that he faced a much superior rebel army, ordered a relief force from Fort Miller of over six hundred German troops under Lieutenant Colonel Heinrich Breymann. Breymann had been in command of the German Reserve Corps—their light infantry, grenadiers and jagers—in Vermont, so this seemed like an ideal situation for someone of his background. However, rain forced him to move slowly, following a route similar to that of Baum through Cambridge to the Walloomsac, where Baum was now fortified.[43]

The New Hampshire general, with the advice of Warner and a council of war, prepared to attack Baum the next day, but continuous rain made it impossible to use weapons and the attack was postponed until the following day. Stark did send out skirmishers, who succeeded in inflicting casualties and reporting on the state of the fortifications Baum was erecting.[44]

When Stark delayed attacking Baum because of rain, Thomas Allen, "the Fighting Parson of Pittsfield, Massachusetts," complained to him that "the people of the Berkshires, have been frequently called to fight, but have never been led against the enemy," and he threatened

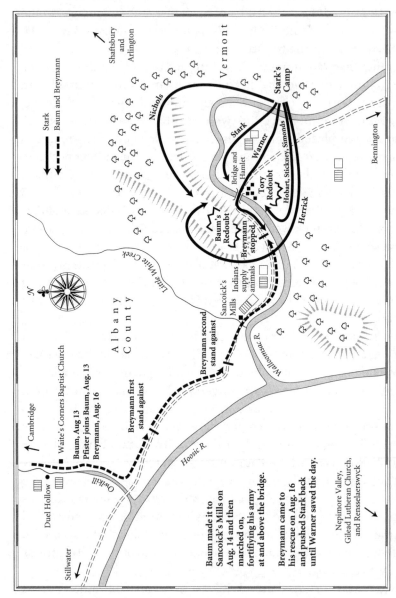

The Battle of Walloomsac, August 16, 1777

that if Stark would not let them fight, they would "never turn out again."[45] Of course, Stark put the Berkshire County militia to work the next day when the sun shone, but Allen's words did reflect the frustration of militias being relegated to their traditional duties of obstruction, policing, and continuously marching back and forth.

The morning of August 16 was clear, and Stark ordered Colonel Moses Nichols to penetrate the woods, get behind Baum's entrenched position on the height, and attack him from the rear, while Lieutenant Colonel Samuel Herrick was to lead a similar force of rangers to outflank Baum on the right.[46] The two parties were able to combine and strike at three p.m. For the next two hours the battle raged. The Indians collected under Claude Nicholas de Lorimier were on the left and were pushed off the hill by the rebel fire and into the ravine, near the baggage field.

In a separate action, the New Hampshire militias of Colonels Thomas Stickney and David Hobart, along with Simonds's Berkshire County militia, penetrating undercover, surprised the "Tory redoubt."[47] Langdon's Light Horse Volunteers were there, but dismounted. The fighting parson, Reverend Thomas Allen, was in the lead of the Berkshire County militia and reputedly performed his religious duty by asking the Loyalists to lay down their arms and receive good quarter, but they, including those of the Gilead Lutheran Church, responded with a volley; he retreated to the lines and joined in what would be a bloody contest. Stickney's, Hobart's, and the Berkshire men responded in kind, and Pfister was mortally wounded. The Loyalists in the redoubt fled and were forced to escape by dropping down the banks and wading through the river, leading to many being captured or missing.[48] Pfister would be taken to a hospital in Shaftsbury, where he died. In his Parliamentary defense in 1779, Burgoyne singled Pfister out as one of his best, meaning bravest, Loyalist officers. After the rout of the Loyalists, the rebels occupied the Widow Whipple's house, using it as a fort at the bridge, but Baum's cannon reached it and burned the structure, eliminating the hiding place.

Meanwhile, at Baum's hilltop redoubt, the advancing Cambridge militia looked like possible Loyalists and were able to move up the hill and get close to Baum's men before Baum's men realized their mistake and fired on them. A hot exchange of fire followed, but the Germans ran out of ammunition and were forced to defend themselves with swords, until they were overwhelmed by superior numbers.

Baum was fatally wounded and taken to the same Shaftsbury hospital as Pfister, where he also died.[49] Among the Germans, casualties were heavy and prisoners were taken.

At the moment of apparent victory, however, Heinrich Breymann's reinforcements including two six-pounders and a band, suddenly appeared on the road to the west and began skirmishing with the rebels about a mile from Baum's position. Stark's dispersed and pillaging militia, of whom Herrick's men were notable, were being driven back to Baum's position, and Breymann might have turned the tables on them when, unexpectedly, Warner's 130 Continentals from Manchester appeared to strengthen the rebel resolve against Breymann's command.[50] Led by Major Samuel Safford, they had arrived in the vicinity the night before, and Warner had joined and rested them after their march from Manchester. They had not yet appeared in the action, and while small in numbers, they were fresh and disciplined Continentals, ready to turn the tide.

Seventeen-year-old David Holbrook of East Hoosic, a private in Colonel Simonds's Berkshire County militia, was present as Breymann's force appeared. He described how victory was snatched from the jaws of defeat.[51] From his perspective, after Baum's position had been taken, he and a companion hid behind a haystack until Breymann's men appeared, then discharged their pieces and ran, joining other rebels who were also retreating and trying to form to resist the German reinforcements. He noted the rebels, "in pursuing those who escaped from the entrenchments, had got scattered and fatigued, and but few assembled at first, but kept falling in continually until a line was formed along a fence on the northeast side of the meadow in which was the haystack." He continued: "Firing commenced as soon as [Breymann's men] came within musket shot, but the [rebels], not being sufficiently strong to keep the ground, retreated from tree to tree, firing as they left the trees, until they came to a ravine where was a log fence . . . and held the ground." Breymann's men came up and "firing then continued some time without cessation, when Colonel Warner, with the remains of his regiment, came up, and some of his men, understanding the artillery exercise, took one of the field pieces taken in the first engagement and formed at the right [and fired the gun] which was seconded by a yell, the most terrible [I] ever heard . . . it was the voice of Colonel Warner, who thundered, 'Fix bayonets. Charge." Warner's Continentals saved the day. Holbrook and his compatriots followed Warner's men rushing on the Germans, who "took to their heels and were completely routed." Holbrook could not participate any longer because he was exhausted and could not walk, having been wounded in the earlier engagement. He recovered in Bennington.

Actually, there was no rebel pursuit of Breymann, as darkness had set in and both sides were exhausted. Breymann retreated with the remains of Baum's force to Cambridge. His force returned to Burgoyne's army by way of the Batten Kill, where Burgoyne ordered much of the army to come out to give them full support.[52]

In the days following the battle, the remains of Baum's and Breymann's forces continued to drift into Burgoyne's camp. The day after the battle, a German officer wrote: "Many of the [Indians], Canadians and [Loyalists], . . . together with Major Campbell and Captain Charret, arrived at camp [on the Batten Kill] having made their retreat through the densest woods and the most impassable roads. In the evening and during the whole night, wounded soldiers, as well as those who were completely exhausted from terrible fatigue, periodically arrived in their battalions."[53] Captains Alexander Fraser and Samuel McKay likewise returned and even brought along several Indians and Canadians. Only Fraser and seven of his picked marksmen rejoined Burgoyne. Following Francis Pfister's death from his wounds at Bennington on August 18, Burgoyne appointed Captain McKay to command the remains of his Loyalists. This would cause controversy because Peters considered that Pfister's men had been assigned to his corps by Baum.

The dead of both sides needed to be buried. When John Weir left Cambridge supposedly to join Stark, he had advised his wife to remain inside the house with their child and bolt the door. Deborah Weir heard the noise of the Battle of Walloomsac, and she wanted to see what was happening, so with child in hand she mounted a horse and passed Cowden Tavern, which had been turned into a hospital for the Cambridge wounded, who included Cambridge militiamen Daniel Crossman, Thomas Comstock, and twelve others.[54] She passed farther on to the battlefield and found her husband busy, burying the dead. Such a chore was only compensated by the fact that one could plunder them. John then rode to Bennington to join Stark, but his presence in the battle is unclear, for he does not seem to have belonged to the Cambridge militia. Despite his apparent conversion to the rebel cause, Weir did not involve himself further in the war, living quietly in Cambridge to the ripe old age of eighty-four. The ambiguity of John Weir's family in the conflict leads to the conclusion that they were neutrals.

Stark's army had suffered losses of 30 killed and at least 126 wounded. Bennington's two militia companies lost men: Nathan Clark's son, John Fay, and Henry Walbridge of the Bennington Committee of Safety were among the dead.[55] Although he lingered for many months, Ethan Allen's brother Heman died in March 1778 from exposure at the battle. The New Hampshire Committee of Safety ordered Josiah Bartlett, the New Hampshire political leader, and Dr. Nathaniel Peabody to go to Bennington to assist the sick and wounded in Stark's brigade and to obtain an accurate account of the battle. Technically, all booty, including the two cannon, belonged to Stark's New Hampshire militia—not to Vermont's government or to the Continental Army.

The German colonels had suffered 766 men killed, wounded or captured, about a third of that number being killed, chiefly in the hand-to-hand fighting on the hill.[56] Dead officers, besides Baum, included the master of horse Reineking, Captain von Shieck, Lieutenant Muhlenfeldt, Lieutenant d'Annieres, and Hagermann, color bearer. Certainly half of the two German forces were casualties or prisoners, and Baum's men suffered more than Breymann's.

Loyalist causalities were reported by the rebels at 55, the bulk of whom were prisoners. Peters, who was wounded, brought off his men with Breymann's retreating army, while Sherwood, Carscallen, and Robert Leake, now commander of Pfister's force, took their men through the woods and met Breymann at Cambridge. Peters estimated a much higher figure for just his losses than the rebels, claiming his unit had been devastated, reduced by more than half, from 291 to a mere 117.[57] Macomb claimed that 106 of Pfister's men were taken at the Walloomsac. By August 29 the Vermont Council of Safety had a list of fourteen Vermont Loyalists, half of whom were taken at the battle. They include James Reynolds, Ephraim Mallory, John Davoe, Solomon Millington, Bartholomew Wennicks, and George Tibbets. By late October Chittenden's council was requiring only an oath and fine for Loyalists who wished to be pardoned. The Loyalists had been new recruits; for many this was their first military action, and like militia, they were more concerned with escaping than holding their position. Some actually returned to the Vermont regiment from which they had deserted after the fall of Ticonderoga. Despite Pfister's bravery, in this early test of Loyalist recruits, they did not perform well, and many certainly went home or were contrite before Chittenden's council.

According to Baum's survivors, "the fury of the Rebels, some of whom were drunk by the way, had especially focused on captured [Loyalists], whom they . . . treated with all imaginable cruelty." J. F. Wasmus added that the Loyalist prisoners were treated "like cattle, . . . tied to each other with cords and ropes and led away; it is presumed that they will be hanged."[58] Some Loyalists were executed and thrown into a common grave, as it was thought they were trying to escape. At the request of Riedesel, Burgoyne wrote a letter to General Gates, complaining of "the bad treatment the [Loyalist] soldiers in the king's service received after the affair at Bennington." He went on to claim that some had been refused quarter after having asked for it. He requested the rebel commander observe "those maxims upon which all men of honor think alike." Gates responded that "nothing happened in the action at Bennington, but what is common when works are carried by assault." While the Loyalists suffered casualties, the insinuation of indiscriminate executions by the rebels does not seem valid.

By early October Peters's numbers were already higher at 154, and Macomb asserted that 318 of Pfister's men made it to Burgoyne's camp.[59] In the camp, Peters suffered as much from attrition of his men to other Loyalist units as he had from losses on the Walloomsac. The rebels offered quick paroles to many Loyalists who agreed not to resume participation in the hostilities, but some ignored their oath and made their way to Burgoyne's army. There they had no reason to respect Peters, and many defected to Hugh Munro's bateaux corps or to McKay's corps, new units that were just being formed. Peters's losses had more to do with recruiting than what happened at the Walloomsac.

AFTERMATH OF THE WALLOOMSAC BATTLE

Philip Skene has received much criticism for the Walloomsac debacle, beginning with Burgoyne himself, who laid the blame on his once trusted adviser.[60] Certainly there is something to this. Skene's choice of Bennington as the objective makes sense only if he wanted to destroy it as a strong center of rebel resistance and independent Vermont sentiment—a goal that was not among the reasons for undertaking the foray. With Arlington, Castleton, and Manchester in the grasp of the king's Loyalists, that should have been the direction in which Baum moved. Skene's intelligence on Loyalist support was on the mark, but he missed a crucial detail: the unexpected arrival and size of Stark's army, which was appearing in Manchester as he, Burgoyne, and Riedesel were planning the foray. No one in the British camp seems to have realized the numbers under Stark, for if they had, they would have at least combined Baum's and Breymann's men at the beginning of the foray. In his defense, Skene did find the Loyalist support he expected along the way to the Walloomsac. Baum had probably achieved most of his goals by the morning of August 16, for by then almost half of his cavalry was mounted. Had Stark's extensive army not existed—which is what Burgoyne's intelligence told him—they might have succeeded.

But the rest of the blame must go to Baum. He was headstrong, delaying his request for further support because he thought he could take on Stark's larger army alone, being spirited by the success he had thus far achieved. His instructions included the advice that if he were intercepted by the enemy, he was to "take as strong a post as the country will afford, and send the quickest intelligence to" the main army. [61] However, the placement of his defenses left much to be desired. Instead of concentrating his smaller force, he dispersed it among separate fortifications. It was as if each unit fortified itself without an overall command. In an exposed position, the Loyalist redoubt was easily overrun, a humiliating experience for all the newly formed Loyalist units. The dramatist Burgoyne somehow found this to be the high point of Loyalist support for his campaign, since the brave Pfister was killed and Sherwood was wounded. However, bravery did not count for much in a civil war.

Burgoyne, Baum, and Breymann did not realize whom they fought at the Walloomsac. They simply thought the countryside did not support them, ignoring the work that had been done during Riedesel's and Baum's pacifications. Loyalist were numerous; the Loyalists in Peters's corps, both at the Battle of Bennington and after it, outnumbered the entire Vermont contingent that Warner was able to put together for the battle. In contrast, the numbers of militia from Cambridge or Bennington participating in the battle were negligible. The British explanation for the defeat in Burgoyne's army failed to identify Stark's New Hampshire force, instead claiming that it was those who had taken the oath of loyalty to the king at Castleton and Cambridge

who made up the extensive army that attacked Baum.[62] This turncoat theory was fiction, for the New Hampshire militia that made
victory possible were from elsewhere and had never been exposed
to pacification or Burgoyne's army. As the blame for the defeat was
dispensed, the turncoat explanation perpetuated the rift between
Burgoyne and his Loyalists.

LOYALISTS STILL JOINING BURGOYNE

After the defeat at the Walloomsac, Burgoyne's policy toward Loyalist
recruiting may have been subdued, but his Loyalists captains continued
to thrive on recruiting and their growing combat role. The New York
countryside remained friendly, and numbers of Loyalists appeared,
many bent on filling the ranks of a Loyalist corps. Stepped-up activities
by the Albany Committee of Correspondence failed to catch a particular
group of Loyalists before they reached Burgoyne's army. This was the
case of four men, seven women, and seventeen children from Stillwater who "were persons of wealth who had hid their household
goods and clothing until Burgoyne arrived."[63]

More Loyalists got through to Burgoyne's army—like those who
arrived two days after the Battle on the Walloomsac. They consisted
of "more than 100 Albanians, who offered their services to the army;
. . . they had already had a few small, unsuccessful skirmishes with
the Rebels." Less than a week after the defeat at the Walloomsac, in
Burgoyne's camp it was observed that

> more and more families, who were afraid of the rebels and
> their acts of violence, fled Albany to come to our army out
> of the woods. They occupied dwellings on either side of the
> Hudson River with the cattle they had brought along; ten or
> more families could at times be found there. All assured us
> that the rural population of Albany, of whom a large part is
> of German descent, had only been prevented by the rebels'
> extreme use of force and the personal ambitions of their men
> in power from declaring themselves for the party of the crown.
> We would not only find all possible assistance to fill all our
> needs in Albany, but also see how the people who fled from or
> were taken by force by the Rebels would come back to their
> old possessions in great numbers."[64]

Arrivals continued as "between 30 and 60 daily entered headquarters to take another loyalty oath and quite a few of them decided to take up arms together with us for the general good. These numbers greatly reinforced our good opinion of the Albanians and we hoped in the near future to see an entire regiment of them under the command of one Peters to be incorporated in our army." Either these Loyalists were unaware of the Battle of Walloomsac or the Albany Committee's high-handed methods encouraged them to join Burgoyne.

Rensselaerswyck continued to be a source of Loyalists, most of them tenants, with the opportunity at last to serve with Burgoyne's liberating army. Jeremiah French's brother Gershom, who had gone with Jeremiah to Canada late in 1776, had returned to his home in New City (Lansingburg) and gathered ninety-four recruits that he brought to Burgoyne. At New City, Gershom was also one of Pfister's recruiters, who gathered them in the woods, awaiting the British invasion. His activities had been opposed by militia organized by the Albany Committee that had been monitoring him since the attempted uprising of the manor Loyalists in May.[65]

Born in Southbury, Connecticut, Gershom French had moved to the Rensselaerswyck area in 1775 and was an active rebel, living in New City and signing "the Lansingburg Declaration of Independence." However, like Schuyler and Duer, he favored peaceful reconciliation, and this led him to become a Loyalist. He went back to his native Connecticut to raise a regiment of Loyalists, the Prince of Wales American Volunteers, and with the help of Francis Hogle, recruited 216 men.[66] Bizarrely, his authorization came from the governor of New Providence Island off the coast of Florida, Montfort Browne, who had been taken from the island and was now a prisoner in Connecticut. French and Hogle led their men to join Burgoyne, although they lost many recruits along the way. Burgoyne integrated French's recruits into the Queen's Loyal Rangers, where French became a lieutenant and acting adjutant.

On August 27 Loyalists led by Henry Simmons arrived at the Batten Kill River, after an eleven-day journey from the Claverack area in the lower Rensselaer Manor.[67] By September 8 his men were armed, and within two weeks they would serve in the Battle of Freeman's Farm. Simmons also sent two men back to bring in more recruits from an area that been ready to join Burgoyne since May. At the same time, Peter Van Alstine and Guisbert Sharp brought in thirty recruits from rebellious Kinderhook, who would make themselves useful as bateaux men.

Fraser's marksmen had been decimated by their casualties at the Walloomsac. However, on September 23 Burgoyne reauthorized them to be recruited as before from his British regiments.[68] But his regiments were already a thin red line, reduced in numbers, and consequently recruits had to be drafted from the grenadier and light infantry companies as well as the Loyalist corps. The initial strength of the revived marksmen company was at best seventy. Andrew Skene, who had been serving with his father, was appointed to the renewed marksmen unit. From the Loyalist standpoint, they now had the option of serving in this elite independent company.

Despite the debacle on the Walloomsac, by September 1 there were 682 Loyalists in Burgoyne's camp, mostly combat ready rather than protectionists—certainly a considerable improvement over the original 83. They were described critically by a British officer as "inhabitants of that country, assembled under officers who were to have had different commissions, provided they had ever amounted to certain numbers."[69] He concluded, "I know they were not all armed. We had not arms for them"; but they were soon armed. As late as September 22, after the Battle of Freeman's Farm, fifty Loyalists appeared in Burgoyne's camp, joining him by traveling over one of his newly constructed bateaux bridges on the Hudson.

Not all those Loyalists who joined Burgoyne were men; Loyalist women and children also came in alone or in various parties, revealing the families of Loyalist recruits. On September 2 the Albany Committee of Correspondence announced to General Gates that it was emptying its jails of nineteen Loyalist families that hopefully would be exchanged with Burgoyne for rebel prisoners. The list reads like a who's who of Loyalist wives: Jannetje Glen (Mrs. Abraham) Cuyler, Catharina Lydius (Mrs. Henry) Cuyler, Mary (Mrs. Daniel) McAlpin, Elizabeth and Abigail (Mmes. Ebenezer and Edward) Jessup, Marie Talbot (Mrs. John) Munro, Elizabeth (Mrs. James) Gray, Deborah Wing (Mrs. Daniel) Jones, Katherine Greene (Mrs. John) Amory of Boston.[70] For other wives we know only their husbands' names: Mrs. Gershom French, Mrs. John Morral of Cambridge, Mrs. Jacob Muller, Mrs. Lawrence Leedings, Mrs. Isaac Mann with a husband in the Loyal Volunteers, Mrs. Casper M. Halenbeck, Mrs. Alexander Crukshank, Mrs. Robert Hoakesly, Mrs. Beaton. There is no record that Gates pursued an exchange, but one of the wives, Elizabeth Gray, with her children was brought to Ticonderoga by Vermont rangers on October 27, where her husband was a member of the garrison. Many of the other women would be released to go to Canada in the following months.

Burgoyne sent the foray toward Bennington mainly to pacify the countryside and recruit Loyalists and mounts for his troops—food was not his primary goal. Burgoyne's soldiers did harvesting and farmers sold cattle and wheat to Burgoyne. It seems safest to say that the area's farmers supported neither the British nor the rebels, looking upon both armies as predators. The Battle of Walloomsac was Burgoyne's first defeat, a sign that numerous New England militias were now alerted and ready to oppose him. The victory belonged to John Stark and his New Hampshire militia, for Vermont lacked militia to protect its own settlers. The situation fulfilled Anburey's prophecy at Crown Point that "I have fears, as the New England Provinces are most violent in their principles of rebellion."[71] The ability of New Hampshire to raise troops in a crisis after the fall of Ticonderoga was a condition that Burgoyne and even Skene seem to have failed to contemplate. What began with Stark raising his New Hampshire militia would continue till the Battles of Saratoga, as New England militia would give the rebels an overwhelming superiority in numbers.

The heavy losses to both German forces at the Walloomsac was a check that Burgoyne could ill afford. The defeat ended his pacification policy in Vermont, although conditions in New York remained amicable. Surprisingly, Loyalists would still join Burgoyne, despite the fact that they had been routed at the Walloomsac. This contradicts one of Burgoyne's favorite explanations for his defeat, that his Loyalists and Indians abandoned him when adversity appeared. Instead, in the aftermath of the Battle of Walloomsac, he needed to decide how to give a more important role to the rising number of Loyalist recruits, so they would have a reason for staying and not returning to their farms.

PART IV

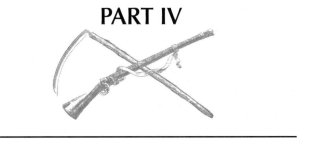

THE BATTLES OF SARATOGA

11

BURGOYNE OUTNUMBERED

The goal of Continental generals was to meet the British on a battlefield and defeat them with the volley and bayonet in a European-style confrontation. The Continental Army consisted of men who had enlisted for a term of a year or more to serve under George Washington; its numbers were limited because the soldiers were expensive to maintain. The age-old militias, raised in each state for a short duration, were potentially more numerous. Disagreement existed among rebel generals as to the use of these two sources of manpower, especially when confronting a European army. Long-standing rivalry among the states also prevented rebel unity, especially between New York and emerging Vermont. Furthermore, monitoring the numerous Loyalists in the region tied down the rebel militia, further diluting its resources. Supply was not a given, either. Rebel credit was spotty, and while considerable supplies were collected by Schuyler, they were concentrated at the Continental Store in Albany. Here they disappeared with amazing rapidity, without ever being sent north to the army opposing Burgoyne. Such disunity and corruption had to be overcome if the rebels were to prevent Burgoyne from advancing toward Albany.

THE ARRIVAL OF HORATIO GATES

In early August, while he was confronting Burgoyne, word came to Schuyler that Congress had relieved him of command of the Northern

Department and replaced him with Horatio Gates.[1] Gates had spent months in the halls of Congress blatantly lobbying for the position. It never seemed to occur to him that service in the field would enhance his candidacy. Meanwhile, Schuyler had retreated from Fort Edward to the Moses Kill, then to the Saratoga plantation, then to Stillwater, and finally to Van Schaick's Island, only eight miles north of Albany. Congress feared that all would be lost.

Gates's appointment as commander of the Northern Department was announced to the Northern Army on August 20 at Van Schaick's Island in the midst of the Hudson River.[2] The army that Schuyler handed to Gates was still in the making. Schuyler had confirmation that further troops would arrive from General Washington and Governor Jonathan Trumbull of Connecticut. Using Fort Edward figures in July, the rebel army consisted of at least 6,359: 3,925 Continentals and 2,434 militiamen—although a large number were not fit for duty. This army had come from Schuyler's own command of 2,100, the remains of St. Clair's army of 1,700, John Nixon's brigade of 600 sent by Washington, and the Albany County militia, which at the time fluctuated between 1,000 and 1,600 men. Over the next month, Glover's Continental brigade of 1,300 would arrive from Washington and General Benjamin Lincoln would begin to build another force of 2,000 in the Grants. In all, there were at least 8,000 men in Schuyler's army; certainly it was now larger than Burgoyne's force. Moreover, Washington had promised that Morgan's Continental light infantry of 500 would soon arrive. Thus, Schuyler turned over a much improved army to Gates.

Five years older than Schuyler, Gates is usually regarded as the general who patiently brought Burgoyne's army to a halt and then bided his time while Burgoyne exhausted himself in trying to dislodge him. Gates was a skilled administrator, certainly one of the best in the Continental Army. In the early years of the war he rebuilt several disorganized rebel armies.[3] Before the war, Gates also had been involved in political activities in Bristol, England, and New York City, where he developed the political aspirations of a Whig republican. His republican values had served him well with Congress.

Born in Maldon, Essex, England, in 1727 of working-class parents, Gates did not have the court and family connections of Burgoyne.[4] Like Montgomery and St. Clair, he joined the British army, seeing service as an officer as a means of making him a gentleman and securing his livelihood. He learned to cultivate the great in both England and

North America, knowing how to make friends with those of higher social and political status. But early in his career he found he lacked an income for advancement in the army. He was nowhere near as rich as Schuyler; not until much later after the war, with his second marriage to wealthy Mary Vallance, would he be financially secure.

Gates's military background was similar to that of Burgoyne's officers. He served in Europe in the War of Austrian Succession and as a captain in North America during the Seven Years' War, where he was wounded during Braddock's humiliating defeat.[5] He was often based in New York City, becoming a member of the Whig Club made up of Yale graduates William Livingston, William Smith, and John Morin Scott. These men were in the forefront of New York's early hostility to the Stamp Act and efforts to prevent imperial taxation, though Smith eventually became a Loyalist.

For Gates, the Seven Years' War culminated when he became the protégé of a powerful British general, Robert Monckton. On March 20, 1761, Monckton was made governor of New York, arriving in the city in October.[6] A year older than Gates, Monckton and he were close in temperament. Brigadier Monckton had been Wolfe's third in command at the Plains of Abraham, where he had been seriously wounded by a ball to the lungs. He recovered in New York City over the winter of 1759–60, and there must have first made his acquaintance with Gates. Brigade Major Gates became Monckton's right-hand staff member, and Gates introduced Monckton to his friends in the Whig Club. Gates prepared Monckton's campaign of 1762 that left from New York for the West Indies. Gates was with Monckton when he conquered Martinique and went on to help him subdue Havana. Monckton sent Gates to London to announce the victory, and in recognition of his service, the king gave him a purse to purchase the rank of major. After this respite, Monckton returned as governor of New York in June 1762 and was popular because he invested in a privateer, the *General Monckton*, following the example of many New York merchants.

With the war over, however, Gates found his military career stalled when he returned to England in 1762.[7] Monckton's patronage seemed to offer him a promising career, but this did not materialize because during peacetime the army's reduction in size and narrow traditions offered few opportunities. In September 1763 Gates and his family settled near fashionable Bath. Three years later, he moved them to a quiet and less expensive country estate near Bristol, and in 1768 he moved again to Sandridge near London to be closer to his mother, who had complained about his distance from her. At this time, except for his officer's half pay, he had no sources of financial support.

His frustration with finding a fulltime promotion, along with the growing North American crisis in the 1760s and 1770s, led him to associate with radical groups in England and even consider a political career. He thought of running for Parliament, and he shared his aspirations with a friend from service in Nova Scotia, John Hale, who had formed a group of Whig radicals, the Demoniacs.[8] In Bristol from 1765 to 1766, Gates became involved with anti–Stamp Act Whigs who gathered at Mrs. Perry's Coffee House. Here he met Henry Cruger, a colonial, who represented his great New York merchant family in Bristol. In 1768 Gates attended a dinner hosted by Benjamin Franklin, which included Monckton and the radical Charles Lee, a future Continental general. As a result, in 1770 Gates was called a "red hot Republican." Like Hale who contemplated a move to America, Gates was a frustrated republican, and he left England forever in 1772, sailing from Bristol to Virginia. A year later, with the money from the sale of his major's commission, he purchased a modest farm near Leetown in western Virginia. Within a few years he doubled the size of his original one-and-one-half-story limestone farmhouse and called it Traveler's Rest, a sign of his modest prosperity.

Gates's Generals and Army

When he was appointed to command of the Northern Department, Gates lacked subordinate major generals to carry out his plans. This situation was his own fault, and he may have wanted it that way. He specifically snubbed Philip Schuyler, who was his only general officer with in-depth influence and knowledge of the area.[9] Gates could not match Schuyler's connections, for the New Yorker had been raised in an important Albany family, had been a leader in promoting the area's settlement, had ample business connections for supply, and in a pinch could offer his own personal credit to sustain a military request. While Schuyler did smart in private from losing the command, he was enough of a gentleman to be ready to use his skills and connections to find supplies and men for Gates's army.

Despite his best efforts, Gates also could not get along with Major General Benedict Arnold, whom he would constantly restrict from taking the field against Burgoyne.[10] Yes, Arnold was headstrong and after personal glory, but what good officer is not? An able commander would have harnessed Arnold's talents and used them when action was needed. Arnold was second only to Schuyler in experience in the region, having served at Fort Ticonderoga, Quebec, and the Battle of Lake Champlain. He was also a New Englander, making him acceptable to the militia from that area.

Another major general was Benjamin Lincoln, an officer whom Gates inherited from Schuyler, who had met Lincoln on July 30 at Fort Miller and given him an independent command in Vermont. Lincoln was immensely popular with George Washington and with the people of his home state, Massachusetts.[11] While not a brilliant soldier, his even temper allowed him to get along with touchy generals and even militias and he avoided the personality conflicts that abounded in the Northern Army. Alas, Lincoln was still fulfilling his independent command in Vermont when Gates organized his army, leaving Gates to command one wing of the army and Arnold the other, a situation that was explosive. If Gates had brought Lincoln to his army sooner, for the Battle of Freeman's Farm on September 22, Lincoln might have mediated between Arnold and Gates. The new commander of the Northern Department seems to have been jealous of his major generals and therefore avoided giving them important roles in halting Burgoyne.

Gates needed subordinate generals in a battle situation because he remained in the rear during battle, never actually coming to the field and joining in the combat, depending on his subordinates to use their own initiative in an assigned area. While a commander overseeing the actions of subordinates was an ideal of European battlefields, the terrain to the north of Bemis Heights was so broken that no commander had clear indication of where his troops or those of the enemy were.[12] Once maneuvers commenced, it was left to Gates's brigadier generals and regimental commanders to form against the enemy and to attack or retreat as immediate conditions dictated.

One of these officers was Brigadier General Enoch Poor of New Hampshire. As noted, John Stark was immensely jealous of him because Poor had been promoted by Congress ahead of him. Stationed at

Ticonderoga since Carleton's invasion of Lake Champlain, Poor had more service in the region than most generals. He was described by the opinionated Dr. Lewis Beebe as "very sociable and popular; but of absolute, despotick turn of mind. As to his principles, respecting religion, it is very difficult to determine. . . . But in my opinion he had none at all."[13] He was born in 1736 in Andover, Massachusetts, into a respectable family and had served as a private in Nova Scotia during the 1755 expulsion of the Acadians. Upon his return he eloped with Martha Osgood and they settled in Exeter, New Hampshire. He was an early rebel, protesting the Stamp Act and was twice elected to New Hampshire's Provincial Assembly. After Lexington, Poor was named colonel of the 2nd New Hampshire Regiment, which was then absorbed into the Continental Army. The regiment joined Montgomery's invasion of Canada, and after the defeat Poor led the survivors back to Ticonderoga. When Carleton abandoned Crown Point in November 1776, Poor's regiment was sent to serve with Washington at winter quarters in Morristown, New Jersey. With a brigade of New Hampshire and New York troops, Poor would then go back to defend Ticonderoga against Burgoyne's invasion. He was with St. Clair in the withdrawal from Ticonderoga on July 5. When Gates became commander, his brigade was further extended by the addition of two regiments of Connecticut militia.

Another of Gates's brigadier generals was Ebenezer Learned. Born in Oxford, Massachusetts, in 1728, Learned had lived there all of his life, was married, had nine children, ran a farm and tavern, and was a selectman and militia officer.[14] During the Seven Years' War, he had served briefly at Fort Edward and Lake George. When conflict erupted at Lexington, he marched his militia regiment to the siege of Boston, gaining Washington's respect by holding the strategic position of Dorchester Heights. After the British evacuated Boston, Learned was eased from the militia into the Continental Army, becoming colonel of the 4th and later 3rd Massachusetts Continental Regiments. In May 1776 ill health forced him to leave the army and return to Oxford. However, almost a year later he was recalled by Congress, made a brigadier general, and ordered to command a brigade in the Northern Department. Like Poor, he originally commanded militias but had been drawn to the Continental Army as the war progressed, giving him an understanding of how to command both types of men.

In conspicuous support of the generals was forty-two-year-old Colonel Daniel Morgan from Virginia's Shenandoah Valley. In September 1776 Washington recommended to Congress that Morgan, who had just returned from imprisonment as a result of the loss at Quebec, be named commander of a newly raised riflemen regiment.[15] In January 1777 Morgan began to recruit this regiment, dressing his riflemen in hunting shirts and leggings, but since he was a stickler for neatness, the unit reputedly always looked professional. Finding accurate marksmen proved to be difficult, and he was only able to gather 180. To solve the dilemma, Washington made him colonel of an already existing light infantry regiment with 500 men. They had been chosen from Continental regiments, and most hailed from Pennsylvania, Maryland, and Virginia. Officially they were armed with rifles and pikes, although there is no evidence the last were ever issued. The regiment first saw action against General Howe in New Jersey, but when the word of Ticonderoga's fall came to Washington, he sent Morgan's light infantry to bolster the Northern Army, first to Peekskill and then to Albany. They arrived at Bemis Heights on August 30, where Morgan had dinner with his Virginia neighbor and now commanding officer, Horatio Gates.

A key subordinate in Poor's brigade was Joseph Cilley, who had been named colonel of the 1st New Hampshire Continental Regiment when Stark resigned in March 1777. He was an officer quite unlike the touchy commander at the Walloomsac. Born in 1734, he represented New Hampshire's seaboard interests in the Portsmouth area, becoming an influential lawyer, businessman, and farmer. With John Langdon in 1774 he participated in the symbolic seizure of Fort William and Mary's arms in Portsmouth Harbor.[16] He was a major of New Hampshire Continentals in the invasion and retreat from Canada and as a result was named lieutenant colonel of the 1st New Hampshire Regiment. Early in 1777 his regiment was recruited anew, and in May it was sent to Ticonderoga, where he served under St. Clair, retreating with him to join Schuyler's army. He and his regiment would serve with distinction at the Battles of Freeman's Farm and Bemis Heights. Considering the temperamental Stark and the mixed quality of New Hampshire troops, Cilley was a contrasting steady and brave regimental commander.

Further down the lists was another New Hampshire officer, twenty-six-year-old Henry Dearborn, one of the youngest majors in Gates's army. Born in Hampton, New Hampshire, by the time he was twenty-one he was practicing medicine and a captain in the New Hampshire militia.[17] In 1775 he took his company to Boston, where they served at the Battle of Bunker Hill. He then gained experience in Arnold's march to Quebec and the siege of the Canadian stronghold. Like Morgan, he was captured at Quebec and exchanged in March 1777. He returned to serve at Ticonderoga and was in St. Clair's retreat. He was a major in the 3rd New Hampshire Regiment of Colonel Alexander Scammell but transferred to the 1st New Hampshire Regiment of Joseph Cilley. Gates tapped him as commander of his light infantry, to be teamed with Morgan's special unit at the battles of Freeman's Farm and Bemis Heights.

Overall Gates's officers were experienced Continentals, but there was considerable difference in their backgrounds and social skills. They could not all be gentlemen in the mold of Philip Schuyler. The year before in the retreat from Canada, straight-laced Dr. Lewis Beebe came to the conclusion that rebel officers were a sorry lot, for among them "drunkenness, is a great beauty, and profanity an ornament of an officer. . . . The whims, caprice, and vanity of this set of being [officers] is ridiculous to the last degree. Children are not often guilty of such scandalous behavior, without severe correction."[18] Beebe further described how "our officers and soldiers in general, are remarkably expert in a swearing way, nothing comes more handy, or gives such power and force to their words as a blasphemous oath." He also saw no difference between the conduct of the men, who learned from their officers. Beebe made fun of military procedures as well. He had been stopped by rebel guards for the password, which he had forgotten, and could not resist observing that the entire army at Mount Independence was alerted because an ox had wandered into the fortifications and "was taken for one of the enemy, for not giving the countersign when demanded." Certainly, the officers of Gates's army were not universally thought of as honorable gentlemen.

Some Continental officers had developed a sense of honor that bound them together, enforcing a social hierarchy that separated them from their men.[19] The officers' living conditions, punishments, medical care, burials, and treatment as prisoners set them apart from the soldiers. Rank had its jealously guarded privileges in a society that settled scores by duels for honor. Actually, Continental officers had more respect for the officers of the enemy than their own rank and file. In incidents during the Saratoga Campaign, Gates would apologize for bombarding the burial of British general Simon Fraser at the Great Redoubt, and Schuyler could think of no greater honor after the British surrender than entertaining Burgoyne at his Albany home. While Continental soldiers occasionally challenged their officers, on the whole the military hierarchy survived the War of Independence unscathed by forms of democracy.

BURGOYNE'S ARMY ON THE MOVE TOWARD ALBANY

Burgoyne's army would travel on the roads to Albany on both sides of the Hudson River, with their supply bateaux on the river paralleling the army. Although the river was in places easily navigable, it was also continually falling from its headwaters in the Adirondacks, causing dangerous rapids and eddies that had to be portaged. Thus the army could not move on it, but the supply bateaux could managed on it relatively safely. The roads were far from ideal for military uses, and the closer Burgoyne's army came to Albany, the worse they seemed to get for soldiers marching with their packs, because the rebels had destroyed the bridges and otherwise obstructed the roads.

The terrain near the river would also become a problem for Burgoyne's army. British volunteer Thomas Anburey noted, "This road is bounded on one side by the river, and on the other by perpendicular ascents, covered with wood, where the enemy might not only greatly annoy, but where one night, they could throw impediments in our way that would take nearly the whole of the next day to remove."[20]

From September 13 to 15, near Schuyler's Saratoga plantation, Burgoyne left the east side road and crossed the Hudson River to its west bank over a bateaux bridge. Burgoyne had chosen the western road because it was on the same side as Albany, and he feared to make a crossing nearer the city where the river was wider and the chances for opposition greater. Unopposed, he occupied Schuyler's plantation, which would be the scene of heavy fighting a month later. German troops occupied the barracks that Schuyler had constructed in the village, while Burgoyne found quarters in Schuyler's house.[21] Plans were made to fortify a nearby island and the flat promontory behind it. To give the army greater protection, the Loyalist units of Peters and Jessup, along with Fraser's newly recruited marksmen, were sent on scouts. Here it was confirmed that St. Leger had been forced to break off the siege of Fort Stanwix and retreat, but it was now hoped he would return to Canada and come to Burgoyne's aid by way of Lake Champlain.

After three days the bateaux bridge was dismantled as the army moved down the west side of the river, southward toward Stillwater.[22] This was symbolic because Burgoyne purposely cut his supply line with Lake George and Ticonderoga. His troops and bateaux now carried supplies for a forty-day dash to Albany. Thus Burgoyne was completely unorthodox, deliberately cutting and abandoning his supply lines with Ticonderoga so he could make a quick move on Albany. Ideally, Burgoyne hoped to treat his entire army as fast-moving light infantry. This was risky because sources of additional supplies could be in the hands of rebels.[22]

Burgoyne's army moved southward in three wings: on the Hudson were the supply bateaux, manned and protected by Loyalists, naval ratings—men attached to the navy who were normally noncombatants but who had skills in maintaining ships—and boatmen, who in turn were defended by the 47th Regiment, which traveled on the flats immediately along the river. The boatmen were soon placed in their own unit and trained to defend themselves and the bateaux, taking the burden off the 47th. A second wing was slightly inland on the road itself, where the bulk of the army traveled along with the supply carts and artillery, often stopping to repair the bridges. Third, Fraser's advanced corps occupied the heights above the road, confronted with the difficulty of marching through a broken ground of continuous ravines.[23] However, his position was deemed worthwhile because he protected the flank and often had a view of the entire army moving southward. Effort was made to keep the three wings moving together.

Except for the rebels' foraging parties, Burgoyne's army had seen little of the enemy.[24] Burgoyne did not realize that he would soon be confronted by the rebels at major fortifications that Gates was erecting at Bemis Heights, north of Stillwater. The extensive fortifications were being designed by Colonel Thaddeus Kosciuszko and included, where the river was narrowest, a battery of cannon that could command the road, the flood plain, and the river. The defenses ran inland and were a continual work in progress, even during the fighting with Burgoyne. He gained enough information to realize these river fortifications were too strong to directly attack, so he would have to develop a more subtle strategy to dislodge the rebels from their strong position.

The Battle of Freeman's Farm

Burgoyne decided he had to move the bulk of his army into the hilly, broken, mixed forest and fields to the right and thus outflank the rebels and storm the Bemis Heights defenses from the west, where they were unfinished. On the Heights, the Neilson house, barn, and farm outbuildings were on the left of the extensive works; the tiny house would shelter Generals Arnold, Poor, and John Paterson, commander of a brigade of Massachusetts Continentals and militia.[25] Gates established his headquarters farther back, at Captain Ephraim Woodworth's farmhouse. He now had a slightly larger force than Schuyler's, totaling 9,000, easily outnumbering Burgoyne.

On September 19 Burgoyne divided his 6,000 men into three columns as he advanced along the Hudson River. Two of the smaller columns under Fraser and Hamilton headed through the hilly terrain to his right, while the third column under Riedesel held the attention of the enemy on the river road.[26] Gates in conference with Arnold responded by sending out Colonel Daniel Morgan's and Dearborn's light infantry to probe the enemy movement. As they reached the Freeman farm, the light infantry ran into the advance party of Fraser's column, made up of Indians, Loyalists, Canadians, and Captain Fraser's marksmen, and drove them back with a deadly volley. Then the Loyalist corps of Peters and Jessup, as well as Fraser's marksmen, rallied and advanced farther right to give Burgoyne's army greater security on the right flank.

But Morgan's riflemen rushed after the enemy, losing the advantage of their order and were scattered through the woods, leaving Morgan almost completely alone. Emotional, with tears in his eyes, Morgan used a turkey call to rally his men, who were no match for British regulars firing in volleys. However, Dearborn's light infantry was still on his left, and the New Hampshire Continentals of Poor's brigade, with Scammell's and Joseph Cilley's regiments, came to Morgan's rescue on his left. They split their troops to fight both Hamilton's and later Fraser's men. Thus stiffened by New Hampshire Continentals, Morgan's re-formed. The center under Burgoyne and Hamilton, consisting of the 9th, 20th, 21st, 24th, and 62nd Regiments, was now completely enveloped, and cannon were placed at the edge of Freeman's farm to support them. The rebel force was now slightly larger. Digby claimed "the heavy artillery joining in concert like great peals of thunder, assisted by the echoes of the woods, almost deafened us with noise."[27]

In the center, Benedict Arnold attempted to collect and bring his entire wing into the fray.[28] When he tried to go with his wing, Gates called him back and he obeyed, so that he was not present on the field in the conflict at Freeman's Farm. While Arnold could not have been directly involved in combat, his leadership in bringing troops to the action was later complimented by Poor and his colonels, Cilley and Scammell.

The farm of John Freeman, Sr., had now become the center of fighting that was far more than a probe.[29] It was a 170-acre farm, leased from landlord Philip Schuyler in 1769, but like so many tenants Freeman had not followed his landlord, instead becoming a Loyalist. Five of Freeman's sons were in Burgoyne's army. John Freeman, Sr., guided Burgoyne's army, and his twelve-year-old son, Thomas, belonged to Jessup's King's Loyal Americans, who were in the vanguard. However, the Freemans were no longer in possession of the farm, as the lease had recently been sold.

Before the confrontation of September 19, a Quaker Loyalist, Isaac Leggett, had purchased the lease and improved it with his son, Ebenezer.[30] His daughter, Mary Maxwell, lived on the farm at the time of the battle, evidently without her father and brother. Mary, her mother, and sisters left the farm as the armies appeared, supposedly burying $300 in gold under the cellar floor. Before they got away, Gates and Arnold summoned the ladies to learn if their father, Isaac, as a supporter of the king, "had not he sold provisions to the enemy." Mary denied knowing anything, upsetting Arnold, though Gates, the gentleman, intervened and she was released.

Now with difficulty Fraser tried to form a uniform line, but the rebels attempted to cut the line between him and Hamilton. Fraser's men were forced to make several bayonet charges, in which they usually excelled, but they found the rebels unmoved and sustained high casualties.[31] The battle seesawed back and forth for most of the afternoon. Gates then sent Learned's brigade in to help on the field, but Learned's men had trouble with the broken terrain, got lost, and finally stumbled into Fraser's column, losing thirty-five men. A lack of coordination existed among the rebels on the battlefield.

As yet Riedesel, with the third and largest column of Burgoyne's army, had not been involved. He had been moving according to his orders down the river road, attempting to probe the rebel defenses that commanded the river. Late in the afternoon, Burgoyne sent orders to him to attack the right of the rebel line. Riedesel quickly moved one regiment, two companies, and artillery to his right and into the fighting. When he saw the British regiments in trouble, he charged bravely with the van, much as he done at Hubbardton. His attack upon Morgan and the New Hampshire regiments was a surprise that drove them back into the woods. The Hesse Hanau artillery under Captain Georg Pausch came up and placed two cannon in the British line. They fired fourteen shots into the rebels with grape at close range. So effective was the artillery that the rebels ceased firing and withdrew. Saved again by Riedesel, in this section of the battlefield Burgoyne was suddenly triumphant. The rebels withdrew and Burgoyne's army camped on the battlefield as a sign of victory. For the army as a whole, however, it was "a dear bought victory." [32]

The British army remained on the field overnight and the next morning, burying their dead and tending their wounded. Burgoyne made a relatively accurate account of his losses: they consisted of about 600 men, killed, wounded and captured, the bulk of them in three British regiments, the 20th, 21st, and 62nd. Rebel causalities amounted to about half that number, 319. True to their need for manufactured items, it was observed that Burgoyne's "Indians had a fine time the next morning in plundering and . . . scalping" the enemy. Anburey claimed "the artillery made the difference," but he was also generous to the Continentals: "The courage and obstinacy with which the Americans fought were the astonishment of everyone, and we now became fully convinced they were not the contemptible enemy we had hitherto imagined them."[33] Burgoyne's insistence on an artillery train had paid off. Fraser's vanguard of Indians and Loyalists had served credibly.

The day after the battle of Freeman's Farm, Phillips and the Frasers urged Burgoyne to contemplate a second attack on the rebel defensive position.[34] While the troops of both armies were exhausted, the discipline of the British force was greater, since regulars were used to winning battles bit by bit, rather than in a single action. After a day of rest and reorganization, Burgoyne seemed ready to attack on September 21. But he had received a message from General Henry Clinton in New York City, dated September 12, that he was moving up the Hudson against Forts Clinton and Montgomery in about ten days. So Burgoyne, thinking that Gates would have to send reinforcements south to defend Albany against Clinton, felt he did not need to make an immediate attack. In this he was mistaken.

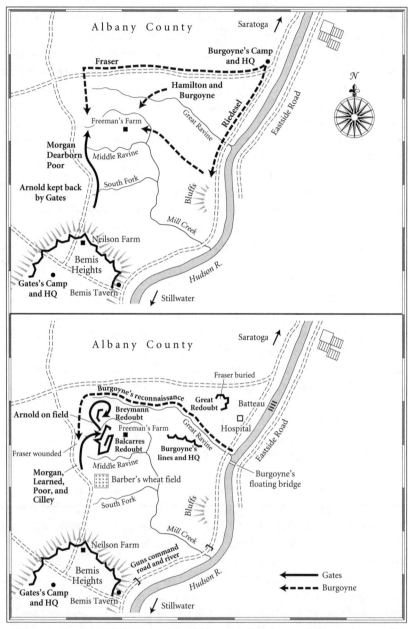

The Battles of Freeman's Farm (September 10) and Bemis Heights (October 7, 1777)

While Gates continued to fortify Bemis Heights, Burgoyne began to fortify the position he occupied at Freeman's farm, foolishly wasting his opportunity to advance. Two redoubts were built: the Balcarres on the farm and the Breymann near it.[35] The Balcarres was the larger of the two, with walls fourteen feet high, mounting eight cannon and holding up to 1,500 men. It was the strongest position in the British line, which stretched to the river. In contrast, the Breymann had walls only six feet high, mounted but two cannon, and was defended by a mere 600 men. It guarded the British right flank and the road to the hamlet of Quaker Springs. The anchor for the defenses on the left, overlooking the river, was a hilltop fort, the Great Redoubt. A bridge of bateaux across the river completed the left flank. A field of Indian corn was even found, to provide for the army's horses. Burgoyne's overriding assumption for his defense was based on the belief that Clinton would soon be in Gates's rear. Burgoyne's army was still dangerous, but it was now operating largely on local foraging and the supplies it carried, a perilous situation no matter what Burgoyne chose to do.

BURGOYNE COPES WITH HIS PROBLEMS

On August 27 a German officer claimed "that up to the present time there has never been an army in which desertions have been so scarce."[36] This was in contrast to the rebels, who had been deserting since Ticonderoga fell. A month later, however, Ensign Anburey commented that "the rebels had sent agents into the English camp who endeavored to induce soldiers, by all kinds of representations to desert; and it being known that the Americans treated their prisoners very kindly . . . the agents here and there found a willing ear." Certainly some of Burgoyne's soldiers defected: this was especially true late in the campaign, when Wilkinson reported that fifty or sixty Germans deserted to the rebels. The Germans had no understanding of the political situation and were impressed by the region's farms, while British soldiers had built up a well-defined hated of the rebels. British soldiers who had been disciplined by their officers also tended to hold a grudge and desert. However, British officers in America did not strictly enforce the military code, preferring leniency toward their men, cutting down on this type of discontent.

Burgoyne's regular regiments had become depleted as he dispersed them to posts like Ticonderoga and as they suffered casualties at the Battle of Freeman's Farm, as well as from the effect of desertion and disease. On September 21 he was forced to integrate Loyalists into each of the regiments to bolster his ranks.[37] From the Loyalist corps of Peters, Jessup, McAlpin and McKay, "120 men of proven loyalty and courage" were transferred to fill the regular regiments. Just so they knew that this situation was temporary, Burgoyne gave Loyalists a certificate saying that they were not allowed to actually serve in the regiments for "any longer than Dec. 25 of this year." This integration involved only a fraction of the men in the Loyalist corps, and those not drafted continued to serve within their own units.

The "batoe service" was another area in which the Loyalists could serve. A force was needed to parallel Burgoyne's army on the Hudson River, charged not only with carrying but defending supplies. The first fifty men had been organized at the time of the Battle of the Walloomsac by Brigadier Fraser, who had placed them under the command of Loyalist Captain Hugh Munro. A fellow Scot and veteran of the Seven Years' War, Munro had a sawmill on the Hudson River, was related to the Anglican reverend Harry Munro, was a friend of the Jessups and Abraham Wing, and had provided Burgoyne with Indian corn. Hugh Munro had been an adjunct to Jessup's corps, but Brigadier Fraser transferred his bateaux corps to Captain McAlpin, causing the usual struggle between Loyalist officers over the possession of recruits.[38]

The bateaux corps was oversubscribed, not only from Loyalists but from naval ratings and Canadians, and it rose to at least seventy, including Jeptha Hawley.[39] The corps's first duty was to ferry supplies from Fort Edward to Burgoyne's various camps. As noted, they had to cope with the Hudson's rapids, currents, falls, and frequent portages, in which supply barrels had to be taken out of the bateaux, while they were guided past obstruction and then repacked. Sometimes the bateaux had to be completely pulled out of the river and moved by land on log rollers. The corps also had a gunboat, which served to gather intelligence, and they were involved in the construction of floating bridges. It was this unit that provided provisions and intelligence that Burgoyne needed if he was to advance rapidly toward Albany.

On September 22 "fifty loyal Albanians, who were either hard pressed or had opted for the King, came over to [Burgoyne's army] across the newly constructed bateaux bridge."[40] The auxiliary groups continued to serve, for "the Indian, Canadian and Albanian volunteers . . . have their outposts in front of the whole of this part of the line." In the evening Indians returned from scouting. They brought in with them a prisoner who, although alive, was half dead from fear and anguish. They also had taken two scalps, "after their own neat fashion!" The Loyalists now made up perhaps a fifth of the army. A report of October 1 stated that their numbers had declined to 456, but the figure did not include 200 loyalists stationed near Fort Miller. Doubtless some were lost, but some were joining anew. Still, the Loyalist additions were unquestionably fewer than Gates's hundreds of militia reinforcements.

LINCOLN'S COMMAND AND BROWN'S RAID

Not all military activity in September would be concentrated at Freeman's farm. Conflict continued around Burgoyne's communications line, which was still viable from Ticonderoga, down Lake George and below. However, because the Continental army was not respected in this area, the diverse forces seemed to operate independently, without any overall coordination. Remember, before Burgoyne cut his supply line in September, Major General Benjamin Lincoln of the Continental Line had been sent by Washington to help Schuyler. He had specifically assigned Lincoln to Vermont, for he was a native of Massachusetts and supposedly had an understanding of their militia's motives. He was technically in command of the Manchester front where he arrived on August 2, two weeks before the Battle of Walloomsac.[41] However, he was ignored by Warner, even though he had a plan to use the Manchester troops in irregular strikes at what was then Burgoyne's existing supply line. Lincoln was also there when Stark arrived, and he passed on Schuyler's orders that Stark refused to follow. Lincoln went to Schuyler to discuss his plan to threaten Burgoyne's supply line. While Lincoln was with Schuyler, however, Stark and Warner, on their own, left Manchester and moved against Baum and Breymann on the Walloomsac. It is not clear that Lincoln ever returned to Manchester, but if he did, it was only briefly, as he developed a base at Pawlet, just within the Grants, to carry out the strikes he planned to sever communication between Burgoyne's army and their bases at Lake George and Ticonderoga.

Lincoln was able to get respect from about 2,000 men, chiefly Berkshire County militia under Simonds and Brown. He planned three attacks on Ticonderoga and its dependencies. Each thrust involved about 500 men, while he held 600 in his reserve.[42] Colonel Enoch Woodbridge was to move against Skenesborough and then, with reinforcements from Lincoln, turn southward toward Fort Edward. However, Woodbridge found Skenesborough abandoned, though the empty post did contain stored food, and he returned. The second effort of Colonel Thomas Johnson was to dislodge the enemy at Mount Independence. When Johnson arrived there, however, he abandoned the effort, having made no impression on its garrison. The third force, consisting chiefly of Berkshire County militia from Stockbridge, with some of Herrick's Rangers, was under the command of Massachusetts colonel John Brown. It was aimed at raiding the crucial portage and Lake George landing at Ticonderoga. Lincoln was more pleased by the results of this third effort.

John Brown, was a pale equivalent of Francis Marion or Thomas Sumter in the South. Brown was born in 1744 in Haverhill, Massachusetts, but at the age of eight his family moved to Berkshire County, where his father was a local magistrate under the crown.[43] In 1767, at the rather advanced age of twenty-three, John entered Yale College, from which he graduated four years later, having in the meantime married. While in New Haven, he came to know of Benedict Arnold because his sister Elizabeth had married Oliver Arnold, a cousin of Benedict and attorney general of Rhode Island. Brown began practicing law, but not in New Haven, rather in newly created Tryon County in New York's Mohawk Valley. His stay there was brief and in 1773 he was practicing law in Pittsfield, Berkshire County.

In Pittsfield, Brown slowly began to notice events that were taking place in what he regarded as distant Boston.[44] He was chosen by Pittsfield leaders to respond to the Massachusetts General Court over the Boston Tea Party. Taking an independent stand—as they did in the Berkshires—while he denounced British taxes, he was opposed to the destruction of property when the tea was thrown overboard into the harbor. He became a member of the Berkshire County Committee of Correspondence, a delegate to the County Congress at Stockbridge, and then a delegate to the Massachusetts Provincial Congress. Late in 1774 the Provincial Congress sent him to Canada to gather information on how Canadians viewed the political situation in Massachusetts. The mission was meant to be peaceful and assure both French and English Canadians of the good will of New England. Back after this experience, he conspired with Mott and Easton in Pittsfield to seize Ticonderoga and was with Ethan Allen at its capture, but he failed to support Allen in his ill-planned attack on Montreal, where Allen was taken prisoner. Brown was now a lieutenant colonel of Berkshire County militia and capable of an independent command.

At Ticonderoga, Brown would face Brigadier Henry Powell, who like commanders before him could not defend the extensive works. He had less than 1,000 men stretched to protect the fort, the French Lines, Mount Independence, and Mount Defiance, with a further command of troops and workers stationed at the Lake George landing and the connecting road's defensive post at Fort Mt. Hope.[45] Strategic Mount Defiance was held by only a corporal and four men.

Earlier when Brigadier Hamilton commanded at Ticonderoga, he had set precedent when he placed most of his 100 rebel prisoners in a barn at the Lake George landing, a decision based on the need for them to haul supplies, not consideration of preventing their escape. Thus, Brown surprised the Lake George landing contingent on September 18, releasing the prisoners and taking 293 prisoners of his own, chiefly Canadian artificers, but also British troops from the 53rd Regiment and naval ratings.[46]

The British blamed the surprise on their sentinels at LaChute bridge, who thought the rebels to be Canadian teamsters and were overpowered before they could spread the alarm to the sprawling fortifications. Brown even had the audacity to demand the surrender of Fort Ticonderoga, which Powell firmly refused, and no siege emerged, as by September 21 Brown was ready to take his raiders elsewhere.[47] The prisoners were marched to Skenesborough and then Castleton and Pawlet. Brown may have learned that British reinforcements from St. Leger's army were only a day from Ticonderoga.

At the Lake George landing, Brown gathered 420 men and confiscated a sloop, placing cannon on it, which gave him the makings of a navy to control the lake. On September 22 his fleet left the landing to capture the chief British post on Lake George, Diamond Island, twenty-five miles to the south.[48] But in this endeavor he proved to be no sailor.

The post at Diamond Island had been established from Fort George in early September when Burgoyne sent his excess supplies, baggage, artillery, and, it is said, his cash box to the island, signifying the abandonment of his Skenesborough supply line. Anburey described the newly created post: "About the center of [Lake George] are two islands, on the largest of which, called Diamond Island, are encamped two companies of the 47th Regiment, under the command of Capt. Aubrey, for the purpose of forwarding provisions across the lake."[49] The 47th Regiment manned gunboats, the breastworks, and cannon. It was a safer and more strategic location for control of the lake than Fort George, which anyway could be occupied from Diamond Island if necessity required it.

Private Thomas Wood was with Brown at the capture of the Lake George landing, and he continued with Brown's fleet against Diamond Island, where he was told "Burgoyne had deposited large sums of money designed for the payment of the British troops." The fleet, however, was delayed by high winds and forced to put in for the night at Sabbath Day Point, and the attack on the island did not come until the morning of September 24. In the fighting in the midst of Lake George, Wood reported: "This engagement was with cannon and a very severe one. A considerable number of our men were killed, and the said colonel [Brown] ordered a retreat, the sloop being very much disabled by the shots of the enemy. Our vessels moved down the outlet of Lake George into [Dunham's] bay, on the south side, where they were burnt."[50] Riedesel claimed that Brown had been "bravely received by the commander, Captain [Aubrey] of the 47th, [and] compelled to make a precipitate retreat having lost about sixty men killed and wounded. Captain [Aubrey] pursued, and recaptured [Brown's] ship and bateaux." From there, Brown's force retreated to Fort Ann, Skenesborough, and finally Pawlet, where Wood was discharged.

The day after their defeat at Diamond Island, booty remained a prominent concern of Brown's men. Brown and Herrick requested that the Vermont Council of Safety send teams to them to bring off the plunder they still held. This referred not only to cattle but to "a large quantity of European goods" that had been found in a Ticonderoga storehouse.[51] As Private Wood eagerly observed, these goods were deposited in the Wilson house at Pawlet, for probable distribution. At this time Gates intervened, thinking it was best for Lincoln's separate command to cease its harassing activities on the lakes and join his army at Saratoga.[52] To Gates it may have become evident that there was no longer a British supply line by way of Skenesborough. More important, he wanted to overwhelm his foe by gathering a superior number of troops. Lincoln collected Woodbridge's men and sent them and his other forces to Saratoga between September 22 and 29.

Lincoln did not arrive at Gates's headquarters until a week later, the day of the Battle of Bemis Heights, where he technically was given a command. The next day as he traveled from his meeting with Gates to rejoin his men, he was confronted by an enemy patrol and wounded in the ankle.[53] He was immediately sent to Albany, as it was felt his wound was life threatening, and he would not see action in the rest of the campaign. While a secondary front along the east side of the Hudson extending all the way to Ticonderoga may have been forming, without Lincoln's leadership and ability to coordinate with Gates's army, its value would be limited.

GATES'S ARMY AND THE NEW ENGLAND MILITIA

While Burgoyne fortified his army and remained hopeful of help from Clinton, Gates moved to make his army decisively larger than that of the invaders.[54] In calling on the militia, Gates chose a path that most Continental generals avoided. Militias were known for being uncontrollable because they were dominated by concern for their enlistment term, and thus it seemed they left an army as soon as they arrived, often in the midst of a crisis for which they were needed. Besides, Continental quartermasters could not wait to see them leave, as they were so wasteful and expensive to maintain. Since militiamen supposedly supplied their own arms, they often had none or weapons that were in need of repair. The New England militias elected their own officers, a practice that even spread to New York. It meant that the leaders of their communities, more versed in politics than in war, were chosen, and many lacked battlefield experience. Any talented person who was serious about becoming an officer joined a Continental regiment—not the militia. It is noteworthy that while Gates needed the militia in September, he dismissed most of them as soon as Burgoyne capitulated because he could not afford to maintain them.

Gates followed the practice of adding militia regiments to his Continental brigades.[55] He knew militias did poorly when standing alone, but if he mixed them with Continentals, who were already under strength, he would be able to stiffen their resolve. Furthermore, the militias would not straggle in the rear but would be introduced to a formal battlefield situation in which they had to sink or swim. Thus by using the militia, he was able to strengthen his Continental brigades and gain an overwhelming superiority in numbers.

Most of the militias coming to Gates were from Massachusetts, New Hampshire, and Connecticut and they reflected New England's strong commitment to the rebel cause. Gates was supposedly popular with New England's militia leaders, although evidence shows he was most popular with the New England delegates in Congress. In Philadelphia, New York delegate Gouverneur Morris wrote a warning to his friend Philip Schuyler that the word was out that New England troops "would not march while you had command," while they would accept serving under Gates.[56]

Gates was often no better than Schuyler at keeping the militia in the field. Stark's 1,500 New Hampshire militiamen had made victory on the Walloomsac possible—but it was also true that after his victory Stark remained as insubordinate to Gates as he had been to Schuyler. He continued his independent status, making excuses to avoid joining Gates's army. His brigade, minus Stark, who claimed to be ill, finally took a position on the east side of the Hudson, across from Stillwater, almost a month after his victory on the Walloomsac.[57] Stark himself arrived a week later as the Battle of Freeman's Farm was imminent, announcing that his men's enlistments had expired and thus he had to lead them back to New Hampshire. To make up for their return, New Hampshire's Committee of Safety tried to reinforce their "army in the Grants," putting their reinforcements under the command of the "Continental General nearest Bennington." In Bennington Josiah Bartlett of the New Hampshire legislature tried to get Stark to delay, but he knew Stark would not tarry. It is clear that New Hampshire authorities had lost what control they had over him. Gates also offered a bounty to militiamen who would stay, but it had no impact, and Stark left at the crucial moment. In October, Stark would again return to participate in cutting off Burgoyne's path to Fort Edward, but it was clear that he was a militia commander upon whom Continental generals could not depend.

The appearance of thousands of New England troops at Saratoga was not a new phenomenon; twenty years before, in 1758, during the Seven Years' War when the French threat seemed acute, over 9,000 New England provincials had joined the king's troops for Abercromby's army, and close to 5,000 had joined Amherst's force a year later.[58] Burgoyne's policy of appearing to threaten the Connecticut Valley had now hit home as a danger that New England would face, if its militias did not hold the line in New York. Also, roads like those for Crown Point, Mount Independence, Skenesborough, and Kinderhook had been developed as a result of the Seven Years' War and now facilitated the movement of the militia.

THE BATTLE OF BEMIS HEIGHTS

Near Bemis Heights, Burgoyne waited in vain for more than two weeks for a report of Clinton's presence at Albany. The weather had been fair and dry since September 26, and Burgoyne's troops had been occupied by foraging for hay, while his Loyalists and Indians sparred with rebel rangers. On October 6 they confronted a large number of rebel rangers for two hours, driving them back to their pickets, with only a trifling loss to the Loyalists. A day later Burgoyne proposed a "reconnaissance in force" of the rebel position, again aiming at the rebel left where hills could command the Bemis Heights fortifications, although by this time the rebels had seen their vulnerability and fortified these places.[59] Burgoyne's need for solid information on the enemy was not for lack of trying, but the broken terrain made it impossible for scouts from either side to come up with an exact picture of their positions. While Burgoyne was scouting the rebel position, he did not expect to engage the entire rebel army. Because a height that commanded Bemis Heights was the objective of the reconnaissance, the ensuing battle was given the name "Bemis Heights."

At 1 P.M. Burgoyne led only 1,700 men from the British camp in three columns toward the rebel left. They consisted of Balcarres's light infantry, Auckland's grenadiers, the 24th regiment and picked force of Germans, led by Loyalist rangers and Indians. Remembering its effectiveness at the Battle of Freeman's Farm, they carried two twelve-pounders, two howitzers, and six six-pounders.[60] They advanced from Freeman's Farm less than a mile, to the edge of one of the Barber farms, where the field was cultivated with wheat, and in the lull his soldiers began harvesting the grain—one of the goals of the reconnaissance.

In Gates's army his Continentals were now outnumbered by militiamen, and he integrated them into the Continental brigades: John Patterson's brigade contained John Ashley's Berkshire County regiment and Storer's York County regiment, and Jonathan Warner's brigade contained Brown's Berkshire County regiment among other Massachusetts militias. John Glover's brigade had Albany, Dutchess and Ulster County militias, Poor's brigade had the Connecticut militia, and Nixon's brigade had a Hampshire County regiment of the Massachusetts militia. Only the Albany County militia would fight as a single brigade. With these militias present, Gates ordered Daniel Morgan's regiment "to begin the game," sending them along with Leonard's and Poor's brigades to the Barber farm, where they ended the British harvesting by driving the flanks of their line back.[61]

As the British grenadiers advanced, it was the turn of Poor's brigade to face them and give them a devastating volley. The grenadiers retreated to the defenses that had been erected around the Freeman farm, leaving their Major John Dyke Acland behind, wounded in both legs. Balcarres's light infantry received the same punishment and retreated, but the Germans held and did not fall back until ordered to. This time, Captain Pausch, who posted two six-pounders on a rise, was surrounded and could not bring his cannon off, and it became every man for himself when his gun crew retreated. As they fell back, Brigadier Fraser tried to form another line, but bravely exposing himself in the forefront of the army, he was mortally wounded.[62] As if to flaunt their superior numbers, the episode was concluded by a volley from the brigade of the Albany militia, over 1,800 strong, a larger force than Burgoyne's entire reconnaissance. At this moment, Burgoyne sent an officer to order an end to the action, the reconnaissance obviously having failed. However, his messenger was mortally wounded and captured, and thus the action continued.

Among the close to 8,000 rebels on the field was militia private Samuel Woodruff of Southington, Connecticut. He had served in Westchester County, New York, substituting for his brother Jason before August 1777, when he volunteered to go with Colonels Thaddeus Cook's and Jonathan Latimore's Connecticut militias that marched to Albany. From there they advanced to Bemis Heights, where Woodruff saw the battle unfolding. He described how Fraser's men were repulsed and Fraser wounded, and that they retreated to Freeman's farm but still "kept up a respectable fire, both of artillery and musketry."[63] Woodruff testified that Benedict Arnold appeared on the field, although he did not know that Arnold was again without an active command because, as the two were not speaking, Gates had relieved him of it. Arnold led Poor's brigade against the Germans who were holding the center, finally forcing them to retreat to the Balcarres Redoubt at Freeman's farm. Believing he had them cornered, Arnold then initiated a series of attacks against the Balcarres Redoubt with Poor's, Patterson's and Glover's men, and with Ten Broeck's Albany County militia in the reserve. Despite hand-to-hand combat, Arnold's effort was repulsed with heavy losses. Some of the brigade commanders felt that Arnold was wasting their men in futile attacks to enhance his personal reputation.

From Woodruff's perspective, at this crucial moment Benedict Arnold changed direction, "galloping up and down our line upon a small brown horse which he had that day borrowed of his friend Leonard Chester, . . . [Arnold] received a musket ball which broke his leg and killed the horse under him. He was at that moment about forty yards distant from [me] in fair view." [64] He helped "to extricate Arnold from his fallen horse, placed him on a litter, and sent him back to the headquarters of General Gates." Clearly his perspective of Arnold in the smoky field may have been blurred, for he makes no mention of Arnold leaving the hopeless attack on the Balcarres Redoubt and moving instead against the weaker Breymann Redoubt, and he implies that Arnold's leg was wounded by the same bullet that killed his horse.

When Arnold changed direction, he joined Learned's and Nixon's brigades along with Morgan's and Dearborn's light infantries in storming the Breymann Redoubt. Some say as Arnold entered the rear of the redoubt his horse was killed and the animal pinned him, crushing his leg—a less heroic explanation of his wound.[65] Breymann, of Walloomsac fame, was killed when the redoubt was taken, crucially leaving the British flank completely exposed. Darkness brought an end to the general fighting, allowing Burgoyne to withdraw from his precarious position. But it was not over; in the evening Lieutenant Colonel Wilhelm von Speth and his Germans made a desperate attempt to recapture the now symbolic Breymann Redoubt. He was thwarted and captured by the rebels.

Burgoyne's army retreated behind its lines, where Hamilton commanded, and then was regrouped in the relative safety of the Great Redoubt and its dependencies. Gates did not order a pursuit. Actually, only a fraction of Burgoyne's army had participated in the bloody action that culminated at the two redoubts. Baroness Riedesel had prepared dinner for returning officers in her new log cabin, but she found in the afternoon that her early guest was the mortally wounded Fraser. The dinner table was removed and Fraser was placed in a bed,

"View of the West Bank of Hudson's River 3 Miles above Stillwater," and burial of General Frazer, 1777, by Sir Francis Carr Clerk. Reproduction, Library and Archives Canada/Bibliothèque et Archives Canada, Ottawa.

and he asked Burgoyne to bury him in the Great Redoubt. He died in the early morning, but was buried by Chaplain Edward Brudenel and Burgoyne's officers with the pomp of a "great captain" at six o'clock in the evening—as Gates's artillery fired cannon balls over the mourners' heads.[66]

Meanwhile, the evening after the battle, Woodruff provided water and comfort for two hundred rebel wounded brought from the battlefield, who "were placed in a circular row on the naked ground."[67] It was a clear, frosty night, and they suffered because they had no bedding. About seventy of the wounded died overnight. At daybreak Woodruff participated in the melancholy task of burying the dead on the battlefield, which also offered opportunities for plunder. Three days after Burgoyne surrendered, Woodruff's Connecticut militia company was disbanded and he was home by November 1.

In the Battles of Freeman's Farm and Bemis Heights, the Continentals were in the thick of the fighting and carried the day. Militias had played only a supporting role, occasionally firing a volley as they held their place in line. However, militias did provide Gates with depth so that he had ample troops to plug any gap or to stiffen resolve and could ignore his losses. The former British officer who had used his influence in Congress to undermine Schuyler's command had proven to be a formidable adversary for Burgoyne.

The professional war, the type that Burgoyne thought his army best at, was now going badly. Burgoyne had to face the fact that his mad dash to Albany had been stopped and his army was becoming increasingly isolated. He had moved southward with the supplies he could carry in his bateaux on the Hudson or in his road cartage, which depended upon fodder for his animals. He had a scare when John Brown's militia captured the Lake George landing and threatened Ticonderoga's elaborate defenses, although the British remained in control of Lake George when Brown was driven from Diamond Island. At Freeman's Farm Burgoyne did win a tactical but costly victory and decided to fortify his position, waiting for word from Clinton's army moving north from New York City. It was a lost opportunity that ended his march down the Hudson. In early October his reconnaissance was soundly defeated at the Battle of Bemis Heights. His army remained intact, and while weakened by defeat, it was still dangerous. Burgoyne now had to show his skill in doing something he had not expected: conducting a retreat.

12

To Retreat, Escape, or Surrender

On July 23 General William Howe embarked with 13,000 men from New York City, with Philadelphia as his destination. In London Lord Germain was uncertain as to Howe's whereabouts, and Howe was equally uncertain of Burgoyne's plans after he had taken Ticonderoga. Howe would be too occupied with Philadelphia to return personally for a demonstration toward Albany. However, after a week at sea he wrote to Sir Henry Clinton in New York City, "If you can make a diversion in favor of General Burgoyne's approaching Albany, I need not point out the utility of such a measure."[1] This suggestion was offset by the fact that Clinton had only 7,000 men, nearly half of them Loyalists, to defend the New York City region, which included Long Island, Staten Island, and Paulus Hook. Howe is regarded as having been so obsessed with the capture of the seat in the Congress, and yet lethargic in undertaking the expedition to Philadelphia, that he could not effect events elsewhere. Going by way of Chesapeake Bay rather than the Delaware River, he did not reach the Philadelphia area until September, and his forces were weakened by the longer sea voyage.

Back in New York, Clinton received reinforcements from England on September 24, changing his situation. New York's royal governor, William Tryon, had already produced an ambitious plan that allowed troops to travel up the Hudson River rapidly, by alternating water transport with marching. As Clinton had promised Burgoyne, he would make an effort toward Albany. He led a force of 3,000 troops and three frigates and other ships, under Captain Sir James Wallace, from New York City north toward the Hudson Highlands. Clinton's first objective was the rebel Forts Montgomery and Clinton, which commanded the river.[2] His force included not only regulars from the 52nd, 57th, and 63rd regiments but also Loyalists of the New York Volunteers, Emmerick's Chasseurs, and most notably, Colonel Beverly Robinson's Loyal American Regiment. The forts' defense was in the hands of Brigadier General George Clinton—a distant cousin of Sir Henry and the politician who had recently defeated Schuyler for the governorship of New York State.

On October 6 the British disembarked at Stony Point, with their army in three divisions: Major General John Vaughan's against Fort Clinton, Lieutenant Colonel Archibald Campbell's against Fort Montgomery, and Governor and Major General Tryon's troops serving as a reserve and rear guard. The forts were taken, although Campbell was killed, but he was replaced by Robinson, who showed himself the equal of a regular officer. In addition, the rebel defensive fleet of two frigates, two galleys, a sloop, and all their cannon and stores was captured. The following day the British fleet continued northward and took Fort Constitution. On October 9, unopposed, Tryon's force destroyed the Continental Village, the Continental Army base, burning a barracks for 1,500 men, several storehouses, and loaded wagons. This rout was the beginning of George Clinton's reputation as a less than able military commander.

Sir Henry could rest on these laurels and at this time he returned to New York, leaving the expedition in the hands of Vaughan and Captain Wallace, who continued the advance up the river. They came to the port of Kingston on October 16 and found it so heavily defended that they could not avoid attacking it, for fear of it being left in their rear. Vaughan also noted its infamy, because "[the New York legislature and Governor] Clinton had taken refuge there that morning and its being a town notorious for harboring the most rebellious people in that part of the country."[3] Vaughan succeeded in driving the rebels into the town, and when they fired on him from the cover of its houses, he had no choice but to begin a fire that spread, destroying two to three hundred houses. Scattering without an adjournment, the new legislature and Governor Clinton were unable to complete their first session. The Senate and Kingston refugees fled to Hurley, about three miles inland.

Meanwhile, fifty miles north in Albany, the Albany Committee of Correspondence prepared for the city's defense against Vaughan and Wallace. A delegation was sent to Gates to confer on the defense of the city, and they returned with the general's opinion that they had sufficient troops for the task. Gates did not want any of his men diverted from the Saratoga front. On October 17 the Albany Committee sent a message to the committees and field officers of the districts south of Albany in Coxsackie, Kinderhook, Claverack, and Livingston Manor to assemble their militia on the banks of the Hudson, to send their flour and stores to Albany, and to drive their cattle into the interior.[4] It is unclear as to what extent this happened.

Burgoyne surrendered at Bemis Heights the day after Kingston was burned, neither he nor Vaughan being specifically aware of the condition and location of the two armies. On his arrival at Kingston, Vaughan had tried to get information on Burgoyne's situation, detaching two messengers to him and receiving a messenger from him the next day—but it was too late to help him. Vaughan did not tarry at Kingston; on October 17 and 18 he moved forward, and on both sides of the Hudson River he burned rebel homes, storehouses, and barns, such as those of the rebel elite, Abraham Ten Broeck. At Livingston Manor, Vaughan fulfilled the promise of May that the British would support the rising of tenants against their rebel landlords. Robert Gilbert Livingston, Jr., Margaret Beekman Livingston, and her sons, Robert R. Livingston and John Livingston, would see their homes and outbuildings destroyed.[5] The Livingstons did not delay; along with young Stephen Van Rensselaer and his mother, they fled with their possessions in carts to Sharon and Salisbury, Connecticut. At Sharon the Livingstons had a cottage and could feel safe in the obscure village. The opposition of Major General Israel Putnam and militia that is often referred to did not stop Vaughan's ship-based forays.

Only after this high point, about forty miles from Albany, did Vaughan begin his withdrawal toward New York City, continuing to destroy rebel property on the river, until he arrived at Fort Vaughan on October 26. Clinton had ordered Vaughan's retreat, as Howe now wanted 4,000 more reinforcements for the Philadelphia Campaign. One can imagine what Burgoyne would have said, had he known this. The Hudson River expedition was a complete tactical success and Clinton, Vaughan, Wallace, Robinson, and the army's Loyalists deserved the honors they received. However, the two British armies, one at

Saratoga, the other above Kingston, a distance of about seventy miles, remained too far apart to directly affect each other.

Burgoyne's Retreat

Unaware of what was happening below Albany, a German soldier in Burgoyne's camp declared, "At no time did the Jews await the coming of their Messiah with greater expectancy than we awaited the coming of General Clinton."[6] After his defeat at Bemis Heights, it became evident to Burgoyne that he would have to move in the opposite direction from Clinton's expedition. He decided he had to abandon the Great Redoubt and retreat northward to Schuyler's plantation during the night and morning of October 9. The movement was protected by his still active artillery and was not impeded by Gates. The retreat was led by Indians and Loyalists under Captains Fraser and McKay. The army covered the eight miles to the plantation, completing their evacuation of men and bateaux by the evening of the 9th. They left their hospital behind to the protection of the rebels and broke up their latest bateaux bridge across the Hudson, limiting their movements to the west side of the Hudson. Heavy rain slowed their efforts, but they were not pursued; the only rebels they saw were Berkshire County militiamen on the east side of the river.

The East Side Army

With Lincoln gone, there was no overall coordinator of the militias on the east side of the river, but the Berkshire County militia under Brigadier General John Fellows and the New York militia under Brigadier General Jacob Bayley were there. Fellows's 1,300 Berkshire County militiamen had already crossed the river to the Saratoga hamlet on October 8, taken the barracks that Burgoyne had occupied in mid-August, and begun to entrench themselves, unaware of the Battle of Bemis Heights or Burgoyne's decision to retreat. Communications were delayed. Gates's aide, James Wilkinson, intercepted Fellows's request for instructions from the now absent Lincoln, and evidently with Gates's approval, he pointed out to Fellows the danger of his position and suggested he retreat back to the east side of the river. Fellows took the advice, after burning the barracks in the hamlet.[7] Meanwhile, Burgoyne sent ahead a detachment under Lieutenant Colonel Nicholas

Southerland of the 47th Regiment, and it had no difficulty in moving though Saratoga, discovering Fellows's entrenchments and camp "entirely unguarded, that he marched round without being hailed." By the time Burgoyne's full army arrived, Fellows's militia was back across the river and began firing on his men from the heights. At Fish Kill on the south and to the west on the slopes above the village, Gates's army did not appear, so Burgoyne's army was certainly not surrounded.

Forty-three-year-old Brigadier General John Fellows was a wealthy, well-connected member of the western Massachusetts gentry from Sheffield.[8] In 1762 he had married Mary, the daughter of the influential John Ashley, Sr. Fellows and John Ashley, Jr., were officers in the local militia regiment, and he was given seniority over John because he was two years older. Early in 1773 Fellows had signed the Sheffield Resolves, which finally identified the town as supporting the rebellion in Boston but also brought the land issue to front by opposing the boundaries of New York's Livingston Manor. On July 1, 1777, in the midst of the alarm of Burgoyne's invasion, Fellows was purchasing a slave woman, named Ton, from another member of the Berkshire gentry. Like most militia officers, Fellows was too tied to local activities and his property to take on the professional responsibilities of serving as a Continental officer.

Fellows shared his east side duties with Brigadier General Jacob Bayley, a fanatical Congregationalist who had founded Newbury in 1764 on the northern Connecticut River, in what became Vermont. Unlike John Peters, who lived nearby and chose to be a Loyalist, Bayley chose to be a rebel, but under the jurisdiction of New York. He had served in the Seven Years' War, and in 1772 he had obtained at his own expense a confirmatory charter for Newbury from New York. As a result, in August 1776 New York appointed him as commander of the militia of Gloucester and Cumberland Counties, with the rank of brigadier general.[9] He had been invited to the New York Provincial Congress in 1775, although, like many others, the distance was too great for him to attend. He did correspond with them until mid-June 1777, when he confessed that it seemed impossible to establish New York's authority in his area.

The crisis produced by Burgoyne's capture of Ticonderoga induced Bayley to raise his regiment in Newbury, Ryegate, and Barnet and travel to the Saratoga region.[10] Ryegate had been settled by Presbyterian

Scots, who had often heard the preaching of the visiting reverend Thomas Clark of Salem, as they did not have a minister. On their way to Saratoga, Bayley's militia digressed to visit Clark in Salem, where he held a prayer meeting in their honor. While Bayley gravitated away from New York's authority, that did not mean he accepted the new Vermont government, which placed him on significant committees constantly and begged that he attend meetings, while he studiously avoided contact with them. The Vermont Council of Safety had no control over Bayley or his men. For example, on September 18 the council—of which Bayley was supposedly a member—wrote to Lincoln, asking him, if he thought proper, to request Bayley to return home and raise more militias for Gates's army. Bayley's major concern would be the crucial defense of northern Vermont, for which his participation at the Siege of Saratoga would make him highly recommended to Continental generals.

On the day of the Battle of Bemis Heights, Private Simeon Alexander was stationed on the east side at Schneider's Mills on the Batten Kill, near where it emptied into the Hudson. To Alexander's credit, after a week at home in Northfield, Massachusetts, word circulated that the rebel army was desperate, and he and fifty of his neighbors reenlisted.[11] His company's immediate commander was Brigadier General Bayley. After the battle, Gates ordered Bayley's men to move up the Hudson River to Fort Edward, but he then called them back to join Fellows's militia opposite Saratoga, where the heights commanded Burgoyne's entrenched army.[12] Alexander participated in the siege of Burgoyne's army at Saratoga, observing the artillery duel in which both sides suffered. Part of the reason the British would find no opposition to their probes toward Fort Edward may be that Bayley's militia was not there in force, as most of them were involved in the siege. Therefore, they were not a position to stop Burgoyne's retreat.

THE SIEGE OF SARATOGA

Burgoyne now faced a siege, a situation for which he seems to have been physiologically unprepared. At the beginning of the siege there were many opportunities for his army to retreat to Diamond Island and the reinforced Ticonderoga, which his officers urged him to take. But Burgoyne, claiming to be under orders to reach Albany, was fixed on the south and the possibility of Clinton's successful foray advancing the British to Albany—a dilemma that influenced his conduct during the siege.

In the confusion of the initial British retreat from the Great Redoubt to the Schuyler plantation, the rebels had captured most of the British supply bateaux. Sharing responsibility, Edward Jessup, Daniel McAlpin, and Hugh Munro led the bateaux men and Loyalists below the Saratoga plantation on the 9th, recapturing eighteen bateaux from the rebels. They brought them up Fish Kill with their ammunition and provisions intact, a bright spot in a campaign that was verging on disaster. From the neighboring heights on the opposite side of the river, the bateaux that were anchored in the river were frequently fired upon. Some of them were lost, and several men were killed and wounded defending those that remained. On October 11 the enemy continued their attacks upon the bateaux, and several were taken and retaken until "it was judged necessary to land the provisions and send them up the hill, as it was impossible to secure them by any other means: this was effected under a heavy fire and with the greatest difficulty."[13] With the supplies on land, the boatmen were released from their duties as bateau men and soldiers, and for the first time in the campaign, Burgoyne was without his supporting bateaux contingent.

The main British army had crossed the Fish Kill near Schuyler's house late on the 9th and taken post around Saratoga hamlet. Burgoyne's army dug in, the Germans having an especially difficult time because they were located on stony ground. From the next morning until a truce was called on the 15th, Burgoyne's exposed army in Saratoga, including the scattered houses where the sick and wounded lay, became the target of the rebels' east side batteries. The Germans answered with cannon and easily silenced the rebel six-pounders. As one German officer summed it up, the rebels "had inflicted little damage on us while they had suffered great losses from our cannon (as they later admitted)."[14] Still, the rebels would replace the guns. Lt. William Digby surmised that the rebels, by limiting themselves to an artillery barrage, meant to starve them out, the classic model of a siege.

Gates's army was as exhausted as the British, and since Gates assumed that Burgoyne was on his way to Fort Edward, the rested rebel army did not appear before the Fish Kill until late in the afternoon of the 10th. Gates's aide James Wilkinson described the scene,

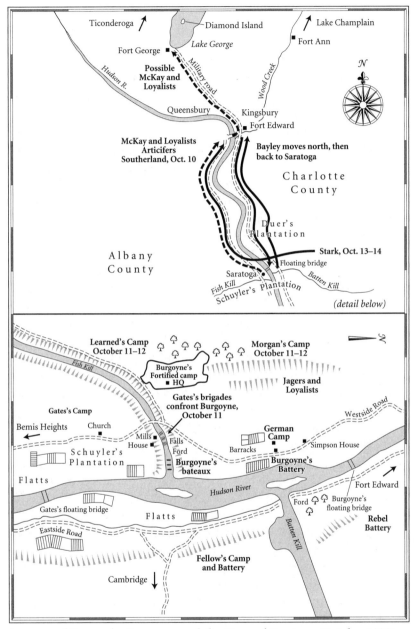

Avenues of Escape for Burgoyne and the Siege of Saratoga, October 1777

noting "the bateaux of the enemy at the mouth of the creek, with a fatigue party busily employed unloading and conveying their contents across the plain to the heights."[15] Gates felt that by this time Burgoyne's army was well north of Saratoga, leaving only a guard to delay him. Thus, on the morning of the next day, in a heavy fog that enveloped the steep Fish Kill gorge, he ordered Morgan's light infantry to begin an attack on the British defenses.

Learned's, Nixon's, and John Glover's brigades followed Morgan toward the top of the gorge, obscured by mist. Suddenly the fog lifted and Burgoyne's army, bristling with artillery, appeared, inflicting losses on the rebels.[16] Wilkinson claimed he saved the day and Gates's honor by convincing the brigade commanders to retreat before they became hopelessly exposed in the gorge. It was at this time that Schuyler's house and the barracks on the south side of the Fish Kill caught fire and were destroyed. Gates seemed less capable in leading an advance against Burgoyne than he had been in defending Bemis Heights. The British remained firmly entrenched on the north bank of the Fish Kill.

Riedesel's wife, Frederika, wrote of the siege from the house of Mr. Sampson of Albany. Built in 1770, the Sampson house did have a large cellar for protection, but it soon became overcrowded with wounded and families. She suffered with her children and then two other wives who were still with the army. Despite claims by the Germans that the guns had been wiped out, the rebel cannonade from the east side of the river seemed to target her dwelling because the rebels falsely assumed that it housed important British and German officers.[17]

Frederika Riedesel described how "the commissaries had forgotten to distribute provisions among the troops. There were cattle enough, but not one had been killed. More than thirty officers came to [her], who could endure hunger no longer. I had coffee and tea made for them, and divided among them all the provisions with which my carriage was constantly filled; for we had a cook who, although an arrant knave, . . . often in the night crossed small rivers, in order to steal from the country people, sheep, poultry and pigs."[18] On account of the cook's effort, a large amount of fresh meat was distributed among the officers, who up to this time had received only salted provisions, which had aggravated the condition of the wounded. The cook constantly supplied those in the house with water and made them soup from the fresh meat. Knowing her husband's views, she claimed, "the whole army is for a retreat, and my husband promised to make it possible, provided only that no time was lost."

Digby confirmed that as early as the morning of the 10th preparations were being made, "to push for the heights of Fort Edward." Burgoyne, however, was not convinced. He called an officers' council for the first time in the campaign to decide on what course of action to follow.[19] While a retreat toward Fort Edward was certainly among the proposals discussed, Burgoyne insisted that cutting away on the enemy's right and marching south to Albany was still a viable option.

To Riedesel and the German officers, the path to Lake George was open, and they urged the army not to tarry at Saratoga and take this route instead. Even before the action at Bemis Heights, Riedesel had hinted that retreat to Lake George should be considered a serious option, and he would propose it again at a meeting with Burgoyne on October 11.[20] Riedesel's proposal was enhanced by information from a scout, led by Lieutenant Colonel Southerland, made on October 10. His force had been ordered north to repair bridges, open the road on the west side of the river, and probe the enemy around Fort Edward. Southerland's scout included the engineer, Lieutenant Twiss; Southerland's regiment, the 47th; Captain Fraser's marksmen; Loyalists and Canadians under Captains McKay and Boucherville; and a detachment of artificers.

Southerland moved north and began to reconstruct the bateaux bridge across the Hudson at Fort Edward.[21] To him, the road to Lake George was open and the base on Diamond Island could provide transport and supplies for an army arriving at Fort George. Furthermore, the westerly direction toward Lake George took a retreating army further away from the possibility of harassment by the New England troops, who were south of them, concentrated around Saratoga. However, the next day Burgoyne suspended Southerland's work on the bridge and ordered him to return with most of his men to help defend Saratoga, because the enemy was now strongly posted on the heights above it.

Burgoyne was not focused on further retreat. He still believed that Clinton was advancing, and he wanted to be as close to Albany as possible to receive him.[22] At a second council meeting, the retreat toward Fort Edward was actually approved. Preparations for the army to retreat were made on October 12, but at eleven p.m. Burgoyne suspended them, for he could not bring himself to accept further retreat if Clinton was near Albany. His difficulties increased when his Canadian wagon drivers disappeared and made it through the rebel lines. He used the excuse that his troops lacked supplies for a retreat, but Riedesel noted that his Germans had them. It was argued that the army should have crossed the Hudson on Southerland's bridge to Fort Edward and then destroyed it, remaining as briefly as possible at Saratoga. With hindsight, the Germans later blamed Burgoyne for a series of mistakes that prevented the army from retreating, a situation that furthered hostility between the German and British commands.

Meanwhile, Captain McKay, whose corps was now largely made up of recruits from Peters's and the Jessup brothers' units, had been left by Southerland to guard the artificers still working on the bridge at Fort Edward. There they now skirmished with Bayley's militia, and what happened next depends on accounts that are contradictory.[23] McKay stated that he was outnumbered and cut off from Burgoyne, so he began a retreat toward Ticonderoga. The artificers told a different story: upon very slight enemy fire, McKay and his men disappeared, leaving them to escape as they could, without the possibility of their finishing their work. Notoriously independent, McKay and a hundred Loyalists and Canadians ran away, wisely toward Ticonderoga, which they reached without difficulty on October 17—the day Burgoyne surrendered. McKay defended his decision to leave for Ticonderoga, but he would eventually lose his command because of dereliction of duty in making this retreat.

At the last moment, on the evening of October 13, John Stark descended from the east to the north of Saratoga with a New Hampshire militia of perhaps 2,000, which had been raised anew by the New Hampshire legislature, inspired by visions of another Walloomsac victory. Gates knew of their existence on October 14, when he wrote to Bayley about their appearance. As expected, Stark operated completely independently of Gates, Fellows, and Bayley, leading his men across the Hudson, near the mouth of the Batten Kill, putting himself between Burgoyne at Saratoga and Fort Edward.[24] He erected an artillery battery on the road to Fort Edward near an outcropping afterward named Stark's Knob. However, there is no evidence that his presence prevented any Loyalists, Canadians, or bateaux men from escaping, and his arrival was much too late to affect Burgoyne's decisions.

Burgoyne's Surrender

By October 14, Burgoyne's indecision and his choice to dig in at Saratoga caused him to be surrounded by Gates's army, and his route of retreat was cut off. He knew he had to negotiate favorable terms, so that day he sent a flag of truce to Gates. As a formality, Gates first proposed unconditional surrender, which Burgoyne firmly rejected. The rebel commander was now prepared to be generous in negotiating with Burgoyne because he was aware that Vaughan was advancing toward Albany. A letter on the 7th from Governor Clinton had confirmed that the Highlands defenses were taken, and on the 15th word came that Vaughan's fleet was approaching Kingston, leading Gates to be even less demanding and accept terms that Burgoyne offered. Burgoyne proposed that the articles be called a convention, not a capitulation, and that his troops would not become prisoners, but instead be allowed to leave North America rapidly on condition that they would not see further service in the war.[25] And while the rebels noted that they could be used in other parts of the British Empire, freeing up troops for North America, Gates did give him everything he wanted, Boston being designated as the port from which the army would sail. Burgoyne still stalled on the 16th, claiming that Gates was moving his troops to meet Vaughan's invasion, but Gates would have none of it, and the next day Burgoyne signed the convention and surrendered. His British troops stacked and his Germans grounded their arms in a field overlooking the Hudson River, just north of the Fish Kill.

During the negotiations, Burgoyne claimed again that Loyalists had been persecuted after they surrendered at the Walloomsac, and he wanted to avoid this. Privately, he felt that the Loyalists and Canadians were equipped mentally and physically to escape through the countryside, while his regulars, he was afraid, would lose their order and discipline and thus had to be surrendered.[26] He may also have feared that the Loyalists would be treated as regulars because more than a hundred of them were now serving in the ranks of his regular regiments.

Loyalists had already been slipping through the rebel lines, but on the day before the surrender, Burgoyne officially gave permission for Jessup's, McAlpin's and Peters's units to leave the army and get through the surrounding rebel lines—officially because he feared the treatment they would receive.[27] Suspicious that he might be thought a deserter, Peters would not leave until he received written orders to go, and when these came from Phillips on October 14, Peters moved north by way of Lake George, arriving at Ticonderoga with thirty-five followers, including men from Simeon Covel's company. Others left just before the surrender ceremony, going up the Hudson River in the bateaux, and like previous Loyalists, Canadians, and Indians, had little difficulty at penetrating the rebel militias and arriving at Diamond Island. Technically, the rebels would consider the Loyalists to be exiles, whose persecuted and imprisoned families would be sent after them to Canada.

The Jessups ignored Burgoyne's permission and surrendered with the regulars under what came to be called the Convention of Saratoga. However, Burgoyne's terms had allowed for Canadians of all types to return to their homeland, separating them from the regulars, and this allowed the Jessups to follow other Loyalists to Canada unscathed. Immediately after the surrender, they were conducted "to the first British post on Lake George [Diamond Island]" and then joined their compatriots at Ticonderoga.[28] They were still under the Convention obligation of not serving against the rebels, but this obligation was soon put aside as it became clear that the Congress would not accept the Convention agreement, so it was no longer in effect. Actually, Burgoyne's efforts to keep his Convention Army clear of Loyalists and Canadians ensured their role in the continuing war.

In 1779, after Burgoyne had blamed the Loyalists for his defeat, Peters countered with a suggestion similar to that of Riedesel, that Burgoyne could have retreated. Peters's contention focused on Fort Miller, which he noted was a major crossroads between New York and New England.[29] He thought that Burgoyne should have waited there and reevaluated his situation in terms of meeting Clinton, before sending out the Walloomsac foray or proceeding with the army to Saratoga. Peters suggested that if Fort Miller had been held, Burgoyne could have easily returned to Ticonderoga, rather than capitulating. Burgoyne, however, was not about to follow a Loyalist's advice, for he had European concepts of honor and his own reputation as a professional soldier that guided how he would behave.

REGROUPING AT TICONDEROGA

Brown's raid at the Lake George landing in mid-September had left Ticonderoga with barely 700 men, causing Brigadier Henry Watson Powell to not only tighten his security but become paranoid of a surprise attack. However, the situation soon changed in Powell's favor. With most of Lincoln's men drawn to Saratoga, on September 27 Colonel

Barry St. Leger arrived at Ticonderoga with 500 men to fill the gap. In fact, the reinforcements made Burgoyne's possibilities of a retreat to Lake George stronger than ever.

St. Leger had completed the logistical feat of covering the vast distance from Lake Ontario, to the St. Lawrence, to Lake Champlain in a matter of weeks.[30] Ignoring his failure to capture Fort Stanwix in the Mohawk Valley, he brought several companies of the 34th Regiment and close to 300 of Sir John Johnson's Royal Regiment of New York, plus Captain Gilbert Tice's Rangers and Indians. In addition, Governor Guy Carleton—though he had earlier denied Burgoyne's request for help in garrisoning Ticonderoga—finally came through with troops, as it appeared that Burgoyne was in difficulty. He sent Brigadier Allan Maclean with his brigade of Highland Emigrants and companies of the 31st Regiment to further reinforce Ticonderoga. They arrived on September 30, although Maclean left in a few days to post himself at strategically important Chimney Point, across from Crown Point, so that following Carleton's orders he would have an independent command. As a result, Powell began to consult with Carleton as if he were his commanding officer, though he was still technically responsible to Burgoyne. Powell's garrison would be further strengthened by Canadians and Burgoyne's 796 Loyalists, who escaped or were conducted through the rebel lines. The question was whether Powell, as senior officer, would take advantage of his new opportunities.

Burgoyne was aware of the late September reinforcements at Ticonderoga and urged them to join his weakened army.[31] He wanted St. Leger to go to Diamond Island and from there make contact with him at Fort Edward. Powell, however, informed St. Leger that no bateaux existed at the Lake George landing or horses to carry supplies there. This was surprising in that LaChute portage was specifically designed to reinforce the landing, and it appeared that bateaux and supplies were being held in front of the fort for travel to the north. Later, Powell stipulated that St. Leger could only go to Burgoyne if he had a direct order from him. Powell was stalling, for he wanted St. Leger to stay and strengthen the Ticonderoga garrison, rather than be risked in making contact with Burgoyne. Finally, on September 30 Powell ended his posturing and urged St. Leger to join Burgoyne. It was seen at last that contact would provide exact intelligence of Burgoyne's plight and possibly facilitate preparations for his further retreat.

To this end, Sir John Johnson had sent a proposal to Burgoyne with Kingsbury Loyalist Captain John Jones suggesting the King's Royal Regiment of New York join his army.[32] On account of the supposed lack of bateaux, Sir John's men would not navigate Lake George but rather would march overland. Jones returned with the news that Burgoyne had accepted the offer, but Sir John still needed Indians to guide him over the mountains, and evidently Tice's unit from the Mohawk Valley was unable to help. At Burgoyne's Saratoga defenses, it was still rumored on October 9 that St. Leger was coming with nine hundred reinforcements. In fact, no further action on the part of St. Leger or Johnson took place. The efforts originating at Ticonderoga to make contact with Burgoyne in force never materialized, and Burgoyne did not treat them with the same interest as reports of Clinton's and Vaughan's progress.

By October 16, intelligence that Burgoyne was going to surrender began to seep through to Powell at Ticonderoga. He now wrote to Carleton, hoping that he would not want to defend the post and asking him for orders to evacuate it.[33] On October 17 McKay arrived with his Loyalist refugees from Fort Edward. Some Loyalists, like Lieutenant Henry Simmons, had already left Ticonderoga on October 17, when news of Burgoyne's defeat began to surface. He and his men spent three weeks walking to Montreal. Finally, on October 20, Captain Alexander Fraser appeared at Ticonderoga with a signed copy of the Articles of Convention, definite news of Burgoyne's surrender. At Ticonderoga the Loyalists became preoccupied with recruiting and reorganization. Johnson found Burgoyne's Loyalists to be ideal recruits for the King's Royal Regiment of New York. John Munro was the prize of his recruiting effort because he already had a captain's commission in Maclean's regiment. Richard Duncan and Samuel Anderson also made their way to Ticonderoga with Burgoyne's escaping Loyalists to fulfill an earlier pledge as captains in Johnson's regiment.

At Chimney Point Maclean was Carleton's man, and he kept the Canadian governor informed of the state of affairs at Ticonderoga. Powell tried to lure Maclean to Ticonderoga, noting that if he were to hold it, he would need every soldier he could get.[34] Maclean did send men to help bring off stores and did try to encourage Powell to be more forceful in his role as overall commander, but he was not enticed.

For weeks Powell had been ready to abandon Ticonderoga. Maclean reported to Carleton on November 1 that Powell was overprotective because no more than two hundred rebels were within striking distance of Ticonderoga. Powell had yet to receive an answer to his letters from Carleton.[35] He hoped that Carleton would recommend a return to Canada, just as he had done at Crown Point late in 1776, rather than face a winter at Ticonderoga. However, when Powell finally heard from Carleton, he was given no direct orders but had the decision put firmly on his shoulders.

This was enough for Powell, who lost no time in planning the evacuation of Ticonderoga, including Diamond Island, Crown Point, and Chimney Point. On November 1 he had at Ticonderoga at least 1,642 men, and there were more at Chimney Point, other dependencies, and on patrol. Thus perhaps 2,000 men, the majority Loyalists, were put to work destroying the fortifications that the rebels had worked so diligently to build. To his credit, Powell did bring off most of the ample stores and livestock held at Ticonderoga. [36]

After a week of preparation, at which Powell seemed far more meticulous than he had been in supporting Burgoyne, on November 8 he abandoned Ticonderoga and Mount Independence and headed for St. Johns by water and land. The withdrawal was marred by an ambush conducted by Captain Ebenezer Allen of Herrick's Rangers at the Bouquet River. Fifty New York Loyalists, mainly McAlpin's men, who were driving a cattle herd toward Canada, were captured. While pleased with their booty, the rangers did fail to get a money chest that the Loyalists were said to be carrying.[37] Although some of these New York Loyalists claimed to be protected under the Convention, Gates sent them as prisoners to Albany, evidently assuming they had broken their parole.

Most authorities portray Powell's retreating army as demoralized, and doubtless at the moment they were.[38] But the remains of Burgoyne's and St. Leger's armies had a definite future, which would bring them only glory. Powell's diverse army would be the nucleus of a striking force that would defend Canada for the next five years. While they were leaving now, many of these men would soon return to Lakes Champlain and George. Neither Burgoyne nor most of his regulars were to play a further role in the region.

THE QUICK DISPERSAL OF GATES'S ARMY

It has been mentioned that Gates sent his all-too-willing militia units home the day after the surrender. What is less known is that the Continental Army left Saratoga as well, moving as rapidly as possible to the defense of threatened Albany and the Hudson Highlands.[39] From here even the Continental brigades of Poor and Learned, as well as Morgan's crucial riflemen, were sent south at the request of Washington to defend Philadelphia. By November 7, the day before Powell's evacuation, Gates in Albany had essentially only Nixon's brigade. Congress in York, Pennsylvania, had received confirmation of his victory the week before and sent congratulations, but it also ordered him to remain in command at Albany and drive the enemy from the northern posts. Clearly this was unrealistic, considering Gates's nonexistent resources, and Gates himself left Albany to take post with Israel Putnam at the endangered Hudson Highlands.

By early January 1778 Gates had gone all the way to York to defend his repudiated Convention and to take the new post of chairman of the Board of War, which Congress had created. It was at this time that Washington, like Schuyler, became suspicious of Gates's maneuvering in Congress. Washington had been ignored by Gates in sending news of his victory and been left to surmise it through rumor, well after Congress received the official confirmation. Because of these rivalries, the Northern Department was in no condition to threaten Powell had he remained at Ticonderoga.

The Battles of Saratoga brought no glory to the British arms or Lord North's government because Burgoyne's modest army was never able to cooperate with other British armies. As Burgoyne found the rebel opposition firmly entrenched on the upper Hudson, his success became dependent upon Sir Henry Clinton's advance up the Hudson, an endeavor over which General Howe had the final say. Clearly, there was a breakdown in cooperation at the highest levels of the British command.

Overwhelming numbers of New England militia continued to give Gates the advantage as Burgoyne retreated and dug in for the siege of Saratoga. While British and German troops fought doggedly, Burgoyne ultimately was more concerned for his reputation than the welfare of his men. The week-long Siege of Saratoga was his own doing, as gradually the rebels were able to cut off his avenues of escape. He would not consider retreating to Ticonderoga, even though it had been reinforced and remained an option until the very end.

By the time of the battles of Saratoga, Burgoyne's Loyalists numbered at least eight hundred, ten times their original count and far more than his Indians and Canadians combined. Loyalists fought well in both Saratoga battles, and as the siege of Saratoga opened, they achieved a singular victory in recapturing supply bateaux. Burgoyne's concern for his Loyalists' safety as he contemplated surrender had far greater implications than he realized, for most of his Loyalist corps ended up safely in Canada. Over half of Powell's army that retreated from Ticonderoga consisted of Loyalists who would serve as the nucleus for future invasions and continuation of the civil war.

PART V

AFTER SARATOGA

13

Intensifying Civil Conflict

The most recent accounts of the Saratoga Campaign and the interpretation at the Saratoga National Historic Park, which oversees the battlefields today, emphasize the Battles of Saratoga as the turning point of the War of Independence, the victory that the French respected enough to give recognition to and form an alliance with Congress.[1] Thus, winning the war was a result of a combination of French military aid, rebel leadership, and the will of King George III and the British ministry to continue the conflict.

Logistics expert Arthur Boland claims that after the Saratoga Campaign "the Americans did not again attempt to draw Canada in the Revolution, and after 1777 the British mounted no further serious operations from that base."[2] Following this interpretation, most accounts of the war in the Hudson-Champlain region finish their narrative with a quick chapter on the war from the defeat of Burgoyne until the end, the surrender of Cornwallis in October 1781. It is usually mentioned that the focus of the overall war shifted to the south. Admittedly, Loyalist and Indian raids made life in the Hudson-Champlain borderland difficult, but, the claim is made, the depredations were deceitful and of little consequence in determining the region's future. Historians who believe this wish to skip the rest of the war and get on to the development of the new nation in the late 1780s. This is not the perspective found here.

To look at what came after Burgoyne's defeat, the persistence of five conditions should be recognized. First, the region continued to be invaded from Canada by British forces every year after Burgoyne's defeat. There was no decline of the British initiatives, the largest and most successful invasions coming in 1780 and 1781. In contrast, the rebels were never able to mount another invasion of Canada, although this was often contemplated by Congress. Second, a stream of emigration to Canada was created by the expulsion of Loyalists, including Indians. It consisted not just of men but entire families, who would permanently settle as far west as Lake Ontario. Some came of their own accord, especially when shepherded by British invasion forces, but most were forced out by rebel policies of detection and confiscation of their property.

Third, the British held control of an extensive portion of the Hudson-Champlain region. Dominance of Lake Champlain by the Royal Navy was a given, offering British commanders a perfect avenue of access into the rebel borderlands. Ticonderoga and Lake George were occupied by the British at will, and the 1780 invasion penetrated farther than Burgoyne—to Saratoga, Ballston Spa, and even Salem. Thus the region was not lost to the British Empire after Burgoyne's capitulation; instead, it was an area that the rebels could not control. Fourth, the British were able to detach Vermont's governing leaders from the rebel cause by negotiating a truce with them from 1780, which effectively made them neutrals, lured by opportunities of trade with Canada.

Finally, the rebels proved to be divided on the defense of the borderland to the point that Vermont seized territory from New York and New Hampshire, claiming that it was better able to defend that territory. Vermont's government would reap a whirlwind of hostility from Congress on its policies that would prevent recognition of it as a state until 1791—a decade beyond the war. The era of the new nation was not peaceful, as regional discord over land, politics, and ethnicity continued as it had before the war. This is the perspective that will be unveiled here.

After Burgoyne's surrender, conditions around Saratoga did not improve for the rebels. John Neilson's home had been occupied by rebel officers and his fields destroyed, and while he filed a damage claim with the Albany Committee in May 1778, he never received compensation. Instead, the civil war renewed with intensity as the countryside remained, according to Neilson's son Charles, "over-run with spies and traitors. Robberies were frequent, and the inhabitants . . . carried prisoners to Canada."[3] John provided his foremost military service to Congress three years after the Battles of Saratoga, when Sir John Johnson in April and May of 1780 raided Johnstown and carried off the families of Johnson's supporters. He was in a party ordered by Governor George Clinton to scout toward Schroon Lake to intercept Johnson's force, though they found no trace of them. Governor Clinton had made it a point of honor that New York would not be invaded again or fail to retaliate as it had in the previous years. Clinton led Continentals and militia in pursuit of Johnson all the way to Ticonderoga and Crown Point, but he would be frustrated in his attempt to catch the Loyalist force. In the renewed civil war it was simply impossible for the Neilson family to defend their homes.

Triumph of the British in the Continuing Civil War

One reason the British cause in Canada was reinvigorated after Burgoyne's surrender was that a new Canadian governor appeared, who provided superb leadership. Frederick Haldimand, the governor designate, arrived in Quebec from England in June 1778.[4] He received Guy Carleton's parting blessing and began a term that would cover the next eight years. Carleton would follow Burgoyne to England, both of them licking the wounds caused by partisan politics. Haldimand was a new breed of British commander, reflecting a shift in policy as a result of Burgoyne's defeat. He was first and foremost a professional soldier who avoided the political intrigue that fascinated Burgoyne and victimized Carleton. He would carry on a war that used fewer resources but was more effective than either Burgoyne's or Carleton's invasions. Ultimately, he would lead Canada through the last years of the war and open new areas for settlement by Loyalists from the Hudson-Champlain region and other British strongholds.

Born in Yverdon, Switzerland, in 1718, as a young man Haldimand left home to serve as commandant of the Swiss guards in the Dutch army during the War of the Austrian Succession. He then served in the British army in North America during the Seven Years' War. Along with other Swiss officers, Haldimand had come to the British colonies in 1756 to form the Royal Americans, a regiment recruited in the colonies.[5] He led his regiment with Abercromby at Ticonderoga, at Fort Edward, at Oswego, and in Amherst's conquest of Montreal. When hostilities ceased, he gained Canadian administrative experience as acting military governor of Trois-Rivières. His knowledge of French made a difference with the habitants, and among other projects he promoted the St. Maurice Iron Works. As a Swiss, he was discriminated against by British authorities in London who saw foreigners in the army as untrustworthy; this was offset by the fact that, like Burgoyne, he was popular with officers and men in the field. The authorities sent him to the most difficult posts, choosing him to administer the distant Floridas. He honestly felt the army should abandon Florida and leave it to the navy, but he responded dutifully, and in 1772 he was rewarded by being named colonel of the Royal Americans and a major general.

The North American commander, Thomas Gage, who had known Haldimand in Canada, then called him to be acting commander in strategically crucial New York City. There he handled army relations with the city's rebellious civilians coolly, preventing violence such as happened in Boston and gaining the praise of Lord North. On this basis, in 1775 Gage called him to Boston to help with his confrontational situation. However, Haldimand was kept out of the decision-making process and did not even know about Gage's orders for the march to Lexington and Concord. And when Haldimand was called back to England to be honored for his service, in reality it was because the authorities felt that, as a foreigner, he was unsuitable to lead military forces in a North American civil war. However, when Carleton resigned in spring 1777 because Burgoyne had been given command of the invasion, Haldimand was at the center of power in London, and Germain quickly named him as Carleton's replacement. He was an obvious choice, as he was already familiar with Canada's geography, cultural diversity, and governmental organization. He should have been Burgoyne's superior in Canada, but navigational delays in England prevented him from arriving until 1778.

According to instructions from Lord North's ministry to Haldimand, his principal duty was to keep Canada within the British fold, preventing an invasion from the south and suppressing internal discord.[6] Using the Quebec Act, the example of Carleton's administration, and a respect for French-Canadian culture, he was able to do this admirably. He would ignore the defenses of Quebec City, instead focusing his effort to the west, on the Champlain-Hudson region and the Great Lakes. He found the best way of preventing invasion from the south was to carry the war to the rebels, putting them on the defensive and preventing them from gathering an invasion force.

Haldimand saw what Schuyler and Washington feared, that if he could maintain British control over Lake Champlain he would be able to easily penetrate the borderland. From 1778 to 1784, the British succeeded in controlling the lake by their superior naval power and the effective use of their limited army. Soon after his arrival, Haldimand had the fortifications and barracks improved at the Isle aux Noix and St. Johns to serve as bases for penetration throughout Lake Champlain.[7] To the north, where the Richelieu River met the St. Lawrence at Sorel, he developed an important supply base, avoiding the need to go to Montreal. He introduced the permanent use of two patrol vessels that traveled to Crown Point and provided assistance to Loyalists. He wisely decided not to use his limited resources to permanently restore and garrison the posts at Ticonderoga and Crown Point, for his control of Lake Champlain allowed him to use them as temporary bases when he wanted.

Because Haldimand's regular army was smaller than Carleton's or Burgoyne's invasion forces, he had to depend more on Loyalists and Indians. In 1778 he estimated that he had only 2,500 British and German regulars and about 3,400 Loyalist or Canadian troops to oppose a rebel invasion of Canada.[8] At least 900 of these were stationed in the Great Lakes posts, while most of his British and German regulars were the remains of Burgoyne's and St. Leger's armies that had retreated to Canada when Powell abandoned Ticonderoga. Haldimand's modest armies of rapidly advancing and retreating parties of Loyalists, Indians, and regulars were meant not only to invade the Champlain-Hudson Valley but to directly continue the civil conflict. He authorized a policy toward the south that would force the rebels to abandon their farms and prevent rebel farmers from supporting a Canadian invasion or their own defense. His raiders seemed even to have perfected the discrimination of friend from foe. It was observed after one of his raids in the Mohawk Valley that the path of a Loyalist force was clear because the Loyalist farms had been left untouched while those of the rebels were burned out. Thus, Haldimand's strategy was a return to the tactics of Canadians before and during the Seven Years' War, their petite guerre, which put emphasis on continual and diverse raiding to destroy the logistical ability of the enemy to make war.

To form these mixed bands, Haldimand needed the additional manpower that Loyalists provided. The early ambivalent British policy toward Loyalists had prevented their organization for permanent military service. Burgoyne had only established his Loyalist corps for the duration of his campaign, and he preferred that Loyalists perform manual labor and deliver supplies rather than actually serve in combat. Carleton also feared that using them would intensify hostilities that would make reconciliation impossible. With Haldimand, Loyalists were no longer an afterthought, for he commissioned them as permanent officers to carry out expeditions against rebel posts and communities. As he became more dependent on Loyalists, he took an interest in their organization and training in the irregular tactics adopted to fight the rebels.[9]

Haldimand now had the definite support of Lord North's ministry in bringing Loyalists from the periphery to the center of his defenses. In London in 1778, the ministry had a new approach to winning the war by shifting the burden from regulars to Loyalists in the belief that they were the key to winning the hearts and minds of the people.[10] The new emphasis was also helped by the fact that British resources were strained now that France had entered the war. It is true that the ministry's emphasis covered up a range of opinion among British military leaders as to how to use Loyalists. Some favored a strictly military role of spreading destruction and terror to the rebels, while others felt that that the protectionist and neutral base of the population should be expanded through integration with the Loyalists, using persuasion rather than force. Burgoyne had wrestled with these choices during his campaign.

Haldimand ignored the two poles and came up with his own policy, which took something from each. His mixed forces, with regular officers in command, prevented Loyalists and Indians from indulging in the worst activities of terrorism.[11] In Vermont, from late in 1780, his expeditions minimalized destruction and became increasingly benevolent as he negotiated for Vermont's return to the British Empire. At the same time, Haldimand's brilliant, irregular tactics gave the region's populace the impression that they were never safe from the threat of destruction by his raiders, who could choose numerous targets for an invasion.

Haldimand welcomed Loyalist families to Canada, rather than trying to pacify the populations of New York and Vermont as Burgoyne had. At first, most Loyalist fathers and sons had left their families behind to maintain the farm, hoping that they would be able to return with a British rescue force, but also exposing their loved ones to rebel harassment. After Burgoyne's surrender, with their menfolk in retreat and faced by the growing persecution of rebel authorities, many families did their best to go to Canada or British-held New York City. The heavy male makeup of the first wave of migrants after the surrender was to an extent a matter of rebel policy. They tried to draft all boys over twelve into the militia, making it a priority among Loyalists that such teenagers be sent to Canada to avoid the draft.[12] There, boys younger than fifteen years and old men received a measure of security by being attached to Loyalist units with their kin, even though they were not capable of being full-fledged soldiers. Thus male kinship was a characteristic of the makeup of Loyalist corps. Recruiting also came to involve returning to one's home to protect, enlist, or bring off one's sons and ultimately one's family. From 1778 on Haldimand gradually took full responsibility for Loyalist refugees, establishing refugee centers, the most noted being Machiche and Sorel. He would welcome refugees and produce 10,360 daily meals for the refugee families.

While no admirer of their savage excesses, Haldimand knew from his previous experience in Canada that Native Americans were necessary for the British army to carry on its effort against the rebels. He understood the necessity of the expense of continual councils and the giving of presents to keep them supportive and counteract rebel influence.[13] He also ended the rivalry between the Indian Affairs and Quebec Departments, fostering cooperation that allowed for a unified policy toward Indians. Remembering Burgoyne's problem, Haldimand placed restrictions on them, forbidding the practice of scalping when they participated in a raid and trying to avoid having them attack without the presence of a British or Loyalist officer. At this he was never completely successful, but his own officers did claim that their Indian allies were much better behaved than previously. Ultimately Haldimand hoped that, like the Loyalists, his Indian refugees would settle in Canada and cultivate the land. Administratively, in 1782 he replaced indolent Guy Johnson with Sir William's more competent son, Sir John Johnson. While the British government ignored Indians at the peace table in Paris, Haldimand attempted to make up for the loss of the Six Nations' lands in New York by offering Canadian land grants and helping them to resettle. To this end, he would provide them with hoes and corn seed and had grist- and sawmills built near their new Canadian home villages.

STATE OF THE REBELS

While Haldimand was putting a new face on the British forces in Canada, in the region the rebel military situation was far from promising. Leadership in the Northern Department was definitely lacking. Gates, the conqueror of Burgoyne, had left the Northern Department quickly to join Congress in Pennsylvania as president of its newly created War Board. From there he used Congress as his power base to snipe at Washington. Schuyler was still the obvious choice for commander of the Northern Department, but he remained in limbo while Congress carried out a review of his and St. Clair's conduct during the fall of Ticonderoga.[14] By the end of 1778, a review board on the conduct of the army during Burgoyne's invasion, chaired by Benjamin Lincoln, had exonerated both Schuyler and St. Clair with honor. Washington then asked Schuyler to again assume command of the Northern Department—but Schuyler was fed up. He had resigned his commission as Major General only a few days before, and in the succeeding months he even refused to take the seat he had been elected to in Congress. While he remained the most knowledgeable person about Canada and the Saratoga region, officially he would only continue to serve as an Indian commissioner, dealing with the Oneidas and Tuscaroras. A guard, established in June 1777 from periodic drafts of the 1st New York Continental Regiment, continued to protect him at his Albany and Saratoga homes. This was now the extent of Schuyler's military command.

Late in 1777, while in Pennsylvania, Horatio Gates had hatched his own plan for an invasion of Canada. It was an about-face, since Gates had made no effort to move against or interfere with Powell's evacuation of Ticonderoga. Without consulting Congress, Washington, or Governor Chittenden in Vermont, Gates depended upon Continental colonel Moses Hazen and former Continental colonel Timothy Bedel, now of the New Hampshire militia, to put together an invasion force in northern Vermont, coordinating with support from the Abenakis at Odanak Mission. Bedel was the New Hampshire colonel who had been expelled from the Continental Army for his incompetence during its retreat from Canada in 1776. Hazen's influence was dependent upon his supposed ability to raise French Canadian volunteers.

The expedition never got off the ground. Gates found himself isolated, and in April 1778 he was removed from the War Board and exiled to Fishkill on the lower Hudson to serve as commander of the Northern Department and oversee Stark's similar position in Albany. It was at this time that Gates began to lose touch with reality. He wrote to Stark that the failure of his and Congress's initiatives against Canada meant nothing, for "the period is not far distant when [Canada] must join the great confederation, without any force being raised to effect it; or if any, such only as is merely necessary to take possession." [15] No wonder Gates was soon dispatched by Congress to the south, where in August 1780 his army was crushed at Camden by General Charles Lord Cornwallis. After this defeat, Congress did not even allow him the courtesy of a hearing to defend himself, and he never again held a command in the Continental Army. Such was the fate of a general who was too involved in fickle politics.

Congress did pursue its own plans to conquer Canada. Marie Joseph, Marquis de Lafayette, appeared briefly in Albany in February 1778 to lead the congressionally sponsored invasion of Canada, but he was embarrassed to find no army or supplies ready for such a feat. [16] Resources were inadequate for the minimum of 5,000 troops necessary to bring off an invasion. Units that were to have been raised by the Vermont Committee of War, like Herrick's reconstituted rangers, were delayed in recruiting. New York was in no position to provide supplies for an army, since it had to feed its own population. The remaining inhabitants of the state petitioned the new state government for relief because of the damage of 1777. Two thousand bushels of grain were provided, chiefly taken from Loyalist lands, a special burden placed upon them that was to increase during 1778.

Previous to Lafayette, Congress had also offered John Stark the command of the secret Canadian expedition. From Livingston Manor where Stark was in exile, James Duane made the congressional offer, which appears to have included a commission of brigadier general in the Continental Army. [17] In early January Stark replied by letter affirmatively, although he did not go to Albany. Late in January 1778, Gates informed Stark that Congress had replaced him with the higher ranking Lafayette, and Gates asked that Stark provide "officer-like assistance" for Lafayette. When the expedition failed to materialize, Stark was placated with command of the Northern Department at Albany, a position in which he lasted about seven months. He disbanded the New Hampshire militia he had raised for the invasion of Canada, and came alone to Albany—to Congress's disappointment. He found the commissaries at Albany and Bennington to be cesspools of corruption. As to Bedel's Continental regiment, in which Gates had put so much hope, he reported that "no man knew where it was" because as soon as it was mustered, the whole immediately retired to their homes and yet claimed Continental "wages and provisions." Bedel's regiment was disbanded by November 30, 1779. Furthermore, it was on Stark's watch that Christopher Carleton led a force of British regulars and Indians down Lake Champlain to Ticonderoga, destroying farms and hamlets on either side of the lake and returning unscathed. Somehow, throughout these trials and tribulations Stark did not revert to his old ways, remaining obedient to Gates, Washington, and even Schuyler, with whom he worked on Indian affairs. Without the patience of a Schuyler or Gates in organizing, Stark was much relieved to leave Albany in November.

The presence and influence of Gates, Lafayette, and Stark in the region was the result of Congress and its Board of War. Washington was not directly consulted until June 1778, and anyway in Washington's mind Schuyler remained the key figure in the defense of the region. In fact, there would be no immediate replacement for Stark, as Washington and even Congress tried to encourage Schuyler to fill the Northern Department position. The landlord had quickly rebuilt his burned Saratoga plantation house and barracks on a site farther from the Hudson River.[18] Though smaller than the previous structure, the new house had fresh brick nogging in the walls. Schuyler used it not only as a business hub but as an intelligence center, aimed at gathering information on what was going on in Canada. Evidently, he financed his intelligence network himself. Even though he had resigned from the Continental Army at the end of 1778, Schuyler continued to provide Washington and other generals with information.

Only Washington and Schuyler understood that the key to the defense of the borderland was to find a way to cope with the superior British fleet at St. Johns. In November 1778 Washington wrote to Schuyler, "I am clear also that neither force nor stratagem can give us a well grounded hope of a decisive superiority in naval strength upon Lake Champlain, where the enemy are, at present, so powerful."[19] Schuyler proposed building two large ships on Lake Champlain, the beginning of an effort to wrest control of the lake from the British, but Washington pointed out that it could never be done in secrecy and might even be threatened by the superior enemy. While Washington ordered that the sawmills at Forts Ann and Edward prepare plank for bateaux and larger vessels, he saw "mastery of Lake Champlain" as an impossibility and instead hoped to use these materials at Oswego to build ships to challenge the British on Lake Ontario. By the end of 1778, Haldimand's control of Lake Champlain remained secure, making a rebel invasion of Canada unthinkable.

With Schuyler holding no Continental position, Governor George Clinton held the chief responsibility for New York's defense from 1779 to 1781, as he was both a brigadier general of New York militia and of the Continental Army.[20] He was beholden to soldiers because they had voted for him in the contest for governor and determined to keep the militia in the field and prevent the loss of territory to the British. His resources, however, were limited. The British held New York City and controlled the borderlands, so that, in fact, rebel New York was limited to the central Hudson Valley. Demands from other fronts, furthermore, put a strain on Clinton's ability to defend New York. Washington, for example, had just finished a starving winter in 1778 at Valley Forge, and he asked Clinton for food to feed his beleaguered Continental Army. To this end a bill was passed in the New York State Assembly that included the establishment and maintenance of several storehouses to supply the Continental Army. Clinton would coax his legislature to pass tax laws that were more equitable than before and in this way obtain more revenue for the war. It was in his ability to put New York on a wartime footing, rather than his command of troops, that he would excel.

THE SLOW RECOVERY FROM BURGOYNE'S CAMPAIGN

The entire region had suffered damage, and not all of it had been done by the British. Even the victorious Continental Army was called to account for vandalism and looting. On April 4, 1778, the Albany Committee met and resolved, "Whereas many depredations have been committed in this city and county by the troops under command [of] General Gates, and whereas many fences and other effects have been destroyed in and about thus city by said troops. . . . That a committee be appointed to draw up a slate, of the depredations committed . . . and the same be transmitted to . . . the Governor."[21] In addition, there were refugee problems caused by the abandonment of farms in the face of Burgoyne's invasion. A week after the depredations list was drawn up, the Committee reported that nine Charlotte County families, altogether twenty-seven inhabitants, were in the city and "had requested the aid and assistance of this board to forward them in their journey." They were given $100 and flour to support their return to Charlotte County.

Loyalists remained a problem, even without the presence of Burgoyne's army. Still active was Reverend Samuel Swertfeger, the Lutheran pastor of the Loyalist congregation in Brunswick, Rensselaerswyck. While some in the congregation had fought at the Walloomsac and were now in Peters's corps in Canada, Swertfeger continued to conspire in the Albany area. He had the itinerant duty of preaching to Lutherans in Albany and as far away as Schenectady. He especially ministered to Lutherans in Rensselaerswyck's rugged Helderberg Mountains, to the southwest of Albany. In 1778 and 1780 he was questioned and then accused by the rebels of trying to "inculcate doctrines tending to disaffect the minds of well disposed persons" in the Heldebergs.[22] He was asked not to travel unless he was fulfilling his preaching duties and required to post a bail of £100. Needless to say, he was spreading Loyalism and opposition to the rebel Van Rensselaer landlords. It is worth keeping in mind that when the Anti-Rent War began in the 1820s, it was the Helderbergs and Brunswick that would be epicenters for the movement.

In the far northeast of Albany County, Cambridge was now split three ways between moderate and vindictive rebels, as well as Loyalists. Baum's expedition had divided the community, as many had taken a loyalty oath to the king and joined the Queen's Loyal Rangers. After Burgoyne's surrender, Cambridge rebels split into two parties, with diverging views on how to treat Cambridge's Loyalists: one group sought to physically abuse them by public whippings, the other, while not excusing the infamy of their actions, sought to rehabilitate them and bring them back into the community.[23]

The abusive group was led by Edmund Wells, Jr., and James Cowen, active members of town government, although not leaders of the militia. Wells came from the only patentee family that settled in

Cambridge in 1773.[24] A twenty-two-year-old graduate of Yale in 1768, he was elected town clerk and treasurer in 1777 and the next year replaced John Younglove as supervisor of the town. James Cowen had been one of the original thirty settlers who came to Cambridge from 1761 to 1763. At a town meeting held at his house in 1777, he was elected poor master. The equally illustrious rehabilitators were represented by the long-serving town supervisor, major of the Albany County militia, and commissioner of sequestration, John Younglove, and wealthy Phineas Whiteside. Both were also members of the Albany County Committee of Correspondence.

During the winter in Cambridge, when imprisoned Loyalists were released from jail, they were forced to run a gauntlet in which Wells's and Cowen's followers beat them. In January 1778 Younglove called for a new election of Cambridge's Committee of Correspondence in the hope of expelling the vindictive hotheads and replacing them with leaders who were more humane and respected forgiveness. Whiteside reported to the Albany Committee of Correspondence that Wells and Cowen "had flogged and otherwise ill treated . . . inhabitants of the [Cambridge] district to correct them from being Tories and Protection Men."[25] The Albany Committee responded immediately, declaring "that inflicting . . . any corporal punishment or depriving any of the subjects of this state of their property without the proper authority is an infringement of privileges of the people . . . in direct violation of all law and justice," vindicating the viewpoint of Younglove and Whiteside.

Younglove and Whiteside were also generous to Loyalists who had already left, including community leaders like Simeon Covel, the first elected supervisor of Cambridge, at whose house the district meetings had been held in 1774 and 1775. Serving in the Queen's Loyal Rangers, he had gone to Ticonderoga and Canada after Burgoyne surrendered but had left his three children in Cambridge.[26] In October 1778, Younglove gave permission for the removal to British territory of Covel's three children, along with Elizabeth and Jane Hogle, respectively the wives of John and Francis Hogle. Younglove's kindness was appreciated, and he was reelected supervisor in 1779, although Wells and Cowen continued to be active in town affairs. Still, with divisions like this, post-Burgoyne Cambridge was in no condition to be a rebel bulwark.

One way of avoiding the factionalism that Cambridge experienced was to peacefully heal the discord within a community. The

Waite's Corners church, south of Cambridge, had been split by the appearance of Baum's expedition against Bennington, which had led half of its members to declare themselves Loyalists. In 1778 Elder William Waite began the process of healing the Baptist Church through revivals.[27] Informal prayer meetings that could last for several weeks were held, allowing groups of the faithful to rededicate themselves to Christ. By November he was willing to comment, "the Lord was pleased to revive his work among us." By February 1779 the church was reorganized, and four months later Waite was called by the elders to be their pastor—a position he would hold for the next fourteen years. The members of this community were once again united and stable, convinced that it was dangerous to participate in politics.

Vermont's Condition

Vermont was no better off. Governor Thomas Chittenden wrote that Burgoyne's campaign had already had its effect in 1777 because "the inhabitants of Vermont were prevented from planting winter grain . . . the flax harvest was neglected as well. Their sheep were also lost to marauding British troops, [so that] their backs & their bellies have become Co Sufferers."[28] Herrick's Rangers had already been discharged in November 1777 because the Vermont Council of Safety did not have the funds to maintain them over the winter. On May 12, 1778, Ethan Allen focused on the problem of the disaffected: "The [Loyalists] & friends of [Loyalists] give us . . . trouble yet; they contribute to the anarchy which now reigns among us, and I am of the opinion that we shall never be at peace, while one of them is suffered to remain in the country." Chittenden found this situation continuing into March 1779, so that northern Vermont was empty.

After Burgoyne surrendered, the rebels were unable to sustain further military efforts not only against Canada but to reoccupy Ticonderoga and other abandoned posts. The Saratoga Campaign had devastated the region, and dealing with Loyalists remained a problem. Meanwhile, vigorous Frederick Haldimand replaced Guy Carleton as Governor of Canada. Haldimand was a reformer who reintroduced the old Canadian policy of petite guerre, using mixed forces of Loyalists, Indians, and regulars, which were carefully coordinated to strike multiple targets at the same time. Congress wanted to continue the momentum of the Saratoga victory and thus invade Canada, but an array of generals from Gates to Lafayette to Stark was involved with invasion plans that never got off the ground. Although he resigned his position as major general in the Continental Army, Philip Schuyler continued to be involved in regional affairs, still effective because of his friendship with Washington. Governor George Clinton became the leader of New York's effort to protect itself from invasion, but he found his state to be much reduced in resources because the Lake Champlain and New York City areas belonged to the British.

14

THE LOYALIST DIASPORA

Loyalists had already begun leaving in the aftermath of Burgoyne's Campaign. When Burgoyne invaded the region, a strong possibility remained that the British might regain control and that Loyalists could return to their homes. Many Loyalists in the countryside had come out into the open, so there was no going back to neutrality. After Burgoyne's defeat, the chances of keeping their homes became increasingly dim, and Loyalists left of their own accord and sought protection in Canada, Britain, or other parts of the British Empire. Thus the possibility of living in and participating in forays from Canada became a growing reality to the region's settlers. The emerging exodus to Canada was directly tied to conditions like imprisonment and the confiscation of property that forced Loyalists to leave.

In the months immediately after Burgoyne surrendered, Loyalist family members left separately, seeking to be reunited on Canadian soil. Women like Betsey Fisher of Munro's Meadows were encouraged by their families to follow their Loyalist menfolk, who in the fall of 1777 retreated to Diamond Island, then Ticonderoga, and finally Montreal.[1] Betsey had gone home to the meadows but had been burned out of it by rebels, seemingly at the orders of John Williams. Earlier, she and her infant son had traveled with the guidance of a farmer driving his single cow to Burgoyne, and she had been reunited with her husband at Fort Edward. In Burgoyne's camp she was able to buy "everything my child and I needed," and thus they stayed with

Burgoyne's army until the surrender. Independent, she refused to leave with her husband, Donald, when he retreated north with the Loyalists to Diamond Island, where he found her father, the Reverend Henry Munro, among the refugees. Munro asked for her, and at his insistence, Fisher went back to Hebron, where Betsey had taken refuge, and convinced her to join her father in what would become a march to Canada. The Fishers were thus reunited at Diamond Island and then Ticonderoga, where she found her father. It was a happy reunion, but then they spent eleven difficult days in an open boat on Lake Champlain, arriving in Montreal on November 22. They found Montreal crowded with refugees and rents and firewood dear, but by spring her husband had purchased a house and established a merchant business. At her father's insistence, Betsey finally named her son after him, Harry Munro Fisher.

While Betsey Fisher's migration to Canada seemed relatively painless, this was not the case for Loyalists who found the distance to Canada and weather conditions formidable obstacles. The John Freeman family, whose farm had been at the center of the Battles of Saratoga, had served with Burgoyne until his surrender, when they attempted to escape to Canada.[2] On their own, however, they languished on the banks of Lake Champlain in the winter, and John, his wife, four of his sons, and two daughters perished there of exposure, leaving twelve-year-old Thomas and two of his sisters to survive and make their way to Canada. Destitute and orphaned, two years later young Thomas, on behalf of his sisters, applied to Major General Riedesel for charity.

Loyalist women now came to the conclusion that they must take their families and join their husbands in Canada. The Jessups' families left late in 1777, arriving in Canada by December. Ebenezer brought his family, a group he described as "a brood of unfortunate women and children," to Quebec City.[3] It consisted of his wife, a fifteen-year-old son, Henry James, and five daughters, Leah, Sarah, Elizabeth, Deborah, and Mary-Ann-Clarendon, none of whom was or would be married, as late as 1789. By 1780 Ebenezer's family was living on charity in Quebec, while he completed his company. In contrast, his brother Edward had only a daughter and a son, eleven-year-old Edward, Jr., who was already serving in his father's unit. The third Jessup brother in Canada, Joseph, was involved in public works and would retire as a pensioner in public employment.

Back in Salem, Colonel John Williams was determined to stop the migration of Charlotte County Loyalists to Canada. In late April 1778 he reported to Governor Clinton that Loyalists were joining the enemy, who was rumored to be coming from Canada. He estimated that Charlotte County was "one half disaffected" Loyalists and that most would join the enemy if they appeared. He affirmed that "no quarter would be given them."[4] Notwithstanding Williams's concern, Loyalists who left in late 1777 or 1778 were having only minimal difficulty from rebel authorities in going to Canada.

The Exodus from Vermont

Vermont Loyalists were also poised to leave as soon as Burgoyne's army surrendered. In October and November 1777, those who had openly supported Burgoyne's army gathered their families and kin and walked north along the east side of Lake Champlain, now convinced that they would have to live in Canada. The total exodus has been estimated as numbering between 562 to 700 persons and took several months to complete.[5]

Earlier, Sarah Bothum Sherwood had found out that her wounded husband, Justus, was at Ticonderoga, and she decided to join him, as their farm was now relatively secure in her father's name. But brother Simon and her father warned her that she could not go directly to the fort, rather she had to first go to Bennington and ask for a safe conduct pass on humanitarian grounds. She went to Shaftsbury, where her father arranged for her to meet with Bennington's "Grand Council of Safety."[6] She was quickly granted safe conduct, only a week after Burgoyne surrendered, though she could take only necessary clothing and one bed. From Shaftsbury, Sarah, her children, and a slave were driven by wagon to Skenesborough. From there they were rowed to Ticonderoga, but when they arrived, they found they had just missed Powell's evacuation of the post. Sarah's rebel escort attempted to take her to the nearest British fort, Pont au Fer at the northern end of Lake Champlain, but about thirty miles from there, the escort panicked, abandoning Sarah's family on the west side of the lake. Aided by her slave, Caesar Congo, she hid her belongings, and with her toddlers she succeeded in walking to Point au Fer. Caesar recovered her belongings and they traveled by bateau down the Richelieu River to St. Johns. There Sarah met Justus and they began a new life in Canada.

As long as Loyalist property could be confiscated, the Vermont Council in Arlington was actually helpful in facilitating Loyalist migration to Canada. This was especially true with Arlington's Loyalist families. On October 29, 1777, the council gave Philo Hard's wife, Currence, and their child permission to join her husband at Ticonderoga, so she would be among her kin.[7] Similar permission was given to Mrs. Samuel Adams. Philo and Samuel Adams, Isaac and Nathan Brisco, and Caleb Henderson were already involved in the retreat to Canada. They joined Jehiel, Jeptha, and other members of the Hawley family. The move to Canada was too arduous for Jehiel, however, who was now in his sixty-fifth year, and he died on November 2, 1777, and was buried near Shelburne on Lake Champlain. His wife, Abra, may also have succumbed on the march to Canada. As Andrew, Jehiel's eldest son, remained in Arlington, Jeptha, a firm Loyalist, would now take on the role of family patriarch.

Currence Hard and Mrs. Samuel Adams did not actually go to Canada until spring. In March 1778 the council in Arlington ordered Captain Isaac Clark to transport the Arlington families of Samuel Adams, Isaac Brisco, Caleb Henderson, and Philo Hard to Ferrisburgh, near Lake Champlain, from whence they would be transported to Canada.[8] Over the winter, Mrs. Adams prepared her children and household furniture, bedding, kitchenware, and apparel. Ruth Hawley, Mrs. Isaac Brisco, was able to take with her feather beds, sheets, pewter plates and platters, and a wardrobe chest. Although household items were sequestered in other Vermont communities, in this case the council allowed the Loyalist wives to take some household goods. Unlike the situation that would develop in New York, the Vermont Council in Arlington made no effort to prohibit the migration, readily giving permission for spouses of Loyalists to leave, even with a modest amount of household goods.

The Hawley kinship network that had been transferred from Connecticut to Arlington held up remarkably as intermarried families prepared for exile in Canada. This was especially true for women who valued their family circle and kinship ties and chose to travel with their kin to Canada. Of Jehiel's children, Jeptha, Ruth, Anna, and Abijah participated in the exodus. As noted, Ruth had married Isaac Brisco, Arlington's town clerk, who from 1774 to 1777 bought thousands of acres in the area to keep it from "Greedy New Yorker land-grabbers." The Briscos were wealthier than Jehiel, giving up a house, two mills, two barns, and stock.[9] Anna was married to Phineas Hard, Philo's brother, also a firm Loyalist, who moved to Canada. Abijah, Jeptha's older brother by two years, was unmarried and went to Canada. Jehiel's nieces and nephews also migrated to Canada, including Abel's son, Abel, and Josiah Hawley's son Gideon and the aforementioned daughter Currence. Several of Jehiel Hawley's grandchildren participated in the exodus, including Andrew's sons Adoniran, Eli, Jehiel, Zadock, and Andrew, Jr.

The need for these migrating Loyalists to join the military intensified because they were now one of the few sources of Loyalist recruits in Canada. Hawleys had served in Ebenezer Jessup's King's Loyal Americans, in Burgoyne's bateaux corps, and as members of Samuel Adams's company.[10] Jeptha was attached to both Jessup brothers' units, serving at Saratoga in the highly esteemed position of captain of bateaux. Among Jessup's Rangers in 1781 were Ichabod and Martin Hawley, respectively Jeptha's nephew and eldest son. Ichabod had served in both the rebel army and in Loyalist units from 1777. Many of the next generation of sons and especially grandsons also served in Loyalist units, leaving them with no alternative but to settle in Canada. As younger sons, most in their early twenties, the possibility of Canadian land grants in reward for military service was more attractive than remaining in Arlington.

Vermont's Practical Policy on Loyalists

Vermont saw the value of retaining some Loyalists as settlers. Not until February 1779 would the Vermont Assembly pass the Act of Banishment, so that the exodus that had been voluntary until then was now mandatory for certain individuals. Named in the act from Arlington were Jehiel Hawley (although he had died), Philo Hurlbert, Isaac Brisco, Samuel Buck, and David Williams; from Manchester, Jeremiah and Andrew French; from Pawlet, Reuben Hawley; from Dorset, William Marsh; from Bennington, James Breakenridge, Jr.; from New Haven, Justus Sherwood; and from Shaftsbury, John Munro.[11]

Even with the most extensive Loyalist properties, the Vermont courts or the council did not confiscate all acreage, leaving enough land and livestock for a widow or spouse who remained in Vermont to eke out an existence. Wives were capable of maintaining farms and families on very slender resources. Because of this leniency, some of the wives of Loyalists stayed in Arlington and Sunderland while their husbands lived in Canada. Jehiel's nephew, Abel, went to Canada, and his three hundred–acre Sunderland farm was confiscated. This left Abel's wife, Mary Folsom Hawley, alone in Arlington. A widow by April 1779, she petitioned the Vermont Council of Safety for payment of the cost of a cow, which was customarily left to a widowed victim, so she would not be destitute.[12]

In another case of November 1777, Jeptha's wife, Esther, petitioned the same Council of Safety requesting confirmation that she could remain in Arlington at peace, though her husband was serving in a Loyalist unit. The council was willing to support her farm through the winter of 1777–78, including the care of two cows, one horse, one colt, three yearlings, four sheep, and eight swine, as well as providing firewood and twenty pounds of sugar. In April 1778 Jeptha's estate was confiscated, and three months later the council had his house and farm repaired, including the cost of a pair of iron hinges, a well critch, and forty-five rods of fence—all this evidently to make the estate more attractive to a buyer.[13] In 1779 and 1780 his confiscated land was sold in separate parcels to Ebenezer Bartlet and Jacob Hinds. Another relative, Esther's brother, David Castle of Pawlet, escaped to Canada late in 1777, and in February 1779 a customary cow was given to his wife for her maintenance at the pleasure of the council.

This humane policy toward Loyalist women finally outran the council's patience or resources, and on November 11, 1779, it appointed a committee, made up of militia captains Matthew Lyon, Ebenezer Wallace, and Jonas Galusha, to investigate the possibility of selling the Loyalist-occupied farms, like that of Phineas Hurd's widow, and moving the families elsewhere.[14]

THE ARLINGTON JUNTA

During the Burgoyne invasion, a convention at Windsor on the Connecticut River was drafting Vermont's first constitution. However, when the members of the Windsor Convention heard that Burgoyne had taken Ticonderoga, the convention adjourned and the delegates scattered to save their families and property from the impending invasion. These were dark days, and as Ira Allen put it: "The Government was not organized, as the constitution was not fully completed, and near three quarters of the people on the west side of the Green Mountains were compelled to remove, and the rest were in great danger . . . the Council of Safety had no money or revenue at command."[15]

In the Convention's place, provision had been quickly made for a small Council of Safety with dictatorial powers to govern and complete the constitution. Despite defections from the council to the enemy by members like Benjamin Spencer, a few members carried on. Thomas Chittenden, Jonas Fay, Ira Allen, Nathan Clark, Paul Spooner, Moses Robinson, and Matthew Lyon ruled Vermont as members of the council, which has been called, notoriously, "the Junta."[16] After Ethan Allen's return from imprisonment, while he was not actually appointed to the council, he had easy access to it and was involved in the formulation of many of its policies.

Once the Junta was entrenched, it was difficult to reduce its influence. To make certain the governor in council had no rivals in the raising of funds for military affairs, on March 9, 1778, the council disbanded local Committees of Safety, like that of Bennington. Three days later, the governor in council, operating as the Committee of Safety, replaced them as Vermont's chief political authority. For the next ten years, in practice, the first three members of the state Council of Safety—Chittenden, Jonas Fay, and Ira Allen—would dominate Vermont, mainly from Arlington.[17] The Junta was thus a collective leadership that, with its strong personalities and ability to manipulate the political system, remained in power for an excessively long time.

In the later years of the War of Independence, Arlington became the seat of the Junta, making the former Loyalist stronghold the center of Vermont's executive power. Beginning in the spring of 1778, leaders of Vermont's independent government arrived in the Arlington area, settling with the remaining Loyalists. Their choice of Arlington was not accidental. Arlington's Loyalism had been weakened by Herrick's devastation of the Batten Kill Valley after the Battle of Walloomsac. Its large concentration of developed Loyalist properties were now vacant or ruined, so they could be easily confiscated and sold, the proceeds hopefully becoming the chief means of sustaining the new Vermont government. The Junta also came to appreciate their ability to deal with the British through Arlington's lingering Loyalist kinship connections. Furthermore, in Arlington the Junta could operate on a day-to-day basis without interference from the Vermont Assembly or the Bennington leadership, two rival authorities that did not always approve of its actions.[18]

The Arlington Junta began meeting there on April 9, 1778.[19] Its leader was Thomas Chittenden, a land speculator like the Allens, who had come to the Grants late in 1774 to develop property at Williston, far to the north but conveniently in the Allens' Onion River Patent. When the Continental forces withdrew from Canada in 1776, Chittenden gave up living on his property and moved south to Danby. He continued southward when Burgoyne invaded in 1777, first taking his family to the safety of Pownal and then in August to Williamstown, Massachusetts, where many New Yorkers had taken refuge. Finally in 1779, having purchased Jehiel Hawley's house and some of his property, he permanently placed his family in Arlington. Meanwhile, this barely literate but shrewd politician had managed to participate in most of the conventions that created the Vermont constitution, and in 1778, under the new constitution, he was elected president of the Vermont Council and "Captain-General, Governor and Commander in Chief" of Vermont. Like Governor George Clinton in New York, he would be popular and would retain this position into the postwar era.

By the time the Junta met in Arlington, Ira Allen had already purchased confiscated Arlington and Sunderland Loyalist estates, including a gristmill, and he had erected a sawmill and opened a land office. Ira held the crucial positions of treasurer and secretary of Vermont's governing Council.[20] His extensive official authority contrasted with his brother Ethan's more casual approach to politics. Ethan would hold only temporary commands in the Vermont militia, but his personal influence remained important. He had been released from a British prison in March 1778, exchanged, and came to Arlington to visit his three daughters and wife, Mary Brownson Allen, who were living in Sunderland with her brothers, Timothy and Gideon Brownson. His relationship with Mary was a cool one; it was clear that she was residing with her brothers because Ethan could not support his family. He stayed only briefly and returned to Bennington, where he rented a house, though he visited his relatives and friends in Arlington often in 1778 and 1779, and in 1780 he finally moved there. He was not yet focused on farming, an activity that he did not take up seriously until seven years later when he obtained a Burlington farm in retirement.

Beyond the two Allens and Chittenden, the supporting roles in the Junta fell to Timothy Brownson, Jonathan Fassett, and Matthew Lyon, all members of the Commission of Sequestration, which confiscated Loyalist property.[21] Ethan Allen's brother-in-law, Brownson represented Sunderland on the council and on the commissions. Fassett and Lyon had also settled in Arlington, and Fassett was appointed to represent Arlington in the Assembly in 1778 and 1779. In the latter year, Fassett was also named to the Governor's Council and as commissioner of sequestration for the Town of Arlington. He would control Loyalist land sales in support of the Junta's policies. He cemented his power with a family alliance, marrying his daughter to the governor's son, Noah Chittenden. Fassett was the son of John Fassett, Sr., the Bennington political and Separatist church leader. The son had left Bennington, unimpressed with the conciliatory attitude of the Bennington Committee of Safety toward New York.

Matthew Lyon, who in 1777 had commanded the militia in the Arlington skirmish over cattle, by now had lost interest in a military career.[22] Born in Ireland, he came to Connecticut in 1764 as a fifteen-year-old indentured servant and eventually purchased land in Wallingford, the Grants, where he settled in 1773. In Arlington he would serve as clerk of the Court of Confiscation, secretary to the governor and council, and a representative to the Assembly. Lyon, Brownson, and Fassett were in direct charge of the confiscation of Loyalist estates, enforcing the policies of Chittenden and the two Allens.

During the Burgoyne invasion, Ira Allen had suggested that the Vermont Council of Safety establish a Commission of Confiscation because of the upsurge of Loyalism created by the invaders. The Junta, acting as the council, assumed the task of confiscating Loyalist property, the proceeds from the sales becoming the Vermont government's chief source of revenue. At first, in July 1777, only movable property was seized, such as livestock, crops, household goods, and farm equipment. The proceeds were used purely for defense, as the Junta had no other way of raising money for Herrick's Rangers and the Vermont constitution was not in place. Two months later the effect of the policy was seen in Arlington, where Jonas Fay of the Council of Safety now controlled a flock of sequestered Loyalist sheep. Rebels who claimed to have lost sheep could apply to the council to have them replaced from the "Tory herd."[23] By November 1777, the council ordered that hay be provided at Arlington for Thomas Chittenden's cattle, evidently a confiscated herd being maintained for him.

Not till March 1778 was the confiscation of real estate approved by the council, making the rewards more lucrative and possibilities of land speculation more inviting.[24] Ethan Allen was named a judge and Matthew Lyon the clerk of the court of sequestration, an ad hoc body that existed only as long as it had public business. The Commissioners of Confiscation were busiest taking lands on the west side of Vermont; from October 1778 to February 1779, they sold thirty-three farms in Bennington County, many of them in Arlington. When the Vermont General Assembly passed the Act of Banishment in 1779, a special court was established to permit Loyalists to speak against the confiscation of their property. This was also Junta business, as Ethan Allen and Matthew Lyon directed this court. Probably the most heart-wrenching part of this activity for Allen was when he denounced his brother Levi as a Loyalist to the Court of Confiscation, leading Jonathan Fassett to publically advertise the accusation of Levi's Loyalism.

Among the first properties confiscated by the court in Arlington in April 1778 was Jehiel Hawley's estate of 3,000 acres. Additional Arlington properties that were taken included those of Abel Hawley, Jr., Jeptha Hawley, Reuben Hawley, Isaac Brisco, Philo Hurlbert, James Hard, and Phineas Hard.[25] Later confiscations included the estates of Abijah Hawley, Ichabod Hawley, and Dr. Samuel Adams. Also confiscated were the properties of Justus Sherwood in New Haven, Reuben Hawley in Pawlet, William Marsh in Dorset, John Munro in Shaftsbury, and those of no less than twenty-nine individuals in Clarendon who included Benjamin and Hazelton Spencer. The most lucrative actions went against the properties of absent or dead Loyalists, ranging from the 13,000 acres of Justus Sherwood to the 300 acres of Benjamin Spencer.

While Vermont militia officers like Ebenezer Allen and his associates purchased Sherwood's New Haven property, the Junta itself was a leading buyer of the confiscated lands. By dominating the Commissions of Confiscation and Sequestration and the courts, the Junta was first in line to purchase Arlington's or other Loyalist property. Both Ethan and Ira Allen purchased land from William Marsh's confiscated estate. On June 10, 1779, Thomas Chittenden purchased 617 acres of Jehiel Hawley's confiscated property from John Fassett for a substantial £3,000. Fassett, as a commissioner of sequestration, had been the first to purchase the Hawley property.[26] As a result, Chittenden moved into Jehiel Hawley's wood-frame house, which he would inhabit for almost a decade. A Junta kinship group, with Chittenden acting as the new patriarch, had now replaced the Hawleys as leaders of Arlington.

The Junta aimed to control the sequestration process so they could buy the best land for themselves.[27] As state treasurer and state surveyor general, Ira Allen had abundant opportunities to feather his nest, and his careless keeping of the treasury's records always seemed to benefit himself. As a surveyor he took his salary in land, amassing more than 100,000 acres by the end of the war, chiefly in the Champlain Valley. Those who sought land in Vermont learned quickly that they had to grease Ira's palm.

The career of Matthew Lyon shows how members of the Junta enriched themselves as they gained political and economic power. Lyon felt justified in seeking profit, ignoring the concept of serving the public good.[28] He was on Arlington's Committee of Safety with Chittenden, and the two of them made the Junta's headquarters in three confiscated Loyalist homes, Lyon's and Chittenden's being connected by a long vault, which served as a jail. From April 23, 1778, Lyon in his capacity as clerk of the statewide Court of Confiscation had first-hand knowledge of the parties who were found guilty and the estates that were confiscated. Nine months after his appointment, Lyon purchased the property of Isaac Brisco, which had been confiscated during the court session, from Jonathan Fassett, the commissioner of sales and his fellow conspirator. Later that year, Lyon placed £400 as security with the Court of Confiscation, directing Fassett to sell to him "any farm or farms in his district." This allowed him to acquire even more of Brisco's property when it was taken by the court two years later. Such a setup was only for Lyon and was an obvious conflict of interest, for he was acquiring Arlington Loyalist property for future speculative gain rather than settling it.

Other lucrative possibilities came in March 1780, when as a member of the Committee to Defend the Northern Frontier, Lyon asked the Vermont Assembly to grant five or six townships to raise money for defense.[29] Lacking funds, the Assembly expanded the number of granted townships to fifty, and Lyon petitioned for and got five of the townships himself. Since it was required that the proprietor settle the land and Lyon had no resources to accomplish this, he was again speculating, hoping to sell the land to another party at a profit. Ultimately he did plan to settle in one township, New Haven, where by January 1781 he had put together over four hundred contiguous acres. New Haven, of course, had been the home of Justus Sherwood, whose property had been among the largest confiscated by the commission.

While the confiscation program appeared to enrich the Vermont treasury, it never was a steady source of income. It was one thing to take property and another to sell it. Although the Junta and its cronies certainly bought confiscated land, there was always far more land than buyers. With Vermont's history of controversy over land tenure, there was no reason for an outside entrepreneur to consider such lands a worthy investment—as they might have in New York. By the end of the war, many confiscated but unsold Loyalist properties existed in Vermont.[30]

CONFISCATING LOYALIST ESTATES IN NEW YORK

As a result of the enduring war, Governor George Clinton and the New York legislature had begun to put aside their attempts to rehabilitate Loyalists and instead adopt a policy of expulsion. At first Clinton personally handled Loyalist cases, but then he supported a series of laws that made Loyalists the object of persecution. Clinton began by regulating the travel of Loyalist husbands, wives, and children to either New York City or Canada to prevent them from being reunited as readily as they been after Burgoyne's surrender. He used his authority as governor harshly in specific cases of prisoner exchange. He removed the Fraser family from Hoosic to Albany in 1778, where he held them prisoner until May 1780, when he finally allowed them to be exchanged and sent to New York City. They survived an abortive passage to London, ultimately reaching Ireland, and by 1785 they were all reunited, living in Scotland.[31] Clinton also targeted Quakers as pacifists, for the state's new constitution did not offer them the protection of hard-won colonial legislation.

New York's confiscation of Loyalist estates went hand in hand with its detection of Loyalists. It required over four years of legislation to hammer out a state confiscation policy. The process began as early as March 6, 1777, when New York's Provincial Congress appointed commissioners of sequestration to take the personal property of Loyalists—though not land—and sell it at public auction.[32] On October 22, 1779, their authority was replaced in the constitutional legislature's more comprehensive Act of Attainder, which created a statewide Committee of Forfeitures that oversaw abandoned Loyalist property and sold their crops to raise revenue, though not yet the property itself. Commissioners of Forfeitures were appointed by the governor, to administer the law in the southern, middle, western, and eastern parts of the rebel-controlled state. Alexander Webster of Hebron had been named a commissioner for the Eastern District, making him the most important official in Charlotte County regarding the confiscation of Loyalist estates. After several votes in the Assembly, the Commissioners of Forfeitures finally were charged to sell confiscated lands, with tenants being given priority in the purchase of lands, and on occasion the commissioners could offer land grants to deserving persons. By 1780 the legislature urged that confiscated lands be sold to support the war effort, especially to provide apparel and provisions for the troops. It also authorized that certificates used to pay New York troops in lieu of currency could be accepted to purchase confiscated estates at the same value as specie. Unfortunately, most of the troops with an interest in Charlotte County lands sold their certificates to speculators like John Williams or Alexander Webster, who did not hesitate to buy them at a fraction of their worth.

The Confiscation Act of October 1779 was labeled by Clinton's opponents like John Jay as "a disgrace," because he favored a more moderate course.[33] Still, Clinton saw to it that fifty-nine prominent Loyalists lost their estates. Among the properties taken in Charlotte County were those of John and Daniel Jones, John Morehouse, Gilbert Harris, Jr., Alexander Campbell, and Donald Fisher, and in Albany County those of Gershom and Benjamin French, Francis Hogle, John Macomb, Hugh Munro, and Francis Pfister. All had been involved in Burgoyne's invasion. By 1780 the Commissions for Detecting and Defeating Conspiracies had begun to sell a backlog of confiscated Loyalist properties to fill the empty state treasury.

Admittedly, Clinton would try to finance New York's war effort through revised property taxation, more than the confiscation of Loyalist property.[34] However, Clinton's persecution of Loyalists increased each time the British foiled his clumsy attempts to protect New York's borderland from invasion. Those Loyalists who managed to survive these measures would still face the Disfranchisement Act of May 12, 1784, which allowed them to stay but eliminated their political rights.

An idea of who the buyers of confiscated property in Charlotte County might be comes from a study of the confiscation of Loyalist estates in Tryon County, where the Johnsons had been the dominant family. It concludes that Loyalist confiscations during the last years of the War of Independence, 1780–83, were purchased by men of substance because lesser men had little Continental currency. It was a means for the astute to get rid of the worthless currency, investing in the more lasting value of land, because the currency had to be accepted. From 1784 to 1788, confiscations intensified and peaked.[35] In this postwar era, more middle-class buyers, especially from New England, joined the elite in purchasing confiscated lands. Confiscation activity fell considerably after the commissioners of forfeitures ceased operation in 1788, but forfeiture activity continued under the surveyor general and did not technically cease in New York until 1823. The Tryon County analysis concluded that increased revenue and persecution of Loyalists always took precedence over any democratization of land tenure. It was also impossible to determine whether the activities of the commissioners had an equalitarian effect on New York's land holdings, since other factors, such as anti-rent sentiment, may have had a much greater impact.

With this outline of Tryon County's activities as a start, did members of Salem's Commissioners for Detecting and Defeating Conspiracies profit from the confiscation of Loyalist properties? Using evidence of land purchases and sales from the 1780s to the early 1800s, most members did not, showing that their decisions were not driven by personal profit as in the case of the Arlington Junta. However, Alexander Webster was the exception, as he was definitely a land speculator who took advantage of confiscation opportunities. Holding the position of commissioner of forfeitures between 1783 and 1800, Webster sold nineteen parcels of Charlotte County land and was still involved in land sales in the early nineteenth century.[36] In 1779 he also claimed the right to collect rents from the Loyalist estate of Oliver Delancey and Peter Dubois because he held their power of attorney, after Dr. Clark declined to continue as their rent collector. Clark had acted as the rent collector since his congregation came to Salem in 1765. It is likely that the war left most of the tenants unable to pay their rents, but Webster may have been banking on the future and certainly was willing to use his power of attorney from the two Loyalist estate holders to gain a share of the rents.

John Williams did not serve on the Commission for Detecting and Defeating Conspiracies or as a commissioner of forfeitures, and yet he would gain more land from confiscated estates than anyone else in Charlotte County. For a start, he was involved in an unpopular court-martial aimed at punishing Charlotte County militia members who had not turned out during Burgoyne's invasion. Many were convicted—unfairly, they felt, because Williams favored the village's New Englanders over the Scots-Irish. Williams's conduct with his militia command came to the attention of the New York senate, in which he served. Because of the expense incurred in the trial, he was found guilty of payroll discrepancies and expelled from the senate. For solace, he joined Washington's army and attempted to reestablish his medical practice in Philadelphia. Yet his influence in Salem and Charlotte County does not seem to have been diminished by his misfortune. Locals considered his militia payroll problems insignificant. Charlotte County's leaders came to realize they needed an affluent and unselfish gentleman like Williams, who could use his credit to help supply the militia. By 1780 even his rival Alexander Webster was writing to Governor Clinton begging that he replace him as commander of the militia and reinstate Williams.[37] Williams was elected to the Assembly in 1779, and he followed this by a return to the Senate in 1780, where he remained until 1795 with only a single year's respite, 1781–82, when he again served in the Assembly. This was despite the fact that he had too many commitments to consistently take his seat in the legislature, thus lacking the respect of some legislators because his attendance was spotty.

With his political career revived after the war, Williams eventually owned, in terms of newly created Washington County towns, nearly all of Hampton; more than half of Salem; half of Putnam, Whitehall, and Hebron; and much of Granville.[38] Admittedly, except for Webster, Williams had little competition in acquiring confiscated Loyalist estates and rebel soldiers' certificates and bounties.

When Williams was serving his first term as a New York State senator in 1778, Skenesborough was captured and burned by the British. But this did not stop him from acquiring the prized Philip Skene estate. A year later Williams, Joseph Stringham, and John Murray purchased Skene's confiscated estate for £14 10s, a pittance, as conveniently there were no other bids.[39] In 1802 and 1803 Williams bought out the other two and became the sole proprietor, a culminating step in making him the region's greatest landholder. As early as 1777 Williams had asked Philip Schuyler if he wanted a share of Skene's estate, but Schuyler turned him down, even though he had been prepared to offer a much higher price than Williams and his partners had paid.

In 1783 Williams bought land in Granville from the Commission of Forfeitures, and a year later he bought sixty-five parcels of confiscated Loyalist land throughout the region, which were recorded on Webster's register of Sales of Forfeited Estates, Act of May 12, 1784.[40] The land had the obligation of a quit rent to the crown, which now went to the owner, so the land would be rented, not sold in fee simple. Williams was a landlord, renting a farm to Robert Chapman on November 1, 1794. He also purchased bounty land from Continental veterans like Phineas Wheeler of Hebron in 1791, and three years later he bought land between Ticonderoga and Crown Point. About 1800 he purchased Putnam Township in Washington County from Alexander Turner. Williams was clearly able to cheaply invest in land as result of the war.

In the face of the poverty caused by the war, well into the 1780s the revenue from confiscation of Loyalist property was in great demand— even for small projects. In 1784 Salem's New England Presbyterian Church petitioned the New York State Assembly for money from the sale of Loyalist property to build a new church, as their church had been destroyed and the remains turned into a fort during the war.[41] However, the legislature felt the revenue should be used elsewhere and turned the church's request down. The profits realized from confiscation were never so extensive that they could cover projects like this.

The Act of Attainder of 1779 had specifically mentioned the confiscation of the estates of prominent Loyalists like Skene and his son Andrew, Robert Leake, Edward and Ebenezer Jessup, Beverly Robinson, Sir John Johnson, Guy Johnson, and Daniel Claus.[42] In places controlled by the rebels in the state, confiscation by the Commissioners of Forfeiture went on, enriching rebels who had the funds to purchase them. Much of the Saratoga area was in the Western District because it included Albany County. Loyalist Pat Smyth's property in Fort Edward was confiscated and sold to Colonel Adiel Sherwood, who we will see as commander of Fort Ann. He may not have been much of a soldier, but he evidently prospered: a decade later, he headed a large household of eleven, including two slaves. The Hoosic, Walloomsac, and Pittstown Patents were confiscated and sold to rebels of wealth. They included members of the Van Rensselaer and Gansevoort families, another case of politically active rebel leaders enriching themselves. The effect of the Act of Attainder was to help rich rebels to obtain land, not the soldier or farmer. While Governor Clinton or the New York Assembly hoped for a more democratic situation, during the war the only people who could afford to purchase the confiscated estates were the wealthy, who had been able to absorb the terrible cost of the war's devastation and use the depreciated currency that ruined the average farmer.

The Loyalist exodus from New York and Vermont commenced soon after Burgoyne surrendered. The exodus would be further fueled by the confiscation of Loyalists property—at first only personal property but later the land itself. Differences developed between Vermont's and New York's treatment of Loyalists, not so much in terms of legislation, but rather the ways in which similar legislation was interpreted. Governor Clinton made certain New York's legislation was vindictively enforced, while Governor Chittenden followed the more moderate John Jay, always being willing to help a Loyalist widow or accept the return of a Loyalist husband. By the time the Vermont and New York constitutions were fully functioning, new government institutions were in place with formidable executive powers, based partially on their ability to confiscate and sell Loyalist property. In Vermont the governor in council was dominated by the Arlington Junta and initiated the confiscation of Loyalist property, which was especially extensive in that area because of its numerous Loyalists. While Vermont's and New York's governments projected that the confiscation of Loyalist property would help to finance government, in reality the proceeds fell short of what they expected. Rebels with credit did expand their landholdings. Meanwhile, as the confiscation of Loyalist property and their expulsion occupied the rebel leadership, Haldimand decided to invade, a policy he would carry on for the rest of the war.

15

HALDIMAND'S FORAYS

Burgoyne's defeat had not been followed by a rebel effort to retake Ticonderoga and Crown Point. In fact, the entire northern theater of the war was denuded of Continental troops, and even Warner's Continental regiment would eventually be discontinued. The defense of the frontier was left to John Stark and, informally, the civilian Philip Schuyler.[1] The militia also faltered, and at the beginning of November 1778 the New York legislature was forced to create new night watches in Albany, Charlotte, Dutchess, and Ulster Counties to make up for it. Males between sixteen and sixty years—slaves and Indians excepted—were ordered to do watch duty. The only other defensive resource was the independent Vermont militia, controlled by the Junta, which, beyond Herrick's constantly recruited rangers, was never funded to remain in the field for long. Furthermore, the continuing controversy over jurisdiction brought Vermont and New York close to their own war, preventing the rebels from forming a united front to oppose the British.

PERFECTING PETITE GUERRE

In contrast, the British military in 1778 was in the strongest position on Lake Champlain and Lake George since the war had begun. It has been claimed that rebel militia units, sniping at the heels of the British army, ultimately won the War of Independence.[2] This assumes that the rebel militia was better than the British army at irregular warfare—

breaking up the British line to use terrain for protection rather than the marching lines and firing volleys of European armies. Perhaps this was true at Lexington and Concord, but by 1778 Washington had developed a European-style Continental Army that could meet British regulars on a battlefield and trade volleys, such as they did after Saratoga at the Battle of Monmouth. Moreover, while some militiamen were capable of serving as rangers, the vast majority were not experienced in irregular or forest warfare, and their ability to use any firearms has been a subject of hot debate. In fact, in the Hudson-Champlain region, the roles were reversed, as it was the British who were best prepared for irregular warfare while the rebel militias faltered more than ever.

As noted, Haldimand would stretch his resources with mixed forces of regulars, Loyalists, and Indians that would carry out constant forays against the rebels. The attacks were carefully orchestrated by Haldimand and his officers so that rebel militia found it difficult to confront them. The multiplicity of British raids left the rebels in the wrong place at the wrong time. Haldimand's new policy drew on the expertise of others who had served in the area. Guy Johnson, the superintendent of Indian affairs to the Iroquois, believed that petite guerre was clever because while it "does not admit of any thing capital, it is still of much importance . . . in keeping the Rebels in a continued state of alarm and apprehension, and destroying their resources."[3] Burgoyne's belief that light troops were the best for North American conditions also supported the policy. Following ideals that Burgoyne was not fully able to put into effect, Haldimand's army expanded the use of light infantry tactics and marksmen units to meet American conditions.

As governor, Haldimand was an administrator, for he never actually led any forays. Field commanders like Christopher Carleton were crucial to the governor's success in petite guerre. Carleton turned out to be an especially talented partisan, certainly as good as Seven Years' War predecessors like Robert Rogers and George Augustus, Lord Howe. One thing he would not be was a northern equivalent of Banastre Tarleton, notorious for his cruelty. While he would adapt his regulars to surviving the woods, he would also restrain his Indians and Loyalists when dealing with civilians. From a military family, Carleton was born in Newcastle, England, in 1749 but was orphaned at the age of four when his parents were lost at sea.[4] He entered the army at twelve, having been brought up by his uncles, Guy Carleton, governor of Canada, and Thomas Carleton, the first governor of New Brunswick. He came to Canada as an ensign of the 31st Regiment, and he visited Johnson Hall, where he admired how Sir William Johnson interacted with the Mohawks. In the early 1770s he lived as an Indian at the Kahnawake and Kanesetake missions and learned their language. He was not only involved in village politics, but he dressed as they did, had his body tattooed, had a ring placed though his nose, and took an Indian wife. He claimed this was the happiest time in his life.

To prevent him from becoming a complete Indian, young Carleton was sent back to England, where he was when the War of Independence broke out. He returned to Canada in May 1776 with the rank of captain, as part of the relief force that his uncle used to drive the rebels from Canada. In his uncle's campaign along Lake Champlain, he commanded the detachment of four hundred Indians. As Governor Carleton advanced up Lake Champlain, the young captain led a reconnoitering party on the lake. He knew how to gain the confidence of the mission Indians, especially as he could speak several native dialects. Surprisingly, his white colleagues also found him to be "refined, gentle, friendly, well-mannered and unaffected."[5] In 1777 he purchased a major's commission in his uncle Thomas Carleton's regiment, the 29th, and two years later he made a suitable marriage to Anne Howard, sister of Maria, wife of Guy Carleton. By 1780 Christopher held the crucial position of commandant at St. Johns.

The process of adapting to petite guerre led each segment of an expedition to learn from the other. One of the first activities Christopher Carleton ordered upon entering the Lake Champlain basin in September 1778 was that his regulars practice "treeing," "the manner of hiding themselves behind trees, stumps etc."[6] A regular officer, Lieutenant John Enys, noted the difficulty the regulars had with such training: "Our awkwardness diverted the Indians and [Loyalists] who are by far better hands at this work being bred in the woods from their infancy, and accustomed to this manner of hiding themselves in order to shoot deer and other wild beasts." Carleton was pleased by the progress of his regulars, for such training was becoming standard practice. Now familiar with the woods, regulars were not going to be devastated by an Indian ambush as they had been in the Seven Years' War.

The Makeup of the Expeditions

Blacks were present in Haldimand's mixed expeditions. The forces that Mohawk leader Joseph Brant was able to put together were largely made up of renegade Loyalists and blacks because he actually had minor influence in the Iroquois councils or in recruiting Six Nations warriors. Brant's followers, the Reverend Henry Munro's students, Joseph Bettys's recruits, Sir John Johnson's and James Gordon's slaves, freed at Ball's Town, contributed to raiding parties. All the Loyalist corps had blacks in their ranks, many being officers' servants. In 1780 Captain John Munro reported that his guides mentioned four hundred Schenectady and Albany blacks who wanted to join the king's troops, confirming that they were only waiting for a sign to aid the British.[7] The New York City policy of freedom for blacks who joined the British army was not in effect in Canada, but blacks in the Albany area may have thought it was and thus hoped to join Haldimand's raids. In 1781 Haldimand ordered Sir John to prepare a census of slaves brought to Canada by scouting parties. There were forty-one, of whom nineteen were owned by Sir John and fifteen by rebels. They alleged the right to freedom following the New York City policy. However, Sir John was not about to give up his valuable property, and some blacks were certainly returned to their Loyalist master.

The Loyalist Units

After Burgoyne's surrender, Loyalism continued to develop in the Hudson-Champlain region, inspired by Christopher Carleton's raids of 1778 and 1780, and also after 1780 by Justus Sherwood's and John Meyers's espionage activities. Until the Peace of Paris in 1783, support for Loyalism remained high because of the success of petite guerre and diplomacy with the Arlington Junta.

While Haldimand would be magnanimous toward Loyalist refugees, he also saw that the ranks of most Loyalist corps were not full. As an administrator, he knew he could not afford to support all the embryonic Loyalist corps and furthermore that some units technically belonged to Britain's Central Department (New York City), not his Northern Department (Canada).[8] This lingering division had been used by Carleton to refuse support for Burgoyne's expedition until the very end. Officers of the fragmented Loyalist corps were still not commissioned or paid, and their men were treated in Canada as refugees, not part of the standing army. Only the two largest Loyalist regiments, Sir John Johnson's Royal American Regiment of New York and Brigadier Alan Maclean's Royal Highland Immigrants—which became part of the regular establishment as the 84th Foot—were treated as part of the Canadian standing army. Strengthening these two regiments made sense to Haldimand. Obviously, Jessups, Peters, and Adams did not share this view, as they still had to scramble to recruit their under-strength corps. The best possibility open to them was to join in the forays against New York and Vermont so that they could continue to recruit.

Jessup's King's Loyal Americans and their growing number of dependents were sent to Quebec in the spring of 1778 to work on its fortifications.[9] Then they were stationed around Sorel at the mouth of the Richelieu River and at Machiche encampment near Trois-Rivières. They also garrisoned Dutchman's Point at the extreme end of Grand Isle on Lake Champlain. None of these assignments, however, helped their officers to fill their ranks because they were still in Canada and their status remained cloudy. Jessup's corps continued to be treated as an entity that Burgoyne had created only for his campaign, which the authorities were under no obligation to support, except as refugees. Facing the problem of recognition and seeking to be reimbursed for the expenses of raising the battalion, Lieutenant Colonel Ebenezer Jessup agreed to have his King's Loyal Americans subordinated to Sir John Johnson's favored and long-established regiment. But his corps did not disappear. In July 1780 the Jessups' and other Loyalist corps continued to participate in the raids as their own units.

It was the same situation with Peters's corps, the Queen's Loyal Rangers, where Justus Sherwood was a captain. Peters had lost many recruits at the Battle on the Walloomsac and during the last days of Burgoyne's campaign, when he had hesitated to leave Saratoga and escape to Ticonderoga. When he got to the fort, he discovered that Samuel McKay had taken many of his recruits. In Canada his options for recruiting were limited, and in November 1778 he also asked that his men be integrated with Sir John Johnson's regiment.[10] This seemed compatible with Haldimand's policies of strengthening that regiment, but Haldimand was disappointed in the conduct of Peters and his corps, and he turned the request down. Finally, in July 1780, Peters's understrength corps was placed under command of Sir John, and it was in this situation that most Vermont Loyalists served.

To his credit, Haldimand did discriminate as to the quality of Loyalist officers. Some like Sir John, Sherwood, and Edward Jessup, received his favor, while others, who he felt were lacking like Ebenezer Jessup or John Peters, would be relieved of their command or demoted.[11] Additionally, an area that Haldimand found Loyalists ideally qualified for was espionage and here he used them more effectively than his predecessors.

Continuing the Use of Native Americans

In 1778, mission Indian support for the British at first seemed soft. The surrender of Burgoyne had caused uneasiness with the Canadian Indians because it was followed by an alliance between the rebels and France against the British. The Kahnawake and other mission Indians had not forgotten their French "father" and had ties to the rebels in the Mohawk Valley, where their ancestral homeland was now under the control of rebels like Samuel Kirkland. While most sachems at Kahnawake remained loyal to the British, a few led by Colonel Louis Atayataghronghta had continued to travel south to the Oneidas and provide the rebels with intelligence.[12] Colonel Louis would attract support in Kahnawake and Akwesasne, but his following was actually made up of Oneidas. Daniel Claus, still smarting from the loss of his position in Indian affairs to Major John Campbell, felt the Akwesasnes would be firmly in the British camp if they could be treated along with the Six Nations, a suggestion that is not surprising because it put them outside of the Canadian superintendent's jurisdiction.

Elsewhere, Odanak, Becancour, and Lorette also had rebel learning factions that led them to favor neutrality, rather than uniting behind the British.[13] Against this neutrality was the firm support displayed by Oswegatchie, Kanesetake, and ultimately Akwesasne, where most looked forward to participating in Haldimand's new raids.

To lead the Indians in petite guerre, the Canadian Department of Indian Affairs utilized British officers, who were placed in each mission village to recruit warriors for expeditions and to prevent the village from falling under rebel influence. These officers varied in their quality. After his 1778 raid, Christopher Carleton took an interest in placing the officer for Kanesetake, where he had once lived. He complained that the natives of Kanesetake had been abused since he had lived among them. According to their best chiefs, two "low fellows" were living with them as Canadian Department officers, speaking their language and taking advantage of them.[14] He suggested another officer be appointed to visit the Kanesetake from time to time. He assigned the task to Lieutenant Conrad Brown, who had been at Kahnawake previously, feeling Brown would be the ideal officer to continue the close relationship and be a representative who would please their chiefs. Considering the officers' corruption, Carleton felt he had to intervene in the affairs of the Canadian Department.

For his forays of 1778 and 1780, Carleton knew how to restrain his Indians. He consulted with them frequently and managed them effectively. They were only allowed to plunder Fort George after the garrison had been removed and was protected by the Loyalists and regulars— a great contrast with the massacre at Fort William Henry that had happened nearby only twenty years before.[15] However, at Fort George scalps were taken, which was not part of the understanding Carleton had with his Indians. Rebel militiamen who came to the site became too ill to participate in burying the slain. The grotesque condition of the bodies really had nothing to do with Indian mutilation, for the bodies were found after days of exposure, showing the typical but ugly signs of decay. Furthermore, restraint on scalping also did not prevent Carleton's Indians from filling an entire Lake Champlain schooner with plunder on their return to Canada.

Even while the Indians were marauding, when their desire for plunder might have gotten out of hand, the officers of the Indian Departments now had the influence to restrain them. In Carleton's 1778 foray into Vermont, Lieutenant Enys felt that the accompanying Indians were unusually well behaved, refraining from scalping, instead focusing on the capture of cattle and oxen at Otter Creek, for which they were promised eight dollars apiece. Besides, when a settler's home was raided, the settler was allowed supplies or a cow for his or her sustenance, and only then were Indians permitted to plunder the house, an act, Enys noted, which "they always look upon as their undisputed right."[16] A few Indians even returned plunder to residents they empathized with. This was a great contrast to the reputation for savagery they had gained during the Burgoyne Campaign.

By 1780, however, most of the Six Nations and the Canadian missions no longer wavered, definitely supporting the British because of the Clinton-Sullivan Campaign. The previous year, the rebel effort to strengthen their deteriorating position in upper New York had culminated in a thrust against the Six Nations, organized by Washington.[17] The Clinton-Sullivan Campaign successfully devastated much of the homeland of the Six Nations. However, the Iroquois disappeared before their villages were attacked, and there was no decisive confrontation or destruction of Iroquois manpower, which regrouped at Fort Niagara and other Canadian posts. The rebel campaign made the Six Nations firm allies of the British. Only the Oneidas and Tuscaroras would continue to provide warriors for the rebels.

The Regulars

The 2,500 regulars that Haldimand had in Canada were still from Powell's force at Ticonderoga or troops left in Canada when Burgoyne invaded Lake Champlain. Ready for Haldimand were the 8th, 29th, 31st, 34th, 53rd, and 84th Regiments, all much reduced in numbers.[18] The 29th, 31st, and 53rd would make up the bulk of Christopher Carleton's force in October 1778, and the 29th, 34th, 53rd, and 84th would make up more than half of Carleton's force in October 1780. For the Germans, the Brunswickers and Hessian jagers were in Canada, these last German marksmen still being in great demand. The Hessian jagers were usually the only German unit that participated in Haldimand's forays.

THE CONTINUOUS FORAYS

In the year following Burgoyne's surrender, several raids made it clear that Lake Champlain and the area south of it were still being invaded. On March 21, 1778, three Loyalists from Ball's Town and Tryon County and a hundred mission Indians came from Canada and surprised Skenesborough, capturing the garrison of thirteen and killing a man and his wife, burning several buildings, and retiring up the lake on the ice.[19] A week earlier Shelburne, Vermont, on Lake Champlain had been attacked and burned by Loyalists and Indians, who killed an officer of the militia. Then, in August, Peters and Sherwood raided into Vermont, with thirty-four men of the Queen's Loyal Rangers and some Indians. They hid their bateaux and advanced through the forest to seize the garrison of the Onion River blockhouse, which they burned along with a number of barns and mills. This was the first raid that Haldimand watched closely, for it offered Peters the first opportunity to show his abilities since the debacle on the Walloomsac. But Peters had difficulties with his Indian allies, who threatened to leave, probably because of the restrictions that Haldimand had placed on them, and Peters was ultimately forced to bribe them with a supply of rum upon their return. When the expedition was back in St. Johns with its prisoners and loot, Haldimand was disappointed because of the limited scope of destruction, and Peters would never again figure as prominently in Haldimand's plans.

Christopher Carleton himself led a force in October 1778 that consisted of 324 to 390 regulars—including Hessian jagers—30 of Johnson's Royal Regiment of New York, and 80 to 100 Indians from Kahnawake and Kanesetake. Justus Sherwood was with him as guide, and Lieutenant Richard Houghton commanded the mission Indians. Haldimand wanted the foray to take place as late in the season as possible, because he predicted the rebels would have weakened their guard by then and be unable to respond. Before Lake Champlain began to freeze, ships, gunboats, and bateaux left Ile aux Noix, conveying the raiders southward. Carleton's foray would last for three weeks and baffle the militias of Vermont and New York. On November 6 troop details attacked Reymond's Mill on Beaver Creek in New York and Middlebury and New Haven on Vermont's Otter Creek. They moved to Lake Champlain's Buttonmould Bay, where more raiders were sent to Monkton and Moore's Mill near Vergennes, where they skirmished with Warner's Continentals and Vermont militias. Sherwood led the thirty regulars who destroyed Moore's sawmill and took captives on Putnam's Creek, just south of Ticonderoga. From St. Johns, Brigadier Powell bolstered Carleton's force with additional men for the gunboats and a blacksmith, familiar with the area, to set up shop at Ticonderoga.[20] A number of Loyalist families from Albany County and the Connecticut River Valley were rescued and arrived in St. Johns in October.

After Carleton returned to Isle aux Noix, he assessed on November 14 that his force had destroyed "enough supplies for 12,000 men for a four month campaign."[21] He had taken seventy-nine prisoners and destroyed a sawmill, a gristmill, forty-seven houses, forty barns, twenty-eight stacks of wheat, seventy-five stacks of hay, and over eighty head of cattle. Except for the accidental drowning of seventeen men from a bateaux on Lake Champlain, his losses were insignificant.

Haldimand's Forays and Espionage, 1778–1782

The rebels had no strength to oppose Carleton. Warner's Continentals at Fort Edward, Benjamin Whitcomb's rangers at Rutland, and the Charlotte County militia under Alexander Webster failed to even confront him. In late November Webster concluded a letter to Governor Clinton with the comment, "If more men is not stationed for the ensuing campaign than has been this, I do not believe any of the inhabitants will stay, as the enemy intends the most cruel usage of us."[22] Again, the rebels had lost any possibility of mounting an attack on Canada. Carleton was so thorough that in late November he took Sherwood with him to revisit the sites of his victories on Lake Champlain and noted that the places remained devastated and had not been rescued or rebuilt.

At Isle aux Noix in January 1779, mission Indians asked for another raid and Powell passed on the request to Haldimand, who answered cautiously, "I shall have no objections provided it be to procure intelligence and that they proceed to no greater length than taking prisoners, but you must insist upon their containing themselves within the bounds of humanity . . . , otherwise they must not be suffered to go."[23] On Lake George on July 15, a scout of twenty-seven Loyalists and Indians caught a rebel party of Warner's Continentals, women, and children picking huckleberries on Fourteen Mile Island. Some, like Major Wait Hopkins, were killed, and about half the party, including Captain Gideon Brownson and Captain Simeon Smith, were taken prisoner. Brownson, who was wounded, was a particular loss, since he had served under Warner since 1775, had also been wounded at the Battle of the Walloomsac, and had been with Ethan Allen in his abortive attempt to take Montreal in September 1775.

The defense of the south end of Lake George in 1779 fell on Warner's Continental regiment, which held Fort George. The crucial road between Fort George and Fort Edward had been the scene of ambushes since the Seven Years' War. Warner himself in September 1779 was nearly cornered on the road by a party of Indians near the famous "Bloody Pond" of the Seven Years' War.[24] His two companions were killed and he and his horse were wounded, but he made his escape on the dying horse to Wings Falls and then returned exhausted to Fort George. Thus the level-headed Vermont hero was almost a casualty of the forays, well after the Burgoyne Campaign.

Following the model of Major Carleton's expedition the year before, in November 1779 British craft came down Lake Champlain and discharged troops, including Jessup's corps and Indians, who raided the shore settlements as far south as Orwell, and then moved inland to Brandon and Middlebury, the latter Carleton having destroyed the year before.[25] So effective were the raids that, in New York, rebels reported that "we are at present compelled to procure private guards to secure" our persons and property from Loyalist incursions.

THE YEAR OF THE BURNING

In March 1780 Indians under Lieutenant Andrew Skene, Philip's son, attacked the rebels at Skenesborough, this time young Skene having no regrets about ravaging his family home. He took several prisoners back to Canada.[26] Two months later a force of 528 men under Sir John Johnson was conveyed by warships to Crown Point. The expedition consisted of his own regiment of Royal Yorkers, Jessup's and Peters's corps, 50 regulars and Hesse-Hanau jagers, the Kanesetake mission Indians, and Fort Hunter Mohawks. Their goal was a foray against Johnstown and Caughnawaga in the Mohawk Valley, moving by way of the western Saratoga area. After successfully completing his foray, Sir John retreated the way he had come. It was at this time that John Neilson of Bemis Heights and Alexander Webster, Joseph McCracken, and Brinton Paine of Charlotte County were called out with the militia by Governor Clinton to pursue Sir John. Governor Clinton led them all the way to Ticonderoga, but they failed to find Sir John's elusive force. This brief moment was the last time in the war that the rebels would occupy Ticonderoga in force.

On August 9 twenty-one Indians attacked Barnard, Vermont, and took at least three farmers captive to Canada. Fifty men from Barnard pursued them but could not find them. A week later "the militia officers and other principle gentlemen" of the area agreed to raise "forty volunteers" for the long-term defense of Barnard and Pomfret. They were to join Major Ebenezer Allen's newly raised rangers and "continue until the first of December next unless sooner discharged."[27] They carried on scouts to search and oppose "skulking" Loyalists, who continued to pick off a man or two in the Wethersfield area. It would be difficult, however, for Vermont's Board of War to find money to keep these men in the field longer.

In October 1780 the greatest invasion force thus far of the post-Burgoyne era was assembled in Canada under Major Christopher

Carleton. It consisted of 518 British and German regulars, 150 Loyalists, 108 mission Indians, and 30 Fort Hunter Mohawks. Eight ships and twenty-six boats bore Carleton's force.[28]

Haldimand was now willing to give a measure of recognition to his numerous Loyalist officers. He stipulated that Loyalist officers who were wounded in action were "entitled to the same gratuity of one years advanced pay as officers of the Established army," that officer's ranks were to be permanent in America, and that new recruits were to receive a cash bounty as an inducement.[29] He also made it clear to the Jessups that with such support from the crown, they should be able to fill their corps.

The Loyalists in the foray included the newly raised and still recruiting King's Rangers, under James Rogers, the brother of the famous Robert Rogers.[30] James Rogers had come to Quebec in 1779 with the blessing of Sir Henry Clinton to recruit a Loyalist regiment in Canada, much to the annoyance of Haldimand, who already had enough problems with understrength Loyalist units. However, by distancing himself from his obnoxious brother and by sheer determination, James gained Haldimand's respect and was allowed to recruit in 1780. The King's Rangers were inspected at the end of the year. In addition, David Jones was there as a lieutenant of the King's Loyal Americans, his task being to sweep the area south of Fort Edward. John and William Tuttle were in a company of Fort Edward and Kingsbury Loyalists, who were returning to see what had happened to their homes. Jeptha Hawley was involved in the expedition, in the capacity of a commander of bateaux men.

Rebel officers were completely surprised when Carleton's force appeared. Rebel Captain Silas Child at Granville, who had warned of the March foray, was the first to report Carleton's presence at Ticonderoga, which he passed on to Colonel Alexander Webster at Salem.[31] Webster knew the militia of the Charlotte County regiment were understrength and could not be in several places at once. He was helpless against the brilliant British campaign, which left rebel officers confused as to where the danger really lay.

Carleton's fleet landed at abandoned Skenesborough. They advanced to Fort Ann, which was garrisoned by seventy-five New York militiamen and a few Continentals under the command of Colonel Adiel Sherwood.[32] Sherwood was an officer of experience, having served from 1776 as a lieutenant in the First New York Continental Regiment, but he had ended his service abruptly, resigning over a promotion squabble. He then joined the state militia, where late in 1777 he was given the command of Fort Ann.

On October 10 Carleton destroyed an unoccupied blockhouse and sawmill before he reached the fort, which he then surrounded and asked for its surrender. While short on ammunition, Sherwood refused Carleton's summons at first but then decided it was wiser to yield, provided the women in the garrison were allowed to return to their homes.

When Governor Clinton received word of the surrender, he was outraged at Sherwood's conduct; he wrote to Washington that the fort "appear[ed] . . . to have been surrendered thro' treachery or cowardice."[33] Only the day before, Sherwood had dined at Fort Edward with thirty-year-old Colonel Henry Livingston, commander of the 3rd New York Militia and former major of a New York Continental regiment that served with Brigadier General Richard Montgomery in his invasion of Quebec. When Livingston received word of the enemy's advance from Governor Clinton, Sherwood had returned to his post, not realizing how close Carleton was. Soon farms were being destroyed within view of Livingston, who hid timidly behind Fort Edward's walls. A local family, the Bitelys, fled from their farm, which was under the fort's guns, thinking the garrisoned fort would offer a measure of protection, but when they returned, their buildings were all burned, their grain consumed, and their livestock slaughtered.

Livingston called for the militia, including Webster's Charlotte County regiment, to turn out at Fort Edward. In Webster's attempt to raise men, he went so far as to request help from Governor Chittenden. Afterward Governor Clinton was furious at him for dealing with the Vermont governor, denying he had given Webster such authority.

Carleton dispatched a party under Lieutenant David Jones of the King's Loyal Americans on the west of the Hudson River to Saratoga, devastating rebel farms but also being greeted by his neighboring Loyalists. In Kingsbury he received a warm welcome as expected from Gilbert Harris, Jr., who had put together a party to intercept rebel families fleeing southward. Ironically one of the houses destroyed by the raiders was that of Colonel John McCrea, brother of the heroine Jane, who had been betrothed to Jones. Recruiting went well for Jessup's King's Loyal Americans, which reached a strength of 133.[34]

Carleton dispatched another party, made up of the new regiment of the King's Rangers led by Captain James Rogers, bypassed

Fort Edward, and moved down the east side of the river to Duer's Plantation, burning hay and grain barracks in farms on both sides of the river. Some of the King's Rangers may have reached Salem, which had been largely abandoned, and Fort Williams and some houses were burned. The King's Rangers were even more successful than Jessup's corps in recruiting, for their numbers rose from about fifty to ninety-five as a result of the many prisoners they took in the foray. Overall, Carleton's men had devastated Queensbury, Kingsbury, Fort Edward, and Salem and destroyed six sawmills, a gristmill, thirty-eight dwelling houses, thirty-three barns, and fifteen hundred tons of hay. The foray was essentially unopposed, even by the rebel garrison at Fort Edward. No wonder the rebels called it "the Year of the Burning."[35]

Fort George remained and was the strongest of the rebels' garrisoned posts because of the quality of its Continentals. As noted, the fort and Lake George had been assigned to Seth Warner's independent Continental regiment in 1778, moving them from their traditional base in Vermont. After Saratoga, Warner was never able to recruit his regiment to anything like its authorized strength. In 1778 he suffered from the competition of the higher pay offered by states for their militias, and he even found Washington stealing some of his recruits and sending them to Rhode Island.[36] Warner was able to recruit only about two hundred men, chiefly stationed at Fort George and also token companies at Bemis Heights and Bennington. Samuel Safford, who had been named his second in command at Dorset in 1776, was still with him after Hubbardton and the Walloomsac, a remarkably supportive subordinate.

Now, in October 1780, a further calamity befell Warner's regiment when Carleton's men appeared on the road to Fort George. The fort was occupied by Captain John Chipman with seventy soldiers of Warner's regiment, the rest being off scouting Lake George. Chipman sent to Fort Edward for badly needed provisions, but the rider ran into what he thought was a small Indian party.[37] Not having heard that Carleton was in force in the area, Chipman sent Captain Thomas Sill with fifty men to destroy the marauding Indians. In fact, what Sill ran into was Carleton's main body, and though he attacked them, he soon found himself overwhelmed by numbers and was killed. Only fifteen of Sill's men escaped. Captain Chipman, having lost most of his force, could not defend the fort and surrendered. Thus a majority of

Warner's Continental regiment was lost. As for Carleton, to return to Ticonderoga, he had to raise from the lake bottom bateaux that had been sunk by the rebels, and even with them prisoners and booty had to be marched over the west side of the lake.

On October 12, at Fort Edward, Colonel Livingston received his requested reinforcements and began a tardy pursuit of Carleton, who by this time had vanished into thin air. Washington reviewed the Continental losses at Fort George and Warner's increasing inability to command because of illness, and at the end of the year the regiment was discontinued, fatefully ending its existence and Warner's career in the Continental Army.[38]

THE OFFSHOOTS OF THE INVASION

Captain John Munro was a native of Scotland who came to North America during the Seven Years' War as a soldier in the 48th Regiment. He received a grant as a disabled soldier after the war and became a Schenectady merchant and landholder, developing farmlands, mills, an ashery, and a nail factory at Shaftsbury near Bennington.[39] Here he had been confronted by the Green Mountain Boys and struck by Seth Warner and prevented from taking Remember Backer to Albany. He relocated in Albany, where he joined the Presbyterian Church. When the war came, he joined his cousins, the Reverend Henry Munro and bateau captain Hugh Munro, in becoming a Loyalist. As Sir John Johnson was forced to leave Johnstown, Munro was imprisoned, for he had accepted a commission in the Royal Highland Emigrants. He was sent to a Kingston jail on the Hudson River, from which he was able to escape in October 1777. He went to Ticonderoga and met Sir John, who convinced him to become a captain in the King's Royal Regiment of New York, leading Munro to ignore his previous commitment to the Royal Highland Emigrants. Munro would not completely leave the Hudson-Champlain region until 1784, when he settled in the Lunenburg district of Upper Canada.

This Loyalist would command a foray that went through the Saratoga area with the possible destination of Schenectady. Munro's mixed force left Carleton at Bulwagga Bay, near Crown Point, traveling in a more westerly direction by way of the Schroon River valley toward Schenectady.[40] The force consisted of his own and Joseph Anderson's companies of the King's Royal Yorkers, about 130 men, 34 of

Captain William Fraser's Independent Company, 30 of Claus's Rangers and Fort Hunter Mohawks under Captain Deserontyon, perhaps 250 in all. At St. Johns, 72 mission Indians from Kanesetake also joined Munro, led by the familiar Captain Alexander Fraser, deputy superintendent of Indian Affairs. On the way to Schenectady, the expedition stopped at Ball's Town, fifteen miles west of Bemis Heights, and decided that it would be a worthy objective, as it had a log fort, with 200 Schenectady militia to defend it and was the home of one of the area's leading rebels, Colonel James Gordon, who had previously led the militia that in 1777 seized the property of Daniel McAlpin and drove his wife Mary from their farm.

Munro's challenge was to destroy property throughout the Ball's Town area and capture Gordon without disturbing the fort's considerable militia garrison. Ball's Town's inhabitants had been under apprehension of an attack and had been leaving their houses at night and camping in the woods. As no enemy appeared, however, they had relaxed their vigilance and were back in their houses.[41] Gordon had just returned from the New York legislature in Poughkeepsie, where he represented the area. On the evening of October 16, he was awakened by the breaking of his chamber windows, so that any defense of his wife and daughter proved impossible, and he was seized while his house was plundered. He, his family, two servants, and three slaves were taken captive. Other houses were broken into, including that of militia Captain Tyrannis Collins, and families and slaves taken, in all perhaps twenty prisoners and captives. Thanks to the intervention of Loyalist officers, only two were killed by Indians, and the captives who could not keep up with the rest were returned to prevent them from being executed by the Mohawks and Kanesetakes.

At daylight Munro's force began to retreat northward, breakfasting on the sheep and cattle they had taken. Munro had orders to return by way of Saratoga, where it was known that a group that his raiders could rescue had been gathered in the barracks, awaiting exchange. But he was already overloaded with booty and prisoners like Gordon's family, so he chose not to go to Saratoga and return the way he had come. To ward off pursuers, Munro stated that if he discovered a pursuit, then his prisoners would be executed. Schenectady militia from the fort, under Captain Stephen Ball, did follow, but upon hearing of Munro's execution order and also reports that he commanded five hundred men, they dropped prudently back. Munro's victorious force and their prisoners were back at Bulwagga Bay on October 24. They rejoined Carleton with his fleet resting at Crown Point. There they awaited the pursuing rebels, who did not come. Commodore Chambers insisted that the season was too far advanced, and when the wind was right, the two forces sailed triumphantly north to Canada.[42] The effect of these forays against rebel defenses was long-term. Less than a year later, Governor Clinton ordered that Loyalist families and their effects be removed from Ball's Town to "interior parts of the country" to prevent further incursions.

To keep the rebels further confused, a third raid was conducted by Lieutenant Richard Houghton, who been with Carleton in 1778. He landed at the mouth of Vermont's Onion River with three hundred mostly mission Indians and Loyalists. A lieutenant in the 53rd Regiment, Houghton, following the policy of the Indian Department, in 1778 had been placed in charge of the crucial mission of Kahnawake, in which position he must have gained the confidence of Christopher Carleton. This raid had not been originally planned as part of Carleton's expedition; but so many Indians had gathered at St. Johns that Brigadier Powell insisted that they be used on a foray up the Onion River. Besides Kahnawakes, Houghton's allies included a few "Upper County" Indians, under French interpreter Joseph Marie La Motte, who acted independently and were "supposed to be more barbarous and cruel than Canadian [mission] Indians."[43] Indian auxiliaries also came from the Akwesasne mission, headed by Lieutenant William Johnson of the 47th Regiment and the Quebec Indian Department. More Kahnawakes, who were hunting along Lake Champlain, also joined Houghton, who welcomed them as their resident officer. Canadian Indians, then, were now confident in their British allies and willing to initiate forays with their resident officers.

Houghton's raid into Vermont was significant because it showed that a truce between Haldimand and the Arlington Junta was still not in effect. On October 15 Houghton's forces moved down the Onion River toward the Connecticut River, destroying Tunbridge, Sharon, Middlesex and Royalton—an attack that was expected after the Barnard raid in August.[44] At Royalton they struck at dawn on October 16, and four to seven people were scalped and thirty-two taken captive. The town and stockade fort were burned; the loss included twenty-eight dwellings, three barns, and one each sawmill and gristmill, while black cattle, sheep, and pigs were butchered. The raiders then began to return, burning Randolph—which was largely abandoned—on the way. Hough-ton's force was now burdened with plunder, cattle, horses, and male captives. One of the captives from Randolph, twenty-two year old Zadock Steele, later composed a popular account of his captivity.

Benjamin Witcomb's rangers were in the vicinity, but they seemed unable to do anything. Rebel scouts were sent out from Barnard and Bethel, but they could not find the enemy. A larger relief force of perhaps four hundred did materialize, but as might be expected, given Vermont's inability to raise troops, it was chiefly made up of Simonds's ever dependable Berkshire County militia, including Simeon Alex-ander of Northfield. Colonel John House of Hanover, New Hampshire, was elected the relief force's commander. They ran into Houghton's camp after advancing only two miles, and a warm exchange of fire followed. However, House ordered his men to halt, cease firing, and wait till dawn, probably to organize them for a more coordinated attack on the enemy. But by daylight Houghton's force was long gone, and House became the scapegoat for the failure to catch him. The Massachusetts and Vermont militias were frustrated, and as one scout commented, the enemy made off by "flying into Canada."[45] Actually, Houghton's force, with their captives and booty, returned by way of the Onion River and Lake Champlain to the Kahnawake mission.

In Vermont from 1778 to 1780, Haldimand's raiders specifically took fathers and sons as prisoners, those who could be exchanged for equivalent Loyalist prisoners, from youngsters in their teens to men in their fifties, sparing only females and young children. Separated from their families, mothers and their children were urged by the British to retreat to the nearest settlement. Christopher Carleton's men were under orders to burn rebel property, but Lieutenant Enys claimed they enforced the policy only sporadically. On occasion they left a home site immediately, purposely letting women extinguish the flames that were supposed to consume their homes.[46] Still, women left at home were unable to farm without their husbands and sons, and they faced the probability of becoming refugees and abandoning their households. As with Loyalist women who had lost their men, some of these women chose to stay on their farms, heading families of young children, eking out a bare existence but maintaining their husband's crucial claim to the land.

The rebels could not defend against the multiple incursions, for the task of even finding the enemy was difficult. The effect of Haldimand's raids was to push Vermont's border back to where it had been in July 1777 at Castleton. In 1779 the Vermont governor and Council, acting as a board of war, were forced to abandon the north and establish a more limited defense line at "the North line of Castleton, the west and north lines of Pittsford to the Green Mountains."[47] Any place north of that could not be protected. Ira Allen noted that without assistance from "our friends," the state could not maintain even this defensive frontier. Appeals for help again went to New Hampshire and Massachusetts, but those states could not be expected to continue to rescue Vermont. Although they would pretend to be more prepared than John Williams, Alexander Webster, or Governor George Clinton, the Arlington Junta had very little wherewithal to defend Vermont from British invasions.

New York: A Struggle between the Enemy and Domestic Necessity

New York was no better than Vermont in the protection of its borderland. As early as April 1778, Colonel John Williams was already feeling the effect of Haldimand's aggressive policy. From Salem, Williams saw clearly the enemy's design. They "are to present themselves in the frontiers in order to receive the disaffected [Loyalists] that will join them and then return to St. Johns and as soon as [our] militia are returned home, they are then to return and penetrate the country by parties in order to detect as many as they can and return."[48] Williams saw that the continuous British raids would make disaffected Loyalists part of their army.

Understanding the enemy's objectives did not mean that Williams or his militia could confront them. In May 1778 Governor Clinton gave Williams wide latitude in equipping and turning out his regiment "on the approach of the enemy without waiting orders" from him. Two years later Clinton still called out the Charlotte County militia, but their officers replied that in the past two years there had been an "unabated Struggle betwixt the Enemy, and Domestic necessity."[49] Without Continentals or long-term state levies, it was impossible for Clinton to rely on such militias, who had to support their family farms as well as defend the borderland.

The Salem district in Charlotte County had problems not only of religious and ethnic diversity but of increasing hardship and poverty.

John Armstrong, who had been the presiding officer at the court-martial of Williams's regiment, had come to Salem before the war and with his brother Thomas bought two lots north of Salem village in the Turner Patent.[50] The winter of 1780 was brutal, and with Armstrong away on militia duties, he took on a twelve-year-old Scot, Donald McDonald, to help his wife manage the farm. Donald's father, a veteran of the Seven Years' War in America, after losing two spouses to illness had returned to America in 1773 and leased land in the Salem area. Donald's winter duties included cutting browse, rounding up the cattle to feed on the browse, and bringing in firewood to cut. Both he and his father had all they could do to survive, let alone contribute to the war effort. Furthermore, Armstrong's wife was as niggardly as possible in treating Donald. She fed him a diet of mush and milk, which was not only skimmed but watered. After four months in the Armstrong household, Donald was described as skin and bones and at death's door. His father discovered his state and took him away. Such were the conditions, even when one lived in the household of one of Salem's rebel leaders.

In contrast, Cambridge's Phineas Whiteside would become wealthy during the war. He added to his existing eight hundred acres a further six hundred that he had been renting and now was able to purchase as confiscated Loyalist property. He was generous to the rebels, subscribing £1,000 to support them. He also, however, got involved with some deserters, friends of his from the Charlotte County militia whom Williams and his militia officers had court-martialed in 1778.[51] In court, Whiteside obtained an acquittal for the men and a reprimand to the officers, including Williams. With such divisions within the rebel leadership, it seemed the whole borderland would have to be abandoned.

In addition, Cambridge's militiamen felt that they were overextended in turning out for the governor's alarms. On May 6, 1780, the commanding officers of Cambridge's 16th Regiment—Colonel Lewis Van Woert, Lieutenant Colonel John Blair, and Major James Ashton—wrote to the governor of their plight. They had joined Clinton in chasing Sir John Johnson's expedition and now returned home, ready on "the Shortest notice" to defend the frontiers.[52] They had also done their part in public drafts for campaigns, in detachments and taxation. For April they had had orders to list and equip every thirty-fifth man to be posted as frontier guards, and this had been done. "But now we are called upon to raise one eighth part of our militia and provide them with arms, ammunition and provision. They are to take permanent post on the frontier, through periodic reliefs." This last request to support levies was the proverbial straw that broke the camel's back.

Cambridge was still so divided that it was impossible to expect a large and consistent turnout of militia. Despite the reconciliation proposed by Younglove and Whiteside, Loyalist raids continued around the settlement, making reconciliation difficult. Among the militia were known protectionists and Loyalists like George Telford. Moreover, its militia leaders could "neither raise nor equip these soldiers. When they got arms, they were unable to purchase ammunition. Also, they could not victual themselves on the frontier and leave sufficient to support [their] families at home."[53] Only outside financing and supply would have allowed the Cambridge militia to defend the place. Yet outsiders like Salem's Ebenezer Clark thought that Cambridge was "our only support in case of sudden invasion," implying that Salem's inhabitants would have to flee to the protection of Cambridge if they were attacked by Indians.

Clark did not know the realities of Cambridge. In September 1779 Cambridge petitioned for permission to trade wheat for salt with New Englanders, an embargo having been placed on the export of wheat by New York authorities, as it was needed for home consumption and Washington's army. They were unable to break the embargo and thus were left short of salt in the coming year, which anyway was one of crop shortage.[54] Many families chose to leave, making Cambridge a fragile place to defend, even though it was south of more exposed Granville and Salem. Cambridge was also left with considerable unoccupied land, and the abandoned lands were not sold to new settlers until after the war. From 1789 to 1790, Younglove would continue his effort to heal the split by reviewing affidavits as a judge of those who were "obliged to leave" the town during the war, excusing them from paying the accumulated quitrent. It appears that some were rebels who had given up their farms in the face of Haldimand's forays, but some, like Thomas Ashton, had been Loyalists. Clearly Younglove wanted no questions asked, for Cambridge's population had diminished during the war and it needed settlers. A population decline may be true of many Albany and Charlotte County communities.

Seeking to hold a defensive line, the Albany Committee organized collections "for the ruined settlers of the frontiers of this state."[55]

With Stark now serving with Washington, in October 1780 Washington had named James Clinton, brother of the governor and leader of the Clinton-Sullivan Campaign against the Iroquois, as commander of the Northern Department. By the time Clinton arrived at Albany, Carleton had done his work. At the end of the year, New York's line of settlement was effectively thrown back to Saratoga and Salem to avoid the British incursions. In that year Justus Sherwood would suggest to Haldimand that the influential John Williams should be brought into the secret negotiations with Vermont because he understood "the designs of Allen and Chittenden" and might be further cultivated. The war was far from over.

Haldimand's policy of petite guerre might have pleased Burgoyne, although he would have been disappointed that British light infantry did not play a more important role. Haldimand succeeded where Burgoyne had not by using mixed forces, depending more on his Loyalists and Indians. None of his raids should be seen in isolation as petty warfare; they were part of a well-organized and successful effort to invade rebel territory. From Lake Champlain the mixed forces would continually raid, with Loyalists returning to their homes, bringing their relatives and friends away, while dealing retribution to their rebel neighbors. Thus, civil war was rekindled every time Haldimand sent out a raid. His effort culminated in the Year of the Burning, during which Warner's Continental regiment was eliminated and all rebel posts north of Saratoga were abandoned. Ultimately the area of Burgoyne's invasion no longer belonged to the rebels, but rather it had become a borderland controlled by the British from Canada.

16

DISCORD AMONG THE REBELS
The Need for Protection in
Eastern New York

As we have seen, after Burgoyne's Saratoga Campaign the defense of the New York–Vermont borderland was of primary concern to Washington, Schuyler, Stark, Chittenden, and George Clinton. The borderland was incessantly invaded by British forces from Canada. Most of the Continental troops had been sent elsewhere, leaving the defense to local militia and finally longer-term levies. This meant that the defense of the devastated region fell on the farmers and others who remained there, who complained that as militia men they were so continuously under arms that they were unable to farm their land and support their families.

In Charlotte County, Governor Clinton had continued to be unable to defend farms and settlements. Not only was the line of settlement thrown back to avoid the British incursions, but remaining in homesteads became almost impossible as families were dispersed and did not have enough labor to farm. As a result of the British forays, the reduced number of rebel militia units remaining could not possibly protect places like Granville, Fort Miller, and Salem, instead asking the New York legislature for defensive aid. Major Joseph McCracken, Charlotte County militia commander at Salem, noted that since the Burgoyne expedition, the region had often been devastated, leaving the people "so long kept under arms" that they were obliged to neglect their crops and withdraw from their settlements unless immediate relief was given.[1] Such succor was impossible for the New York legislature to provide for, especially as its resources were being diverted in several directions. To solve the problem, in 1781 Governor Clinton ordered the populace to move south toward Saratoga, where they could be defended, but this meant that those north of Saratoga would have to abandon their farms, always an unpopular measure. With the ability of families to maintain households in the borderland threatened from several directions, they became open to seeking protection from beyond New York State and Congress.

SECESSION IN NEW YORK

The secessionist movement by the New York towns was a gradual process, spurred by the nearby presence of Arlington's Junta. The Junta justified their action with the theory that some New York towns had been taken from the State of New York when Philip Skene was named lieutenant governor of Ticonderoga and Crown Point in 1774 and hence they were now free to join Vermont. This disregarded the fact that it was unclear as what Skene's title meant and that he had only used it for less than a week, during Colonel Baum's march to the Walloomsac. On April 11, 1781, the Vermont General Assembly called a May convention at Cambridge for New York towns east of the Hudson to agree to articles of union with the independent republic of Vermont.[2] Newly arrived New Englanders who settled in the New York towns of Granville, Cambridge, Hoosic, and elsewhere were sympathetic to the call and convened in Cambridge five days later to review the articles of union presented by the Vermont Assembly. After acceptance of the articles, the New York towns were to elect representatives to take seats in the Vermont Assembly.

A few days later it was reported to Governor Clinton that Ethan Allen had visited the Cambridge area and was "deluding the people."[3] The report rightly accused Allen of corresponding with the British. It claimed that "the great distress is the want of provisions" and it was such that "the inhabitants are moving off every day, notwithstanding every argument is used to keep them on their farms." Rumors flew, for Governor Chittenden reacted by claiming that New Yorkers were actually forcing settlers out of the area. In response, New York militia officers affirmed to Chittenden that they were doing their duty in raising a militia for defense and that he had no authority in New York State.

On May 8 Ira Allen had made a point of informing Haldimand that "the people east of Hudson's River . . . will be represented in the [Vermont Assembly]."[4] Ira would argue that the annexation of the New York towns was a step in the development of a special relationship with the British. As we will see, the Junta's negotiations with Haldimand had also created an apparent lull in hostilities that made it seem that the British were being restrained from attacking Vermont. It suggested that New York's towns might be better protected if they were part of Vermont.

In March and April 1781, petitions were sent to Chittenden from citizens in Cambridge, Granville, and the Camden Valley, asking to join Vermont because New York had neglected guarding the northern region. The Junta chose Cambridge as the meeting place, and no less than Ira Allen visited Cambridge to prepare for the meeting held there from May 9 to 15, to be attended by a committee of the Vermont legislature and representatives of the seceding New York towns. Town meetings were to be called, at which delegates would be elected to go to the Vermont Assembly. Yet John Younglove, the supervisor of Cambridge in 1780, felt the division on the annexation question was "half & half."[5] In Cambridge, the subscribers to the Allens' proposal were Colonel John Blair, commander of the militia; Phineas Whiteside, the wealthy and conciliatory rebel of West Cambridge; and Colonel Joseph Caldwell. The latter two would be elected representatives from Cambridge to the Vermont Assembly. Blair had been in the process of raising levies for the New York militia, but he halted his activity as he now switched his allegiance to Vermont. Younglove asked his second-in-command, Major James Ashton of Ashgrove, to take Colonel Blair's place, but Ashton avoided this now highly controversial duty.

Receiving reports of these activities, Governor Clinton had few resources to support those loyal to New York, and he could only urge Cambridge's John Younglove to avoid altercation and wait patiently for the reestablishment of New York's authority.[6] The situation was further complicated when one of Sherwood's agents, Lieutenant James Parrot, on a raid to capture rebel leaders, decided to abduct Younglove. On July 30, 1781, Younglove's house was surrounded and his guards taken, and a demand for his surrender by Parrot was followed by a volley against the door. When his wife opened it, Younglove was seen apparently mortally wounded. Parrot retreated with the guards as prisoners and the expectation that Younglove had died of his wounds. In fact, he survived. He had, of course, been a strong supporter of New

York's jurisdiction over Cambridge, and he would be out of the picture while he recovered. The incident, however, made it seem as if Loyalists like Parrot and representatives of the Junta were working together.

Governor Chittenden had already made an effort to fulfill obligations to the gathered New York towns. On April 25, 1781, the Vermont Board of War recommended that 1,500 men be raised for their defense, that a cheap barracks be erected for them, and that scouts be sent to "cover the inhabitants of Skenesborough, Granville, etc."[7] A committee was set up to arrange civil and military departments in the New York towns. Thus, Chittenden prepared to protect the seceding New York towns from New York State's forces.

At Salem, the watchful Major Joseph McCracken informed Philip Schuyler that "Ethan Allen had some days ago been [there] attempting to seduce the inhabitants from their allegiance to [New York]." When he asked Allen what part Vermont would take if "the enemy attempted to penetrate into the country," Allen replied "that he would neither give nor take any assistance from New York" but would operate independently.[8] Despite the presence of Allen in Salem for three or four days, McCracken and John Williams maintained Salem's loyalty to New York. Williams, however, would warn Clinton on June 5 that "we shall be compelled to submit ourselves to Vermont if nothing is done."[9] New York had no troops, no provisions, and no money in the area, while Vermont was actually supplying the Cambridge militia with ammunition. To the north, Fort Edward was abandoned because there were no supplies for the troops. New Yorkers were being asked to leave their farms and retreat behind Stark's lines at Saratoga, while Allen was claiming they could remain on their farms and be protected where they were.

On June 15 and 16, 1781, the Vermont Assembly, meeting in Bennington, was informed that the delegates were ready to take their seats and voted to confirm the union with the delegates elected from ten communities in seven districts along the New York border.[10] This was definitely not all the towns that had been invited to join the Assembly. As expected, there were representatives with no constituencies: Colonel Gideon Warren, who supposedly represented Greenfield, in fact, had just moved there from Vermont and was unknown in Greenfield.

It was an explosive situation, as New York's and Vermont's militias were poised to confront each other. Congress and John Stark, Northern

Department commander at Saratoga, tried to prevent this, asserting that a violent confrontation would seriously undermine the rebel cause. In August Stark wrote to Chittenden, advising him that the best course to achieve Vermont's independence was to avoid engaging itself in the governing of either New York or New Hampshire.[11] Privately, Stark wrote to Meshech Weare, president of New Hampshire, in no uncertain terms: "I deem the late riotous conduct of the state of Vermont, in extending their pretended claim to the westward, and threatening to support it by military force" to be in "violation of the rules of Congress."[12] The hero of the Walloomsac was not about to see his own New Hampshire or New York dismembered.

By December 1781 Governor Clinton was able to head off the annexation by putting together a force to invade independent Vermont. The move was the result of a provocative incident in Hoosic at a public house, where Colonel John Van Rensselaer of the Lower Manor had openly denounced the effort to annex the town to Vermont.[13] In Green Mountain Boy style, a mob seized Van Rensselaer and his supporters and took them to nearby Bennington, evidently to humiliate them. There the conservative Bennington magistrates promptly released them, and the incident made Van Rensselaer a hero in the manor, as Hoosic refused to send delegates to the organizing conventions or to the Vermont Assembly.

However, Van Rensselaer was an officer of the militia and reported the incident to the commander of the Albany County militia, the hero of the siege of Fort Stanwix, Peter Gansevoort. Governor Clinton saw the incident as Chittenden's strengthening the authority of the Vermont militia while he moved toward an alliance with the British. Gansevoort called out the Albany County militia, a body that had sent 1,800 men to do battle with Burgoyne. In this case, however, only about 200 responded.[14] In fact, some authorities have seen the poor turnout as a continuation of militia insubordination that had commenced with John Williams's effort to turn out the Charlotte County militia in 1777. The array of New York militia officers was at least impressive, at one time including Henry K. Van Rensselaer of Fort Ann fame, Colonel John Van Rensselaer, and Colonels Peter Yates and Cornelius Van Vechten.

Both Gansevoort and Ira Allen claimed to be opposed to civil war, but soon the states' militias were facing each other. Captain John Abbott collected Vermont militiamen to oppose Gansevoort near Hoosic,

New York, where he established a fortified camp.[15] Ira visited Abbott and now upped the stakes by calling the Vermont militia of Colonel Noah Lee from distant Rutland. Ira, continuing to rattle his saber, placed Colonel Ebenezer Walbridge in charge of the force gathered just within New York, telling him to avoid contact with John Van Rensselaer. An original Separatist settler of Bennington, Walbridge had served on its Committee of Safety and established the famous ammunition magazine that was Baum's objective. He was a veteran of Warner's Continental regiment and had been named lieutenant colonel of the Vermont militia in 1778. He certainly was more at home sparring with the British than New Yorkers. On his own, Samuel Robinson, Jr., of Bennington raised a militia to oppose New York at the Walloomsac River. Certainly, the forces of the two states were poised for combat.

On December 18 Gansevoort asked Walbridge, "What was the objective of the movements into the interior parts of New York?"[16] Walbridge replied that he was there to defend those who owed allegiance to Vermont, especially if they had been taken prisoner by Gansevoort's men. He conceded that his activities only involved those New York towns that had demonstrated a desire to join Vermont. Gansevoort had gone to the Continental commander, John Stark, and asked for troops and field guns to aid him, as Governor Clinton had none. Stark refused because his resources were limited and he was not happy with the prospect of civil war between the two states.

When Gansevoort returned to muster militia at Schaghticoke and Hoosic, he found Colonel Peter Yates in full retreat with only eighty men.[17] At Sancoick Mills, he was told that he faced a force of as many five hundred Vermont militiamen, terrorizing those who refused to take the oath of allegiance to Vermont. It was said that Ethan Allen, the great propagandist, accompanied the Vermont militia. Gansevoort was left without an army and thus ended the phony war. New York had shown a lack of will and resources to either control or defend its border towns, while Vermont had challenged Governor Clinton, annexing several, if not all, of New York's eastern towns.

The possibility of bloodshed between New York and Vermont was thus avoided, but this was not the only front on which the Junta operated. It was not just New York towns they wished to annex, but also those to the east in New Hampshire. Yes, New Hampshire, the very state that had saved Vermont at the Battle of the Walloomsac!

The idea had actually been broached earlier in March 1778, when sixteen New Hampshire towns in the Connecticut Valley, discontented over the domination of the state's eastern seaboard, suggested annexation to Vermont. The towns petitioned the Vermont Assembly to receive them into union, and the Assembly was receptive. However, at that time the Arlington Junta saw the new towns as packing the Vermont Assembly with representatives from areas that were too far away for them to control. How many of the leaders of these towns would be as independent as Jacob Bayley? In addition, the action upset the rest of New Hampshire, especially powerful president Meshech Weare. Ethan Allen had supported the annexation in June but changed his mind when he apologized to Weare in October for "the imbecility of Vermont in the matter of the union."[18] By February 1779, the Junta had maneuvered the Vermont Assembly into rejection of the proposed connection.

Two years later, however, another attempt to annex the same New Hampshire towns developed, and this time it was spearheaded by the Junta. Weare acted decisively, and the New Hampshire House of Representatives issued a proclamation, giving their revolted towns forty days to go before a New Hampshire magistrate and swear their recognition of the Connecticut River as the western boundary of New Hampshire.[19] Additionally, a thousand New Hampshire militiamen were called up to go to the disputed area, to protect the inhabitants and allow for the exercise of New Hampshire's civil authority. Again, the Junta's policy of annexation had led to the expansion of civil war.

Congress had already firmly rejected Vermont's demand for recognition on June 20, 1780, and the annexation efforts made matters worse. On October 20, 1781, Ira Allen wrote to Loyalist Justus Sherwood, his new ally, explaining that a committee of the Vermont Assembly had rejected Congress's demand that the annexed territories be restored.[20] Haldimand was again being told that annexation would smooth the way to restoring Vermont to the British Empire.

However, the Vermont Assembly was exasperated and separated itself from continuation of the Arlington Junta's annexation policies, which were creating lasting friction with New York and now New Hampshire. Catching Ira and Ethan unaware, on February 23, 1782, the Assembly on its own dissolved the short-lived union with New York and New Hampshire towns.[21] The boundaries of Vermont returned to what they had been. The Assembly followed the termination of union by sending a delegation of moderates to Congress, consisting of Jonas Fay, Moses Robinson, Paul Spooner, and Isaac Tichenor. They found the damage done to Vermont's reputation in Congress beyond repair, and on March 1, 1782, Congress reiterated their earlier reasons for not allowing Vermont into the union of the thirteen states. Here was a sign that the Vermont Assembly would take a more independent role in their future relationship with the Junta.

In New York the Vermont Assembly's action left Granville, Cambridge, and White Creek to end their relationship with Vermont and petition the New York State legislature for clemency. In the words of the Granville petitioners, we "have been for the last three campaigns almost constantly in alarms, which hath rendered" us "in a most deplorable condition, so that there are numbers of families now amongst us who have scarce one bushel of grain to support them, nor is there any to be purchased within twenty miles distance. That under these distressing circumstances, and the insinuation of artful and designing men [the Allens and Thomas Chittenden], your petitioners were seduced to swerve from their allegiance, not from any desire of leaving the State, could we have been protected."[22] Representatives involved in the annexation to Vermont—including Middle Granville's Asaph Cook and John Glover as well as South Granville's David Blakesley—all contritely signed the petition.

In 1782 the New York legislature reacted favorably to the prodigals' petitions, giving the districts full amnesty and welcoming their return.[23] In fact, they coupled the Amnesty Act with a second "for Quieting the Minds of the Inhabitants" of the area, which was also meant as an olive branch to Vermont grant holders. The Quieting Act was another attempt to bring Vermont back to New York. It confirmed New Hampshire land grants that had been made before those of New York. New Hampshire grants could not be voided because conditions, like settlement, had not been met. Squatters were even allowed to have the right of up to 500 acres on ungranted land. The only stipulation to enjoy these privileges was to renounce the authority of independent Vermont. It was the best try New York had ever made to reconcile its differences with Vermont, but it should have come much earlier. Vermont was now independent, had confiscated Loyalist property, and was carrying on negotiations with Canada's Governor Frederick Haldimand.

Never again would the New York towns come this close to joining Vermont. In 1784 the New York legislature created Washington

County from the old Charlotte County in recognition of the growing importance of the rebellious towns, and two years later the new county numbered 4,456 inhabitants.[24] As we have hinted, rivalry appeared over where the new county seat should be located, with Salem and Fort Edward vying for the honor.

The Arlington Junta's attempt to annex the adjoining portions of New York and New Hampshire made those states more hostile and fueled civil conflict. New York could not protect itself against Haldimand's petite guerre, and Vermont's resources for defense were even less. Chittenden's orders to defend the borderland were only on paper: it proved impossible to raise a militia to defend against the British forays and pursue them. However, the need for protection in New York's eastern towns made them ripe for annexation.

The entire annexation episode showed that the New York–Vermont borderland remained torn by civil war, a lawless region with an absence of local government. It was not controlled by either New York or Vermont, let alone Congress, and the most powerful military presence in the area remained Haldimand's forces. The War of Independence would fail to settle the land problems between Vermont and New York.

17

HALDIMAND AND THE ARLINGTON JUNTA

From Crown Point in October 1780, Christopher Carleton, at the height of his power over the region, wrote to Ethan Allen guaranteeing that he would restrain his forces from further depredations if Allen and Chittenden would consider a proposal from Governor Frederick Haldimand.[1] The bearer of Carleton's message and Haldimand's letter was Justus Sherwood, who was now the Loyalist officer most involved in Haldimand's secret service. By October 29 Allen had received the former Green Mountain Boy in Castleton and replied to Carleton, assuring him of a truce with the Vermont militia under his command while the letter was being considered. Bluffing as usual, Allen had very few militiamen on hand, and initially it was the defenseless state of Vermont that led the Junta to treat with Haldimand.

Actually, the British feelers to Ethan Allen had begun earlier, at the end of March. Lord George Germain in England and Sir Henry Clinton in New York City had chosen Beverly Robinson, a prominent Hudson Valley Loyalist involved in the 1777 expedition that had taken Forts Montgomery and Clinton, to write Allen asking if he might be interested in negotiations. Robinson had heard that Allen "would willingly assist in uniting America again to Great Britain, and restoring that happy constitution we have so wantonly and unadvisedly destroyed."[2] He also offered to establish secret communications between Allen and Sir Henry Clinton. Allen had received Robinson's letter in Arlington in July and brought it to Chittenden and the rest of the

Junta for discussion. So the matter of negotiations had already been broached by Robinson when Carleton sent his letter.

The crucial go-between in these negotiations was Justus Sherwood. He had access to his rebel relatives Adiel and Seth Sherwood, the former responsible for the surrender of Fort Ann in 1780, and to Loyalists to the south. Justus Sherwood had been named commissioner of prisoners and refugees by Haldimand, operating from early 1779 out of St. Johns, when he delivered Robinson's letter to Allen. The Arlington Junta grasped at the opportunities Haldimand offered. In early May 1780 Ira Allen had written directly to Haldimand about his conversations with Justus Sherwood concerning a prisoner exchange. It was to be followed by a truce between independent Vermont and the British. Two months later in another letter to Haldimand, Ira revealed more of the conditions under which Vermont might return to the empire. He commented, "The citizens of this state are emigrants from Connecticut and would choose charter privileges similar to that government."[3] As to the mood of Congress, he complained, they "wished to keep this state in suspense to the end of the war and then divide her territory amongst the claiming states." Such opinions were certainly heartening to Haldimand. The prisoner exchange went through in September at Skenesborough, where Sherwood delivered 117 men, women, and children to the Vermont authorities, who exchanged them for 23 Loyalist families.

Sherwood was so successful in negotiations like this that by July 1781 he would begin to build the Loyal Blockhouse, the most forward permanent British base on Lake Champlain, at Dutchman's Point, North Hero Island. At the new blockhouse he would command a unit of the Queen's Loyal Rangers and establish a system of Loyalist scouts and agents throughout Vermont, New York, and western New Hampshire.[4] Previously, Haldimand had formally appointed him as the officer in charge of his secret service, a role he had already been performing. Among his prerogatives would be the requirement that all secret agents were to stop at the Loyal Blockhouse and be cleared by Sherwood before they journeyed south. He or his agents would continue to approach the Junta in Arlington, carrying Haldimand's correspondence to them. This relationship flourished as he and his superiors offered Vermont support against New York and Congress, encouraging Vermont to become a territory within the British Empire.

From June 1781 Sherwood had a refugee Loyalist assistant, and then more formally a deputy, who helped him keep track of the rebels, especially in New York State. The deputy was Dr. George Smyth, the brother of Pat Smyth of Fort Edward.[5] George Smyth had come to North America from Ireland in 1770 with his wife and two sons, Terence and Thomas. They had settled near his brother in Fort Edward, but then, as George practiced medicine, he and his family left for Claverack in Rensselaerswyck and finally to Albany, where they lived in a townhouse. In Albany George was interrogated and warned several times by the Albany Committee because of activities favoring the enemy. He was jailed during the Burgoyne invasion, finally being paroled to work in the Albany military hospital. During his residence in Claverack and Albany, aided by his family, he acted as a bailsman for Loyalists, and despite the surveillance of the Albany Commissioners for Detecting and Defeating Conspiracies, he sent a constant stream of intelligence to Canada. He used the code name of Hudibras—from a poem by Samuel Butler—a name by which he was known in Loyalist circles.

By late May 1781, the Albany Committee for Detecting and Defeating conspiracies had had enough.[6] They ordered the arrest of Smyth and his son Terrance, but the authorities were unable to find them. George had escaped to New City (Lansingburgh), where his friends asked Brunswicker Adam Beam to secretly convey him to the comparative sanctuary of Bennington, which not only was outside New York's jurisdiction but was the territory of the Junta. Smyth, however, was captured by rebels and again imprisoned in Albany, only to be rescued from jail by Mathew Howard, one of Sherwood's agents. After an arduous journey up Lake Champlain, he arrived in St. Johns. He would serve as a doctor at the St. Johns hospital, and ultimately, in late 1782, he would personally carry Justus and his family through a bout with smallpox. A well-educated and gregarious man, Smyth would become Sherwood's friend as well as his best spymaster.

At the same time, Sherwood and Smyth acquired a familiar immediate superior, Major General Friedrich von Riedesel, who had been imprisoned as a member of the Convention Army and then paroled to New York City, where he was exchanged for Benjamin Lincoln, who had surrendered Charleston, South Carolina, to the British. After a stint on Long Island, Haldimand asked that Riedesel return to serve in Canada. Previous to his arrival, the Lake Champlain command had informally belonged to Lieutenant Colonel Barry St. Leger. Sherwood had found St. Leger difficult because he was jealous of Sherwood's close relationship with Haldimand and insisted on reviewing all of Sherwood's correspondence. With Riedesel, however, Haldimand's direct relationship with Sherwood was not a problem.

Riedesel established a comradely rapport with Haldimand, ignoring the fact that he had been warned that Haldimand was "a sour looking morose man, and of a very unsocial disposition."[7] Haldimand appreciated Riedesel because of his thorough reports on defenses of the Richelieu Valley, from Lake Champlain to Sorel, the extent of the German's command. In March 1782 Riedesel inspected Sherwood's force at the Loyal Blockhouse and noted that while the blockhouse was strong, Sherwood's own house would be easily taken in an attack. He emphasized that if the post were about to be attacked by superior forces, Sherwood and his command should retire to nearby Point au Fer, which was a much more defensible position. The team of Riedesel, Sherwood, and George Smyth were now prepared to handle any situation that affected the territory to the south of them.

On October 5, 1781, Smyth received a letter from the south end of Lake Champlain "near Brown Point" from the Reverend John Stuart, the former Anglican missionary to the Fort Hunter Mohawks.[8] While most of the Mohawks had left him for Canada in 1777, he now had with him his family, his slaves, and a number of followers, mostly women and children—altogether fifty souls. They were free to go to Canada, but as the chill of fall set in, they were still awaiting boats in a most exposed position along the shore. Immediately, Smyth left with bateaux on a relief mission to rescue Stuart's party, and on October 9 he was back with Stuart and his flock. When Stuart arrived in Montreal, Haldimand gave him a grant to open a school there, thus providing him with a modest income and offering a new opportunity for Loyalist families. Stuart was also appointed chaplain of Sir John Johnson's 2nd Battalion of Royal Yorkers.

Cooperative as the relationship was between Sherwood and Smyth, there were times of strain. Smyth also appeared to be jealous of Sherwood, an emotion that may have undermined their relationship. Smyth clearly understood that Sherwood was in charge, the man from whom he would have to seek approval.[9] However, the two leaders were often separated, Sherwood at the Loyal Blockhouse and

Smyth at St. Johns, and when one of them was absent, it was impossible for both to confer on the demands of the spy network. What was amazing was that the two managed their far-flung spy network so well. Under their leadership, this intelligence network played a crucial role in Haldimand's aggressive defense of Canada.

A key to Sherwood's success was to maintain long-term contact with his friends in the Arlington area. In a letter in May 1782, Sherwood admitted to recruiting Loyalists in Arlington, especially using his brother-in-law Elijah Bothum of Shaftsbury, an ensign in Jessup's Rangers. In 1783 Sergeant Moses Hurlburt was so open in recruiting Loyalists at a public dance next to Chittenden's house that the Junta had to rescue him from arrest.[10] Sherwood's Arlington agents included Jehiel's grandson, Eli Hawley, who Sherwood respected as "a very active discreet young man." Other Vermont agents were Lemuel Buck of East Arlington, Loyalist scout Samuel Rose of Manchester, and Bennington's Breakenridges, James Sr. and David Jr. Some of Sherwood's agents, like Buck, who represented Arlington in the Vermont Assembly, were still involved in securing Vermont's independence from New York. Of the Breakenridges, James Sr. was a New Hampshire grantee icon, after the famous confrontation at his farm in 1771, where Ethan Allen overawed New York authorities. Now, however, he was part of Sherwood's network.

Sherwood avoided one contact, who it would seem was ideal for his efforts. This was William Marsh, who had gone over to the British in 1777 as result of the Castleton Meeting and was now living in St. Johns. He had connections to the Allens, for he had been a Green Mountain Boy in 1775.[11] However, Haldimand felt that Marsh was to be kept at arm's length because he had loose lips and an exaggerated sense of his own importance. Marsh, carried on his own effort to have Vermont become part of Canada. Late in 1780 he was at Chimney Point urging Haldimand to intensify negotiations with the Junta and claiming he had a letter for the Allens. He did perform a major service in late August 1781, by bringing 130 Loyalist women and children from Vermont to St. Johns. A year later he visited Vermont and claimed that his friends welcomed him and hoped for trade with Canada.

OPPOSITION WITHIN VERMONT TO THE HALDIMAND NEGOTIATIONS

While Ethan Allen and the Junta were negotiating with Haldimand, Ethan wrote letters to rebel leaders John Stark and Philip Schuyler denying any wrongdoing. Still, the Junta's negotiations with Haldimand caused a growing Vermont opposition. In fact, the existence of this opposition was Ira and Ethan's favorite excuse as to why negotiations with Haldimand did not move more quickly. They claimed such resistance had to be won over or eliminated.

Sherwood knew about the Junta's opposition, when he observed: "I have no doubt, but Vermont will be ours as far as Mr. [Chittenden, Allen, and Fay] can put it in our power, but I fear the Benningtonites, especially the two mob Colonels; Warner and Herrick, will find means to overturn the whole system."[12] The Junta's negotiations with Haldimand did not go unnoticed in Bennington, where they were as upset about the Junta's prisoner exchange with Haldimand as was Washington or Governor Clinton. As early as July 1778, petitions from Bennington and Shaftsbury had protested the Junta's Commission of Confiscation because of the sweeping banishments it issued, which included many prominent original New Hampshire grantees. In March 1781, Seth Warner had confronted Ethan Allen on his dealings with Haldimand and Beverly Robinson, but Allen again denied he had any.

A year later Warner and Samuel Herrick organized the Bennington crowd to oppose the Junta's negotiations with Haldimand. Their opposition came to a boil over another exchange of prisoners that was meant to demonstrate the Junta's willingness to negotiate with the British. In May 1782 Ethan and his militia were ordered by Chittenden to go to Bennington and take prisoners held in confinement and march them north to be exchanged with the British. Colonel Warner— worn down by illness that would take his life by the end of the year— and a committee from Bennington came to Arlington to confront Chittenden. They opposed the exchange and threatened to raise men to bring the prisoners back. Chittenden warned them that they would have to clash with Ethan Allen's men, who were operating under his authority. He also maintained that the northern part of the state was united with him and the Council, and he suggested that Warner and the committee should return to Bennington and be quiet.

But the opposition to the Junta's negotiations would not go away. In June Warner was chagrined to learn from Washington, his commander-in-chief, that he was unable to get through to Haldimand to propose a return of prisoners that been taken from Warner's Continental regiment at Lake George in 1780. In contrast, the Junta had easy communications with Haldimand over the matter of prisoners. In July Herrick gathered a mob and demanded that Chittenden give reasons for sending back all the British prisoners and Loyalists he held. Herrick claimed that Chittenden, Ethan Allen, and Major Gideon Brownson were traitors and actually Loyalists. Brownson, who was Ethan Allen's brother-in-law and had served with Seth Warner, ordered Herrick's mob to disperse, and finally they did.[13] Clearly, the Junta's negotiations with Haldimand came with a price, for they split the authority of Vermont government and weakened the Junta's influence over the Assembly and places south of Arlington like Bennington.

As early as November 1780, the Vermont General Assembly felt enough evidence existed to try Ethan Allen for treason in his dealings with Haldimand. Allen objected to the proceedings, and while the complaint was dismissed, Allen resigned his commission as brigadier general of the Vermont militia.[14] His resignation was accepted, and he was thanked for his services. Without a command, in April 14, 1781, Allen wrote a letter to New York's Governor Clinton offering his, Colonel Ebenezer Allen's, and two other minor officers' services to New York—despite his past activities against that state. This was a brazen act, for Clinton was his archenemy, his most ardent foe in keeping Vermont independent of New York. Regardless of the opposition, Allen and the Junta continued to keep the door open to negotiations with the Canadian governor and his agents.

A separate source of opposition to the Junta's policies came from the eastern Vermont towns along the Connecticut River that still harbored pockets of support for New York titles. Lacking respect for the distant Arlington Junta, they now looked to union with New Hampshire as a solution for their problems. As one might have guessed, one of their leaders was the veteran of the Siege of Saratoga, Jacob Bayley of Newbury. Never a supporter of an independent Vermont or the Junta, he was now an outspoken critic of the Junta's negotiations with Haldimand. As military leader of northern Vermont, he still held his New York militia commission and dealt directly with Washington and other Continental officers. Late in 1778 and early in 1779, he worked with the commander-in-chief on yet another invasion of Canada that failed to materialize. In March he went before the New Hampshire General Assembly, representing eight towns on the Vermont side of the Connecticut River that sought to join New Hampshire, or that failing, create a separate state made up of the towns on both sides of the river. Ira Allen was in New Hampshire shadowing him to scuttle his proposal, but as late as August Bayley wrote President Meshech Weare, "I wish your [New Hampshire] would not neglect to support your claim to the grants on this [west] side of the river."[15] It was obvious that Bayley would do his best to undermine the Junta and its authority in Vermont.

With such a record of opposition to the Haldimand negotiations, the capture of Bayley became the object of a plan hatched at the Loyal Blockhouse. It is not clear as to the Junta's involvement, but Sherwood's effort depended upon the cooperation of Colonel Thomas Johnson, also of Newbury, the officer who had failed to take Mount Independence in September 1777. In March 1781 Johnson had been taken prisoner by one of Sherwood's agents.[16] After swearing to be loyal to the crown, Johnson was released on parole and was allowed to return to Newbury with the understanding that he would act as a double agent. However, when Sherwood's agents arrived in Newbury and conferred with Johnson on their plan to take Bayley while he was busy working in his fields, Johnson sent a servant to warn the New York general. In the nick of time, Bayley escaped to the New Hampshire side of the Connecticut River. Thus ended one of Sherwood's least successful endeavors, but it certainly made Bayley as hostile as ever to the Junta. Bayley, who knew the Junta was negotiating with the very agents who had tried to take him, was unshakeable in his support for Congress.

THE CONTINUATION OF HOSTILITIES, 1781 TO 1783

While the war was winding down elsewhere, in 1781 petite guerre continued to dominate the Hudson-Champlain valley. In February Major Edward Jessup was informed that the thirty men in the rebel garrison at Fort Edward were "ripe for a revolt" and needed only a guide to defect to Canada.[17] He was asked to keep it secret, but to send the King's Loyal Americans and Indians to provide whatever assistance was needed to bring the Fort Edward garrison to Canada. However, this first action of the new regiment never took place.

Late in May at Albany, Schuyler's intelligence network informed him that the enemy was occupying Crown Point "in force," that is, with as many as 2,000 men. He expected that the area south to Half-moon and Schenectady would be ravaged. He was reluctant to take his servants from the Saratoga plantation as "the whole country . . . follow my example," but if Bemis Heights were abandoned, he "would order all my people & stock down." Taking into account that the British did occupy Crown Point and Lake George in strength the year before, his current information does appear to have been exaggerated.

Ball's Town was the victim of a second raid on June 4, when Loyalist agent and recruiter John Meyers led barely a dozen of his recruits into the sleeping village.[18] From his farm in Coeymans Patent south of Albany, he had already served as a Loyalist intelligence gatherer and messenger, carrying dispatches to both Haldimand in Canada and Sir Henry Clinton in New York. Myers emptied the Ball's Town jail, which held many Loyalists, captured several militiamen, and then escaped north toward Point au Fer. He jettisoned some of his prisoners only ten miles from Ball's Town, so that when he arrived, he had only fourteen recruits for his corps, although two had to be jailed at Chambly because they were thought to be French deserters. The rebels had been watching Meyers but assumed that he was still near his Coeymans home below Albany. Raids like the one on Ball's Town let the rebels know that they were still on the defensive.

In small groups, Loyalists were still seeking to reach Canada. On July 11, 1781, the Albany Commissioners for Conspiracies reported that five youths had been apprehended. But because of their "youth and inexperience" they were only asked to swear that they would "not aid, comfort, counsel or assist . . . the enemies of the State of New York or the United States of America."[19] Such men were inspired by the presence of Loyalist raiders like David Jones, who in August attempted to capture the rebel commander at Saratoga, Major John McKinstry of the New York militia. The rebel officer was able to foil Jones's plans.

To Support and Reorganize Loyalist Units

To continue the invasions, Haldimand's Loyalist units were put on a more permanent footing and reorganized. Following the king's orders in September 1780, Haldimand announced that Loyalist officers wounded in action were to receive the same year of advanced pay that regular officers did. The king would also make provision for all Loyalist soldiers "disabled from wounds received in his service." In June 1781 Haldimand requested that Loyalist units hold regular religious services each Sabbath in full regimentals, and that no excuses for absence would be accepted. He still faced the problem that most of his Loyalist units, including the King's Loyal Americans, were still not up to strength. [20] He hoped that Jessup's and Peters's regiments could still be filled and that their aspirations of rank achieved, and he encouraged the recruitment of able-bodied young men. At the same time, he found it necessary to appoint Major John Nairne to take command of the various units from September 1780 through the winter at Verchères and Contrecoeur.

This was the situation until November 1781, when Haldimand put into effect plans to eliminate some Loyalist units, causing animosity as he was forced to demote several officers who had long service records. The remaining units were consolidated into a new regiment, the Loyal Rangers, commanded by Major Edward Jessup, while Sherwood was a captain and his brother-in-law, Elijah Bothum, was an ensign. John Peters, however, was demoted to captain of a company of invalids, and Ebenezer Jessup to captain of a company of pensioners. Both these men had been colonels of their own units, and Peters would leave his command to go to England to seek redress. Their distress was offset by the fact that in April 1781 Loyalist officers of the Burgoyne campaign were finally receiving reimbursement for their costs during the 1777 expedition. It was some consolation for Ebenezer Jessup that he was paid over £1,028 for his service in Burgoyne's Campaign. Peters received £664, the deceased Samuel McKay £288, and Peter Drummond of Daniel McAlpin's corps £262. [21]

A profile of the Loyal Rangers gives an indication of where most Loyalist troops came from by 1781. It shows that 75 percent were from New York, of which 40 percent were from Albany County and 20 percent from Charlotte County, leaving 15 percent from the rest of the state. Vermont contributed 11 percent, and the remaining 14 percent were from elsewhere in New England. The majority of the rank and file were freeholders rather than tenants. [22] It is evident this regiment had roots in the Hudson-Champlain region.

Albany Believes it Stands Alone

To the south, no Continental troops remained in the Northern Department, Washington having taken the last by June 1781, in an effort to build up his forces around New York City. [23] The commander-in-chief sent a request to Brigadier General John Fellows for 600 Berkshire County militiamen, with the suggestion that if he was unable to meet the quota, then an appeal should be made to neighboring Hampshire County. The militias were to meet in Albany, but there is no indication they filled the gap. Governor Clinton was having difficulty in turning a portion of his militia into longer term levies, and thus in 1781 he began to ask other states to defend New York. However, the New England states would not be forthcoming with their militia as they had during the Burgoyne crisis in 1777. By 1780 Connecticut's government was bankrupt and shifted the responsibility for recruiting to its towns. The towns were no better at it and were soon themselves bankrupt, and they could not prevent the hemorrhaging sale of the state's provisions to the British in New York City. Once an important player in the Hudson-Champlain region's defense, Connecticut dropped out completely. War weariness set in as it became difficult for states to collect taxes and provide bounties and the decline in value of Continental and state currencies made recruiting and supply unpopular.

On June 25, 1781, Washington again asked John Stark to assume command of the denuded Northern Department, which the New York governor's brother, James Clinton, still technically held. Conditions were worse than they had been in Stark's previous term in 1778. This time Stark established himself at Saratoga, relinquishing the posts that Christopher Carleton had destroyed in 1780 in favor of occupying the sites of the battles of 1777. It was clear to everyone that in 1781 Haldimand would again occupy the lakes and invade southward, perhaps this time as far as Albany. Stark wanted to stop the invasion at Saratoga, but Abraham Ten Broeck, now mayor of Albany, refused to send the Albany County militia there, keeping it to defend the city. Stark had other problems with the city; he quipped that "Albany is a very dangerous place to put men into; for [the Albany authorities] would have one half of them in jail, and the other half to keep them there."[24] He felt his soldiers were being capriciously arrested for debt and drunkenness. Moreover, the civil war between New York and Vermont came to the front in May when the Junta began its effort to annex the towns along its border with New York, preventing coordination between the two political authorities. While Stark detested most Albanians as alarmists, the one bright spot in his command was none other than Philip Schuyler, the once mistrusted Yorker. When no one else seemed able to obtain supplies, Schuyler could, and Stark was often entertained at the Saratoga plantation by Schuyler's family. On October 16 Schuyler thanked Stark for consideration of his family, explaining that Mrs. Schuyler "has detailed the various attentions you and your worthy son have paid herself and her daughters."

Stark's compatriot Philip Schuyler had already been threatened by Loyalists, even though he had his own guard in Albany. In early August a dozen men organized by Sherwood, under the command of the intrepid John Meyers, attacked Schuyler's mansion, The Pastures, on the south side of the city, in an attempt to kidnap him. They entered the rear of the house into the great central hall but were stopped by Schuyler's guards and servants. Schuyler had been warned, and he either escaped from the house or remained hidden upstairs. Meyers, fearing that the alarm had been spread to the city, retreated with two of Schuyler's servants as prisoners and some of his silver plate.[25] Haldimand considered the last a breach of gentlemanly honor, but the silver disappeared in Albany County and he was therefore unable to return it to Schuyler. Thankful for his escape, Schuyler rewarded three members of his guard with a joint tenant's grant in his Saratoga Patent.

Also in August, Mayor Abraham Ten Broeck investigated the report of an Indian servant who had found a dead body in the woods. The report turned out to be a Loyalist attempt to draw him out of the city and capture him, much as they had attempted with Schuyler. Incidents like this kept Albany in perpetual alarm and justified keeping its militia in and about the city.[26]

On September 1 Major General William Alexander, Lord Stirling, was informed by Washington that he been chosen to replace Stark as commander of the Northern Department.[27] Stirling's departure was delayed, and Stark was unaware of his arrival in Albany and the decision until October 20. Stark would remain his second-in-command and took his demotion surprisingly well, perhaps because Stirling brought Continental regiments with him to augment the levies now coming from nearby Massachusetts. Stirling visited Stark at Saratoga, and with his reinforcements, almost 1,500 men reoccupied the Bemis Heights lines by November 2. Such a defensive position, however, did nothing to prevent the enemy from occupying the lakes or aid settlers to the north who were struggling to survive in their homes. Stirling returned to Albany after only four days at Saratoga, apparently to quell the city's fears of invasion. He did not tarry there, and Stark was once more in command of the Northern Department in November. The army they had gathered at Saratoga was quickly dispersed as supplies to support it were lacking. By January 1782, Stirling was at his estate at Basking Ridge, New Jersey, and Stark had gone home to winter in New Hampshire. Without further support, Governor Clinton would reorganize a portion of the Charlotte County militia as levies with longer enlistments, better equipment, and selective physical specifications. Named "nine month men" for their duration of service, by 1782 they were enlisted from towns like Salem and then were divided into companies and kept to garrison Fort Williams in Salem or sent to the Saratoga defences.[28] It was said that the levies were paid from the proceeds of sheep and cattle confiscated from the Argyle Protectionists, showing that the civil war would not disappear. No other defense posts were left in the north, but the longer enlistments seemed to offer a greater measure of security for settlers closer to Albany.

THE INVASION

The preparations at Bemis Heights were meant to ward off an invasion from Canada that never reached the defenders. The situation was similar in Vermont. While the Junta had a truce with Haldimand that was supposed to keep hostilities to a minimum, in fact the British had continued to breach Vermont's security. In March 1781 Peacham and Greensboro, towns in the northeast, were attacked by mission Indians.[29] A blockhouse on Caspian Lake had been erected to protect the road that General Jacob Bayley had built in 1779. Four men in the garrison were surprised by the Indians; two were scalped while two were taken captive and later returned from Canada. Here was a small incident, but also a sign that not all hostilities against Vermont had ceased.

Following the strategy of sending out a force while rebel militiamen were busy with the harvest, in October Haldimand launched the invasion that was so feared in Albany. To lead it, he passed over the brilliant Carleton in favor of Barry St. Leger, a commander who had failed to use his opportunities at Fort Stanwix or to aid Burgoyne from Ticonderoga. He advanced down Lake Champlain in a flotilla to occupy Crown Point, Ticonderoga, and Mount Independence. On October 20—the day that Stark learned he had been replaced by Stirling—St. Leger arrived at Ticonderoga with four gunboats, two ammunition boats, thirty bateaux, more shipping, and over a thousand Loyalists and regulars, including Edward Jessup's King's Loyal Americans. While this was the largest force that Haldimand would send down Lake Champlain, the invasion did not have the destructive objectives of Carleton's raid the year before, for Haldimand had restricted it to demonstrating British military ability to dominate the lakes. In fact, he wanted to revive the pacification policy that Burgoyne had begun at Castleton in 1777, especially now that he was negotiating with Vermont and had a proclamation specifying the conditions for Vermont's return to the British fold.

St. Leger occupied the once-prized rebel stronghold at Ticonderoga for two weeks, sending parties to both sides of Lake Champlain and down Lake George.[30] On October 27 an annoying rebel attack on the guard at Mount Defiance was beaten off. Earlier he had dispatched over three hundred British light infantry, jagers, and King's Loyal Americans, with Edward Jessup commanding, to take control of Lake George and to menace the rebel post at Saratoga. They spent over a week on Lake George and sent agents to gather information from as far away as Argyle and New City (Lansingburgh). Having completed its mission, Jessup's force returned to the Lake George landing on November 1—the day before Stirling arrived at Saratoga.

When St. Leger was at Crown Point, the Vermont militia, in contrast to the rebel force at Saratoga, peacefully occupied Chimney Point, across Lake Champlain, as the truce between Chittenden and Haldimand was in effect. St. Leger, however, wanted to capture a Vermont patrol and then release them to distribute Haldimand's proclamation of the terms by which Vermont could return to the British Empire. This proclamation had been requested in September by Ira Allen and Joseph Fay. Loyalist Dr. Samuel Adams led the party to capture a patrol at Chimney Point, but in taking them they killed Sergeant Archelus Tupper and took the rest of his force prisoners.[31] Realizing Tupper's death violated the armistice, St. Leger had him buried with full honors and released the prisoners, sending them home with the proclamation and every kindness. The Vermont opposition to the Junta was enraged by the Tupper incident; how was it, they asked, that the enemy treated Vermont rebels so well?

This was the only bloodshed in St. Leger's expedition, and it met the test of preserving the truce with the Junta. St. Leger's expedition has been seen as bizarre because of the Tupper incident and a waste of resources in comparison with Carleton's expedition the year before, but Haldimand had been specific in designating the defensive nature of the expedition, hoping to probe deeply into New York, far enough so that Canada's boundary with New York might be considered the vicinity of Lake George. With this accomplished, St. Leger arrived in St. Johns by November 16.[32] It was then that the Loyalist units faced reorganization as the Loyal Rangers, and as a result of his service with St. leger, Edward Jessup was elevated to the command of the consolidated regiment.

Meanwhile, the Franco-American victory over Lord Cornwallis in Virginia in October 1781 had no effect on St. Leger's expedition, because in mid-November Canadian authorities at best considered it an unsubstantiated rumor. Even then it would not affect Haldimand until a new policy was drafted and sent from London. St. Leger's effort on Lake Champlain would be bolstered by the consummate professionalism of Riedesel, who from his bastion at Sorel masterminded the aggressive defense of the Richelieu Valley. Following Haldimand, Riedesel aimed to establish a well-arranged system of defense that would also serve as a base for British control of the lakes. He especially devoted himself to the fortification of Isle aux Noix, using the designs of Burgoyne's engineer, William Twiss, and the labor of his own German regiments, Loyalist units, and Canadians.[33] Like past foreign officers, he discovered the value of snowshoes in the winter and had them issued to his entire command.

Throughout 1782 and into 1783, now that a French army was with Washington, rumors persisted of a Franco-American invasion of Canada. In July 1782 Washington again sent Stirling to command the Northern Department at Albany, but a rebel invasion never materialized. In fact, by the beginning of 1783 the French forces in the United States were being shipped to the West Indies. Similar rumors also persisted that Haldimand would again invade as he had in the past. Having deflected an attempt by Sherwood's agents to capture him, Jacob Bayley was ever watchful, and in October 1782 he reported to Governor Clinton that the British were again going to appear during the harvest season in an expedition down Lake Champlain. Bayley "lay on his arms day and night being in danger both from [Britain] and Vermont."[34] For when the invasion takes place, "Vermont will make a great noise by calling in the militia . . . but you may depend it will not be to oppose the enemy but to deceive the populace and prevent the militia from assisting [Clinton]." The efforts of the Junta to cultivate Bayley had assuredly failed and his keen observations would continue to plague them.

THE PEACE OF PARIS

In March 1783 Haldimand had optimistically shared his thoughts with Riedesel on the peace negotiations in Paris: "Our navy has lost nothing of her luster, and although our expeditions on land have not been successful, everything might again be made right, and even the supremacy of this continent be once more obtained. Notwithstanding, however, peace seems to me to be desirable."[35] While Haldimand was still upbeat in his view from Canada, at the peace table in Paris such sentiments were totally disregarded. The Shelburne ministry sought to bring an immediate end to the war by being overly generous to their former colonies. Their chief goal was to detach the new republic from the French alliance. In doing this, the British peacemakers who signed the document on September 3 disregarded the existing boundaries of British-held territory and totally neglected their Loyalist and Native American allies. The fifth and sixth articles of the treaty stated that the Congress would "recommend" to the state legislatures that Loyalists be given a year in which to regain their rights and properties, and that further confiscation and persecution would end. Such propositions, however, were obviously unenforceable. As to their Native American allies, their territorial rights were also ignored, as if they did not exist in any form, leaving them no choice but to migrate to Canada or throw themselves on the mercy of the new nation's government. The Shelburne government fell during the negotiations, as it was realized they gave away too much, but the war had to be ended and the preliminary agreement was left to stand.

In early June 1783 Riedesel received news from Guy Carleton in New York informing him that the king was sending all his German troops home to Europe without delay.[36] Riedesel and Haldimand busied themselves in preparing for the departure. By August Riedesel, the baroness, and their children were ready to embark from Quebec. Riedesel presented Haldimand with his favorite horse, while Haldimand gave the baroness a muff and sable tippet and their eldest daughter, Augusta, a little dog that she admired. It was the end of Riedesel's career in North America and of the cordial relationship that preserved Canada. It was also a fitting farewell for the most professional general in Burgoyne's army.

Continuing Negotiations with Vermont

The Arlington Junta continued negotiations with Haldimand in 1782 and beyond. The Junta maintained the truce because it protected Vermont from further incursions by Haldimand's forces. Stark had written to Chittenden on November 14 inquiring about the meaning of the Tupper incident, but he was deflected by the governor with the remark that he had written to Washington about it. On first day of 1782 Washington replied to Chittenden about his negotiations with Haldimand: he accepted Chittenden's explanation that the negotiations never led to "any serious intention of joining Great Britain," but he qualified that they had a "certain bad tendency . . . to give some ground to that delusive opinion of the enemy, upon which in a great measure found their hopes of success."[37] Washington and Stark were being fooled by Chittenden, for the negotiations with Haldimand would not cease, although the emphasis was now on trade with Canada, something that was dear to the hearts of the Junta.

Haldimand wrote to Lord Germain seeking instructions on how far to go with the Vermont matter, but as usual the minister avoided a direct answer, leaving the matter to Haldimand's "judgment and discretion."[38] Thus, on April 22, 1782, Justus Sherwood and George Smyth contacted Ira Allen and Joseph Fay to assure them that Haldimand was "still inclined to treat amicably with the people of [Vermont]." They asked if the surrender of Lord Cornwallis at Yorktown had changed the Junta's attitude and proposed to continue negotiations in the vicinity of Crown Point. A month later Ira Allen and Joseph Fay responded with the observation "The doings of Congress have implicitly made Vermont a neutral power by refusing her a confederation . . . from hence we infer that the [United States] must fight their own battles." However, Haldimand was tiring of the continued negotiations and drawing lines as to what could be made public. Six months later he surmised, "The inhabitants of the grants would like to renew their intercourse with this province, and settle again on the shores of Lake Champlain, but I cannot allow it." Smyth and occasionally Sherwood remained at the Loyal Blockhouse till the end of 1782, keeping the channels between the Junta and Haldimand open.

Ever seeking trade, in a letter of May 30, 1783, Ethan Allen had asked the Canadian governor if he could furnish the king's troops with fresh beef, which would be ready in July. He noted that his brother Ira and Joseph Fay would handle the delivery. Almost a month later, Smyth replied for Haldimand that the king's troops were already well supplied with beef and needed no more. However, Smyth noted that he was of the opinion "that should it be worth your while to send any quantity of beef or . . . milk cows to take the chance of the market, that his Excellency would not be adverse to it."[39] In 1783 Ira suggested that wealthy Loyalists being evacuated from New York City be settled in Vermont. The Allens and the Junta also worked with Loyalist James Savage of Albany County to create an asylum for Loyalists in northern Vermont.

Even when the Peace of Paris formally ended hostilities in 1783, it seemed to have little effect on the Junta's overtures, although they were now definitely oriented to trade. Ira and Ethan remained in contact with Haldimand and Sherwood. Ira's resources were now immense, for he was the largest landholder in Vermont, with his own plantation and unlimited supplies of timber. In September 1784 he wrote to Haldimand from St. Johns, claiming that he could not see "why it is not in the interest of the Crown and the subjects of Great Britain to carry on mercantile business with the citizens of Vermont."[40] Ira needed to transfer building materials purchased in Canada to his "plantations" on Lake Champlain. He also offered to drive his cattle on the Onion River to markets in Canada. He and his Loyalist brother Levi would raise and trade cattle for the Canadian market. He proposed the development of a canal to connect Lake Champlain with the St. Lawrence River and Montreal. Here are indications of the continuation of a serious alliance. There was no way that Haldimand would ever be rid of the Allen family's overtures.

In October 1784 the Vermont Assembly, in a rare show of cooperation with the Junta, endorsed the latter's British policy with "An Act for the Purpose of Opening Free Trade to and through the Province of Quebec."[41] Over the next several years, Canada's Governor Guy Carleton eased restrictions on trade between Vermont and Quebec, ignoring the fact that the Privy Council in London had forbade trade between Canada and the United States. Levi and Ira Allen had been commissioned by the Junta in October 1786 to negotiate a commercial treaty between Vermont and Quebec, which the Quebec legislative council approved a year later. However, Vermont's trading status with the British Empire still remained cloudy, and thus Levi was sent to London in February 1789, first to secure a mast contract from the Royal Navy and second to convince the Privy Council to recognize Vermont's special trading status with Canada.

Levi Allen spent over a year in England, where the best supporter of his mission turned out to be none other than Philip Skene. His chief detractor was Ebenezer Jessup, who Levi challenged to a duel that failed to take place. In December 1789, in a letter to Prime Minister William Pitt, Levi went as far as offering "my service to raise a regiment of Green Mountain Boys for his Majesty's Service" to help defend the posts that Britain still held after the peace.[42] Levi's powers from the Junta had always been vague, and in October Ira explained to him that there had been a "revolution of officers of government" when Chittenden temporarily lost the governorship, leaving Ira powerless in the Assembly to support Levi's mission. Finally, in May 1790 the undersecretary of the Royal Navy provided Levi with an agreement that essentially offered Vermont free trade with Canada, ignoring the existence of the United States. Always a Loyalist, Levi felt he had one person in Britain to thank for his success—the one-time victim of the Allen family, Philip Skene.

Haldimand came to realize that it was the rebels' own internal civil conflict that was Canada's best defense against the emerging United States. The Junta's negotiations with Haldimand did give the impression that Vermont had a special relationship with him, which gave Vermont better protection from his forces than New York could expect. Despite opposition, the Junta kept Vermont dealing with Haldimand, creating enmity not only in Vermont and New York but on the part of George Washington and the Congress. Haldimand's negotiations with the Junta were lasting; they continued beyond the war and even beyond his tenure, forging ties that were important for the development of Vermont's economy. Haldimand was never duped by the Allens; he soon realized that he could not bring Vermont into the empire or that he could not trust a government that sustained itself by desperate measures rather than steady policy. The Peace of Paris had little effect on the continuing civil war, although it certainly disappointed Britain's Loyalist and North American allies. Without much direction from British ministers, Haldimand was left alone to look after Canada's future.

PART VI

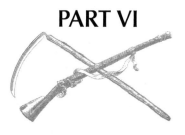

Enjoying the Peace

18

HALDIMAND FORGES A NEW CANADA

On April 27, 1783, the *Quebec Gazette* published news of the end of hostilities between Britain and its colonies.[1] It was then that the whole question of settlement in Canada became preeminent for those displaced from the Hudson-Champlain region. Canada was not every Loyalist's cup of tea, yet a majority of those who resided north of Albany ended up there, and it turned out to be one of the better choices. The Hawleys, Adamses, McAlpins, Jessups, and Joneses were among the thousands of settlers who would leave the region permanently and establish new communities and homes in Canada.

Loyalist families like the Hawleys of Arlington were now seeking permanent homes in Canada. The Hawleys had served in Jessup's corps, the King's Loyal Americans, and finally the Loyal Rangers in both auxiliary and combat positions.[2] Among the extended family, Reuben Hawley, who had lived in Pawlet and worked with Justus Sherwood, now had a contract with British army engineers to improve Canadian fortifications. By 1782 Eli Hawley had left Arlington, his spying days with Sherwood over, and finished the war as a corporal of Peter Drummond's Company of the Loyal Rangers. And Jeptha Hawley would be called upon to hold the important position of caring for the refugees who had been flocking to Canada.

As a first step in the resettlement process, following instructions from London, Haldimand disbanded his Loyalist regiments. The largest, the first battalion of the King's Royal Regiment of New York, was mustered out on December 24, 1783, but the men were allowed to remain in their Montreal barracks over the winter, while preparations were made to settle them in several places.[3] Their wives and children were already in the Yamachiche or Sorel refugee centers or in private homes in St. Johns, Lachine, Chambly, and Montreal. On his own, Haldimand then proposed that townships be developed west of Montreal by the companies of each Loyalist battalion, so that officers and their men would still be together and ready should there be an incursion from the United States. In this sense, official disbandment did not end the regiments, for now that their families were to be with them, settlement and defense would go hand in hand.

THE REFUGEE CENTERS

During the war, Haldimand had provided for Loyalist families arriving in Canada, especially if a member of the family was serving in a Loyalist military unit. Beginning in 1778, Jeptha Hawley was involved in the construction of the Loyalist refugee camp at Machiche (Yamachiche), established near Trois-Rivières on the St. Lawrence River. Conrad Gugy, a fellow officer of Haldimand in the Royal American Regiment and his secretary when he was governor of Trois-Rivières, had suggested to him that a refugee camp be built at his seigneury of Grosbois. A member of the King's Council, he hoped the camp would help to populate his land. On October 6 Haldimand issued orders for buildings to be erected and gave Gugy the authority to maintain order among the arrivals. By the end of the month, using corvées from five neighboring parishes, housing for 240 persons had been erected. The occupants consisted of "women and children, besides some officers and a dozen men to be artisans and a member of the [Samuel] Adams family who claimed to have been a schoolmaster."[4]

In refugee camps like Machiche, the women and children of Loyalist families played the important role of maintaining their households. Loyalist women had previously been on their own, keeping the household fires burning and the children together until it became clear the family had to leave for Canada. It was their responsibility to pack what household goods they could, travel overland together to Lake Champlain, and to have British authorities meet them for transport to Canada. Once there, life in refugee camps like Machiche left them with the task of caring for and educating their children, usually without their husbands, who were only allowed to visit occasionally.[5] This is how women maintained kinship circles that had begun in New England or New York decades before.

The Hawleys and their kinship circle, especially women and children, lived at Machiche, allowing the families that had originally come from Connecticut to maintain their kinship ties and friendships. A return of Samuel Adams's Corps on August 10, 1780, shows places for Jeptha's wife, Esther, and four of his children; his adult son Martin; Isaac Brisco, his wife, and their three children; and the entire Adams family, including his wife and three adult sons.[6] Jeptha was in charge of victualing the entire camp. After 1780 he was reduced to half pay, as he was a volunteer at Machiche, without a place in a Loyalist unit.

Gugy laid out wards and services at Machiche and provided a large garden and pasture for grazing fifty cows and horses. Twelve houses were built for the residents and two hundred beds brought to serve the women and children. As refugees arrived from Fort Niagara and St. Johns, more houses were erected and a school constructed to serve eighty children. Unfortunately, the British approach to the camp followed England's Poor Laws, rather than a sense of public support for the Loyalists. Only deserving refugees—those sick, infirm, women with young children or women whose situation did not allow them to work—were supposedly allowed. They were freely given shelter, food, firewood, medical care, and education for their children, but they were mustered periodically to see if they could do outside work, since like Poor Law administrators, the authorities were afraid of idleness.

The camp peaked with 462 refugees in October 1779, some of these being husbands like Jeptha.[7] Following the guidelines, in January 1781 the husbands and older sons were ordered to leave, and seven months later women were ordered to end "a habit of idleness," by being "struck off the provision list." By September the number of refugees had fallen to 327. While it rose a bit to 355 in January 1782, by December 1783 it was down to 265. Such conditions put a strain on family ties and patriarchal influence as the authorities tried to keep able-bodied husbands and older sons separated from their families in the refugee centers.

Jeptha did not have to leave the camp. At the end of March 1783, with the rank of captain, he was placed in charge of Machiche, where discontent among the Loyalists was now high. His task was to reduce the number of refugees who received provisions and prepare them to be on their own, as it was known that a peace treaty would soon be signed, ending wartime conditions.[8] Among his problems at Machiche was his compatriot, Samuel Adams, who was as contentious toward British authorities as he had been toward the Bennington mob, now demanding that he and his followers be allowed to settle in Nova Scotia. As the war came to an end, the major debate in the Loyalist centers was over where the refugees would go.

Another important Loyalist refugee center developed at Sorel, the village at the confluence of the Richelieu and St. Lawrence Rivers. While a fort had been established there in 1641, the settlement was slow to grow until Haldimand decided to make it into a major Loyalist refugee station. In October 1778 he wrote to Lord George Germain that he wanted to make Sorel a place of strength that would attract Loyalists, who as a mark of favor would not have to pay traditional quitrents.[9] He required government funds to purchase the seigneury owned by English merchants, and the purchase was completed in 1781. Even before this, Sorel had become an English-speaking community where Loyalists were not only interned but encouraged to settle. The place was especially designated for military invalids, and from 1778 a hospital, storehouses, and barracks were built to receive them.

By July 1779 Captain Daniel McAlpin, Burgoyne's corps commander from Stillwater, had become Sorel's commandant, and he reported that 853 loyalists had been received in the village and that 87 of them had decided to settle there. Of these, 300 were from various Loyalist corps, under "Captains" McAlpin, Ebenezer Jessup, John Peters, Robert Leake, and Samuel Adams. All, however, were in need of subsistence. Four years later, with the war over, there were only 132 Loyalists in Sorel, and Haldimand provided them with necessities such as linen and woolen cloth, blankets, stockings, shoes, mittens, and leggings for the winter. A year later it was reported that there were 95 families in Sorel—316 men, women and children—and that 54 of them had cleared acreage. As a sign of the permanence of some of these families, they petitioned the Society for the Propagation of the Gospel for an Anglican minister, and in 1784 the Reverend John Doty arrived, preached his first sermon, and established the first Anglican mission in Canada. A chapel was improvised from a military storehouse. A year later, the village of Sorel was laid out and lots distributed, and within two years 107 refugees had accepted those lots.[10] Certainly, Sorel offered arriving Loyalists the advantages of a renewed settlement in the heart of Quebec.

While Daniel McAlpin was too old to participate in his corps's raids into New York and Vermont, he continued to be active as commander of Sorel. In 1779 he was promoted to major, specifically in command of the corps of older Loyalists at Sorel. He kept a record of the provisioning of all Loyalist families that had entered Canada. It shows that in 1779 Machiche had 196 refugees, while Sorel had 87, Lachine 126, Montreal 208, and St. Johns 209. Ultimately, McAlpin had his duties limited to barrack duty, but he still became ill, and after five months of pain, he died in July 1780.[11]

Burgoyne's other corps commanders, Peters and McKay, had disappeared from the active military lists by the end of 1781. In 1778 Peters found himself financially ruined, ill, and unable to fill his corps with recruits.[12] Three years later, when the Loyal Rangers were formed, he was demoted by Haldimand to captain. After difficulty with Haldimand over where in Canada he should settle, he ultimately went to Cape Breton Island with most of his family. Edward Jessup claimed that Peters, always a problem, tried to undermine Haldimand's resettlement plans. Finally, the Peters family would move to England, where he died in 1788.

McKay had disappeared much earlier. His background that so impressed Burgoyne could not save him. Governor Carleton, in one of his last acts, had removed him from command, ostensibly for his mysterious retreat without orders in the Saratoga Campaign from Fort Edward to Ticonderoga. Definitely in trouble over his conduct, McKay died in April 1779, leaving his widow and children in distress.[13] After his death, his son John served as an ensign in the second battalion of the King's Royal Regiment of New York.

Prominent Loyalists continued to appear in Canada. From Charlotte County, Patrick Smyth, brother of Justus Sherwood's partner, George, joined his brother in Sorel. As mentioned earlier, Patrick's house in Fort Edward had once been the seat of Charlotte County, but it had been confiscated by the rebels. The Smyth brothers had served in the British army in America and after the Seven Years' War came to Albany, where Patrick practiced law.[14] He had remained in Fort Edward, serving as Charlotte County clerk, until after Burgoyne's defeat, when he was taken prisoner by the rebels and confined to Albany, where he lived quietly, although he was able to feed information to the British. In 1781 he, his wife, and five children were expelled from New York and allowed to join George at Sorel, where they lived out their remaining years.

In June 1784 the ever attentive George Smyth vouched for the character of several Loyalist families that had gotten to Ticonderoga and from there were conveyed to St. Johns. They were from the border community of Nobletown, that lightning rod of opposition to the Van Rensselaer and Livingston landlords even before the War for Independence. With the exception of one Englishman, their origin was Hanover, Germany, a state associated with Loyalism because it was ruled by George III's family. Perhaps these refugees had been involved in the premature uprising of May 1777 against their rebel landlords. A tailor, refugee Frederick Fell, claimed he and his family "could not live [in Nobletown] on account of the ill usage he had . . . and several of his family suffered much by imprisonment."[15] All claimed to want to go to the proposed Loyalist settlement at Cataraqui on Lake Ontario, a destination that Haldimand would favor.

The evacuation of New York City in 1783 also produced another influx of Loyalists to Canada that Haldimand had to deal with. Sir Guy Carleton informed him in June that two hundred Loyalist families, organized into eight companies of militia, were about to embark, and they wished to "solicit [Haldimand] for grants in the vicinity of [Cataraqui]."[16] Two or three ships arrived at Sorrel in August with 255 refugees, but the fourth preferred Quebec because they were tradespeople who wished to practice their trade in the urban centers of Quebec or Montreal. Some of these refugees were originally from areas south of Albany such as Ulster County and Kingston.

Resettlement in Canada under Haldimand

Haldimand had received no firm direction from London as to how to handle refugee Loyalists because the British authorities believed that article five of the provisional peace treaty made it possible for Loyalists to stay in or return to their homes in the United States. As noted, this was a forlorn hope, as the state governments ignored the article's obligations. On his own, from the spring of 1783 Haldimand took the responsibility to send agents to look for lands appropriate to providing Loyalists with a home in Canada. As a result he would offer 6,000 refugee Loyalists choices as to where they could settle: at French

Canadian seigneuries like that of the Baron de Longueuil near Montreal, at the Sorel settlement, at New Oswegatchie opposite present-day Ogdensburg on the St. Lawrence River, at the Bay of Chaleur in the Gaspé Peninsula of Quebec. For demanding Samuel Adams, there was even an offer of free passage to Nova Scotia, which was attractive to him because of the supposed trade and fishing opportunities.[17] Some Loyalists made up their mind quickly; Justus Sherwood chose New Oswegatchie, where he was active in surveying it for settlement. But for others the decision was longer in coming, and not everywhere was open to Loyalist settlement.

One place where Haldimand discouraged the settlement of Loyalists was on Lake Champlain at Missisiquoi Bay. He saw settlement there as a security risk. It was simply too close to the newly drawn border between the United States and Canada. Loyalists who resided there would inevitably be raiders, plunderers and spies, carrying on the same activities they had during the war. John Meyers had been one of Sherwood's best spies, who had raided Ball's Town and then tried to capture Philip Schuyler in his Albany mansion. Meyers brought his family to Yamachiche, while he went off preparing a farm on Missisiquoi Bay. He liked to go against the grain and had not been keen on moving west. In March 1784 he led settlers to Missisiquoi, where they built cabins, plowed the land with a yoke of oxen, and put in crops.[18] His comrades were mostly officers from Meyers's own company of Edward Jessup's Loyal Rangers, including Ensign Thomas Sherwood, Justus's cousin, and also the disgruntled John Peters. They thought the Missisiquoi settlement to be ideal because they could maintain the semblance of their disbanded military units. This was enough for Haldimand, and in May he ordered Meyers to meet him at Lachine, where he made it very clear that the settlement could not exist so close to the border. Haldimand would compromise on only one request, Meyers and his compatriots were allowed to harvest their Missisiquoi crops in the fall. By 1785 Meyers and his family had chosen to go west and settle near Cataraqui. Five years later, they ended up further west on Lake Ontario at Meyers' Mills, where Meyers settled permanently and prospered.

LAKE ONTARIO

Among the choices in 1783, Haldimand offered Loyalists a specific homeland where they would be dominant, beyond the Thousand

Islands of the St. Lawrence River, on the north shore of Lake Ontario near Cataraqui. He began by building a fort at Cataraqui, which became the nucleus around which the city of Kingston would grow.[19] Correctly, he made certain that the Iroquois had no interest in the area. While Loyalists would move initially to Cataraqui, the majority took up land grants at the Bay of Quinte, to the west of Cataraqui. Haldimand's program visualized a group settlement pattern of related families, whose men had served in a Loyalist corps. He would encourage the settlers to maintain the social order of the corps, the patriarchal traditions associated with Loyalism, and the camaraderie of their common military experience. Most crucially, the land would be free and the crown would provide initial support to start them in farming and commerce. He put the most popular Loyalist, Sir John Johnson, in charge of the entire settlement process, which would cover land not just at Cataraqui, but from Cornwall on the St. Lawrence to Lake Ontario.

In November 1783, when Haldimand sent an invitation to Machiche families to participate in the settlement of Cataraqui and the Bay of Quinte, only twelve to fifteen responded positively. At the time, Jeptha Hawley was not pleased with the proposal. It was not only the distance, difficulty of transport, and lack of a firm commitment to provide cattle and implements, but that "these allotments [of land] were not to be free donations but were to be leases . . . with the usual reserves, acknowledgements and service to seignors."[20] He wanted fee simple ownership of land as it existed in Arlington, not the manorial tenure that existed under Quebec's laws. Other Loyalists like Justus Sherwood held similar views. The bold New York City refugees gathered at Sorel would request that Haldimand establish a form of government and laws "similar to that which they enjoyed in the Province of New York in . . . 1763." Haldimand had foreseen the problem and was able to answer the complaints, explaining that, while the land had been distributed into seigneuries, the rights had been given to the British crown and the crown would waive them, so in practice the land would be free of manorial encumbrances found in French Canada.

Thus Jeptha and his compatriots at the Machiche camp became more open to settling in the Bay of Quinte. As an added inducement, Haldimand was specific in providing those who gathered for the journey to Cataraqui with clothing. Each man and boy over ten was given a coat, waistcoat, breeches, hat, shirt, blanket, shoes and shoe soles, leggings and stockings.[21] Women and children over ten received two yards of woolen cloth, four yards of linen, one pair of stockings, a blanket, and shoe soles, while their younger children were provided with one yard of woolen cloth, two yards of linen, stockings, shoe soles, and one blanket for every two children. It was expected that women would make their own and their children's clothing.

The former commander of the Loyal Rangers, Edward Jessup, wrote from Montreal that he thought the bulk of his veterans would "go to [Cataraqui], every day more are convinced that it would be to the advantage of the general settlement to allow them their choice; provided they settle in companies and a proportionate number of officers & men together, with whom I would like to take a part of [my] lands and make a beginning immediately." To this end he would promote "the views of government and the well-fare of the loyalists in general" among his men.[22] In October 1783 overall numbers for possible settlements in Cataraqui included 1,289 persons—690 women and children, 543 soldiers, and 56 pensioners.

The Royal Townships along the St. Lawrence

The other great Loyalist destination would be closer to Montreal, the "Royal Townships" along the St. Lawrence on the way to Cataraqui. Here Haldimand developed alternative land grants for those who served in Jessup's Rangers and other Loyalist units. While subjects of the king, the officers were also still Americans in their expectations, and Daniel Jones, John Jones, Justus Sherwood, and Thomas Sherwood signed a letter in July 16, 1783, that protested "a quit rent of one half penny per acre after ten years of development" on lands granted to Loyalists.[23] Less distant from Montreal, the leadership of Sir John Johnson and Edward Jessup would help to settled the St. Lawrence more quickly than Lake Ontario.

Haldimand prepared for settlers to travel to and receive land on the St. Lawrence River west of Montreal or at the Bay of Quinte. During 1783, surveyors had laid out townships and within them two hundred-acre lots that could be split into sections of a hundred acres each, the size of an average farm.[24] Those facing navigable waterways like the St. Lawrence or Lake Ontario were first surveyed because the water-front was more valuable. There lots were rectangular, with a narrow waterfront, the remainder of the land stretching three-eighths of a mile back into the wilderness. The sons of the family patriarch usually took up less valuable inland lots. While a bit different than the distribution of land in Arlington or Kingsbury, it was compatible with similar New England or New York situations. After a loyalty oath, lot tickets were distributed to the head of each family who had served in a Loyalist unit or had additional claims, and it was the duty of each family to discover where their lots were located. Not all awarded lots were taken up, and this allowed for purchase of further lots by those who settled. The process looked orderly on paper and showed the concern of Haldimand to help the Loyalists, but inevitably there would be problems in establishing clear title in a partially surveyed wilderness.

On March 4, 1784, a notice in the Quebec *Gazette* warned Loyalists and disbanded troops who wished to settle land at Oswegatchie and Cataraqui to gather at Quebec, Sorel, or Lachine. During the winter of 1783–84, Loyalists at Lachine had been employed to construct bateaux to carry them westward. Two months later the first party of forty-five men, thirty-five women, sixty-eight boys, and seventy girls left Machiche and went to Lachine, from where they progressed laboriously in bateaux because the St. Lawrence's rapids forced numerous portages. After ten to twelve days they arrived in Cataraqui.[25] In early June, more Loyalists embarked for the west with cargoes that included much of what they had requested: provisions, seeds, tools, grindstones, axes, knives, army tents, and clothing for the needy. Upon arrival at their destination, they took the oath of allegiance and the drawing of lots began. When a person had drawn a lot, the surveyor wrote his name on a corresponding map number, and he was given a location ticket for which a deed was issued within twelve months, on condition that the holder begin to clear the land. In order that families might settle near relatives, some of the tickets were swapped.

THOSE WHO WENT WEST

A profile of the Loyalist families who immigrated to what became eastern Ontario gives an idea of who the refugees were. Men and children predominated, for women made up less a fifth of the refugees.[26] Ethnically, as expected the British Isles were the origin of two-thirds of them, but it was Scots who accounted for two-thirds of that number, with the Scots-Irish and English trailing. While the Scots were certainly the largest ethnic group, surprisingly not far behind them in numbers were the Germans, most probably from the New York manors. Finally, there were as many Dutch as English and a few Huguenots.

Their ethnic diversity carried over into their religious convictions, which were by no means universally Anglican. When Sir John Johnson was settling his first regiment on the St. Lawrence River, he established five townships, each for a different religious group so that the town would have the cohesion of a common faith. The townships were designated for Catholic Highlanders, Scots Presbyterians, German Calvinists, German Lutherans, and Anglicans. In terms of origin, nearly three-quarters were from New York's Tryon, Charlotte, and Albany Counties. The rest were from other parts of New York, Vermont, and Pennsylvania. As to occupation, most were the self-sufficient, family-based farmers who were portrayed in the early chapters on settlement. Half had been tenants, while only a fifth had owned land in fee simple, the rest having mixed obligations or being unidentified. It appears the Hudson-Champlain region had been transplanted to Canada relatively intact.

SETTLEMENT ON THE BAY OF QUINTE

All told, in July 1784, 137 men, 71 women, 214 children, and 12 servants settled on the Bay of Quinte. As members of Jessup's Loyal Rangers, Jeptha, Ichabod, and Martin Hawley, along with Isaac and Nathan Brisco, received lots and settled eighteen miles west of Cataraqui on Lake Ontario in Township No. 2, while Zadock Hawley settled next door in Township #3. This was also the choice for Jeptha and Esther Hawley and their children, Martin, Davis, Sheldon, Russell, Azuba, Amantha, and Esther. Ichabod, Jeptha's nephew, received a lot near him, which was adjacent to the lots of Isaac Brisco. Other Hawleys were Andrew, the son of Andrew, who moved there after his marriage to Urania Leonard and became a farmer. Reuben Hawley, whose land in Pawlet had been confiscated, was also there. Another Arlington refugee was David Williams, Sr., who settled inland from the Hawleys and Briscos.[27] Township #2 was named Ernestown in 1788 in honor of Ernest Augustus, the fifth son of King George III. The diaspora that began in 1777–78 finally ended with families reunited and the Hawleys settled peacefully on the shores of the Bay of Quinte.

Like his father in Arlington, Jeptha Hawley quickly built a house, late in 1784 or early 1785, and cleared three acres for farming. It was a log cabin built of hewn timbers, for no sawmill existed in the area. It was sturdily built, for the structure survives today in Bath, Ontario. Located on the south side of his grant, only about a hundred feet from the Bay of Quinte, the house was a three-bay structure with a central front door surmounted by a transom for light.[28] At the house in July 1785, Reverend John Stuart of Mohawk Valley fame performed the first Anglican services held west of Cataraqui.

Two years later, thirty-inch-thick walls of randomly coursed rubble stone were erected to form an addition on the west side of Jeptha's house.[29] It served as a residence for John Langhorn, who was the first Anglican missionary in the district. A wooden shedlike addition of four bays in the rear completed the house. Although this house was more modest than Jehiel's wood-frame structure in Arlington, it classified Jeptha as a solid middle-class citizen.

SETTLEMENT ON THE ST. LAWRENCE RIVER

The first five townships on the St. Lawrence, closest to Montreal, were established by Sir John Johnson, superintendent of Loyalist settlement, for the families of the King's Royal Regiment of New York. In June 1784 his potential settlements were only clusters of family tents, but two years later the settlements were described by Lieutenant John Enys as having farms "by far better" than those closer to Montreal. Johnson had tenants—now including Scottish Highland emigrants— on acreage a bit inland on the Raisin River and would erect his own country house at Williamstown by 1792. Farther along the St. Lawrence at a point was Johnstown, meant to be the capital of immediate settlements, although lots would not be laid out until 1789 and a local government seat not established until four years later.

The familial nature of the Loyalist corps, in which fathers, sons, and brothers served together, was perpetuated in these settlements. The Widow Jones's family of Kingsbury regrouped on the St. Lawrence River beyond Sir John's land. The family consisted of John Jones and five of his brothers who had served in the King's Loyal Americans until late 1781, when it was combined with other units in the creation of the Loyal Rangers under Edward Jessup. John Jones, one of nine captains in the new corps, arrived at New Oswegatchie in 1784 with his wife Catherine and their children to take up a grant of a thousand acres at Pointe au Baril on the St. Lawrence.[30] By 1796 he had a fine farm, which produced watermelons.

"Encampment of the Loyalists at Johnston [Johnstown], a New Settlement on the Banks of the River St. Lawrence in Canada." Watercolor by James Peachy, June 6, 1784. Reproduction, Library and Archives Canada/Bibliothèque et Archives Canada, Ottawa.

Just to the west of Buell Bay, another Jones brother, Daniel, took up land along Buell's Creek, building a sawmill north of where the creek entered the St. Lawrence. Their neighbors included Elijah Bothum of Shaftsbury, Vermont, Sherwood's son-in-law, who had served as an ensign in Jessup's Rangers. He dammed a stream and built the township's first gristmill. Another neighbor was David Breakenridge, Jr., from Bennington, the son of the man who figured prominently in Ethan Allen's early effort to drive out settlers with New York titles. The son had become an ensign in Major James Rogers's King's Rangers, which had been with Carleton in the Year of the Burning.

Nearby were two more Jones brothers, Solomon and David. Both brothers had served in the King's Loyal Americans and later in the Loyal Rangers. The latter, of course, was famous as the fiancé of Jane McCrea, a man who would never marry, while the former had been chosen by Haldimand to be part of his spy network. Solomon had been an Albany medical student when the War for Independence broke out and had joined the King's Loyal American corps as a surgeon's mate and finished his education in Montreal. After the war, he was surgeon of the local militia, a member of the Court of Requests, and then was elected a member of the second Parliament for Upper Canada. During the Loyalist resettlement, David received choice lots overlooking the St. Lawrence. On one, in 1799 he and Solomon jointly had master mason Louis Brillière from Montreal erect an elaborate stone house with multipaned windows of glass, naming it Homewood. This home was a great improvement over what they had had in New York.[31]

Edward Jessup was enmeshed in the resettlement plans, although he personally took time in deciding where to settle. In September 1783 he was at Lachine, when he was invited to send "Persons of your corps skilled in Land" with Justus Sherwood to lay out the settlement at Cataraqui.[32] By January 1784 Haldimand was asking Edward to help him with the "judicious distribution of [your] people according to their dispositions, characters, and connections with each other, that too much pains cannot be taken in a research of such consequence." Four months later Sherwood reported from Sorel that he had "76 souls of Jessups Corps" that would go with him to Cataraqui. By the end of the year, Edward's disbanded men were settled not only at the Bay of Quinte, but also on the St. Lawrence at New Oswegatchie, and a few were attracted to the Baron de Longueil's seigneury. Edward would personally greet those who chose to settle at New Oswegatchie.

While the resettlement was going on, Edward's brother Ebenezer was in Quebec City with his wife and five daughters, increasingly dependent on his friends and charity. He and Edward had legally lost everything by an act of the New York State legislature in October 1779.[33] To recoup their losses, in 1785 the brothers decided to travel to London to press their claims to the Loyalist Commission, established to reimburse Loyalists for lost property. After two years, Ebenezer decided to bring his entire family to London. He had obtained a position as a government employee in Calcutta, India. Ebenezer's family went to India, and while he visited London occasionally, India remained home until his death in 1818. Thus he continued to serve the British Empire, but in a venue far distant from Canada.

Despite the fact that Edward Jessup presented testimonials from Burgoyne, Haldimand, and naval commander John Schank, he returned to Montreal empty handed; his claim was not recognized by the Loyalist Commission. He spent some time in Sorel, where his brother Joseph lived.[34] As late as 1805 Edward and his extended family—Abigail, Edward 2nd, Edward 3rd, George Covelo, James, William Jessup, and Phoebe and Elizabeth Walker— were listed in the Seigneury of Sorel. But soon after, they settled near their compatriot Justus Sherwood in Oswegatchie's Augusta and Elizabeth Townships. Sherwood had laid it out and granted land to the Jessups more than twenty years before. Edward and his family became leaders in Leeds and Grenville Counties, and Edward represented the latter in the Second Provincial Parliament. In 1810 Edward built houses for himself, his son Edward, and a farm manager, and founded Prescott Village at the head of schooner and sloop navigation. Both father and son had died by 1816, but Susannah Covel, Edward Jr.'s wife, acted as a matriarch over family affairs for another thirty years. She, of course, was a daughter of Simeon Covel of Cambridge, whom Younglove had rescued when she was a girl and sent to Canada. The Jessup family prospered in the British Empire, as if to show their enemies in New York that Loyalists could create successful communities under the auspices of the crown.

By 1786, between Cornwall and the Bay of Quinte, 1,800 families had settled, totaling 4,661 people, with a ratio of 7 males for every 3 females.[35] Loyalist enclaves that survived the war in the new United States would remain a source of immigrants. Many of the Reverend Samuel Swertfeger's Rensselaerswyck congregation had immigrated to Canada in 1777. Ten years later, 444 of Swertfeger's congregation petitioned Guy Carleton, now Lord Dorchester, and his Council to settle at Lake Memphremagog in today's Eastern Townships.[36] It does not appear they were granted the request, but two years later Swertfeger answered a call to be a minister near Niagara at Dundas. Here he established and prospered as the pastor of the first Lutheran church in Upper Canada. In a sense his odyssey in support of the Hanoverian succession was completed, and it is likely that he took some of his congregation with him.

Not only would there be a new nation created by the rebellious thirteen colonies, but simultaneously another, based on Loyalist principles, was forming in what would become Ontario. Loyalists and Indians from the region resettled, and while the effort was certainly no picnic, the success rate was high. They had the guidance and support of Haldimand from the St. Lawrence, west of Montreal, to the Bay of Quinte on the shores of Lake Ontario. These Loyalists formed a prosperous, religious, and stable society, ultimately with political participation under the British Constitution. Today one can visit the historic homes constructed by Loyalists from New York and Vermont—evidence of the loss of population and talent sustained by both states at a time when they were needed. Moreover, the process of settlement in Canada was carried out at a time when conditions in the Hudson-Champlain region still reflected the violence of civil conflict.

19

DEBTOR UPHEAVALS
A Challenge of the Postwar Era

While the Loyalists were reestablishing their society in Canada, the new nation to the south was also going through growing pains. After the War of Independence, the communities of the Vermont and New York borderland experienced no quiet. Homes had been abandoned, crops had been left untended, Loyalists had migrated, and many settlements north of Castleton and Saratoga were in need of redevelopment. Taxes were high in New York and Massachusetts to pay off the extensive debt these states had accumulated as they borrowed money to finance the war. Many investors would never regain the equity that they put into the development of settlements. Edward Countryman, historian of revolutionary New York, has concluded regarding the war's effects that "some people [would] gain to a degree undreamed of at the time of the [war], other people were made happy by modest achievements, and still others' . . . lot would be to endure far worse poverty and exploitation than the eighteenth century ever saw."[1]

THE DEBTOR UPHEAVALS

Like those in Massachusetts, farmers in the nearby Hudson-Champlain region were upset over increasing indebtedness, especially among those who were war veterans. Agriculture had been disrupted by the use of paper money issued by Congress in payment of its soldiers, ruining the financial integrity of the new state governments. As a result, a barter economy had surged, leaving the farmer without cash to pay his mounting debts.[2] Most of the debt was owed to landlords and entrepreneurs like Philip Schuyler, Abraham Ten Broeck, and Philip Van Rensselaer of Albany, or John Williams and Alexander Webster of the Salem area, wealthy rebels who were champions of the rights of property. Not since the tenants of the Van Rensselears and Livingstons chose to be Loyalists had such class division emerged in the region. Once more men of property, even though they had been rebel leaders and supported independence, became an object of scorn to less fortunate farmers and settlers.

The situation in the mid-1780s was explosive. Settlers in the region had purchased land on credit but were unable to pay their debts because of depressed prices for their crops and the lack of hard currency.[3] Landlords and creditors felt they had no recourse but to foreclose on yeoman farmers, using the courts that protected their property rights. But debtors saw their economic situation as only temporary, favoring negotiation and accommodation. They were incensed against landlords whose immediate recourse was legal action, which went outside of the informal bonds of reciprocity that had developed in the 1760s and 1770s as the region was settled.

Civil conflict between the debtors and property owners began in the spring of 1784, as Haldimand was settling Loyalist refugees on the St. Lawrence River and Lake Ontario. A convention of Vermont and Granville, New York, farmers was held in Wells, Vermont, to ameliorate "the general sufferings and embarrassments of the people."[4] The convention scolded attorneys, sheriffs, and justices of the peace who attempted to foreclose for debt and asked the Vermont Assembly to oppose the collection of debts by force for the next two years. Similar protests over the collection of debts and payment of taxes were held in Rutland and Middletown, Vermont, and in Granville. The protestors called for a reduction in the court meetings, the issuance of paper currency, and changes in the tax structure because it fell so heavily on the poorer classes.

In New York State the Granville protestors melted away when they heard that Salem's militia under the command of the region's largest landlord and judge, John Williams, had been called out to march on the town and quell its rioters.[5] By 1786 Williams had been promoted to brigadier general of the Washington County militia, to enable him to prevent anti-court riots. Who the protestors from Granville were remains a mystery, except for the fact that they were not among the town's wealthiest landholders.

Mindful of debtor protest, in newly created Washington County a county court met in 1786, really for the first time since the crown's court had last gathered at Fort Edward, eleven years before. True, appointments had been made to a county court by the legislature during the war, but no courts had actually transacted business. The same was true of Washington County's justices of the peace, who were first appointed by the state in 1786.[6] The names of the justices offer no surprises: Alexander Webster of Hebron, David Hopkins of Hebron, Ebenezer Russell of Salem. Webster and Russell had also been appointed justices of the peace under the crown in 1773 and were still accepted in 1786, while Hopkins was a new state appointment. Williams was behind this, for not only was there now a court to try debtors, but he saw the situation as another reason to make Salem the seat of the new county. He himself acquired the position of justice of the peace three years later.

In Vermont the debtors gained the mild support of Governor Chittenden, who addressed "the freemen of Vermont" with his analysis of the situation in the middle of 1786. He noted that the late war had been the cause of the lack of currency and that Vermont's isolation from the rest of the union had left it without credit to borrow money. During the war, Vermont had commanded its "creditors to stand still while we fought our enemies," and yet at the end of the war the creditors could not collect debts because most debtors were still "destitute . . . of provisions."[7] The problem, he continued, was exacerbated by the practice of purchasing foreign manufactures on credit, rather than raising flax and wool to clothe themselves. As a result, he contended, "law suits became so numerous that there was hardly money sufficient to pay for entertaining the actions," so that many wanted to "kill the lawyers and deputy sheriffs." Chittenden proposed that taxes be laid on lawsuits and imports. He also wished to see the Assembly establish a small bank to loan paper money to debtors and cut down on the number of lawsuits. To enforce his views, Chittenden asked the freemen at large to influence their Assembly representatives to support his proposals.

Chittenden would also submit a series of Betterment Acts in the early 1780s, which were meant to clarify the Redemption Act of 1778. The act allowed Loyalists to buy back their estates, but the Betterment

Acts insisted that legal owners pay for the improvements of smaller farmers and even squatters, if they were ejected from the estate by application of the law. Chittenden insisted on extra payments for improvements in any Loyalist land acquisition, ignoring the fact that English common law treated the squatting farmers as mere trespassers.[8]

Obviously, Chittenden had no use for attorneys, many of whom were now sitting in the Vermont Assembly. Their knowledge and respect for common law he saw as being used solely for their own purposes and bloating the cost of the court system.[9] Assemblyman and attorney Nathaniel Chipman came to the rescue of Loyalists interested in returning but who did not want to pay for additional improvements of squatters. An attorney from Tinmouth, he was a Yale graduate and a veteran of the Continental Army. Chipman was able to delay the passage of the Betterment Acts in the Assembly and water them down, so that compensation for improvements was minimized.

In September 1781 another attorney opposed to Chittenden's policies was Bennington's representative to the Vermont Assembly, Isaac Tichenor. He was portrayed by the Allens as an aristocrat who supported an educated clergy, the rule of law, and respect for the rights of property. A native of New Jersey and a graduate of Princeton University, Tichenor had moved to Bennington in 1777.[10] He had the values of civic-spirited gentlemen like Schuyler, feeling that political leaders should devote themselves to the common good, not their individual political or economic interests. On this basis he was elected by conservative Bennington leaders as their representative in the Assembly. There he found the land title situation still to be in disarray.

The Junta was concerned to protect all settlers, even those who had no legal title to land. The Assembly had adopted the system of English common law and a court system that could recognize legitimate titles, although none of the early judges who sat in Vermont's courts had training in the law and thus failed to execute it properly. The Junta had legislation passed that prohibited trials involving land titles until appropriate legislation had been passed to protect those who had undergone hardship to settle their lands—in other words, they again favored the rights of squatters.[11]

In contrast in the Junta, Tichenor and Chipman insisted that all persons be held strictly accountable to the letter of the law for debt. These two newcomers led the Assembly to protect the rights of property. Tichenor was elected speaker of the Vermont Assembly and was instrumental in blocking the Junta's effort to annex portions of New York and New Hampshire. He had also supported the effort to take the position of state treasurer from Ira Allen, who was unquestionably corrupt.[12] Clearly the Allens were on the wane, though Chittenden remained a force to be reckoned with.

When the Vermont Assembly met in Rutland in October 1786, it looked as if a measure of debtor relief might be imposed on Vermont's courts and creditors. Some Assemblymen lobbied for Chittenden's state bank, paper money, and a general tender act, which would enable a debtor to pay in any form he chose. Others wanted goods accepted in lieu of money to pay for debts. And the creditors had their supporters. Many Protestant churches had come to see indebtedness as a sin, a sign that one was not following God's law. In the Assembly, Nathaniel Chipman blamed the protesting settlers' problems on "Their own shiftless habits."[13] At Rutland, Chipman in alliance with Elijah Dewey, Bennington's veteran of the Battle of Walloomsac, proposed a referendum on the issue of paper money in every town in Vermont, a democratic solution but also a delaying tactic so the opponents of the debtors could form a united opposition. Despite strong resistance from friends of the debtors, Chipman's proposed referendum passed on October 31.

The debate between Chittenden and his opposition took a back seat when the Assembly adjourned and suddenly the reality of mob protest burst into the debate. Debtor protest came to a head in November 24, 1786, when the Rutland County Court attempted to convene.[14] The situation was similar to that in Fort Edward more than a decade before, in which Grants rioters tried to close the New York court because it was only recognizing New York titles. At Rutland the docket was heavy with debtor cases, and the mob wanted to postpone the session. Before the judges reached the courthouse, they were met by six hundred club-wielding men and boys, who sought to temporarily close the court because of its docket. The crowd leaders included Thomas Lee, who had served in Warner's Continental regiment; Benjamin Cooley and James Mead, former officers in Ethan Allen's Green Mountain Boys; and one member of the Assembly, Jonathan Fassett, once a resident of Arlington but now of Pittsford. All were self-styled "colonels," a title implying that they were or had been military leaders. The bulk of the protestors came from the nearby towns of Pittsford, West Rutland, and Ira. One observer commented that "most of the mob were boys, and men of low character, who most probably have been misguided." When the mob was reported to them, Governor Chittenden and the Junta had difficulty in seeing these men as insurgents.

The crowd demanded that the court be adjourned, and when the justices and Rutland County Sheriff Jonathan Bell delayed, they armed and posted themselves at the doors, holding the court hostage inside for two hours before letting them retire.[15] When the justices announced that the court would be held the next day, the mob took possession of the courthouse overnight to prevent the session.

Unable to quell the rioters that night, Sheriff Jonathan Bell called out the Vermont militia from Castleton, Pawlet, Tinmouth, and Wells.[16] The militia units turned out rapidly and in better form than usual. Only Wells, a center of protest, seemed to falter. Colonel Stephen Pearl of Pawlet led the militia from there, advancing by way of Wells, ready to put down the Rutland insurrectionists. The same was true of Colonel Isaac Clark of Castleton and Colonel Samuel Safford—the Benningtonian elected second in command of Warner's Continental regiment at Dorset—now of Tinmouth. Were these militia leaders men of property? It is hard to judge: Pearl kept a store and a tavern, and Samuel Safford and his family had been among the leaders of Bennington from its founding. Isaac Clark was the son of another Bennington founder, Nathan Clark, but he does not fit the conservative mold, as he had married Governor Chittenden's third daughter, Hannah, and become a member of his council. The militia traveled overnight, and much of it was on hand for the opening of the court the next day. In the face of its force, the insurgents gave up the courthouse.

However, the confrontation between the rioters and the militia continued as the two groups paraded in Rutland's streets and shouted their opinions. Near the end of the day, Colonel Clark tried for reconciliation at the courthouse and agreed to meet the rioters on the edge of town at Lieutenant Roswell Post's house. This had the effect of dividing and dispersing the rioters, and many in Rutland were arrested, though Colonel Thomas Lee managed to escape.[17] At midnight Captain Noah Lee of Castleton and James Sawyer were sent to Post's to capture Benjamin Cooley and his followers. Cooley was surrounded and both sides fired on each other, at least one youth being wounded, but the majority surrendered to Lee.

The rest of the week was spent trying the prisoners in court. At least forty of the rioters were tried and fined, having pleaded guilty.

The religious appeal of the revivalist Reverend Jacob Wood was necessary to quell insurgents residing in West Rutland, who had still challenged the militia on their way home. In a stinging rebuke to his neighbors the Fassetts, Elijah Dewey of Bennington moved in the Assembly that for his "seditious speeches" in support of the insurgents, Jonathan Fassett of Pittsford be expelled from his seat.[18] The resolution passed unanimously and again showed that Bennington's leaders were no friends of the Arlington Junta. Fassett also lost his position as a judge of the superior court and even was expelled from the Governor's Council—although Chittenden stood by him and brought him back the next year. The once powerful member of the Junta and confiscator of Loyalist estates was humbled. Overall the sheriff, judges, militia, and Assembly had sustained the rule of law.

Another debtor convention held in the town of Ira fizzled in January 1787, and a month later an Assembly referendum on proposals for debtor relief was defeated. However, the Assembly did pass an act making it lawful to pay debts in "neat cattle, beef, pork, sheep, wheat, rye and Indian corn," as opposed to scarce cash. On March 8 the Assembly also passed "an Act for the prevention and punishment of riots, disorders and contempt of authority"—a piece of legislation that went against everything the Green Mountain Boys had once stood for. The Act made it a crime to impede any civil or military officer. It was punishable by a substantial fine, which if the culprit could not pay, he was then to be indentured until it was paid.[19] Furthermore, a convention of more than three individuals to conspire was unlawful, if it were to fail to disperse when called upon by the authorities. The breaking open of jails to release prisoners was punishable by imprisonment. Freemen were to assist the authorities in dispersing such crowds and were not liable if members of the crowd were injured.

The violence of the debtors, combined with the increasing respect for the rights of propertied leaders like Nathaniel Chipman and Isaac Tichenor, discredited the rioters. They had received indirect support from the Junta, specifically Governor Chittenden, the Allen family, and, as noted, former Junta member Jonathan Fassett. But the Junta now saw the danger of the insurgents to their own position and joined the Assembly in opposition to the rioters.

The anti-court and debtor uprising also spread to New Hampshire in September 1786. The State House at Exeter was surrounded by 200 rioting farmers asking for debt relief and holding the legislature prisoner until Governor John Sullivan calmed them by offering to issue paper money. The rioters retreated to the hills around Exeter, thinking they had won a victory, but in the meantime Sullivan called out 2,000 militiamen from New Hampshire's eastern towns, an overwhelming force. He asked "a gentleman of the first rank and education" to lead them, none other than the veteran of Freeman's Farm and Bemis Heights, Joseph Cilley. [20] He had retired from military service but honored the governor's call and was named major general of the New Hampshire militia with the task of rooting out the insurgents. With the backing of Sullivan and the New Hampshire Assembly, Cilley easily dispersed the insurgent farmers, the leaders were ritually disgraced, and the discord ended by October. Here was a case of a Saratoga commander throwing his lot with the government supporters of law and order at the expense of suffering farmers, who may once have served in the ranks of his Continental regiment. Cilley would not be the only former Continental officer to find himself in this predicament.

Shays's Rebellion

Simultaneously with these upheavals, Shays's Rebellion erupted in western Massachusetts over similar farmers' debts, as yeomen tried to stop the courts from meeting. Their leader was former Continental officer Daniel Shays from Pelham, the hard-scrabble but fiercely independent Massachusetts hill town that earlier had sent Scots-Irish settlers into New York. Many of the insurgents had distinguished records of service in the Massachusetts militia or in fewer cases as Continentals, including the Saratoga Campaign. What held them together was a fierce respect for the local government of their towns against that of the Massachusetts General Court and the belief that the old Puritan morality had been destroyed by attorneys, the courts, and the Massachusetts Constitution of 1780. [21]

Shays besieged the Springfield Federal Arsenal, but General Benjamin Lincoln's army lifted the siege in late January 1787. Lincoln, like Cilley, was a veteran of the Saratoga Campaign. Asked to take on the onerous duty of crushing the insurgents, he responded, "Opposition to the laws, in a free government is a crime which liberty cannot tolerate." [22] His sentiments were against the Continentals and militia he had served with at Saratoga. Neither Continentals nor state militia were part of his force because he and the Boston elite that funded them feared that such troops would go over to the insurgents. His army chased the insurgents, and in February 1787 he caught them at Petersham, where they were defeated by men of property and volunteers from eastern Massachusetts. Both sides had a Saratoga Campaign legacy.

Lincoln still faced pockets of resistance in Berkshire County that had to be snuffed out. From there in mid-February, a Shays lieutenant at Springfield, Eli Parsons, asked his followers, "Will you now tamely suffer your arms to be taken from you, your estates to be confiscated, and even swear to support a constitution, . . . which common sense and your consciences declare to be iniquitous and cruel?" He concluded by begging every friend to rally to Berkshire County "and help us to *Burgoyne* Lincoln and his army."[23] Parsons was a veteran of Saratoga and hoped to see Lincoln caught in a similar trap.

In this final phase of the rebellion the insurgents no longer hoped to reform existing institutions and instead, losing any semblance of being an army, turned to destroying their opposition's personal property, certainly involving class warfare. Hundreds of Shaysites symbolically left Massachusetts, escaping to New York border towns like New Lebanon and New Canaan, and to Vermont. There they rallied, returning on February 27, 1787, to sack Stockbridge, Massachusetts, and take its merchants, attorneys, and shopkeepers prisoner.[24] Federalist attorney Theodore Sedgwick was not there, but his new house drew the pillagers, and only the intervention of his black slave, Elizabeth Freeman, restricted their depredations to taking a horse, clothing, and linen. His law offices suffered more, and his two apprentices, Elisha Williams and Henry Hopkins, were taken as hostages. The homes of thirty of the elite were destroyed and more than twenty were taken prisoner. The remaining Stockbridge mission Indians observed from the sidelines and saw the fighting as a further reason to leave and join their brethren in central New York. Here, as with the Reid plantation on Lake Champlain and the sack of Skenesborough in 1775, the motives of the raiders were to destroy the property of the upper class, based on revenge and envy, rather than to pursue reforming political ideals. The sack of Stockbridge was the last evidence of the intensity of the civil conflict that still existed in the region.

The destruction in Stockbridge put the Shaysite cause into the realm of anarchy, as that evening they traveled as a drunken band south toward Sheffield. John Ashley, who had commanded the South Berkshire militia at the Battle of Bemis Heights, and Benjamin Simonds, who had served over a wide area in the Saratoga Campaign, had been named militia brigadier generals. Their force met the insurgents, and they had the unpleasant task of ordering their men to fire a single volley on the Stockbridge looters. Two Shaysites were killed and thirty wounded, and they immediately fled, preventing further looting and ending the Shaysites' odyssey. Lincoln would praise the effort of Ashley and Simonds in finishing the rebellion in Berkshire County.[25]

Thus the ranks of those who won the War of Independence were split by the debtor upheavals. This time, Lincoln, Cilley, Schuyler, Williams, Chipman, Dewey, Ashley, Simonds, and the Reverend Thomas Allen were on the side of legal authority, supporting the authorization of troops that put down Shays's Rebellion and other debtor insurgencies. Governor John Hancock of Massachusetts, Governor Chittenden of Vermont, the Allens, and Jonathan Fassett showed sympathy for the debtors. The cleavage between gentlemen and common farmers had not subsided because of the War of Independence. Until a new federal constitution could be established, the region was adrift.

The new nation was far from being peaceful and unified. The debtor upheavals covered much of the region, from Exeter in the east, to Rutland in the middle, to Granville in the west, as well as the famous Shays's Rebellion in Massachusetts. They revealed a split between gentlemen of property and the ordinary farmers who had served together in the War of Independence. On the one hand were the courts and paternal authority and on the other were popular demonstrations and debtor relief, inspired by the coming of the French Revolution. The insurgents formed armies, although they disintegrated into plundering mobs near the end, when the Shaysites sacked Stockbridge. The authorities, who included Continental officers like Benjamin Lincoln, chose to ignore the concerns of their former comrades among the rank and file at the Battle of Saratoga. Civil violence did not end when independence was achieved.

Affirmations

In 1851 Sir Edward Creasy, a historian at the University of London, published his monumental *Fifteen Decisive Battles of the World*.[1] The battles covered ranged from Marathon to Waterloo, and the thirteenth chapter was devoted to the only North American contest included, the Saratoga Campaign. While he failed to mention Loyalists and noted the alleged barbarities of Burgoyne's Indians, Creasy was among the earliest to emphasize the recognition the rebels received from France and eventually Spain and Holland as a result of Burgoyne's defeat.

In the foregoing narrative I contend that after Burgoyne surrendered, there was no turning point in the regional war that surrounded and penetrated the Saratoga battlefields. Instead, from 1778 to 1782 we find continued invasion of the region by the British. Lake Champlain and Ticonderoga's ruins remained in their hands, creating a base of operations that allowed them to penetrate deeply into New York and Vermont. The result of the invasions was to force the line of settlement south, well below the lakes, so that most of the settlement gains of the 1760s and 1770s were wiped out. Forts George, Ann, and Edward, which dated from the colonial wars, were abandoned as Schuyler's Saratoga plantation and Bemis Heights became the defensive boundary with Canada. In Vermont the line at Castleton performed the same function. The region's population fell because Loyalists were resettled in Canada.

The rebel predicament was not caused by a complete abandonment of the area by Washington and the Congress. Continental generals like Gates, Stark, Lafayette, Schuyler, and even Washington were constantly involved in efforts to invade Canada that never materialized. Rebel forces also proved much less adept at petite guerre than their British counterparts. Furthermore, the rebels were as divided as ever. Vermont's leaders took the opportunity to annex towns from New York and New Hampshire, while simultaneously ensuring their protection by negotiating with Governor Frederick Haldimand to return to the British Empire. The story has been extended beyond the Peace of Paris to look at the making of the United States and see what sort of consensus was hammered out by the region's leaders as they sought to contend with economic and social upheaval. The civil conflict was, if anything, aggravated during these years, and the region that emerged from the war was poorer, debtor upheavals bringing devastation to places like Stockbridge that had been considered too far south to be reached by invasions from Canada.

My story of the Saratoga Campaign is different from Creasy's in other ways. It has been placed in a much broader context than before. It begins at least fifteen years before the campaign to gauge the degree of settlement and note the conflicts that appeared during this process. The local, physical, and human environment is present. Armies had to deal with topography and the degree of agricultural development that affected logistics. While the Hudson-Champlain region was backcountry, it was far from being the wilderness it had been in the colonial wars. Discord was introduced as settlers established themselves, especially in the future state of Vermont, where the same land was granted by two colonies.

In this account, peaceful action was as important as war. When Burgoyne invaded, he made an effort at gatherings to win the hearts and minds of the inhabitants. As the Independence movement evolved, various rebel committees and commanders also sought to establish their authority over settlers by having them leave the backcountry. Burgoyne sought to have them stay on their farms, come to his army as families, and swear allegiance to the king. In doing this, he was not as forward as British generals like William Howe, but he made a hesitating effort. He finally organized his Loyalists into corps for military action. Indians were valued by both sides, for Gates sought them as much as Burgoyne, but they interrupted pacification efforts because they were independent and could not be controlled.

This presentation of the Saratoga Campaign puts the action in the context of civil war. Eighteenth-century battles were not fought in isolation from existing local animosities. Burgoyne and Gates had to contend with a civil war of local factions and convictions, doing their best to take advantage of or ignore them. The rebels demanded and Burgoyne asked for loyalty from the countryside, but existing religious, ethnic, economic, social, and personal alignments were more crucial in deciding which side one supported.

This is not the first time an effort has been made to recognize the civil war as fundamental to our view of the War of Independence. On May 17, 1775, twenty-four ministers and six elders attended the Presbyterian Synod in New York City. At its conclusion, the Synod's pastoral letter reflected the perspective of the church's leaders after the bloodshed of Lexington and Concord but before the Declaration of Independence. They paid tribute to the king, who they felt had been misled by those around him and denied any "desire of separation from the parent state." At the same time they supported the Continental Congress, now sitting in Philadelphia. What concerned them most, however, was "a regard to order and the public peace . . . so that the evils inseparable from civil war may not be augmented by wantonness and irregularity." To them, if they were drawn into war, it would be a civil war, in which "it is impossible to appeal to the sword without being exposed to many scenes of cruelty and slaughter," for civil wars are carried on "with a rancor and spirit of revenge much greater than those between independent states." It was "therefore the more necessary to guard against this abuse and recommend that meekness and gentleness of spirit, which is the noblest attendant of true valor."[2]

It is left to remember the effect of civil conflict described by the Presbyterian Synod leaders, which began earlier and ended later than the formal conflict of the armies. Local historians did not ignore it, but they defined it as so nasty and complicated that it did not deserve to be analyzed as contributing to the overall conflict. Most military historians disregard the civil war altogether, while focusing on the professional armies.[3] This account of the Saratoga Campaign shows that one does that at one's peril. Looking at the other decisive battle of the war, Yorktown, we have a case in point. After Cornwallis surrendered in October 1781 and the French fleet left, Chesapeake Bay remained in the hands, not of the Maryland and Virginia navies, but rather Loyalist marauders, so-called picaroons.[4] Over the next year and a half, all efforts by the rebel navies and militia failed to prevent Loyalist and British domination of the Chesapeake's waters, in the very sight of the Yorktown triumph. In any account of the War of Independence, it pays to define the civil war and to recognize the extent to which it affected the affairs of great armies.

What other affirmations do we have? In 1776 Carleton's naval victory on Lake Champlain gave the British control of that invasion route from Canada to Saratoga for the rest of the war. This was the most strategic victory of the entire war, for it allowed the British to neutralize Ticonderoga and continually invade rebel territory from Canada.

In Vermont's conflict with New York and New Hampshire, the Allen family was in the thick of it,but as blatant land speculators, for the family's personal interest in the development of Lake Champlain was its highest priority, and this meant that the Allens had to deal with Haldimand. They also watched the Loyalist exodus with anxiety, for the loss of settlers from the region led to the establishment of a community in Ontario that remains loyal to the crown today.

Finally, in the age-old debate over the abilities of militiamen versus regulars, the battle at the Walloomsac has always been a test case. John Stark's New Hampshire militia appears exceptional, having been raised quickly and having done everything expected of it. However, it cannot be overlooked that the last-minute arrival of Warner's Continentals saved the day after the militia failed to form and became consumed by the search for booty. Stark was not a team player with Schuyler or Gates, but after Burgoyne's surrender, when Stark often commanded the Northern Department, he appears to have come round to their pespective. And the debate continues.

NOTES

ABBREVIATIONS

BL	Additional Manuscripts, British Library, London.
BOB	British Orderly Book, Wesleyan University Library, Middletown, Conn.
DCBO	Dictionary of Canadian Biography online.
FTML	Thompson-Pell Research Center, Fort Ticonderoga Museum Library, Ticonderoga, N.Y.
GP	Gates Papers, New-York Historical Society, New York, N.Y.
HP	Haldimand Papers, National Library and Archives of Canada, Ottawa.
NLAC	National Library and Archives of Canada, Ottawa.
NYHS	New-York Historical Society, Library, New York, N.Y.
NYPL	Schuyler Papers, New York Public Library, New York, N.Y.
NYSLM	New York State Library, Manuscripts and Special Collections, Albany.
PPNYSL	John Peters Papers, Manuscript and Special Collections, New York State Library, Albany.
PRO	Public Record Office, London.
RVC	George Russell Collection of Vermontiana, Martha Canfield Library, Arlington, Vt.

PROLOGUE

1. Reid, *Reminiscences*, 14–16.
2. Ibid., 16–17.
3. Ibid., 18–19.
4. Ibid., 19–20.

5. Ibid., 21–23; MacNaughton, *MacNaughtons of Argyle*, 24–25.

6. Gerlach, *Proud Patriot*, 262.

7. Digby, *British Invasion from the North*, 263–65.

8. Burgoyne, *A State of the Expedition*, 133, 160.

9. "Memorandum & Observations relative to Service in Canada submitted to Lord George Germain," CO43/36, 11–17, PRO; Clark, "Responsibility for the Failure"; William B. Wilcox, "Too Many Cooks."

10. Nickerson, *Turning Point of the Revolution*, 77–98. Luzader's Appendix A, "Battle of Bennington Casualties, 352–62, in *Saratoga* is the best explanation of the coordination involved in developing the Saratoga Campaign.

CHAPTER 1

1. Doblin, *Eyewitness Account*, 68; Doblin, *Specht Journal*, 66–67, 77.

2. "Schuyler's Saratoga Daybook," 1764–1770, NYPL; J. Graham to Philip Schuyler, Dec. 19, 1775, ibid.; Kim, *Landlord and Tenant*, 200, 209–10; Doblin, *Eyewitness Account*, 69; Stone, *Memoirs, Letters, and Journals*, 1: 234.

3. Lord, *War over Walloomscoik*, 32–46.

4. Doblin, *Eyewitness Account*, 65; Digby, *British Invasion from the North*, 240.

5. Anburey, *Travels*, 170.

6. Gerlach, *Proud Patriot*, 282–83.

7. Corbett, *Clash of Cultures*, 83–164.

8. Bonomi, *Factious People*, 17–55.

9. A vast literature exists on the settlement of the New England town—e.g., Jones, *Village and Seaport*, 1–10. On the consensus in New England's towns see Greven, *Four Generations*; Charles Grant, *Democracy in the Connecticut Frontier Town of Kent*, 98–103, 172–173; and, more broadly, Gross, *Minutemen and Their World*, chap. 4.

10. Bonomi, *Under the Cope of Heaven*, 51–53, 75–78, 91; Robert Shalhope, *Bennington and the Green Mountain Boys*, 4–13, 35–43.

11. The figures represent Albany County before Tryon, Charlotte, Cumberland, and Gloucester Counties were set off from it. In 1771 Cumberland and Gloucester Counties, covering much of Vermont, contained only 4,669 inhabitants. Even later figures show that the population of Albany County in the period covered here was larger than that of the entire New Hampshire Grants.

12. Census figures are merely a stating point for the discussion of population. On the size of Albany see Corbett, "Introduction"; on the size of Schenectady see Hanson, *History of Schenectady*, 4–8; Smith, *Tour of the Four Great Rivers*, 22–23; on the size of Kingston see Blumin, *Urban Threshold*, 2, 14, 35; Moffat, *Population History*, 120.

13. Kim, *Landlord and Tenant*, 129–80.

14. Corbett, "Introduction," 15–30; this is in contrast to county houses described in Tatum, *Philadelphia Georgian*, 39–40.

15. Kim, *Landlord and Tenant*, 167–68, 235, 238.

16. Ibid., 144–45.

17. Ibid., 145–46; Blackburn, *Cherry Hill*, 7–9, 164–68.

18. On the Palatines in the Hudson Valley, see Cobb, *Story of the Palatines*, 59–303; On their enclaves in the manors, see Barnett, *History of the Gilead Evangelical Lutheran Church*; "John Walden Meyers," DCBO; Fryer, *Loyalist Spy*, 15–18; Broderick, *Brunswick*, 16–17.

19. Runk, *Ten Broeck Genealogy*, 91–92. Abraham is not to be confused with his younger brother Dirck. He lived in Albany, and during the War of Independence he was lieutenant colonel of the Albany militia, a member of the Committee of Correspondence, and a New York State senator. He died in 1780 at the age of only forty-two.

20. Wells, *Population of the British Colonies*, 111–16.

21. Anburey, *Travels*, 170.

22. Kim, *Landlord and Tenant*, 192–93, Brandow, *Story of Old Saratoga*, 28–29, 233; Corbett, *Clash of Cultures*, 108–23.

23. Gerlach, *Philip Schuyler and the American Revolution*, 43–62; Anne Grant, *Memoirs*, 1:86–87, 92–95, 264–70.

24. Bureau for Historic Sites, The Division for Historic Preservation, *Schuyler Mansion, a historic structure report*, 12–16; Corbett, *Clash of Cultures*, 216, 221, 250, 275.

25. Bailyn, *Voyagers to the West*, 576–87; Shy, *Toward Lexington*, 110–11, 122–25, 135–39, 200.

26. The Johnson holdings were described in 1769 by Richard Smith in *Tour of the Four Great Rivers*, 23–25; On the tenants see McLean, *People of Glengarry*, 82–94; Pryde, "Scottish Colonization," 151–53.

27. Morton, *Philip Skene*, 18–37.

28. Philip Skene to Lieutenant Thomas Gamble, Jan. 22, 1764, Business Papers, FTML; Skene to Gamble, June 22, 1765, ibid.; Skene to Gamble, Nov. 25, 1767, ibid.

29. Morton, *Philip Skene*, 22–23, 32, 64.

30. Jones, "King of the Alley," 1–4; Doblin, *Eyewitness Account*, 69; Stone, *Letters of Brunswick and Hessian Officers*, 96, 99.

31. Jones, "King of the Alley," 4–6.

32. Alexander, *Revolutionary Conservative*, 13–51.

33. James Duane, "Journal of a Trip to Princeton in 1765," New-York Historical Society, found as Appendix E in Jones, *Vermont in the Making*, 420–24; Alexander, *Revolutionary Conservative*, 68–72; Lapp, *To Their Heirs Forever*, 22–122.

34. Summary of the several State Electoral Censuses, *Census of the State of New York for 1855*, ix–x.

35. Bureau of the Census, *Heads of Families*, 18–21, 25–26, 187–95.

36. Anburey, *Travels*, 161; Johnson, *History of Washington Co.*, 421–24.

37. Hill, *Old Fort Edward*, 244, 286–87.

38. Ibid., 248–57.

39. Ibid., 279–84.

40. Jessup, Memorial of Ebenezer Jessup, no. 2187, f. 145–46, BL; Fryer, *King's Men*, 180–82;, "Edward Jessup," DCBO; Jessup, *Edward Jessup of West Farms*, 203–70.

41. Fryer, *King's Men*, 181.

42. Ibid., 182;, "Edward Jessup," DCBO.

43. Fryer, *King's Men*, 182;, "Edward Jessup," DCBO.

44. Sylvester, *History of Saratoga County*, 286–93; Saratoga National Historical Park, "Neilson House" brochure, n.p.

45. J. Fraser says McAlpin held 1,200 acres at Saratoga Lake (*Skulking for the King*, 31–32); Dorrough, "Daniel McAlpin."

46. Johnson, *History of Washington Co.*, 252.

47. John Barber, *Historical Collections*; Perry, "Scotch-Irish in America"; Coe, *Line of Forts*, 25–26, 41–44, 174.

48. Johnson, *History of Washington Co.*, 252, 254–56, 260, 266, 271–72, 277.

49. Lapp, *To Their Heirs Forever*, 33, 102–103.

50. Johnson, *History of Washington Co.*, 165.

51. Lapp, *To Their Heirs Forever*, 22–122.

52. Ibid., 102–103, 105, 112–13.

53. Johnson, *History of Washington Co.*, 165.

54. Anburey, *Travels*, 161; Johnson, *History of Washington Co.*, 421–24.

55. Wraxall, *Abridgement of Indian Affairs*, 227; Klopet, "Schaghticoke," 29–33; Niles, *Hoosic Valley*, 26, 88–91, 100–101; Kim, *Landlord and Tenant*, 110–14; Corbett, *Clash of Cultures*, 96–107.

56. Memorial of Robert Leake, Audit Office, PRO; Shy, *Toward Lexington*, 332; Dresler, *Farmers and Honest Men*; on the 60th regiment see Campbell, *Royal American Regiment*,

57. Lapp, *To Their Heirs Forever*, 125–26; Dresler, *Farmers and Honest Men*, 32–33.

58. For John Macomb's early years see Meany, "Merchant and Redcoat"; McAnear, "Albany Stamp Act Riots."

CHAPTER 2

1. Jones, *Vermont in the Making*, 20–66; Hughes, *Journal*, 16–17.

2. Jones, *Vermont in the Making*, 77–88.

3. Ibid., 94.

4. Ibid., 89–109.

5. Charles Grant, *Democracy*, 98–103, 172–73, and more broadly, Gross, *Minutemen and Their World*, chap. 4.

6. Although the Queensbury Patent is usually associated with Dutchess County Quakers led by Abraham Wing, the first settlers in 1762 were actually from New Fairfield, Connecticut.

7. "October 22, 1762, meeting held for the aforesaid naming of the proprietors at the house of Isaac Verinernum, John Seal Moderator," RVC. William Searls's son, William, Jr., resided in Arlington and in September 1777 was accused by the Council of selling oxen to Loyalists, the proceeds of which the Council claimed (Williams, *Public Papers*, 108, 110–11).

8. "Genealogy of Hawley Family, 1880, Arlington Branch," RCV; Petersen, *Seth Warner*, 14. Many of the migrants came from the present day town of

Roxbury. However, this town did not exist until 1796 and hence I used its parent town of Woodbury.

9. Baker, "Remember Baker," 6; Wilbur, *Ira Allen*, 1:60–61.

10. Hemenway, *Vermont Gazetteer*, 2373; Lapp, *To Their Heirs Forever*, 91–92.

11. Arlington Town Records, Proprietors meetings, 1762, RCV; Nye, *Sequestration*, 94–95.

12. Jeptha Hawley, "his flax book," 1773–75, RVC.

13. Van Wagenen, Jr., 164–69; Jones, *Vermont in the Making*, 139; Fraser, *Second Report of the Bureau of Archives*, 434.

14. Jeptha Hawley, "his flax book," 1773–75, RVC.

15. Hughes, *Journal*, 16–17.

16. Shalhope, *Bennington and the Green Mountain Boys*, 3–51.

17. Ibid., 4–9: Brooke, *Heart of the Commonwealth*, 124–25.

18. Shalhope, *Bennington and the Green Mountain Boys*, 12–13, 52–58; Jones, *Vermont in the Making*, 132–34; Corbett, *Clash of Cultures*, 203, 228, 235, 242, 281–82.

19. Shalhope, *Bennington and the Green Mountain Boys*, 54–59; Jones, *Vermont in the Making*, 54–55, 106–107.

20. Shalhope, *Bennington and the Green Mountain Boys*, 60–61.

21. Fryer, *Exploits of Justice Sherwood*, 10–11.

22. Pemberton, "British Secret Service," 130–31; Fryer, *Exploits of Justice Sherwood*, 19–20.

23. Fryer, *Exploits of Justice Sherwood*, 9–10, 23.

24. Johnson and Gilbertson, "Castleton," 67–73.

25. Albers, *Hands on the Land*, 34–39; Watson, *Pioneer History*, 27–30.

26. Bellesiles, *Revolutionary Outlaws*, 83–84, 169–73.

27. Matt Bushnell Jones's account of the Reid settlement in *Vermont in the Making* is the most extensive and evenhanded, 304–305; Webster, *Journal of Jeffrey Amherst*, 154–61; Thomas Davies did his painting of the mill on Otter Creek sometime between 1759 and 1766, (see Hubbard, *Thomas Davies in Early Canada*, 20, 24–25, 30, 33–34); Albers, *Hands on the Land*, 108–109. Maps of Crown Point from the 1760s to 1774 show plans for a large settlement, which was partially executed by the later date (New York State, *18th Century Crown Point Maps*, 10–13).

28. Ethan Allen to William Tryon, Aug. 25, 1772, in Duffy et al., *Ethan Allen*, 1:6; Jones, *Vermont in the Making*, 305–308.

29. Jones, *Vermont in the Making*, 321–22.

30. Pell, *Ethan Allen*, 61; Jones, *Vermont in the Making*, 322–24.

31. "Affidavit of Charles Hutcheson," Nov. 12, 1771, 4:45–46, in O'Callaghan, *Documentary History*; Pell, *Ethan Allen*, 39–40.

32. MacNaughton, *MacNaughtons of Argyle*, 23.

33. Bellesiles, *Revolutionary Outlaws*, 93–109.

34. Pell, *Ethan Allen*, 1–27, 38, 146, 234; Sparks, *Memoir of Colonel Ethan Allen*, 90–91, 95–96.

35. Sparks, *Memoir of Colonel Ethan Allen*, 99–108; Bellesiles, *Revolutionary Outlaws*, 81–85.

36. Shalhope, *Bennington and the Green Mountain Boys*, 51, 88–89.

37. Chipman, *Memoir of Colonel Seth Warner*, 6–7. Bennington and Green Mountain Boys leaders like Warner are recognized in Benjamin Hough's letter.

38. Two residents of the town, but not the village, James Brekenridge and the aforementioned Seth Warner did have connections with the Allens. Brekenridge, however, regardless of the fact that New York authorities tried to take his farm three times, remained law abiding and refused to condone the violence of the Green Mountain Boys.

39. Chipman, *Memoir of Colonel Seth Warner*, 22–25; Petersen, *Seth Warner*, 11–28.

40. Bellesiles, *Revolutionary Outlaws*, 71–72, 100–102, 196, 212, 222.

41. Shalhope, *Bennington and the Green Mountain Boys*, 70–72.

42. Ibid., 84–86.

43. Ethan Allen to William Tryon, Aug. 25, 1772, in Duffy et al., *Ethan Allen*, 1:7.

44. Jones, *Vermont in the Making*, 101; Bellesiles, *Revolutionary Outlaws*, 97–104.

45. O'Callaghan, *Documentary History*, 4:486–88; Jones, *Vermont in the Making*, 181; *Churchman's Magazine* 2 (Oct. 1805), 224; Nye, *Sequestration*, 94–95, contends that Jehiel Hawley did visit England, but her sketch of his life is riddled with errors.

46. Baker, "Remember Baker," 604–608; Fryer, *Buckskin Pimpernel*, 20–22.

47. Ethan Allan and others to Benjamin Spencer, Jan. 11, 1774, in Duffy et al., *Ethan Allen*, 1:11–12.

48. Slade, *State Papers of Vermont*, 38–39; O'Callaghan, *Documentary History*, 4: 523–27; Jones, *Vermont in the Making*, 180–81, 328.

49. New York State, *Colony Laws*, 36–38.

CHAPTER 3

1. Andrew and Jeptha Hawley, but not Jehiel, signed a petition to make Skenesborough the county town of Charlotte County on February 2, 1773 (O'Callaghan, *Documentary History*, 4:496–98); Ethan Allen to John Trumbull, May 12, 1775, in Duffy et al., *Ethan Allen*, 1:22; Williams, *Natural and Civil History of Vermont*, 224; Pell, *Ethan Allen*, 54–55, 24–29, 45–51; Jones, *Vermont in the Making*, 1; Martin, *Benedict Arnold*, 64–65.

2. Smith, *History of Pittsfield, Massachusetts*, 1: 211–25; Mott, "Journal," 163–88; Hall, *Life and Letters*; Martin, *Benedict Arnold*, 66.

3. Martin, *Benedict Arnold*, 67; Smith, *History of Pittsfield, Massachusetts*, 1:225–28; Bellesiles, *Revolutionary Outlaws*, 115–17.

4. Ethan Allen to the Massachusetts Congress, May 11, 1775, in Duffy et al., *Ethan Allen*, 1:21; Sullivan, *Minutes*, 20–21; Martin, *Benedict Arnold*, 67–69.

5. Martin, *Benedict Arnold*, 33–60.

6. Ibid., 61–64.

7. Ibid., 64–69.

8. Pell, *Ethan Allen*, 45; O'Callaghan, *Documentary History*, 4:486–88; Jones, *Vermont in the Making*, 181; *Churchman's Magazine*, 2 (Oct. 1805), 224.

9. Pell, *Ethan Allen*, 79.

10. Morton, *Philip Skene*, 46–47.

11. Ibid., 48.

12. "Philip Skene, Memorial of 1787," Loyalist Transcripts 14:191, NYPL.

13. Heman Allen to the Continental Congress, Apr. 10, 1777, in Duffy et al., *Ethan Allen*, 1:65.

14. Sparks, *Memoir of Colonel Ethan Allen*, 139.

15. Langan to Schuyler, July 21, Dec. 20, 26, 1775, NYPL.

16. Ethan Allen to Noah Lee, May 21, 1775, in Duffy et al., *Ethan Allen*, 1:27–28; Morton, *Philip Skene*, 49.

17. Gerlach, *Proud Patriot*, 1–2, 7–11.

18. Headquarters, Sept. 29, 1776, in Salsig, *Parole: Quebec*, 248–49; Anne Grant, *Memoirs* 1:280–82, 2:11–12, 38, 44, 50.

19. "Schuyler Letter Book," 1:15–17, NYPL.

20. Ethan Allen to the Continental Congress, May 29, 1777, in Duffy et al., 1:31–33, quotes on 31–32.

21. Ethan Allen to Philip Schuyler and Richard Montgomery, Sept. 8, 1775, in ibid., 1:48–49.

22. Ethan Allen to Jonathan Trumbull, July 6, 1775, in ibid., 1:43; Jones, *Vermont in the Making*, 355–56.

23. Allen, *Narrative of Ethan Allen's Captivity*, 47; Sparks, *Memoir of Colonel Ethan Allen*, 139.

24. Ethan Allen to the Albany Committee of Correspondence, May 11, 1775, in Duffy et al., *Ethan Allen*; Ethan Allen to the Massachusetts Congress, May 11, 1775, in ibid.; Ethan Allen to Jonathan Trumbull, May 12, 1775 in ibid., 1:20–22, quote on 20.

25. Ethan Allen and other to the People of the Counties of Albany and Charlotte . . . , Apr. 26, 1774, in Duffy et al., *Ethan Allen*, 1:14.

26. Ethan Allen to the New York Congress, July 20, 1775 in Duffy et al., *Ethan Allen*, 1:45–46; Petersen, *Seth Warner*, 41–42.

27. Ethan Allen to Jonathan Trumbull, Aug. 3, 1775, in Duffy et al., *Ethan Allen*, 1:47.

28. Ethan Allen to the New York Congress, June 2, 1775, in ibid.; Ethan Allen to Richard Montgomery, Sept. 20, 1775, in ibid., 1:35, 51–52; NYPL, Richard Montgomery to Schuyler, Aug. 24, 1775, in ibid.

29. "Orders of New York Provincial Congress," Aug. 15, 1775, and P. V. B. Livingston to Schuyler, Aug. 17, 1775, NYPL; Petersen, *Seth Warner*, 45–46.

30. Salsig, *Parole: Quebec*, 252; Austin, *Matthew Lyon*, 17.

31. Callahan, *Henry Knox*, 40–54.

32. MacMaster, "Parish in Arms," 107–18; Fraser, "Sir John Johnson's Rent Roll"; Corbett, *Clash of Cultures*, 144–46, 150, 160.

33. Sullivan, *Minutes*, 313.

34. Graymont, *Iroquois in the American Revolution*, 81–82.

35. "Schuyler's Letter Book," 2:350–51, NYPL; Gerlach, *Proud Patriot*, 101.

36. "Schuyler's Letter Book," 2:352, NYPL.

37. Graymont, *Iroquois in the American Revolution*, 82.

38. G. Marselis to Schuyler, Jan. 19, 1776, NYPL; Gerlach, *Proud Patriot*, 104–105.

39. Sullivan, *Minutes*, 1:386.

40. Sir John Johnson to Claus, Jan. 20, 1777, in DePeyster, *Miscellanies of an Officer*; Watt, *Rebellion in the Mohawk Valley*, 344.

41. Watt, *Rebellion in the Mohawk Valley*, 47; Burleigh, "Loyalist Refuge," 48–49.

42. Watt, *Rebellion in the Mohawk Valley*, 32; McLean, *People of Glengarry*, 92–97; MacMaster, "Parish in Arms," 118–25; McCulloch, *Sons of the Mountains*, II, 20–21.

CHAPTER 4

1. "Schuyler's General Monthly Return," July 14, 1775, NYPL; Gerlach, *Proud Patriot*, 28–30.

2. Gerlach, *Proud Patriot*, 83; Petersen, *Seth Warner*, 53–58.

3. Reynolds, *Guy Carleton*, 1–7; "Guy Carleton," DCBO.

4. Smith, "Sir Guy Carleton."

5. Paine, *Common Sense*, 1:35.

6. Reynolds, *Guy Carleton*, 59–64.

7. Higginbotham, *Daniel Morgan*, 27–53; Accounts of Arnold's invasion of Canada include Desjardin, *Through a Howling Wilderness*.

8. Bowler, *Logistics*, 214, 219.

9. Beebe, *Journal*, 337–39. Ichabod Hawley had probably enrolled in one of Warner's regiments.

10. "Schuyler's Letter Book," 3:346–47, 4:177–78, NYPL; R. Livingston to R. Varick, Aug. 18, 1776, and J. Porter to Schuyler, Aug. 19, 1776, ibid.

11. "Accounts, Money owed him by the U.S.," Jan. 27, 1776–Apr. 29, 1776, Cherry Hill Papers, 3/22, 3/30; Philip Van Rensselaer to Colonel Barber, n.d., Cherry Hill Papers; Headquarters, Ticonderoga, Oct. 8, 1776, in Salsig, *Parole: Quebec*, 254; Blackburn, *Cherry Hill*, 9–10.

12. Nelson, *Benedict Arnold's Navy*.

13. "Schuyler's Letter Book," 3:482, 485, 345–46, NYPL; J. Wynkoop Memorial to Congress, Aug. 27, 1776, ibid.

14. Baldwin, *Revolutionary Journal*, 35–37; Beebe, *Journal*, 336.

15. Baldwin, *Revolutionary Journal*, 35–37; Specht described the sprawling works in early July 1777 (Doblin, *Specht Journal*, 50–52); Manley, *Geophysical Reconnaissance*.

16. Beebe, *Journal*, 354; Fenn, *Pox Americana*, 75–78; Nelson, *Benedict Arnold's Navy*, 64–65, 77.

17. Saillant, *Black Puritan, Black Republican*, 15.

18. Ward, *War of the Revolution*, 1:390.

19. Digby, *British Invasion from the North*, 107, 122; Starch, "Memoir of the Exploits," 6.

20. Digby, *British Invasion from the North*, 122–23; Stanley, *For Want of a Horse*, 80–81.

21. Nelson, *Benedict Arnold's Navy*, 249–74.

22. Digby, *British Invasion from the North*, 148–64.

23. Beebe, *Journal*, 355–57.

24. Doblin, *Eyewitness Account*, 33; Baldwin, *Revolutionary Journal*, 81, Oct 13, 1776; Stone, *Memoirs, Letters, and Journals*, 1:70–75.

25. Digby, *British Invasion from the North*, 87–88; Recent critics have even blamed Carleton for the British defeats at Trenton and Princeton because had he garrisoned Crown Point, Gates would have been unable to remove troops from Ticonderoga to join Washington's army (Bowler, *Logistics*, 224–25). In fact, Gates brought Washington only eight hundred men, whose enlistments were soon up so they melted away.

26. Bowler, *Logistics*, 214–16.

27. Digby, *British Invasion from the North*, 165–66.

28. Lampee, "Mississquoi Loyalists," 81–96. Lampee's article includes an overview of the region's Loyalists, although he focuses on Peter Miller, who joined Carleton at Crown Point and played a supporting role in the development of Loyalism (Potter-MacKinnon, *While the Women Only Wept*, 38–44).

29. Fryer, *Buckskin Pimpernel*, 28–29.

30. Ibid., 34–35, 42.

31. Lapp, *To Their Heirs Forever*, 126–27; Foster, "Always a Loyal Man," 1.

32. Fryer, *King's Men*, 181–82; Rae, "Jessup's Rangers as a Factor," 123–24; Pierce, "Dr. Solomon Jones: United Empire Loyalist," 437–38. The occupational makeup of the Jessups' new unit was twenty-five landowners and farmers, two merchants (Gershom French and James Rogers, both lieutenants), three former professional soldiers (Lieutenant David McFall, 26th Regiment; Adjutant Mathew Thompson, 31st Regiment; Quartermaster John Ferguson, 29th Regiment); two dependent sons of their fathers (William Lamson and Henry Young); and two doctors (George Smyth and Solomon Jones.) Smyth would become famous as the chief Loyalist spy in the Albany area. Some, like Peter Drummond and Neil Robertson, had actually been recruited at Saratoga Lake by Captain Daniel McAlpin, who was too feeble and closely watched by the rebels to make the journey.

33. Johnson, *History of Washington Co.*, 421–24.

34. Rogers, *Journal Kept in Canada*, 134; Lapp, *To Their Heirs Forever*, 71, 126–28, 163, 185; Burgoyne, *State*, 37.

35. Watt, *Rebellion in the Mohawk Valley*, 56–58. Technically, Maclean's Royal Highland Emigrants might also be included because it was still a provincial regiment and had some New York recruits from the Mohawk Valley.

36. While Carleton mustered his Loyalist units, he left them in Canada when he invaded Lake Champlain. Only Major Gray was to accompany Carleton to recruit the King's Royal Regiment of New York.

37. Watt, *Rebellion in the Mohawk Valley*, 32, 43–45, 56–59.

38. Major General Philips to General Fraser, Nov. 13, 1776, Edward Jessup Papers, 8, NLAC; Jones, *History of New York*, 1:686–92.

39. Major Gray to Major Jessup, Aug. 10, 1785, Edward Jessup Papers, 15–16, NLAC; Rogers, *Journal Kept in Canada*, 69; Jessup to Carleton on Jan. 24, 1777; Fryer, *King's Men*, 182–85.

40. Memorial and Supporting Documents to Lord Sidney, Sept. 6, 1785, CL3576, PPNYSL.

CHAPTER 5

1. Corbett, *Clash of Cultures*, 277, 288–89; Frazier, *Mohicans of Stockbridge*, 127–29; Jackson, *Rogers' Rangers*, 37–38.

2. Kelsay, *Joseph Brant*, 164–66.

3. Corbett, *Clash of Cultures*, 53–55, 86–87; J. Fraser, *Skulking for the King*, 34.

4. Colden, *History of the Five Nations*, 135–61; Jennings et al., *History and Culture of Iroquois Diplomacy*, 39, 163.

5. Corbett, *Clash of Cultures*, 56–82.

6. Doblin, *Eyewitness Account*, 63; White, *Middle Ground*, 315–65.

7. Frazier, *Mohicans of Stockbridge*, 47–51, 84–88; Corbett, *Clash of Cultures*, 162–63, 208–209.

8. Richter, *Ordeal of the Long House*, 54–56, 60–62.

9. Michelson, "Iroquois Population Statistics," 4; Starna, "Mohawk Iroquois Populations: A Revision," 371–82; Richter, *Ordeal of the Long House*, 58–59, 172–73.

10. Richter, *Ordeal of the Long House*, 32–36, 65–74, 81–84.

11. Participation of whites in the captive trade had begun in the colonial wars; see Foster, *Captors' Narrative*, 7–19.

12. Shannon, *Iroquois Diplomacy*, 179–86.

13. Kelsay, *Joseph Brant*, 46–54.

14. "Met according to adjournment," June 24, 1775, Sullivan, *Minutes*, 101–108.

15. Kelsay, *Joseph Brant*, 142–54.

16. Allen, "British Indian Department," 6–26.

17. Watt, *Rebellion in the Mohawk Valley*, 36–38, 44.

18. Ibid., 48–49.

19. Kelsay, *Joseph Brant*, 154–55; Graymont, *Iroquois in the American Revolution*, 66–69.

20. "John Campbell," DCBO; Kelsay, *Joseph Brant*, 157–58.

21. Sparks, *Memoir of Colonel Ethan Allen*, 160–63; Allen, *Narrative*, 17–22.

22. "John Campbell," DCBO.

23. Kelsay, *Joseph Brant*, 159–83.

24. Ibid., 169.

25. Calloway, *American Revolution in Indian Country*, 4, 11–12.

26. Digby, *British Invasion from the North*, 238.

27. Doblin, *Eyewitness Account*, 24; Doblin, *Specht Journal*, 87.

28. Stone, *Memoirs, Letters, and Journals*, 1:47–48.

29. Ibid., 1:50.

30. Ibid., 1:54–55.

31. Ibid., 1:25.

32. B39:360–61, Dec. 28, 1776, HP; Claus to Haldimand, Nov. 19, 1778, in Penrose, *Indian Affairs Papers*, 176–77; Kelsay, *Joseph Brant*, 184–87.

33. Digby, *British Invasion from the North*, 127.

34. Anne Grant, *Memoirs*, 1:146–263; Schuyler, *Colonial New York*; Corbett, *Clash of Cultures*, 109–111, 119–20, 145.

35. "Met according to adjournment," June 26, 1775, in Sullivan, *Minutes*, 109–10.

36. A. Allen to Schuyler, Mar. 19, 1776, "Schuyler's Letter Book," 2:372, NYPL; Graymont, *Iroquois in the American Revolution*, 71–72.

37. Taylor, *Divided Ground*, 52–68, 81–86.

38. Shannon, *Iroquois Diplomacy*, 180–84.

39. Frazier, *Mohicans of Stockbridge*, 193–211.

CHAPTER 6

1. Anburey, *Travels*, 117–18.

2. Luzader, *Saratoga: A Military History*, 33–34; Logusz, *With Musket and Tomahawk*, 42–43, shows the variety of estimates for the size of Burgoyne's army.

3. There are several inadequate biographies of Burgoyne: Howson, *Burgoyne of Saratoga*, 3–129; Hudleston, *Misadventures of an English General in the Revolution*, 1–140. Better is Mintz, *The Generals of Saratoga: John Burgoyne and Horatio Gates*, 3–11, 49–61.

4. Burgoyne, *State*, 76; Urban, *Fusiliers*, 68.

5. Urban, *Fusiliers*, 68, 306; Stephenson, *Patriot Battles*, 46–48.

6. "Simon Fraser," DCBO. His nephew, Alexander Fraser, is not to be confused with him, as Alexander commanded the marksmen in Burgoyne's army.

7. Davis, *Where a Man Can Go*.

8. "William Philips," DCBO.

9. Ticonderoga, July 12, 1777, BOB; Ticonderoga, July 19, 1777, ibid. Also found on the internet at http://62ndregiment.org/sources.htm, as edited by Eric Schnitzer. While the writer of this garrison orderly book remains unknown, Schnitzer feels it is likely to have been the "adjutant" of the fort's commander, Brigade-Major Captain-Lieutenant Michael Kirkman. Also, Digby, "notes," in *British Invasion from the North*, 196–97.

10. Digby, *British Invasion from the North*, 86–87.

11. Ibid., vi–vii, 2–4.

12. Barnard, *New Anatomy of Ireland*, 177–207, quote on 188.

13. Stone, *Memoirs, Letters, and Journals*, 1:24–26.

14. Ibid., 1:26–30.

15. Ibid., 1:34–43.

16. Doblin, *Specht Journal*, 50.

17. "Headquarters, Skenesborough House," July 18, 1777, BOB; Digby, *British Invasion from the North*, 192–201; Doblin, *Eyewitness Account*, 56; Stanley, *For Want of a Horse*, 98.

18. Sylvia Frey, *British Soldier*, 20.

19. BOB, "Headquarters," Skenesborough House, July 18, 1777.

20. On the Canadian militia's service in the Colonial Wars see Corbett, *Clash of Cultures*, 80–82, 259, 262, 264, 265, 267, 270–71; Stone, *Letters of*

Brunswick and Hessian Officers, 22–24; "Charles-Louis Tarieu de Lanaudiere," DCBP.

21. "Rene-Ovide de Rouville," DCBP.

22. "General Orders by General Phillips," Ticonderoga, July 26, 1777, BOB.

23. Negotiation Documents (microfilm), Gates Papers, NYHS.

24. Watt, *Rebellion in the Mohawk Valley*, 56–79.

25. Mintz, *Generals of Saratoga*, 119–30; Nelson, *General Horatio Gates*, 80–88.

26. Knopf, *Anthony Wayne*; Beebe, *Journal*, 358–59.

27. John Langdon to Bartlett, July 15, 1776, in Mevers, *Papers of Josiah Bartlett*, 96; William Whipple to Bartlett, Dec. 23, 1776, in ibid., 140; Bartlett to William Whipple, Jan. 15, 1777, in ibid., 145.

28. Nathan Hale to Abigail Hale, June 6, 1777, www.worldpath.net/~rwhite/histarchive/hale/6-21-77/trans.htm.

29. Mintz, *Generals of Saratoga*, 141–42.

30. Rorison and Boucher, *Major-General Arthur St. Clair*; Wilkinson, *Memoirs of My Own Time*, 1:83–85.

31. A British description of the fortifications is found in Digby, *British Invasion from the North*, 214–15.

32. Chipman, *Memoir of Colonel Seth Warner*, 50.

33. Kim, *Landlord and Tenant*, 412–15.

34. Lynd, "Tenant Rising at Livingston Manor" 170–82, and "Tenant Rising of 1766," 37–54; Dangerfield, *Chancellor Robert R. Livingston*, 20, 53, 81–82, 99.

35. Sullivan, *Minutes*, 823–24.

36. Stone, *Memoirs, Letters, and Journals*, 1:114–16; Digby, *British Invasion from the North*, 204–208; Stanley, *For Want of a Horse*, 103–105; Starch, "Memoir of the Exploits," 6.

37. Doblin, *Eyewitness Account*, 58; Doblin, *Specht Journal*, 50–52; Stone, *Memoirs, Letters, and Journals*, 1:118–19; Bradford, "Lord Francis Napier's Journal," 295; Pell, "Diary of Joshua Pell," 107. Lieutenant Francis Napier's journal remained in manuscript until its publication in 1962. While Napier did analyze on occasion and provided a few footnotes, the journal does not appear to have been turned into the political and literary efforts of Burgoyne and most of his officers. Joshua Pell was a Loyalist volunteer who seemed to be attached to either Fraser's marksmen or Jessup's Rangers. Through his family, he had property in Pelham Manor, Westchester County, New York, which was later confiscated by the New York Commissioners of Forfeiture. After the war, he remained in Canada and settled in the Niagara region.

38. Burgoyne, *State*, 65; Anburey, *Travels*, 142; Bradford, "Lord Francis Napier's Journal," 299.

39. "St. Clair Court Martial at White Plains, New York," Sept. 12, 1778, Revolutionary War Papers, 113, NYHS.

40. Dupuy, "Battle of Hubbardton," 2–57; Williams, *Battle of Hubbardton*.

41. Burgoyne, *State*, 81; Digby, *British Invasion from the North*, 209–13; Napier places Jessup in Fraser's Advanced Corps (Bradford, "Lord Francis Napier's Journal," 298–99); Logusz, *With Musket and Tomahawk*, 120; I have

avoided using Anbury's account of the battle for the reasons that Duling has outlined in "Thomas Anburey at the Battle of Hubbardton," 1–14.

42. Doblin, *Specht Journal*, 54; Doblin, *Eyewitness Account*, 60; Bradford, "Lord Francis Napier's Journal," 301.

43. Doblin, *Specht Journal*, 55; Bradford, "Lord Francis Napier's Journal," 301–302.

44. Smith, *The St. Clair Papers*, 77–78.

45. Anburey, *Travels*, 142.

46. "General Orders by General Phillips," Ticonderoga, July 26, 1777, BOB; Wilkinson, *Memoirs of My Own Time*, 1:123; Austin, *Matthew Lyon*, 18.

47. Walton, *Records*, 1: 135–37.

48. Doblin, *Specht Journal*, 54; Doblin, *Eyewitness Account*, 60; Digby, *British Invasion from the North*, 221–22.

49. Digby, *British Invasion from the North*, 225–26; Bradford, "Lord Francis Napier's Journal," 305.

50. Doblin, *Specht Journal*, 55; Digby, *British Invasion from the North*, 224; Bradford, "Lord Francis Napier's Journal," 304; Bonney, *Legacy of Historical Gleanings*, 1:60–65; Starch, "New Look," 127–34; Johnson, *History of Washington Co.*, 46–48.

51. "Schuyler Letter Book," 5:235, 239–40, NYPL; Johnson, *History of Washington Co.*, 44–45.

52. "Orders, Camp at Skenesborough House," July 10, 1777, BOB; Bradford, "Lord Francis Napier's Journal," 305.

CHAPTER 7

1. Burgoyne, *State*, 133–34.

2. Bowler, *Logistics*, 240.

3. Smith, *Loyalists and Redcoats*, 48–50, 54–55.

4. Digby, *British Invasion from the North*, 201.

5. "Proclamation of June 23, 1777," in ibid., 189–92; Bradford, "Lord Francis Napier's Journal," 295–97; On the hard-liners versus the conciliatory opinions among British officers, see Conway, "To Subdue America," 281–407.

6. J. Fraser, *Skulking for the King*, 41.

7. J. Fraser's *Skulking for the King* is an example, as is "Major Banker informed this Board that a Number of disaffected Persons kept sculking in the woods near [Lansingburg] . . . ," Sullivan, *Minutes*, 799–800, 803, 849, 860.

8. Sullivan, Minutes, 676, 776.

9. Ibid., 721.

10. Ibid., 829.

11. Ira Allen to the Citizens of Poultney, July 10, 1776, in Duffy et al., *Ethan Allen*, 1:57; Baldwin, *Revolutionary Journal*, 101.

12. Ira Allen in the Council of Safety, July 15, 1777, in Walton, *Records*, 1:131–32.

13. "Schuyler Letter Book," 5:331, NYPL.

14. Schuyler's "Manifesto," July 13, 1777, FTML; Stark, *Memoir*, 119–21.

15. Johnson, *History of Washington Co.*, 49.

16. Sullivan, *Minutes*, 820, 830, 832–34.

17. Doblin, *Eyewitness Account*, 69–70; Sullivan, *Minutes*, 870–71.

18. Burgoyne, *State*, 39–40.

19. Stone, *Memoirs, Letters, and Journals*, 1:127–29; Stone, *Letters of Brunswick and Hessian Officers*, 89, 97.

20. Digby, *British Invasion from the North*, 243.

21. Henderson, "Witch of Salem, New York," 3–8.

22. Fitch, *Early History*, 13–18; Johnson, *History of Washington Co.*, 126, 175.

23. Anne Grant, *Memoirs*, 1:79–83, 170, 264–66; Halevi, *Other Daughters of the Revolution*, 75–84; J. Fraser, *Skulking for the King*, 18–20.

24. Halevi, *Other Daughters of the Revolution*, 81–85, quote on 84.

25. "Muster Role of Captain Samuel Adams Company," Jan. 23, 1778, no. 21827, f. 14, BL.

26. Johnson, *History of Washington Co.*, 58.

27. Sullivan, *Minutes*, 960.

28. Bradford, "Lord Francis Napier's Journal," 307; Johnson, *History of Washington Co.*, 248–49.

29. Doblin, *Eyewitness Account*, 66.

30. Anburey, *Travels*, 152.

31. John Williams Papers, Manuscript and Special Collections, HY12382, box 1, f. 2, New York State Library.

32. Johnson, *History of Washington Co.*, 249.

33. Paltsits, *Minutes*, May 15, 1778, 117–18.

34. Johnson, *History of Washington Co.*, 59.

35. Adler, *Their Own Voices*, 71–72.

36. Worrall, *Quakers in the Colonial Northeast*.

37. Easton Book Club, "Some Chapters," 26–28, 34–39.

CHAPTER 8

1. Doblin, *Specht Journal*, 56; Stone, *Memoirs, Letters, and Journals*, 1:121.

2. Morton, *Philip Skene*, 38.

3. Walton, *Records*, 1:165, 198, 208.

4. Morton, *Philip Skene*, 38–40.

5. Digby, *British Invasion from the North*, 233; Stark, *Memoir*, 119; Morton, *Philip Skene*, 55–56.

6. Stone, *Memoirs, Letters, and Journals*, 1:119–21; Doblin, *Specht Journal*, 56–57; Joseph McCracken to Philip Schuyler, July 20, 1777, NYPL.

7. Mintz, *Gouverneur Morris*, 81–82.

8. Petersen, *Seth Warner*, 73–75.

9. Ethan Allen and others to Benjamin Spencer, Jan. 2, 1774 in Duffy et al., *Ethan Allen*, 1:11–12. There were parallels between the Spencers and the Hawleys, even though Spencer was a New York grantee. Both families were Anglican. Jehiel and other Hawleys had signed a letter in early 1774,

offering Spencer a New Hampshire grant at a reasonable price, an olive branch after the depredations to his farm the year before. Jehiel and Benjamin would have the common experience of the region's harsh climate in November 1777 because they both died of exposure during the Loyalist retreat to Canada. Hazelton would perform a role similar to that of Jeptha, going on to become an officer in a Loyalist regiment and a prominent figure in the settlement of Upper Canada.

10. Smith, *Revolutionary War in Bennington County*, 67–73, 131.

11. "Complaint of John Peters against Jeremiah French and his brother Gershom French, Jan. 20, 1781, no. 21827, folios 216–17, BL. Fryer, *Buckskin Pimpernel*, 52, 101, 109. It is difficult to judge the seriousness of the complaint against the Frenches because Peters was an angry man. A second Loyalist with the name Jeremiah French existed. A farmer in New York, he fled to Canada in 1777 and joined the King's Royal Regiment of New York. The uniform he purchased in Montreal as a lieutenant has been preserved; see Chartrand, "French and his Uniform," 42–50.

12. Stone, *Memoirs, Letters, and Journals*, 1:121; Anburey, *Travels*, 152.

13. Stone, *Letters of Brunswick and Hessian Officers*, 89.

14. Ibid., 88.

15. Ketchum, 231.

16. Stone, *Memoirs, Letters, and Journals*, 1:121.

17. Doblin, *Specht Journal*, 56.

18. Stone, *Memoirs, Letters, and Journals*, 1:121, 123.

19. Ibid; Doblin, *Specht Journal*, 57–58; Doblin, *Eyewitness Account*, 64.

20. Stone, *Memoirs, Letters, and Journals*, 1:124; Doblin, *Specht Journal*, 60.

21. Walton, *Records*, 1:147; Wilbur, *Allen*, 100.

22. Ira Allen to John Warner, July 28, 1777, in Duffy et al., *Ethan Allen*, 1:72: At the end of 1777 John McNeil of Tinmouth was exiled from his home by the Vermont Council, and he went to live with Loyalist James Breakenridge in Bennington, which the council allowed. Walton, *Records*, 1:191, 193–94, 198.

23. Johnson, *History of Washington Co.*, 43.

24. On Adams see Palmer, *Biographical Sketches of Loyalists*, 33; Fryer, *Buckskin Pimpernel*, 38, 42. At the Dorset convention on September 28, 1776, when delegates resolved to form a government of their own, it was noted that representatives were not present from "the Town of Arlington [because they] are principally Tories, yet the Friends of Liberty are ordered to . . . choose a Committee of Safety," {Williams, *Public Papers*, 28}; Walton, *Records*, 1:15, 27, 36, 39, 63; Bellesiles, *Revolutionary Outlaws*, 93.

25. It is probable that there were a series of skirmishes in Arlington between the Battle of Hubbardton, July 7, and the Battle of Bennington, August 16. "Action in Vermont," 109; Austin, *Matthew Lyon*, 22; Foster, "Always a Loyal Man," 1–2.

26. Williams, Vermont Council of Safety, Aug. 29, 1777, 93; Potter-MacKinnon, *While the Women Only Wept*, 65. After being abducted by rebels and taken to Bennington, Eastman was permitted to return to Arlington in

January 1778. Hurd was also taken, but seems have been placed in a rebel prison ship near New York, where he died in a fire. His wife received use of his confiscated farm in 1778 from the Vermont Assembly. Andrew Hawley, Zadock Hard, Nathan Canfield, and Caleb Daton were rehabilitated by the Vermont Council and remained in Arlington (Walton, *Records*, 1:163, 174). Jeptha Hawley went to Canada.

27. Austin, *Matthew Lyon*, 22; Foster, "Always a Loyal Man," 1–2.

28. Doblin, *Eyewitness Account*, 64.

29. Doblin, *Specht Journal*, 71; [probably Peters to an unknown], Dec. 9, 1779, Misc. Mss., John Peters Papers, NYHS.

30. By ignoring the regimentalization already started, Burgoyne did not have to recognize the rank and pay of existing Loyalist officers.

31. "Samuel McKay," DCBO; Burleigh, *Captain McKay and the Loyal Volunteers*; Rogers, *Journal Kept in Canada*, 39–43; Doblin, *Eyewitness Account*, 100; McCulloch, *Sons of the Mountains*, 1:16–17.

32. On Howe's use of Loyalists, see Smith, "Sir Guy Carleton," 36–43.

33. List of 20 Loyalists, June 1777, CL3578, PPNYSL; Muster Role of Lieutenant Colonel Peters' Corps for July 23, 1777, CL3582, ibid.; "Muster role," Aug. 23, 1777, CL3601, ibid.

34. "Account of Cash disbursed by Lieutenant Colonel John Peters . . . on the expedition commanded by Lieutenant General John Burgoyne," July 20, 1777, no. 21827, f. 18, BL; J. Fraser, *Skulking for the King*, 46–47, 75–76.

35. Receipt Book, Captain Edward Jessup's Corps of King's Loyal America, 1777–80, transcript Ms 521, NLAC; Rae, "Jessup's Rangers as a Factor," 123–24.

36. Memorial of Ebenezer Jessup, Feb. 1, 1778, transcript MG21, BI67, 161–71, NLAC.

37. Strach, "Notes on the Family of Sarah Dunham Jones"; "In order that the Royalists may be made acquainted with the generosity of his Excellency General Haldimand," Apr. 8, 1781, Edward Jessup Papers, 14, NLAC; Captain Sherwood to Major Mathews, Mar. 18, 1784, in Bruce, *Loyalist Trail*, 64; Johnson, *History of Washington Co.*, 423.

38. Burgoyne, *State*, 133.

39. See chaps. 18 and 19.

CHAPTER 9

1. Burgoyne, *State*, 60.

2. Digby, *British Invasion from the North*, 154, 201, 243.

3. MacLeod, *Canadian Iroquois and the Seven Years' War*, 19–36.

4. "Samuel McKay," DCBO; Graymont, *Iroquois in the American Revolution*, 149, 155.

5. Doblin, *Specht Journal*, 74; Digby, *British Invasion from the North*, 191; Reynolds, *Guy Carleton*, 62–64.

6. Digby, *British Invasion from the North*, 360–61, quote on 360.

7. Doblin, *Specht Journal*, 48–49; Digby, *British Invasion from the North*, 200, 356–60.

8. Digby, *British Invasion from the North*, 356–60; Anburey, *Travels*, 123–26.

9. Doblin, *Eyewitness Account*, 63.

10. "St. Luc de la Corne," DCBO; Doblin, *Eyewitness Account*, 63; Stone, *Letters of Brunswick and Hessian Officers*, 92–93; Corbett, *Clash of Cultures*, 131–32, 135–37, 146, 151–52, 157, 229–30, 262, 267, 289.

11. "Charles Michel Mouet de Langlade," DCBO; Doblin, *Eyewitness Account*, 63; White, *Middle Ground*, 230–31, 402.

12. Anburey, *Travels*, 123–26; Doblin, *Eyewitness Account*, 52; Pell, "Diary of Joshua Pell," 107.

13. Pell, "Diary of Joshua Pell," 108; Doblin, *Eyewitness Account*, 63; Thomas Craige, Pension Application, 1833, in Dann, *Revolution Remembered*, 55; Barrett, *Berkshire County's Army of Obstruction*, 30–34, 42.

14. Doblin, *Eyewitness Account*, 63; Doblin, *Specht Journal*, 57, 87; Simeon Alexander, Pension Application, in Dann, *Revolution Remembered*, 108.

15. Doblin, *Eyewitness Account*, 25; Bradford, "Lord Francis Napier's Journal," 305.

16. Stone, *Memoirs, Letters, and Journals*, 1:134; Stone, *Letters of Brunswick and Hessian Officers*, 91–93; Anburey, *Travels*, 158–59; Digby, *British Invasion from the North*, 254–55; Bradford, "Lord Francis Napier's Journal," 308; White, *Middle Ground*, 366–70.

17. Doblin, *Eyewitness Account*, 69–71. Doblin, *Specht Journal*, 65–66.

18. The Mohawks "were driven from their village by the Americans, and have joined our army: they have come with their women, children, cattle, horses and sheep, and are encamped at the creek from whence this place takes its name; when the army cross the river, the squaws and children are to go to Canada, and the men to remain. [I visited them in camp] Their children are in a manner amphibious; there were several of the men bathing in the creek, and a number of little children, the eldest could not be more than 6 years old" (Anbury, *Travels*, 167); Doblin, *Specht Journal*, 69; Graymont, *Iroquois in the American Revolution*, 147.

19. Doblin, *Eyewitness Account*, 69–70; Graymont, *Iroquois in the American Revolution*, 147–48; Watt, *Rebellion in the Mohawk Valley*, 302–303, 406.

20. Bradford, "Lord Francis Napier's Journal," 311, 313; Kelsay, *Joseph Brant*, 208–209; Graymont, *Iroquois in the American Revolution*, 146.

21. Graymont, *Iroquois in the American Revolution*, 147–48.

22. Brown, "Baroness von Riedesel's Journal," 51; Kelsay, *Joseph Brant*, 208–209.

23. Digby, *British Invasion from the North*, 253–55, 84; Doblin, *Specht Journal*, 71; Stone, *Letters of Brunswick and Hessian Officers*, 91.

24. Anburey, *Travels*, 98; Digby, *British Invasion from the North*, 356–60.

25. Digby, *British Invasion from the North*, 122–23.

26. Anburey, *Travels*, 218–19.

27. Doblin, *Eyewitness Account*, 67, 69.

28. Digby, *British Invasion from the North*, 263; Adler, *History of Salem*, 21–22; Burns, in "Massacre or Muster?," 133–45, claims that the Jane McCrea incident had no effect on raising militia for Stark's army.

29. Digby, *British Invasion from the North*, 263–65.

30. On the theory of rebels accidentally shooting Jane McCrea, see Lasselle, "Remembering Jane McCrea," 72–79; Some of the explanation for the incident's popularity was that in the nineteenth century Jane McCrea became a tourist attraction, and publication of Wilson's *The Life of Jane McCrea with an Account of Burgoyne's Expedition in 1777* ensured she would be remembered. On the difficulty of dealing with this legend, see Logusz, *With Musket and Tomahawk*, 163.

31. [probably Peters to an unknown], Dec. 9, 1779, Misc. Mss., John Peters Papers, NYHS.

32. Calloway, *Western Abenakis*, 214.

33. Frazier, *Mohicans of Stockbridge*, 214–19.

34. Glatthaar and Martin, *Forgotten Allies*, 179–84; Graymont, *Iroquois in the American Revolution*, 149, 155.

35. Glatthaar and Martin, *Forgotten Allies*, 184–86.

CHAPTER 10

1. Burgoyne, *State*, 53–54; Doblin, *Specht Journal*, 66, 75; Bowler, *Logistics*, 225.

2. General Orders by General Phillips, Ticonderoga, July 19, BOB; General Orders by General Phillips, Ticonderoga, July 26, ibid.

3. General Orders by General Phillips, Ticonderoga, July 26, ibid.; Stanley, *For Want of a Horse*, 118; Stone, *Letters of Brunswick and Hessian Officers*, 94.

4. General Orders by General Philips, Ticonderoga, July 26, BOB.

5. Burgoyne, *State*, 143–46, Digby, *British Invasion from the North*, 233, 239; Bradford, "Lord Francis Napier's Journal," 305.

6. Bowler, *Logistics*, 225–28.

7. Roberts, *Rabble in Arms*, 486–93; Burgoyne, *State*, 54.

8. Doblin, *Specht Journal*, 60–76; Bowler, *Logistics*, 227–28.

9. Stone, *Memoirs, Letters, and Journals*, 1:127–29; Stone, *Campaign*, 277–78; Stone, *Letters of Brunswick and Hessian Officers*, 89, 97.

10. Stone, *Campaign*, 277–85. Arlington is identified as the destination on 278.

11. Stone, *Memoirs, Letters, and Journals*, 1:128.

12. Doblin, *Eyewitness Account*, 68; Anburey, *Travels*, 133–34.

13. Burgoyne, *State*, 99; Paltsits, *Minutes*, 1:417–18.

14. Peters to unknown, Dec. 9, 1779, misc. mss., John Peters Papers, NYHS; Stone, *Memoirs, Letters, and Journals*, lxix–lxx, 1:129.

15. Burgoyne, *State*, 99; Pell, "Diary of Joshua Pell," 108.

16. Doblin, *Specht Journal*, 65; Doblin, *Eyewitness Account*, 68; Johnson, *History of Washington Co.*, 54.

17. Stone, *Memoirs, Letters, and Journals*, 1:134; Doblin, *Eyewitness Account*, 69–70; Doblin, *Specht Journal*, 66.

18. Doblin, *Eyewitness Account*, 69–70; Doblin, *Specht Journal*, 68.

19. List of Men in Covel's Company, Oct. 25, 1777, CL3604, PPNYSL; List of Capt. Simon Covel's Company, 1777, MG23, James Parrot Papers,

NLAC; Sullivan, *Minutes*, 1:3–4, 781, 901–902; Johnson, "History of Washington Co.," 255–56; "Forage Money wanted for the Queens Loyal Rangers commanded by Lieut. Colonel John Peters commencing 12th May and ending 24th October 1777 inclusive," 21827, ff. 28&29, BL. Peters commanded from August 14.

20. Fitch, *Early History*, 13.

21. Wallace, "American Revolution and Cambridge," 101; Johnson, *History of Washington Co.*, 254, 256, 277. Cambridge, New York, sent a militia company to the Walloomsac to join Stark. It was Captain Robert Gilmore's single company, probably numbering no more than thirty rank and file. Among them were Lieutenants Jonathan French and John Miller, Quartermaster John Baker, with privates Thomas Whiteside, John and Julius Collins, Graham Woodworth, Caleb Wright, Robert Weir, William Hay, several members of the Heath family, Daniel Crossman, and Thomas Comstock. Despite this company, Cambridge had welcomed Baum only a few days before and had formed a unit of Loyalists that were with him. The rebel militia company had to bypass Baum in order to join Stark. Gilmore was one of the first settlers of Cambridge in the early 1760s, and in an early town meeting in 1774 he was named overseer of the poor, a collector, and a constable. His men were lesser worthies: Thomas Whiteside, the fourth son of wealthy Phineas Whiteside, worked a two hundred-acre farm his father had given him. Comstock was killed at the Walloomsac. Their presence definitely shows that the community was divided.

22. Wallace, "American Revolution and Cambridge," 102; Johnson, *History of Washington Co.*, 59, 123, 130, 175, 252, 255, 271–74.

23. Sullivan, *Minutes*, 489; Niles, *Hoosic Valley*, 240–41, 261; Stanley, *For Want of a Horse*, 98, 103; Broderick, *Brunswick*, 47; Johnson, *History of Washington Co.*, 54.

24. John Macomb, Audit Office, class 13, vol. 56, ff. 113–14, PRO; Sullivan, *Minutes*, 488.

25. Hugh Fraser, Audit Office, class 13; Sullivan, *Minutes*, 489.

26. Stone, *Memoirs, Letters, and Journals*, 1:130; Johnson, *History of Washington Co.*, 56, 252, 255–56.

27. Stone, *Campaign*, 280; Doblin, *Eyewitness Account*, 67.

28. Fryer, *Buckskin Pimpernel*, 57–58.

29. Doblin, *Eyewitness Account*, 57; Stone, *Memoirs, Letters, and Journals*, 1:130.

30. Doblin, *Eyewitness Account*, 72; Stone, *Memoirs, Letters, and Journals*, 1:130–31.

31. Stone, *Memoirs, Letters, and Journals*, 1:132; Stanley, *For Want of a Horse*, 135.

32. Philip Schuyler to Ira Allen, July 16, 1777, in Duffy et al., *Ethan Allen*, 1:68–69, quote on 69.

33. "Schuyler's Letter Book," 5:230–32, 234, 240, NYPL.

34. Ira Allen to the New Hampshire Council of Safety, July 15, 1777, in Duffy et al., *Ethan Allen*, 1:66.

35. Meshech Weare to Ira Allen, July 19, 1777 in ibid., 1:70–71; Ward, *War of the Revolution*, 1:198.

36. Mayo, *John Langdon of New Hampshire*; Stark, *Memoir*, 46–47.

37. Josiah Bartlett to William Whipple, Mar. 26, 1777, in Mevers, *Papers of Josiah Bartlett*, 153–54; Burns, in "Massacre or Muster?,"135–36, contends that the Stark's militia was not inspired to avenge the Jane McCrea incident.

38. Benjamin Lincoln to Gen. Schuyler, Aug. 4, 1777 (microfilm), Benjamin Lincoln Papers, Massachusetts Historical Society; "Schuyler's Letter Book," 5:328–31, 330–33, NYPL.

39. Seth Warner to Brigadier General Stark, July 24, 1777, in Stark, *Memoir*, 121–22; Walton, *Records*, 1:135–39; Nicholson, 227–29.

40. Lord, *War over Walloomscoik*, 36. Asa Douglas owned land on both sides of the New York/Massachusetts border and was active in local politics in both states, but his captain's commission came from New York, and he ended up in Stephentown. See Matthew Vissher, Return of Officers of Sixteen Regiments in New York, Oct. 1775, in Force, *American Archives*, series 4, 3, 1118; Hoerder, 345–46. Bennington had two militia companies, altogether about a hundred men, headed by Captains Elijah Dewey and Samuel Robinson, Jr. The captains belonged to Bennington's social establishment, Dewey, a tavern keeper, the son of the pastor of the First Church, having been a private in Bennington's first militia muster of 1764. Robinson, the son of the founder, had continued his father's policies of legal opposition to New York's authority. The militia companies probably represented every able-bodied man in Bennington. It should be remembered that these companies were recruited and maintained by the town fathers and were not former Green Mountain Boys.

41. Lord, *War over Walloomscoik*, 35–36.

42. John Stark to the Council of New Hampshire, Aug. 18, 1777, in Stark, *Memoir*, 126–27; Lord, *War over Walloomscoik*, 6–7; Doblin, *Specht Journal*, 68, n. 98; Doblin, *Eyewitness Account*, 72–73.

43. Lord, *War over Walloomscoik*, 9.

44. Burgoyne, *State*, l–li, 135–36, 151; Stone, *Letters of Brunswick and Hessian Officers*, 99–100.

45. Niles, *Hoosic Valley*, 337–38.

46. John Stark to the Council of New Hampshire, Aug. 18, 1777 in Stark, *Memoir*, 127.

47. John Stark to the Council of New Hampshire, Aug. 18, 1777 in Stark, *Memoir*, 127; Baldwin, *Revolutionary Journal*, 116; Doblin, *Specht Journal*, 69; Stone, *Letters of Brunswick and Hessian Officers*, 102–103; Niles, *Hoosic Valley*, 341. The Berkshire County militia came at the "Tory Redoubt" from the south, while Hobart's and Stickney's men attacked it from the east. To see the Loyalists who fought at the Walloomsac, consult Roll of the Officers, non-commissioned officers & privates of the Royalists who have served under General Burgoyne's last campaign; and those who came in for protection; and those who were taken prisoner at Bennington and at Different places; and killed, Dec. 20, 1777 (WO 28/10, reel B-2867, 17–18, NLAC).

48. Newcomer, "Yankee Rebels," 156–65; Doblin, *Specht Journal*, 70.

49. Stone, *Memoirs, Letters, and Journals*, 1:130–31; Lord, *War over Walloomscoik*, 10–11.

50. John Stark to the Council of New Hampshire, Aug. 18, 1777, in Stark, *Memoir*, 128; Lord, *War over Walloomscoik*, 11–12.

51. David Holbrook, Pension Narrative in Dann, *Revolution Remembered*, 87–91, quotes on 90; Deering, *Orderly Book*, 50–51.

52. Stone, *Letters of Brunswick and Hessian Officers*, 102.

53. Ibid., 102–104; Bradford, "Lord Francis Napier's Journal,", 308–309.

54. Wallace, "American Revolution and Cambridge," 102.

55. Committee of Safety to Josiah Bartlett and Nathaniel Peabody, Aug. 23, 1777 in Mevers, *Papers of Josiah Bartlett*; Josiah Bartlett to Levi Bartlett, Sept. 22, 1777, in ibid., 171, 174.

56. Rae, "Jessup's Rangers as a Factor," 30–31; Fryer, *Buckskin Pimpernel*, 61–62; Luzader, "Battle of Bennington Casualties," in *Saratoga*, 378–79; Major General Lincoln to the Massachusetts Council, Aug. 18, 1777, in Stark, *Memoir*, 133. Lincoln reported the prisoners as "thirty-seven British soldiers, three hundred ninety-eight Hessians, thirty-eight Canadians, and one hundred fifty-five Tories." If we accept these figures, over half the Germans and threequarters of the marksmen were taken prisoner. The Loyalist figure is closer to what Peters claimed, the bulk of them being prisoners.

57. Digby, *British Invasion from the North*, 260–65; Stone, *Letters of Brunswick and Hessian Officers*, 109; Vermont Council of Safety, Aug. 29, 1777, in Williams, *Public Papers*, 93–94; Peter Olcott to Vermont Council of Safety, Oct. 20, 1777, in ibid., 163; ibid., 163–72. John Davoe came with Samuel Robinson to survey the Wentworth town of Bennington and settled in Pownal (Luzader, "Battle of Bennington Casualties," in *Saratoga*, 378–79). While it is has been asserted that Colonel William Marsh, the Manchester tavern keeper, was made prisoner at Bennington, Wilson Brown explains in an e-mail of Dec. 23, 2010, that this prisoner was a younger and different William Marsh.

58. Doblin, *Eyewitness Account*, 72; Burgoyne, *State*, 99; Audit Office, class 13, vol. 56, folios 113–14, PRO.

59. Monthly Regimental Return, Aug. 7–Oct, 2, 1777, CL3589, PPNYSL; class 13, vol. 56, folios 113–14, Audit Office, PRO.

60. Bartlett to William Whipple, Sept, 22, 1777, in Mevers, *Papers of Josiah Bartlett*, 173–74; Broderick, *Brunswick*, 47; Luzader, "Battle of Bennington Casualties," in *Saratoga*, 378–79.

61. Stone, *Campaign*, 284.

62. Burgoyne, *State*, 47.

63. Isaac Lamb and Moses Dorman were among those Albanians who joined Burgoyne: Paltsits, *Minutes*, 2:87, 430–31; Doblin, *Specht Journal*, 71, 76; on Stillwater see Baldwin, *Revolutionary Journal*, 115–16.

64. Doblin, *Specht Journal*, 69; Stone, *Letters of Brunswick and Hessian Officers*, 104; Bradford, "Lord Francis Napier's Journal," 309, 312, 313.

65. Memorial of Francis Hogle and Gershom French, Dec. 9, 1777, no. 21827, f. 92, BL; Smith, *Tour of the Four Great Rivers*, 135.

66. Bradford, "Lord Francis Napier's Journal," 309; Memorial of Francis Hogle and Gershom French, Dec. 9, 1777, no. 21827, f. 92, BL; Muster Roll of His Majesty's Battalion of Queens Loyal Rangers Commanded by Lieutenant

Colonel John Peters Raised by Order of Their Excellencys Sire Guy Carleton and Munfort Browne Esqr., Jan. 29, 1778, no. 21827, f. 142, BL; Complaint of John Peter's against Jeremiah French and His Brother Gershom French, Jan. 20, 1781, no. 21827, ff. 216–17, BL.

67. Ellis, *History of Columbia Co., N.Y.*, 30–32.

68. Stanley, *For Want of a Horse*, 140; Starch, "New Look," 9–10; Morton, *Philip Skene*, 71.

69. Burgoyne, *State*, 86.

70. Sullivan, *Minutes*, 839; Vermont Council to Stephen Washburn, May 28, 1778, in Walton, *Records*, 260–61; Hille, *American Revolution*, 85; Watt, *Rebellion in the Mohawk Valley*, 305, 406–407. By December 1777 two more Loyalists, Elizabeth and Abigail Jessup, had arrived with their families in Canada. Mrs. Jeremiah French had remained, but in May 1778 Chittenden's Council ordered that she be removed to the east side of Lake Champlain with some of her valuables, "where she can go over to the enemy." Mary McAlpin was not reunited with husband in Sorel until December 1778. Most happy reunions of Loyalist families took place well after the Saratoga Campaign.

71. Anburey, *Travels*, 134.

CHAPTER 11

1. NYPL, "Schuyler Letter Book," 5:333–34.

2. Wilkinson, "Returns referred to in Volume I," Fort Edward, July 20, 1777, 1: appendix, in *Memoirs of My Own Time*.

3. Higginbotham, *Daniel Morgan*, 62–63.

4. Nelson, *General Horatio Gates*, 6–22.

5. William Smith to Gates, June 28, 1763, GP.

6. On his correspondence with Monckton in the Seven Years' War, see Apr. 23, 1762, GP; Nelson, *General Horatio Gates*, 21–24.

7. Correspondence with Monckton and his son, H. W. Monckton, Oct. 24, 1767, GP; Feb. 7, 1770, ibid.; July 10, 1771, ibid.; Nelson, *General Horatio Gates*, 25–38.

8. On his correspondence with Cruger, see Nov. 18, 1769, May 11, 1770, June 26, 1770, July 5, 1770, Nov. 16, 1770, and with Hale, Jan. 17, 13, 1769, Nov. 26, 1769, Feb. 5, 1770, Nov. 18, 1770; Thomas Haynes called him a red hot republican (see May 16, 1770, GP).

9. "Schuyler Letter Book," 5:368, 371–73, NYPL; Gates to Schuyler, Sept 14, 1777, GP.

10. Martin, *Benedict Arnold*, 379–81, 383.

11. Mattern, *Benjamin Lincoln*, 33–36.

12. Luzader believes that Gates's position at Bemis Heights was much more ideal ("Battle of Bennington Casualties," in *Saratoga*, 228).

13. Beebe, *Journal*, 39; George Willey, *State Builders*, 1903), 7–10.

14. "Colonel Ebenezer Learned's Regiment," *Massachusetts Magazine*, 73–101.

15. Higginbotham, *Daniel Morgan*, 55–61.

16. Mevers, *Papers of Josiah Bartlett*, 155; Stark, *Memoir*, 335–38.

17. Dearborn, *Journals*, 6–10.

18. Beebe, *Journal*, 32–33.

19. Cox, *Proper Sense of Honor*, 60, 62, 65, 183.

20. Anburey, *Travels*, 161.

21. Doblin, *Specht Journal*, 77.

22. Doblin, *Specht Journal*, 77; Bowler, *Logistics*, 227–30.

23. Digby, *British Invasion from the North*, 267–70.

24. Wilkinson, *Memoirs of My Own Time*, 1:235–36.

25. Ibid., 1:236–37.

26. Digby, *British Invasion from the North*, 272; Starch, "Memoir of the Exploits," 11.

27. Digby, *British Invasion from the North*, 270–73, quote on 273; Pell, "Diary of Joshua Pell," 109; Wilkinson, *Memoirs of My Own Time*, 238.

28. Martin, *Benedict Arnold*, 377–83.

29. Burleigh, *Freemans of Freeman's Farm*, 22–27; Stone, *Visits*, 67–68; Leslie Potter, "Chain of Title for farm no. 3, Great Lott 16 of the Saratoga Patent," files.usgwarchives.org.

30. Stone, *Visits*, 68.

31. Martin, *Benedict Arnold*, 381.

32. Burgoyne, *State*, 162; Stone, *Memoirs, Letters, and Journals*, 149; Digby, *British Invasion from the North*, 273; Stone, *Journal of Captain Pausch*, 119, 152, 137–40: Captain Pausch would claim that it was the superiority of German gun crews over the British crews that made the difference.

33. Anburey, *Travels*, 174–75.

34. Digby, *British Invasion from the North*, 275.

35. Ibid., 276–77.

36. Stone, *Letters of Brunswick and Hessian Officers*, 105; Wilkinson, *Memoirs of My Own Time*, 1:284; Digby, *British Invasion from the North*, 256.

37. Doblin, *Specht Journal*, 82; Stone, *Memoirs, Letters, and Journals*, 1:154–55.

38. Roll of Captain Munro's Company, MG21, B167, 91–93, NLAC; Abstract of Captain Munro's Company, ibid., 94–95; ibid., 130–35; Miscellaneous Papers Pertaining to the Service of Captain Hugh Munro, ibid., 242–45.

39. "In order that the Royalists may be made acquainted with the generosity of his Excellency General Haldimand," Apr. 7, 1781, Edward Jessup Papers, 13–14, NLAC; Judd, "Memoir," 45–46.

40. Stone, *Memoirs, Letters, and Journals*, 1:154.

41. Mattern, *Benjamin Lincoln*, 41–44.

42. Ibid., 46; Wilkinson, *Memoirs of My Own Time*, 1:248.

43. Howe, *Colonel John Brown*, 1–3.

44. Ibid., 3–7.

45. Hughes, *Journal*, 11.

46. Ibid., 12–13; Orders by Brig Hamilton, July 26, 1777, BOB; Orders by Brig Hamilton, July 31, 1777, Ticonderoga, ibid.

47. Hughes, *Journal*, 13–14; Jepson, *Herrick's Rangers*, 15–19.

48. Hille, *American Revolution*, 78–79.

49. Anburey, *Travels*, 158–59, 161. Fort George had been occupied by the British since Schuyler abandoned it in late August. It continued to be occupied, even when most of the British force was concentrated at Diamond Island.

50. Thomas Wood, Pension Deposition, in Dann, *Revolution Remembered*, 94–95, quote on 95; Stone, *Memoirs, Letters, and Journals*, 1:165; Doblin, *Specht Journal*, 85.

51. Wood, Pension Deposition, in Dann, *Revolution Remembered*, 95.

52. Mattern, *Benjamin Lincoln*, 48.

53. Ibid., 49.

54. Wilkinson, *Memoirs of My Own Time*, 1:334–35.

55. Some historians have assumed that Gates's Continental brigades were made up completely of Continentals, when in fact the militia in each brigade was often more numerous and provided them with overall superiority in numbers. See Nelson, *General Horatio Gates*, 142.

56. Gouverneur Morris to Philip Schuyler, Aug. 27, 1777, in Sparks, *Life of Gouverneur Morris*, 1.

57. Josiah Bartlett to William Whipple, Sept. 22, 1777, in Mevers, *Papers of Josiah Bartlett*, 173; Wilkinson, *Memoirs of My Own Time*, 1:248–49.

58. Corbett, *Clash of Cultures*, 281.

59. Anburey, *Travels*, 175; Stone, *Journal of Captain Pausch*, 141; Digby, *British Invasion from the North*, 286; Doblin, *Specht Journal*, 84.

60. Doblin, *Specht Journal*, 89.

61. Gates to Congress, Oct. 12, 1777, GP; Wilkinson, *Memoirs of My Own Time*, 1:268.

62. Stone, *Journal of Captain Pausch*, 166–71.

63. Samuel Woodruff, Pension Narrative, in Dann, *Revolution Remembered*, 102.

64. ibid., 102–103; Martin, *Benedict Arnold*, 400.

65. Pell, "Diary of Joshua Pell," 110–11; Martin, *Benedict Arnold*, 396–400.

66. Digby, *British Invasion from the North*, 293–96; Brown, "Baroness von Riedesel's Journal," 50–53.

67. Woodruff, 103.

CHAPTER 12

1. "Report from Lieutenant General Sir Henry Clinton to General Sir William Howe," Oct. 9, 1777, in *Naval Documents*, 10:345–47, 350; Gruber, *Howe Brothers*, 266; Paul Smith, 52–53.

2. Wilcox, *American Rebellion*, 70–84; Nickerson, *Turning Point of the Revolution*, 334–52; Nelson, *William Tryon*, 156–57; Diamant, *Chaining the Hudson*, 115–20.

3. Report of Major General John Vaughan to Lieutenant General Sir Henry Clinton, n.d., in *Naval Documents*, 10:10–11, quote on 10; Nickerson, *Turning Point of the Revolution*, 405.

4. Sullivan, *Minutes*, 853.

5. *New York Gazette and Weekly Mercury*, Nov. 3, 1777, NYHS; Smith, *Colonial Days and Ways*, 250–60; Kierner, *Traders and Gentlefolk*, 219–20, 228–29.

6. Stone, *Letters of Brunswick and Hessian Officers*, 119; Bradford, "Lord Francis Napier's Journal," 322; Wilkinson, *Memoirs of My Own Time*, 1: 280–82; Stone, *Memoirs, Letters, and Journals*, 1:166, 169, 170–71.

7. Bradford, "Lord Francis Napier's Journal," 308; Wilkinson, *Memoirs of My Own Time*, 1: 280–82. Wilkinson claimed that his warning to Fellows prevented him from being "cut up and captured . . . and Burgoyne's retreat to Fort George would have been unobstructed."

8. Chase, *Ashleys*, 12, 21, 27; "Bill of sale from John Fellows to Theodore Sedgwick for Ton," July 1, 1777, Sedgwick Family Papers, Massachusetts Historical Society.

9. Jacob Bayley to the President of the New York Convention, Feb. 19, 1777, in Walton, *Records*, 1:373–75; Walton, *Records*, 1:30–31, 38, 43, 46, 58, 117, 122, 138, 159; Thompson, 355–60.

10. Walton, *Records*, 1:172.

11. Simeon Alexander, in Dann, *Revolution Remembered*, 104, 109. Before his enlistment under Schuyler was up in August, Simeon Alexander of Northfield saw service in the Hampshire County Massachusetts militia in the Saratoga Campaign. He had rejoined Lieutenant Colonel Samuel Williams's Hampshire County militia regiment in July 1777. Volunteering from Northfield and Warwick, he joined a company that was to go to Ticonderoga. The company marched to the Hudson River and then to Fort Miller, where Generals Schuyler and St. Clair were in command, Ticonderoga having fallen. Alexander commented on the situation, "The army was retreating, but we were sometime stationary for several days at a time."

12. Alexander in Dann, *Revolution Remembered*, 109–10.

13. Doblin, *Specht Journal*, 94–95; Burgoyne, *State*, 174–76; Stone, *Memoirs, Letters, and Journals*, 1: 171.

14. Digby, *British Invasion from the North*, 304–305; Pell, "Diary of Joshua Pell," 111.

15. Wilkinson, *Memoirs of My Own Time*, 1:284–89. We have only Wilkinson's *Memoirs* for this interpretation, and we know that by the time he wrote them, he detested Gates.

16. Ibid., 1:286–89; Bradford, "Lord Francis Napier's Journal," 323.

17. Brown, "Baroness von Riedesel's Journal," 57–63.

18. Ibid., 56–57.

19. Digby, *British Invasion from the North*, 300.

20. Stone, *Memoirs, Letters, and Journals*, 1:161–62; Doblin, *Specht Journal*, 94–96; McCulloch, *Sons of the Mountains*, 2:62–63. Nicholas Sutherland was promoted to major of the 21st Regiment in 1772, lieutenant colonel of the 47th Regiment in November 1776. After exchange, he would command the Sutherland Fencibles in the defense Quebec.

21. Stone, *Memoirs, Letters, and Journals*, 1:173, 177–78.

22. Brown, "Baroness von Riedesel's Journal," 54–55, 57. The baroness published her journal and letters in 1800, and by that time it had become

standard among the Germans who served in the campaign to blame Burgoyne for the failure to retreat; Doblin, *Specht Journal*, 96.

23. "Captain Samuel MacKay's Account" (typescript), MG23, B43, NLAC. While McKay recruited from Peters's and the Jessup brothers' units, many of them were originally from Pfister's Walloomsac force. It should be remember that Pfister was not a designated officer of Burgoyne's army.

24. Gates to Jacob Bayley, Oct 14, 1777, GP.

25. Wilkinson, *Memoirs of My Own Time*, 1:276–78; Stone, *Memoirs, Letters, and Journals*, 1:136, 158; Stone, *Journal of Captain Pausch*, 152–53; Doblin, *Specht Journal*, 100–101.

26. "Permission of General Phillips," Oct. 14, 1777, NYHS.

27. CO42/37, 137–38, NLAC.

28. Ibid., 234.

29. 2:237–38, Historical Section of the General Staff, Ottawa.

30. Powell to Carleton, Sept. 27, 1777, CO42/37, 137–38, NLAC; Hille, *American Revolution*, 82; Watt, *Rebellion in the Mohawk Valley*, 287–88, 292–94. With St. Leger came Captain Gilbert Tice of the Iroquois Indian Department. Born at Fort Hunter in 1739 and christened in the Queen Anne Chapel, Tice later moved to Schenectady, where he married and established a family. He had come to Canada in 1775 with Guy Johnson. The subversion of Iroquois Joseph's pro-rebel effort had been due to Tice's exertions. It has been noted that upon Tice's return from England, he and Joseph Brant had traveled to Oquaga and Fort Niagara. Eventually he would settle in the Niagara area, where he remained after the war.

31. Powell to Carleton, Sept. 29, 1777, CO42/37, 217, NLAC; Powell to Carleton, Sept. 30, 1777, CO42/37, 219, ibid.; Doblin, *Specht Journal*, 83.

32. Powell to Carleton, Oct. 10, 1777, 237, NLAC; Doblin, *Specht Journal*, 95; debate rages as to who commanded the King's Royal Regiment of New York at Ticonderoga: Sir John or Major Gray. Evidence of Sir John's presence exists (see Thomas, *Sir John Johnson*, 77–78, and Watt, *Rebellion in the Mohawk Valley*, 300, 302–303, 305).

33. Brigadier-General Powell to Lord George Germain, Nov. 8, 1777, in Davies, *Documents of the American Revolution*, 14:253.

34. General Order by Sir Guy Carleton, Oct. 19, 1777, SN:083151, HP. This order seems to be misdated, for Maclean reported from Ticonderoga to Carleton on September 30 (Maclean to Carleton, Sept. 30, 1777, CO42/37, 217, NLAC).

35. Maclean to Carleton, Nov. 1, 1777, CO42/37, 260, ibid.; Carleton to Powell, Oct. 5, 1777, Q15, 201–202, ibid.

36. Weekly State of the Garrison, Nov. 1, 1777, CO42/37, 284, ibid.; Hille, *American Revolution*, 85.

37. Hille, *American Revolution*, 86–87; Walton, *Records*, 1:195, 198–99, 200; Watson, *Pioneer History*, 35–36.

38. Watt paints as gloomy a picture as could be possible in *Rebellion in the Mohawk Valley*, 290–309; see also chap. 15 in the current volume.

39. Putnam to Gates, Oct. 31, 1777, GP; Gates to Putnam, Nov. 2, 1777, ibid.; Gates to Washington, Nov. 2, 1777, ibid.; Wilkinson, *Memoirs of My Own Time*, 1:274–75, 323–24.

CHAPTER 13

1. An early account of Saratoga and the French Alliance is in Warren, *History*, 246–47; see also Nickerson, *Turning Point of the Revolution*, 404–16.

2. Bowler, *Logistics*, 230; Luzader, "Battle of Bennington Casualties," in *Saratoga*, 339–49. For contrast see Johnson, *History of Washington Co.*, 57–58, and Sylvester, *History of Saratoga County*, 70. The war in the south certainly drained some resources from the Northern Department. In actuality, it was Washington's Central Department that kept the bulk of the Continental troops from 1778 to 1781. The war in the south was much like the one in the north, using small armies of Continentals and depending upon militia to carry out petite guerre.

3. Neilson, *Original, Compiled and Corrected Account*, 240; Saratoga National Historical Park, "Neilson House," brochure.

4. McIlwraith's *Sir Frederick Haldimand*, 117–35 (an outdated and inadequate account that needs to be improved upon); "Frederick Haldimand," DCBO.

5. McIlwraith, *Sir Frederick Haldimand*, 1–113; "Frederick Haldimand," DCBO.

6. McIlwraith, *Sir Frederick Haldimand*, 121–35.

7. Add. mss. 21826, B.166.9, HP; "The Loyalists of Sorel," *The Loyalist Gazette*, 6–7.

8. "Frederick Haldimand," DCBO.

9. Regimental Orderly Book, Headquarters, Sept. 4, 1780, Edward Jessup Papers, NLAC; Cantonment Orders, June 19, 1781, 11, ibid.; Haldimand to Peters, Sept. 6, 1780, 3, ibid.; Regimental Orders, Dec. 5, 1780, 4, ibid.; Regimental Orders, Dec. 9, 1780, 4–6, ibid.; "In order that Royalists may be made acquainted with the generosity of his Excellency General Haldimand," Apr. 8, 1781, 12, ibid.

10. Shy, *People Numerous and Armed*, 186–88, 206–11.

11. Enys, *American Journal*, 32–35, 40–44; Watt, *Burning of the Valleys*, 91–156.

12. Brigadier Samuel Fraser, "General Order Regulating the Organization of the Provincial Corps," Sept. 8, 1777, 21,874, HP; Henry Reiter to Mathews, May 10, 1780, 21,821, ibid.

13. Enys, *American Journal*, 46; Claus to Haldimand, Nov. 19, 1778, in Penrose, *Indian Affairs Papers*, 174–77; Hough, *History*, 193.

14. Egly, *General Schuyler's Guard*, 2–8.

15. Gates to Stark, July 14, 1778, in Stark, *Memoir*, 181; Stone, *Visits*, 275–82.

16. Burnett, *Letters of Members of the Continental Congress*, 261–67.

17. James Duane to Stark, Dec. 16, 1777, Stark to Duane, Jan. 14, 1778, Gates to Stark, Jan. 24, 1778, Stark to Gates, June 20, 1778, Stark to Gates, June 26, 1778, Stark to Washington, Aug. 21, 1778, Benjamin Whitcomb to Stark, Sept. 14, 1778, in Stark, *Memoir*, 79–80, 142, 166, 170–71, 188, 493; Sketcher, "Haverhill in the War of the Revolution," Annual Meeting of the New Hampshire Historical Society, May 14, 1912, 134; for Carleton's expedition, see chap. 4.

18. Captain S. Sprague's Receipt, Dec. 31, 1777, NYPL; Colonel Yates's Receipt, Dec. 1777, ibid.; G. Ludlow to Schuyler, Jan. 6, 1778, ibid. Brigadier General Edward Hand was eventually suggested as a replacement for Stark, but while he served under Sullivan in the destruction of Iroquois villages in 1779, he evidently never made it to Albany.

19. George Washington to Major General Philip Schuyler, Nov. 20, 1778, and Dec. 18, 1778, in Fitzpatrick, *Writings of George Washington*, 13.

20. George Washington to Governor George Clinton, Oct. 21, 1778, in Clinton, *Public Papers*; Fitzpatrick, *Writings of George Washington*, Nov. 2, 1778, 13.

21. Sullivan, *Minutes*, 958.

22. Paltsits, *Minutes*, 1:161, 551; Huston, *Land and Freedom*, 3–4, 35, 59, 89–94, 98–99.

23. Sullivan, *Minutes*, 1:3–4, 781, 901–902; Williams to Clinton, June 8, 1778, 3, no. 1487, in Clinton, *Public Papers*; Johnson, *History of Washington Co.*, 255–56; see chap. 10.

24. Johnson, *History of Washington Co.*, 68, 177, 252–57, 266, 271.

25. Sullivan, *Minutes*, 901–902.

26. Paltsits, *Minutes*, 1:94, 129, 219, 242, 286, 311. In October 1780 Younglove cited a new legislative act for the removal of families or persons who had joined the enemy. However, the Cambridge district continued to be responsible to the Albany commissioners. Several Cambridge cases came before them, and they generally favored reinstatement of those accused of being Loyalists. For instance, Patrick Buchanan was liberated for good behavior and a monthly appearance to the Commission. In August 1778 it was suspected that John Wood of St. Croix, Cambridge district, has disappeared in order to avoid the act. Wood was a Quaker from New Bedford, Massachusetts, and clerk of his meeting. He was so respected that the annual town meetings militia elections of 1776 and 1777 were held at his house. Yet it appears that he disappeared rather than be questioned by the commissioners. In another case, granted in October 1780, Jane Hogle, wife of Francis, and Simeon Covel's children were allowed to leave, while John Hogle's wife wanted to stay because he had died in the Battle of Bennington (Paltsits, *Minutes*, 2:540).

27. Niles, *Hoosic Valley*, 236–37, 261; Johnson, *History of Washington Co.*, 462–63.

28. Ethan Allen to John Stark, May 12, 1778, in Duffy et al., *Ethan Allen*, 77; Joseph Fay to Col. Herrick, Nov. 20, 1777, in Walton, *Records*, 1:198–99; Thomas Chittenden to George Washington, Mar. 5, 1779, in ibid., 1:292.

29. David Welch, Narrative in Dann, *Revolution Remembered*, 274–77.

CHAPTER 14

1. Halevi, *Narrative of K. White*, 84–87.

2. Thomas Freeman to Riedesel, Nov. 26, 1781, 21, 796, HP.

3. Memorial of Ebenezer Jessup, Feb. 1, 1778, transcript MG21, BI67, 161–71, NLAC.

4. Williams to Clinton, Apr. 22, 1778, in Clinton, *Public Papers*, 3: no. 1309.

5. Peters, "Narrative," PPNYSL; Lapp, *To Their Heirs Forever*, 146–47.

6. Fryer, *Buckskin Pimpernel*, 78–80; Fryer, "Sarah Sherwood," 245–62.

7. Walton, *Records*, 1:193; Williams, *Public Papers*, 171, 244; Nye, *Sequestration*, 243; Lapp, *To Their Heirs Forever*, 154.

8. Walton, *Records*, 1:226.

9. The extent of Briscoe's land is seen in the amount confiscated (Nye, *Sequestration*, 11, 38, 284, 381, 390, 412, 423–26. 439); J. Fraser, *Skulking for the King*, 434–39; Abijah Hawley, Hawley Genealogy File, RVC; Lapp, *To Their Heirs Forever*, 91.

10. Walton, *Records*, 1:283–87, 2:62–63.

11. Ibid., 1:22–24.

12. Walton, *Records*, 1:197, 291, 298.

13. Ibid., 1:197.

14. Ibid., 2:17.

15. Ira Allen, *Natural and Political History*, 68–69.

16. The creation of a junta and the accumulation of political power by a few men is described in Hoyt, *Damndest Yankees*, 161–210; H. N. Muller, "Vermont's Constitution Bred Stability," sec. 3:1, 3; Williams, *Public Papers*, 250–51; Roth, 34–35, 38–39, 68; Austin, *Matthew Lyon*, 21.

17. Walton, *Records*, 1: 228–29.

18. Walton, *Records*, 1:124–25; Williams, *Public Papers*, 250–51.

19. There is confusion over the exact residences of the Allens because many lived in the adjacent Town of Sunderland but carried on business and the Vermont government in Arlington. Jellison, *Ethan Allen*, 188–89; Pell, *Ethan Allen*, 137–39; Wilbur, *Ira Allen*, 1:77, 90–112, 117. In 1778 Ethan Allen was selected as one of Arlington's representatives to the Vermont Assembly, but he could not sit for the town because he refused to take the religious oath (Belleisles, *Revolutionary Outlaws*, 191). Ira Allen lived in the Arlington area until 1785. Mathew Lyon, clerk of the Court of Banishment, purchased some of Isaac Briscoe's confiscated land (Austin, *Matthew Lyon*, 22–23, 26, 30–31); Kalinoski, "Sequestration, Confiscation," 237.

20. Walton, *Records*, 1: 250–57; Chittenden lived in Arlington until 1787: Smallwood, *Thomas Chittenden*, 10–20; Williams, *Public Papers*, 250–51; Kalinoski, "Sequestration, Confiscation," 237–38.

21. Walton, *Records*, 1: 238; Williams, *Public Papers*, 191, 195, 218–19, 239, 251, 392, 398, 405, 455, 473, 520, 568, 650. On the differences between Jonathan Fassett and his father, John, see Shalhope, *Bennington and the Green Mountain Boys*, 54, 58, 78–79, 164, 174.

22. Austin, *Matthew Lyon*, 7–13.

23. Kalinoski, "Sequestration, Confiscation," 236–47; Hollister, *Pawlet for One Hundred Years*, 14; Williams, *Public Papers*, 181; Ira Allen to the Commissioners of Confiscation, July 28, 1777, in Duffy et al., *Ethan Allen*, 1:73–74.

24. Kalinoski, "Sequestration, Confiscation," 236–37; Belleisles, *Revolutionary Outlaws*, 166–70; Pemberton, "British Secret Service," 313–14; Nye, *Sequestration*, 242; Levi Allen to *The Connecticut Courant*, Mar. 2, 1779, in Duffy et al., *Ethan Allen*, 1:89–90. To help a former Green Mountain Boy, Ethan Allen intervened and prevented the sale of some of Justus Sherwood's property.

25. List of Estates Ordered Confiscated by Court of Confiscation, 77–78. The extent of Briscoe's land is seen in the amount confiscated (Nye, *Sequestration*, 11, 38, 284, 381, 390, 412, 423–26, 439); Alexander Fraser, *Second Report*, 434–39; RCV, "Hawley Genealogy File, Abijah Hawley"; Lapp, *To Their Heirs Forever*, 91.

26. Ethan Allen to the Vermont General Assembly, Oct. 26, 1779, in Duffy et al., *Ethan Allen*, 1:95–96.

27. Austin, *Matthew Lyon*, 22.

28. Ibid., 22–24.

29. Ibid., 24–29.

30. In October 1786 Jehiel Hawley's sons Curtis and Andrew, the Arlington executors of his estate, successfully petitioned the Vermont Assembly for the right to take back Hawley confiscated properties that the Council had not sold, and to collect debts, pay creditors, and disburse the surplus among the family. Curtis and Andrew provided an inventory of these small but collectively significant parcels, which remained unsold. The date is significant, for only a month later the rioting debtors attempted to close the Rutland County Court to prevent such actions from taking place (Nye, *Sequestration*, 93–96).

31. New York Act of Attainder, or Confiscation Act, Oct. 22, 1779, in Greenleaf, *Greenleaf's Laws*, 1:26; Countryman, *People in Revolution*, 173–74, 186.

32. Countryman, *People in Revolution*, 175, 186–87, 235–36; Reubens, "Pre-emptive Rights," 1–2.

33. Countryman, *People in Revolution*, 173–74.

34. Ibid., 245–46.

35. Crary, "Forfeited Loyalist Lands," 239–58.

36. Alex Webster to William Roger, June 27, 1788, A80, Washington County Archives; Alex Webster to Samuel Worsher, May 4, 1789, A117, ibid.; Alex Webster to Nathan Morgan, A143, ibid., Alex Webster to James Fleck, Dec. 23, 1789, A303, ibid.; Alex Webster to Alexander Turner, Jr., July 4, 1792, A340, ibid.; Alex Webster to James Rowan, Nov. 13, 1795, B485, ibid.

37. Webster to Clinton, in Clinton, *Public Papers*, 6: no. 229; Clark to Williams, Aug. 4, 1778, 153, John Williams Papers, Manuscript and Special Collections, New York State Library; Adler, *History of Salem*, 29.

38. Johnson, *History of Washington Co.*, 179.

39. Ibid., 474; Morton, *Philip Skene*, 61–62.

40. Agreement, Mill Farm to Robert Chapman, Nov. 1, 1794, John Williams Papers, 1:648, Washington County Historian's Department; Lots Drawn by John Williams between Lake George and Lake Champlain, Feb. 3, 1803, ibid., 1:743; Alexander Webster and David Hopbunes, Commissioners of Forfeitures for the Eastern District, Nov. 19, 1783, ibid., 2:358.

41. Tomasi, *Village of Salem*, 7.

42. The New York Act of Attainder; Crary, "Forfeited Loyalist Lands," 240, 248, 254–56; Yoshpe, *Distribution of Estates*, 7, 117; Bureau of the Census, *Heads of Families*, 186. Other places had rebels who took advantage of their position on Committees to Detect and Defeat Conspiracies. Dutch-descended Cornelius Wynkoop of Stone Ridge near Kingston served as a militia colonel

during the War for Independence, although it appears he never participated in combat. Before the war, between 1766 and 1772 he married Cornelia Mancis and built a substantial, gambrel-roofed stone home in the Georgian style to show his wealth. He would go on to become, in April 1778, a member of the Ulster County Committee to Detect and Defeat Conspiracies. In this position he employed those penalized as suspected Loyalists, like James Robins, who worked for him as a carpenter.

CHAPTER 15

1. Gerlach, *Proud Patriot*, 335–470; Paltsits, *Minutes*, 1:20.

2. Bowler seems to believe that only the rebels practiced petite guerre: (*Logistics*, 240). Higginbotham, emphasizes the rebel militia's ability at irregular warfare, especially in the South ("American Militia," 96–99).

3. Kelsay, *Joseph Brant*, 210.

4. Stone, *Memoirs, Letters, and Journals*, 1: 48, 56; A tradition began with Christopher Carleton that British officers who had served with Indians dressed as them for portraits. John Caldwell, nephew of the commander of Fort Niagara, who served there and at Detroit, was portrayed upon his return to England in 1782 as an Ojibwa chief. Caldwell had been elected a chief and named Apatto. Also, Major John Norton, who had an Indian wife and served in the midwestern forts, was painted similarly by Thomas Phillips.

5. Stone, *Letters of Brunswick and Hessian Officers*, 55.

6. Enys, *American Journal*, 24–26.

7. Kelsay, *Joseph Brant*, 190–94, 222; Wait, *Dirty, Trifling Piece of Business*, 99, 118, 179, 211; Munro did not treat the blacks he took from Gordon as prisoners but rather as slaves, property that could be sold (Winks, *Blacks in Canada*, 30).

8. Haldimand to Germain, Nov. 1, 1779, B54, 266–69, HP; Rogers, *Journal Kept in Canada*, 72.

9. Memorial of Ebenezer Jessup, no. 2187, f. 145–46, BL.

10. Peters, "Narrative," PPNYSL.

11. Another Loyalist regiment, created from 1779 to 1783, was not involved in the Saratoga Campaign. This was the King's Rangers, which was originally established by the famed Robert Rogers, under the authority of Sir Henry Clinton's Central Department, but in practice was recruited in Canada from chiefly Albany and Dutchess County refugees, who formed the second battalion under Rogers's brother, James. The never fully recruited battalion was stationed at St. Johns and served in Carleton's 1780 expedition and in St. Leger's a year later. Haldimand had originally rejected the entire idea as a drain on his slender resources, but James Rogers's diligence and distancing of himself from his brother gradually won Haldimand over and finally, in January 1783, they were made part of the Northern Department. After the war, most of the battalion remained in Canada and settled at Cataraqui and the Bay of Quinte. See Jackson, *Rogers' Rangers*, 181–91.

12. Taylor, *Divided Ground*, 13, 169, 172–73, 182–84, 217, 220–25, 268.

13. Calloway, *American Revolution*, 65–84, and *Western Abenakis*, 204–23.

14. Watt, *Burning of the Valleys*, 93–94, 253–54, 274.

15. Claus to Haldimand, Nov. 19, 1778, in Penrose, *Indian Affairs Papers*, 174–77; Hough, *History*, 193.

16. Enys, *American Journal*, 46.

17. Graymont, *Iroquois in the American Revolution*, 192–222.

18. Enys, *American Journal*, 23–24.

19. Watt, *Burning of the Valleys*, 46–47, 50–51, 94–96.

20. Carleton's Journal, Oct. 24–Nov. 8, 1778, in Washington and Washington, *Carleton's Raid*, 85–91.

21. Carleton's Journal, Nov. 9–Nov. 13, 1778, in ibid., 7–11, 27, 91–93.

22. Webster to Clinton, Nov. 26, 1778, in Clinton, *Public Papers*, 3, no. 1936; Fryer, *Buckskin Pimpernel*, 98–99.

23. Ethan Allen to George Washington, Aug. 16, 1780 in Duffy et al., *Ethan Allen*, 1:100–101; Petersen, *Seth Warner*, 152–54.

24. Petersen, *Seth Warner*, 154–56.

25. Stevens, "His Majesty's 'Savage Allies.'"

26. Watt, *Burning of the Valleys*, 75–80.

27. Herwig and Herwig, *Jonathan Carpenter's Journal*, 73–74, 76–78, 80.

28. Enys, *American Journal*, 32–35; Watt, *Burning of the Valleys*, 91–156.

29. Dresler, *Farmers and Honest Men*, 62–66; Jackson, *Rogers' Rangers*, 183–88.

30. Regimental Orderly Book, Headquarters, Sept. 4, 1780, Edward Jessup Papers, NLAC; Cantonment Orders, June 19, 1781, 11, and Haldimand to Peters, Sept. 6, 1780, 3, ibid.; Regimental Orders, Dec. 5, 1780, 4, ibid.; Regimental Orders, Dec. 9, 1780, 4–6, ibid.

31. Webster to Chittenden, Oct. 14, 1780, in Williams, *Public Papers*, 526–27.

32. Enys, *American Journal*, 40–44.

33. Clinton to Washington, Oct. 18, 1780, in Clinton, *Public Papers*; Captain Sherwood to Henry Livingston, Oct. 17, 1780, in Hill, *Old Fort Edward*, 336–39.

34. Hill, *Old Fort Edward*, 356–58.

35. Enys, *American Journal*, 50–51; Johnson, *History of Washington Co.*, 59–60; Dresler, *Farmers and Honest Men*, 62–64; Muster Role of a Detachment of King's Rangers at St. Johns Commanded by Major James Rogers, Sept. 8, 1780, in Jackson, *Rogers' Rangers*, 196; ibid., 187.

36. Chipman, *Memoir of Colonel Seth Warner*, 74–75; DeCosta, *History of Fort George*, 49–54; Petersen, *Seth Warner*, 153–54.

37. Chipman, *Memoir of Colonel Seth Warner*, 75–77; Enys, *American Journal*, 45–47; Warner to Washington, Oct. 30, 1780, in Petersen, *Seth Warner*, 153–56.

38. Enys, *American Journal*, 45.

39. Ibid., 34–35, 37; J. Fraser, *Skulking for the King*, 64.

40. Sylvester, *History of Saratoga County*, 70, 78–82; J. Fraser, *Skulking for the King*, 68–69.

41. Sylvester, *History of Saratoga County*, 70–72.

42. Enys, *American Journal*, 48.

43. Ibid., 37.

44. Herwig and Herwig, *Jonathan Carpenter's Journal*, 78–79; Goodwin, *We Go as Captives*.

45. Goodwin, *We Go as Captives*, 79–80.

46. Enys, *American Journal*, 29–32; lists and accounts confirm that Carleton and Houghton took mostly male prisoners(Washington and Washington, *Carleton's Raid*, 93–94); Calloway, "Captivity of Zadock Steele" and "George Avery's Journal of the Royalton Raid," 100–58. This is a contrast to the previous colonial wars in which female prisoners usually matched males in number and were more likely to be assimilated and remain in Canada (Ulrich, *Good Wives*, 202–14).

47. Washington and Washington, *Carleton's Raid*, 13–77; Walton, *Records*, 1:306–308.

48. Williams to Clinton, Apr. 25, 1778, in Clinton, *Public Papers*, 3, no. 1313.

49. Clinton to Williams, May 2, 1778, in ibid.; "The Field Officers of Van Woert's Regiment Submit a Grievance to George Clinton," May 16, 1780, 3, no. 1350, 4, no. 2873, in ibid.

50. Lapp, *To Their Heirs Forever*, 36–37.

51. Johnson, *History of Washington Co.*, 255; Wallace, "American Revolution and Cambridge," 102.

52. "The Field Officers of Van Woert's Regiment Submit a Grievance to George Clinton," May 16, 1780, 3, no. 2873, in Clinton, *Public Papers*.

53. Ibid. John Younglove of Cambridge asked that a prisoner with Burgoyne's army who had escaped, Ebenezer Allen, "be reinstated in his Country's favor" by taking an oath of allegiance. Allen is not to be mistaken for the Vermont captain of the same name, for he had served in 1775 in the minor office of Cambridge path master and was a major in Cambridge's militia regiment.

54. Affidavits, Garat Y. Lansing Papers, Manuscripts and Special Collections, New York State Library; McCabe, "Inhabitants of the Embury Wilson Patent"; Wallace, "American Revolution and Cambridge," 102.

55. Sullivan, *Minutes*, 933, 960.

CHAPTER 16

1. Johnson, *History of Washington Co.*, 219.

2. Walton, *Records*, 2:298–301; Johnson, *History of Washington Co.*, 203; Corbett, "Granville in Turmoil," 12–13.

3. Paine to Clinton, Apr. 16, 1781, in Williams, *Public Papers*, 349–50; Chittenden to Paine, June 14, 1781, in ibid., 539.

4. Ira Allen to Frederick Haldimand, May 8, 1781, in Duffy et al., *Ethan Allen*, 113.

5. John Younglove to Robert Yates, Apr. 18, 1781, in Clinton, *Public Papers*; John Younglove to Governor George Clinton, June 20, 1781, no. 3647, no. 3780; Walton, *Records*, 2:297–98; Johnson, *History of Washington Co.*, 62.

6. John Younglove to Governor George Clinton, June 20, 1781, in Clinton, *Public Papers*; Governor Clinton's Reply, June 29, 1781, no. 3780, in ibid.; Wait, *Dirty, Trifling Piece of Business*, 233–34.

7. Williams, *Public Papers*, 311.

8. Clinton, *Public Papers*, 6:890–91; Vermont Historical Society, Collections, 2:131; Fitzpatrick, *Writings of GeorgeWashington*, 22:81–82; J. McKenstry to Schuyler, Aug. 5, 1781, NYPL; *Documentary History of N.Y.*, 4:1004–10. Brinton also wrote to Governor Clinton of the "general dissatisfaction in the minds of your subjects on the east side of the [Hudson] River, which . . . was occasioned by Mr. Allen's spending several days in the different districts."

9. John Williams to Clinton, June 5, 1781, in Clinton, *Public Papers*, 6.

10. Walton, *Records*, 2:301–307.

11. General Stark to Governor Clinton Concerning the Resolution of Congress, Aug. 27, 1781, Williams, *Public Papers*, 548–49, quote on 549.

12. Stark to Washington, Dec. 21, 1781, in Stark, *Memoir*, 303–305, quote on 304.

13. Stark to Heath, Dec. 12, 1781, in ibid., 296–98.

14. Clinton to Gansevoort, Oct. 18, 1781, in Williams, *Public Papers*, 556–58.

15. Walton, *Records*, 2:8, 147, 160, 194, 253, 259, 272; Shalhope, *Bennington and the Green Mountain Boys*, 52, 78, 254.

16. General Gansevoort to Colonel Walbridge, Dec. 18, 1781, in Walton, *Records*, 2:333–35, quote on 334; Colonel Walbridge to General Gansevoort, Dec. 19, 1781, Williams, *Public Papers*, 568–69.

17. General Stark to Colonel Yates, Dec. 14, 1781, in Walton, *Records*, 2:331–32; Stone, *Life of Joseph Brant–Thayendanegea*, 2:205–207; Walton, *Records* 2: 334–35.

18. Ethan Allen to Meshech Weare, Oct. 23, 1778, in Duffy et al., *Ethan Allen*, 85–86; Ethan Allen to Meshech Weare, Mar. 4, 1779, in ibid., 85–86, quote on 86, 90–91; Walton, *Records*, 1:334–35; "Union of New Hampshire Towns with Vermont, in 1778–9," in ibid., 1:405–33; Thompson, 346–47, 374–83.

19. "Commission of the Vermont Commissioners for Settlement of the Boundary Dispute between New York and New Hampshire," Oct. 27, 1781, in Williams, *Public Papers*, 559–60; Thompson, 475–76.

20. Ira Allen to Justus Sherwood, Oct. 20, 1781, in Duffy et al., *Ethan Allen*, 123–24.

21. Walton, *Records*, 2:379–86.

22. Corbett, "Granville in Turmoil," 15–17; Johnson, *History of Washington Co.*, 203; Thirty-seven household heads signed the clemency petition. We can get an idea of who was sympathetic to the Vermont offer if we examine the twenty-three who can be identified. They resided evenly all over Granville: Middle Granville, North Granville, West Granville, South Granville, and the North Bend of the Mettowee. At least three were from the nearby towns of Hebron, Fort Ann, and Salem. This dispersed pattern of households shows the rural nature of Granville's settlement. Most of the signers were originally from Massachusetts and Connecticut, the lone identified New Yorker being from New Lebanon on the border. Five were members of Middle Granville's Congregational Church and two were affiliated with North Granville's Baptist Church, but the majority seem to have no religious affiliation. Thus effort to see the pro-Vermont activities as centering on Middle Granville's

Congregational Church are not substantiated. Nor were they an offshoot of Granville's militia company, for only two or three of the petitioners served as officers of that group. Most were still in Granville eight years later when the first federal census was taken. It showed their typical household to have five or six members, essentially a conjugal family. However, four large households of ten or more members are found, each with three or four mature males within the household. This probably indicates grown sons and their families living under the same roof as their parents. Sons stayed in their father's household anticipating the partition of land to them at death of the patriarch. They also provided the labor needed to run the most extensive farms. This must have been the case of the largest household, with fifteen members headed by Ebenezer Gould. Sixteenth years after the petition, in 1798, seven petitioners were assessed for tax purposes, proving them to be among the richest families in the town. The most affluent household head in the town was David Doane, who lived in Middle Granville with his modest conjugal family household but attended the North Granville Baptist Church. Lesser worthies were Solomon Baker, Ebenezer Gould, David Blakesley—the caller of the 1782 town meeting—Jonathan Harnden, Jesse Atwater, and Eliphalet Parker. They had survived their political flirtation with Vermont, death, and economic hardship to become Granville's leading citizens.

23. Countryman, *People in Revolution*, 176–77.

24. Johnson, *History of Washington Co.*, 63.

CHAPTER 17

1. Christopher Carleton to Ethan Allen, Oct. 26, 1780, and Ethan Allen to Christopher Carleton, Oct. 29, 1780, in Duffy et al., *Ethan Allen*, 1:102–103. On the new emphasis in British policy, see Shy, "Loyalist Problem in the Lower Hudson Valley," 5–6. On Haldimand in Canada, see McIlwraith, *Sir Frederick Haldimand*, 117–310.

2. Beverly Robinson to Ethan Allen, Mar. 30, 1780, in Duffy et al., *Ethan Allen*, 1:108–109, quote on 108.

3. Sherwood, "Justus Sherwood Journal," 101–109, 211–20; Wilbur, *Ira Allen*, 1:427–38; McIlwraith, *Sir Frederick Haldimand*, 197–217. Sherwood bought a portion of the point for himself and retained it after the Peace of 1783.

4. Ira Allen to Frederick Haldimand, May 8, 1781, in Duffy et al., *Ethan Allen*, 1:112–13; Ira Allen to Frederick Haldimand, July 10, 1781, in ibid., 118–19, quotes on 119. Stone, *Memoirs, Letters, and Journals*, 2:108, 112–13, 121; Fryer, *Buckskin Pimpernel*, 155, 169–72.

5. Hill, *Old Fort Edward*, 248–57.

6. Paltsits, *Minutes*, 1:193, 216, 2:435, 477, 721, 726, 728; Fryer, *Buckskin Pimpernel*, 35, 45, 130–74.

7. Orders of Major General Riedesel, Apr. 8, 1782, Edward Jessup Papers, 42, NLAC.

8. Fryer, *Buckskin Pimpernel*, 151, 152, 158; Rev. John Stuart to Dr. George Smith, Oct. 5, 1781, in Talman, *Loyalist Narratives*, 340–41; Pemberton,

"British Secret Service," 138–39. In 1778 the Commissioners for Detecting Conspiracies accused Stuart of corresponding with the enemy, but the charges proved unfounded, and he and his family were paroled to Schenectady. He remained there for three years but saw his farm confiscated in 1781, and he was prohibited from earning a living by opening a Latin school. With difficulty he was allowed to leave Schenectady, arriving as we see in Canada in October 1781.

9. Fryer, *Buckskin Pimpernel*, 136.

10. Wilbur, *Ira Allen*, 1:376, 383, 386; Pemberton, "British Secret Service," 136–37.

11. Duffy et al., *Ethan Allen*, 1:73.

12. On April 12, 1781, John Williams reported to Governor Clinton that Seth Warner had informed him of the letters between Beverly Robinson and Ethan Allen (Williams, *Public Papers*, 350).

13. Williams, *Public Papers*, 91, 421, 426, 517–18; George Washington to Seth Warner, June 20, 1781, in Fitzpatrick, *Writings of George Washington*, 22.

14. Ethan Allen to George Clinton, Apr. 14, 1781, in Duffy et al., *Ethan Allen*, 1:111–12.

15. George Washington to Jacob Bayley, Nov. 25, 1778, Dec. 7, 1778, Jan. 2, 1779, in Fitzpatrick, *Writings of George Washington*, 13; Walton, *Records*, 1: 432–36; Thompson, 421.

16. Fryer, *Buckskin Pimpernel*, 157, 170.

17. R. Mathews to Edward Jessup, Feb. 15, 1781, Edward Jessup Papers, 11, NLAC; Gerlach, "Philip Schuyler and the New York Frontier," 180.

18. Fryer, *Loyalist Spy*, 115–25.

19. Paltsits, *Minutes*, 747.

20. Regimental Orderly Book, Headquarters, Sept. 4, 1780, Edward Jessup Papers, NLAC; Cantonment Orders, June 19, 1781, 11, ibid.; Frederick Haldimand to John Peters, Sept. 6, 1780, 3, ibid.; Regimental Orders, Dec. 5, 1780, 4, ibid; Regimental Orders, Dec. 9, 1780, 4–6, ibid.

21. General Orders, Nov. 12, 1781, 19, ibid.; "In order that Royalists may be made acquainted with the generosity of his Excellency General Haldimand," Apr. 8, 1781, 12, ibid.

22. Potter-MacKinnon, *While the Women Only Wept*, 20–21; Waltman, "From Soldier to Settler," 39–42.

23. George Washington to Caleb Stark, June 25, 1781, in Stark, *Memoir*, 211–12; Caleb Stark to George Washington, Aug. 9, 1781, in ibid., 211–12, 215–16.

24. George Washington to Caleb Stark, June, 25, 1781, Caleb Stark to Major General Heath, Sept. 11, 1781, Abraham Ten Broeck to Major Samuel Logan, Sept. 15, 1781, Caleb Stark to Major General Heath, Sept. 20, 1781, Philip Schuyler to Caleb Stark, Oct. 16, 1781, in Stark, *Memoir*, 211–12, 247–48, quote on 248, 252, 256–57.

25. Gerlach, *Proud Patriot*, 446, 458–62; Fryer, *Loyalist Spy*, 141–47.

26. Paltsits, *Minutes*, 763.

27. Lord Stirling to Caleb Stark, Nov. 6, 1781; Caleb Stark to Major General Heath, Nov. 29, 1781, in Stark, *Memoir*, 288, 293–94; Valentine, *Lord Stirling*, 257–62.

28. Adler, *History of Salem*, 30.

29. "Reminiscenses of Jonathan Elkins," 188.

30. In October Haldimand sent another expedition from Oswego into the Mohawk Valley under Major John Ross, forcing the rebels to again divide their forces (Watt, *Dirty, Trifling Piece of Business*, 314–61, 379–85, 392–93).

31. Wilbur, *Ira Allen*, 1:325–26, 358; Ira Allen and Joseph Fay to Frederick Haldimand, Sept. 20, 1781, in Duffy et al., *Ethan Allen*, 1:122.

32. Watt, *Dirty, Trifling Piece of Business*, 397–402.

33. Stone, *Memoirs, Letters, and Journals*, 2:145–51, 163.

34. DeCosta, *History of Fort George*, 61;Valentine, *Lord Stirling*, 267–68.

35. Wallace Brown, 170–72; Graymont, *Iroquois in the American Revolution*, 259–63; McIlwraith, *Sir Frederick Haldimand*, 304.

36. Stone, *Memoirs, Letters, and Journals*, 2:175–76.

37. Thomas Chittenden to Caleb Stark, Nov. 14, 1781, in Stark, *Memoir*, 286–87; George Washington to Thomas Chittenden, Jan. 1, 1782, Williams, *Public Papers*, 573–75, quote on 574.

38. Justus Sherwood and George Smyth to Ira Allen and Joseph Fay, Apr. 22, 1782, in Duffy et al, *Ethan Allen*, 1:126–28, quotes on 126, 127; Ira Allen and George Fay to George Smyth and Justus Sherwood, May 19, 1782, in ibid., 1:128–29, quote on 129; McIlwraith, *Sir Frederick Haldimand*, 214–17; Stone, *Memoirs, Letters, and Journals*, 2:136.

39. Ethan Allen to Frederick Haldimand, May 30, 1783, and George Smyth to Ethan Allen, June 24, 1783, in Duffy et al., *Ethan Allen*, 1:140–41, quote on 141; McIlwraith, *Sir Frederick Haldimand*, 216.

40. Ira Allen to Frederick Haldimand, Sept. 10, 1784, in Duffy et al., *Ethan Allen*, 1:138; Ethan Allen to Justus Sherwood and Luke Knowleton, Apr. 8, 1783, in ibid., 1:143–44; Ira Allen to Henry and David Van Schaack, Aug. 25, 1783, in ibid., 1:155, 158.

41. Levi Allen to Ira Allen, May 2, 1789 in ibid., 1:298; Levi Allen to Ira and Nancy Allen, May 3, 1789, in ibid., 299–304.

42. Levi Allen to William Pitt, Dec. 25, 1789 in ibid., 1:336.

CHAPTER 18

1. Fryer, *Buckskin Pimpernel*, 184.

2. Abijah Hawley, Hawley Genealogy File, RVC; Lapp, *To Their Heirs Forever*, 91.

3. Add. mss. 21838, B.166.195, HP; Stuart, "Jessup's Rangers as a Factor," 134.

4. Siebert, "Temporary Settlement of Loyalists," 407–408; "A Return of Men, Women and Children Belonging to Capt. Adams Corps," Aug. 10, 1780, War Office, Class 28, 10: f. 193, PRO.

5. Potter-MacKinnon, *While the Women Only Wept*, 113–17; Fryer and Dracott, *John Graves Simcoe*, 94–127; Head, *Irish Palatines in Ontario*.

6. Siebert, "Temporary Settlement of Loyalists," 409–10; "A Return of Men, Women and Children Belonging to Capt. Adams Corps," Aug. 10, 1780, War Office, Class 28, 10: f. 193, PRO.

7. General Orders, July 7, 1781, Edward Jessup Papers, 15, NLAC; Seibert, "Temporary Settlement of Loyalists," 410–11.

8. Seibert, "Temporary Settlement of Loyalists," 410–11.

9. McIlwraith, *Sir Frederick Haldimand*, 255–56; "Loyalists of Sorel," 6–7.

10. Haldimand Papers, Add. Mss. 21826, B.166.9; "Loyalists of Sorel," 6–7.

11. Rae,"Jessup's Rangers as a Factor," 134; Dresler, *Farmers and Honest Men*, 60; McIlwrath, *Sir Frederick Haldimand*, 256, 269; Alexander Fraser, *Second Report*, 87, 90.

12. Narrative of John Peters, July 20, 1778, Misc. Mss., NYHS.

13. "Samuel McKay," DCBO.

14. Hill, *Old Fort Edward*, 257.

15. "George Smyth to Major Campbell, June 15, 1784," in Preston, *Kingston before the War of 1812*, 79.

16. Sir Guy Carleton to Frederick Haldimand, July 5, 1783, in Bruce, *Loyalist Trail*, 93; "Return of Loyalists Arrived from New York," Aug. 16, 1783, in ibid., 95; "Memorial: Mr. Michael Grass and Loyalists from New York," Jan. 1784, in ibid., 110–11.

17. Frederick Haldimand to Lord North, Nov. 6, 1783, in ibid., 104–105; Dresler, *Farmers and Honest Men*, 68. Alburg, Vermont, was held by the British until the Jay Treaty of 1795.

18. Justus Sherwood to Robert Mathews, Mar. 1, 1784, in Bruce, *Loyalist Trail*, 117–18; Fryer, *Loyalist Spy*, 189–210.

19. Samuel Ross to Robert Mathews[?], Aug. 17, 1783, in Bruce, *Loyalist Trail*, 95–96.

20. Frederick Haldimand to Lord North, Nov. 6, 1783, in ibid., 104–105; Josiah Cass to Captain Sherwood, Feb. 23, 1784, in ibid., 113; Mathews to Sherwood, Mar. 8, 1784, in ibid., 116; "Petition of the Associated Loyalists to His Excellency Lieutenant General Frederick Haldimand Governor and Commander in Chief," Jan.[ ], 1784, in ibid., 118–19. In 1786 Sir John Johnson led the effort in the Legislative Council for free land tenure and use of English law in areas of extensive Loyalist settlement (Thomas, *Sir John Johnson*, 121–22); McIlwraith, *Sir Frederick Haldimand*, 267–71.

21. Siebert, "Temporary Settlement of Loyalists," 411.

22. Edward Jessup to Robert Mathews, Montreal, Jan. 29, 1784, in Bruce, *Loyalist Trail*, 113–14, 51, 53; Capt. John Barnes to Frederick Haldimand, Sept. 24, 1784, in Cruickshank, *Settlement of the United Empire Loyalists*, 112.

23. Otto, *Maitland*, 21–23.

24. Robert Mathews to Major Jessup, Sept. 8, 1783, Justus Sherwood to Robert Mathews, Oct. 14, 1783, John Collins' Survey of Kingston Township, Oct. 27, 1783, Justus Sherwood to Robert Mathews, May 23, 1784, in Bruce, *Loyalist Trail*, 99, 102–103, 122–23; Turner, *Ernestown*, 42–43.

25. Siebert, "Temporary Settlement of Loyalists," 412.

26. Potter-Mackinnon, *While the Women Only Wept*, 10–22, 155.

27. Cruickshank, *Settlement of the United Empire Loyalists*, 134; Hawley Family File, H. C. Burleigh Papers, Queen's University Archives, Kingston, Ontario; Canniff, *Settlement of Upper Canada*, 442–43.

28. Queen's School of Urban and Regional Planning, *History and Architecture*, 26–28; Alexander Fraser, *Second Report*, 434; Foster, "Always a Loyal Man," 2–3.

29. On the perspective of Langhorn in the Anglican Church, see Fahey, *Anglican Experience*, 22–24.

30. Otto, *Maitland*, 25–28.

31. "Report by Lieut. David Jones, Oct. 31, 1783," in *Loyalist Settlement*, 18–19.

32. Major Robert Mathews to Major Edward Jessup, Jan. 22, 1784, in *Loyalist Settlement*, 43; Robert Mathews to Major Edward Jessup, Sept. 10, 1783, in Bruce, *Loyalist Trail*, 99. Edward was involved in issues over Loyalists settlement. He sought to have all Loyalist settlers produce barrel staves, as they had been crucial to exports in the Albany area. To this end he asked that settlers be provided with oxen to help in the process. Like the Jones and Sherwoods, he feared that the land tenure of Quebec would not allow Loyalist to own their land in fee simple. Another concern was that widows and the eldest sons of veterans' families be granted land, not just fathers. As noted, Haldimand was able to smooth over most of these concerns.

33. "Memorial of Ebenezer Jessup," in Talman, *Loyalist Narratives*, 388–90.

34. Frederick Haldimand, Mar. 26, 1785, Edward Jessup Papers, NLAC; John Schank, Apr. 1, 1785, ibid.; John Burgoyne, May 9, 1786, 5, 20, 21, ibid; Major Edward Jessup to Major Robert Mathews, May 10, 1784, in *Loyalist Settlement*, 91–92.

35. Wright, "New York Loyalists," 79; Brown, "Baroness von Riedesel's Journal," 192.

36. Broderick, *Brunswick*, 16, 46.

CHAPTER 19

1. Countryman, *People in Revolution*, 295.

2. Jonathan Chu, "Debt Litigation and Shays's Rebellion."

3. Szatmary, *Shays Rebellion*, 2–36.

4. Parks, *History of Wells, Vermont*, 11–12; "Anti-Court Riot," Collections on the Court Closing, Rutland Historical Society, 229–32; Walton, *Records*, 3:357–59.

5. Johnson, *History of Washington Co.*, 179, 203.

6. Ibid., 112–13, 116.

7. Chittenden, "Address to the Freemen of Vermont," Aug. 28, 1786, in Walton, *Records*, 3:343–54;"The Betterment Acts," in ibid., 359–61, quote on 359.

8. "Remarks of Daniel Chipman on the Betterment Acts," in Walton, *Records*, 3:354–55.

9. Chipman, *Life of Nathaniel Chipman*, 18; "Anti-Court Riot," 227.

10. Walton, *Records*, 3:103–104.

11. Ibid., 3:362–66.

12. Shalhope, *Bennington and the Green Mountain Boys*, 190–93.

13. Walton, *Records*, 3:364–66.

14. Walton, *Records*, 3:366–72; "Anti-Court Riot," 228–29.

15. Walton, *Records*, 3:367–69.

16. Hollister, *Pawlet for One Hundred Years*, 220–21; Walton, *Records*, 1:26, 33, 121–22, 128, 160, 225, 228, 3:368.

17. Walton, *Records*, 3:368.

18. "In the General Assembly," Feb. 19–20, 1787, in ibid., 3:370; ibid., Feb. 28, 1787, 3:371–72.

19. "An Act for the prevention and punishment of Riot disorders and contempt of authority," Mar. 8, 1787, in ibid., 3:373–75, quotes on 373–74.

20. Turner, *Ninth State*, 50–52; Szatmary, *Shays Rebellion*, 78–79; Taylor, "Regulators and White Indians."

21. Nobles, "Shays's Neighbors"; Pencak, "Fine Theoretic Government of Massachusetts," 147–49.

22. Minot, 108–18; Mattern, *Benjamin Lincoln*, 171.

23. Minot, 146–47; Szatmary, *Shays Rebellion*, 102, 107; Mattern, *Benjamin Lincoln*, 172–76.

24. Jones, *Stockbridge, Past and Present*, 193–94; Szatmary, *Shays Rebellion*, 109–11; Frazier, *Mohicans of Stockbridge*, 243–44; Chase, *Ashleys*, 23–27.

25. Minot, 148–150; Chase, *Ashleys*, 28–29.

AFFIRMATIONS

1. Creasy, *Fifteen Decisive Battles of the World*, 254–75.

2. Trinterud, *Re-examination of Colonial Presbyterianism*, 247–49.

3. From the nineteenth century we have Crisfield Johnson and Nathaniel Sylvester. Before the Bicentennial, Upton edited *Revolutionary Versus Loyalist, The First American Civil War: 1774–1784*, in which his chief concern was to include the Loyalist story in the American movement for Independence; see the introduction, pp. ix–xiii. On civil war see also Nobles, Fryer, *John Walden Meyers*; East and Judd, *The Loyalist Americans*; and Frey, *Water from the Rock*.

4. Shomette, *Pirates on the Chesapeake*, 255–304; Frey, *Water from the Rock*, 144–71; Corbett, *Revolutionary New Castle*, 71–80.

BIBLIOGRAPHY

ARCHIVAL COLLECTIONS

Additional Manuscripts. British Library. London.
Audit Office and War Office. Public Record Office. London.
British Orderly Book. Wesleyan University Library. Middletown, Conn.
Cherry Hill Papers. Historic Cherry Hill. Albany, N.Y.
Collections on the Court Closing. Rutland Historical Society. Rutland, Vt.
Gates Papers (microfilm). New-York Historical Society. New York, N.Y.
Haldimand Papers. National Library and Archives of Canada. Ottawa.
Historical Section of the General Staff. Army Headquarters. Ottawa.
John Peters Papers. Manuscript and Special Collections. New York State Library.
    Albany, N.Y.
George Russell Collection of Vermontiana. Martha Canfield Library. Arling-
    ton, Vt.
Schuyler Papers. New York Public Library. New York, N.Y.
Vermont Historical Society. Collections. Montpelier, Vt.
Washington County Archives. Washington County Clerk's Office. Fort
    Edward, N.Y.
John Williams Papers. Washington County Historian's Department. Fort
    Edward, N.Y.
———. Manuscript and Special Collections. New York State Library. Albany.

OTHER SOURCES

"Action in Vermont during the Revolutionary War: Dan Kent's Narrative."
    Vermont History 39 (1971).
Adler, Winston, *The History of Salem, 1764–1976.* Salem, Mass., 1976.
———, ed. *Their Own Voices [collected by Dr. Asa Fitch].* Interlaken, N.Y., 1983.

Albers, Jan. *Hands on the Land: A History of the Vermont Landscape*. Cambridge, Mass., 2000.

Alexander, Edward P. *A Revolutionary Conservative: James Duane of New York*. New York, 1938.

Allen, Ethan. *The Narrative of Ethan Allen's Captivity*. New York, 1968.

Allen, Ira. *The Natural and Political History of the State of Vermont*. Rutland, 1969.

Allen, Robert. "The British Indian Department and the Frontier in North America, 1755–1830." *Canadian Historic Sites/Lieux historiques canadiens no. 14* (Ottawa, 1975): 6–125.

Anburey, Thomas. *Travels Through the Interior Parts of America, 1776–1781*. Toronto, 1963.

Austin, Aleine. *Matthew Lyon: "New Man" of the Democratic Revolution, 1749–1822*. University Park, Pennsylvania, 1981.

Bailyn, Bernard. *Voyagers to the West, A Passage in the Peopling of America on the Eve of the Revolution*. New York, 1986.

Baker, Ray Stannard. "Remember Baker." *The New England Quarterly* 4 (1931): 1–12.

Baldwin, Thomas, ed. *The Revolutionary Journal of Col. Jeduthan Baldwin, 1775–1778*. Bangor, Me., 1906.

Barber, John. *Historical Collections Relating to the History and Antiquities of Every Town in Massachusetts with Geographical Descriptions*. Worcester, 1848.

Barbour, Hugh, Christopher Densmore, Elizabeth Moger, Nancy Sorel, Alson Van Wagner, and Arthur Worrall, eds. *Quaker Crosscurrents, Three Hundred Years of Friends in the New York Yearly Meetings*. Syracuse, 1995.

Barnard, Toby. *A New Anatomy of Ireland, The Irish Protestants, 1649–1770*. New Haven, Conn., 2003.

Barnett, J. N. *History of the Gilead Evangelical Lutheran Church, Brunswick Centre*. Troy, N.Y., 1881.

Barrett, Brian. *Berkshire County's Army of Obstruction*. Waukesha, Wis., 2008.

Beebe, Lewis. *Journal of Dr. Lewis Beebe*. Reprint. New York, 1971.

Bellesiles, Michael. *Revolutionary Outlaws: Ethan Allen and the Struggle for Independence on the Early American Frontier*. Charlottesville, Va., 1993.

Blackburn, Roderic. *Cherry Hill: The History and Collections of the Van Rensselaer Family*. Albany, 1976.

Blumin, Stuart. *The Urban Threshold, Growth and Change in a Nineteenth-Century American Community*. Chicago, 1976.

Bonney, Catharina. *A Legacy of Historical Gleanings*. Albany, 1875.

Bonomi, Patricia. *Under the Cope of Heaven: Religion, Society and Politics in Colonial America*. New York, 1986.

———. *A Factious People: Politics and Society in Colonial New York*. New York, 1971.

Bowler, Reginald Arthur. *Logistics and the Failure of the British Army in America*. Princeton, N.J., 1975.

Bradford, Sydney, ed. "Lord Francis Napier's Journal of the Burgoyne Campaign." *Maryland Historical Society Magazine* 57 (Dec. 1962), 295.

Brandow, John Henry. *The Story of Old Saratoga and the History of Schuylerville.* Saratoga Springs, N.Y., 1901.

Broderick, Warren, ed. *Brunswick, A Pictorial History.* Troy, N.Y., 1978.

Brooke, John. *The Heart of the Commonwealth: Society and Political Culture in Worcester County, Massachusetts, 1713–1861.* New York, 1989.

Brown, Marvin, Jr., ed. "Baroness von Riedesel's Journal." In *Baroness von Riedesel and the American Revolution.* Chapel Hill, N.C., 1965.

Brown, Wallace. *The Good Americans: The Loyalists in the American Revolution.* New York, 1969.

Bruce, R. M. *The Loyalist Trail.* Kingston, Ont., 1965.

Buel, Richard, Jr. *Dear Liberty: Connecticut's Mobilization for the Revolutionary War.* Middletown, Conn., 1980.

Bureau of the Census. *Heads of Families, First Census of the United States—1790, New York.* Washington, D.C., 1908.

Burgoyne, John. *A State of the Expedition from Canada, as laid before the House of Commons.* New York, 1969.

Burleigh, H. C. *Captain McKay and the Loyal Volunteers.* Bloomfield, Ont., 1977.

———. *The Freemans of Freeman's Farm.* Saratoga, N.Y. Ontario, 1979.

———. "Loyalist Refuge: Sir John Johnson's Flight in May, 1776, 38–55." *Forgotten Leaves of Local History.* Kingston, Ont., 1973.

Burnett, Edmund, ed. *Letters of Members of the Continental Congress.* Washington, D.C., 1921–36.

Burns, Brian. "Massacre or Muster? Burgoyne's Indians and the Militia at Bennington." *Vermont History* 45 (Summer 1977): 133–45.

Callahan, North. *Henry Knox: George Washington's General.* New York, 1958.

Calloway, Colin. *The American Revolution in Indian Country: Crisis and Diversity in Native American Communities.* New York, 1995.

———. *The Western Abenakis of Vermont, 1600–1800.* Norman, Okla., 1994.

———, comp. "Captivity of Zadock Steele" and "George Avery's Journal of the Royalton Raid." In *North Country Captives: Selected Narratives of Indian Captivity from Vermont and New Hampshire*, 100–58. Hanover, N.H., 1992.

Campbell, Alexander. *The Royal American Regiment: An Atlantic Microcosm, 1755–1772.* Norman, Okla., 2010.

Canniff, William. *The Settlement of Upper Canada.* Belleville, Ontario, 1971.

Cary, Catherine. "Forfeited Loyalist Lands in the Western District of New York—Albany and Tryon Counties." *New York History* 35 (July, 1954): 239–58.

Chartrand, René. "French and his Uniform." *Canadian Military History* 7, no. 1 (Winter 1998): 42–50.

Chase, Arthur. *The Ashleys, A Pioneer Berkshire Family.* Beverly, Mass., 1982.

Chipman, Daniel. *Memoir of Colonel Seth Warner,* Legacy Reprint Series. Middlebury, Vt., 1848.

———. *The Life of Nathaniel Chipman, L.L.D.* Boston, 1846.

Chu, Jonathan. "Debt Litigation and Shays's Rebellion." In Robert Gross, *In Debt to Shays: The Bicentennial of an Agrarian Rebellion*, 81–99. Charlottesville, Va., 1993.

Churchman's Magazine 2 (Oct. 1805), 224.

Clark, Jane. "Responsibility for the Failure of the Burgoyne Campaign." *American Historical Review* 35 (Apr. 1930): 542–59.

Clinton, George. *Public Papers of George Clinton.* Albany, 1899–1914.

Cobb, Sanford. *The Story of the Palatines: An Episode in Colonial History.* New York, 1897.

Coe, Michael. *The Line of Forts: Historical Archeology on the Colonial Massachusetts Frontier.* Hanover, N.H., 2006.

Colden, Cadwallader. *The History of the Five Nations Depending on the Province of New-York in America.* New York, 1727.

"Colonel Ebenezer Learned's Regiment." *The Massachusetts Magazine* (Apr., July, Oct., 1912): 73–101.

Conway, Stephen. "To Subdue America: British Army Officers and the Conduct of the Revolutionary War." *William and Mary Quarterly*, July 1986, 281–407.

Corbett, Theodore. "Granville in Turmoil." *Journal of the Washington County Historical Society*, 5–25. Fort Edward, N.Y., 2007.

———. "Introduction." In Louis C. Jones, *Murder at Cherry Hill*, 15–30. Albany, N.Y., 1982.

Countryman, Edward. *A People in Revolution: The American Revolution and Political Society in New York, 1760–1790.* New York, 1981.

———. *Revolutionary New Castle: The Struggle for Independence.* Charleston, S.C., 2012.

Cox, Caroline. *A Proper Sense of Honor.* Chapel Hill, N.C., 2007.

Crary, Catherine Snell. "Forfeited Loyalist Lands in the Western District of New York." *New York History* 35 (1954), 238–58.

Creasy, Edward. *Fifteen Decisive Battles of the World.* London, 1851.

Cruickshank, Ernest Alexander. *The Settlement of the United Empire Loyalists on the Upper St. Lawrence and the Bay of Quite in 1784: A Documentary Record.* Toronto, 1966.

Dangerfield, George. *Chancellor Robert R. Livingston of New York, 1746–1813.* New York, 1960.

Dann, John, ed. The Revolution Remembered, Eyewitness Accounts of the War for Independence. Chicago, 1980.

Davies, K. G., ed. *Documents of the American Revolution 1770–1783.* Dublin, 1976.

Davis, Robert. *Where a Man Can Go: Major General William Phillips, British Royal Artillery, 1731–1781.* Westport, Conn., 1999.

Dearborn, Henry. *Journals of Henry Dearborn, 1776–1783* (Cambridge, Mass., 1887).

DeCosta, B. F. *The History of Fort George.* New York, 1871.

Deering, Frank, *Orderly Book.* Saco, Me., 1832.

DePeyster, John Watts. *Miscellanies of an Officer.* New York, 1838.

Desjardin, Thomas. *Through a Howling Wilderness.* New York, 2006.

Diamant, Lincoln. *Chaining the Hudson: The Fight for the River in the American Revolution.* New York City, 1994.

Dictionary of Canadian Biography online. www.biographi.ca.

Digby, Lieutenant William. *The British Invasion from the North, Digby's Journal of Generals Carleton and Burgoyne from Canada, 1776–1777*, ed. James Baxter. New York, 1970.

Division for Historic Preservation. *Schuyler Mansion, a Historic Structure Report*. Albany, 1977.

Doblin, Helga, trans. *The Specht Journal, A Military Journal of the Burgoyne Campaign*. Westport, Conn., 1995.

———, trans. *An Eyewitness Account of the American Revolution and New England Life: The Journal of J. F. Wasmus, German Surgeon, 1776–1783*. Westport, Conn., 1990.

Dorrough, Richard. "Daniel McAlpin." Heritage Hunters, Saratoga NyGen-Web Project, 1996.

Dresler, Horst. *Farmers and Honest Men*. Bedford, Que., 2007.

Duffy, John, Ralph Orth, J. Kevin Graffagnino, and Michael Bellesiles, eds. *Ethan Allen and His Kin, Correspondence, 1772–1819*. Hanover, N.H., 1998.

Duling, Ennis. "Thomas Anburey at the Battle of Hubbardton: How a Fraudulent Source Misled Historians." *Vermont History* 78 (Winter/Spring 2010): 1–14.

Dupuy, R. Ernest. "The Battle of Hubbardton, The Revolution's Only Engagement Fought in Vermont." *Vermont Life*, Summer 1963, 2–5, 56–57.

Easton Book Club. "Some Chapters on the History of the Town of Easton." In *History of Washington County, New York*, 26–28, 34–39. Fort Edward, N.Y., 1959.

Egly, Theodore, Jr. *General Schuyler's Guard*. 1986.

Ellis, Franklin. *History of Columbia Co., N.Y.* Philadelphia, 1878.

Enys, John. *The American Journal of Lt. John Enys*, ed. Elizabeth Cometti. Syracuse, N.Y., 1976.

Fahey, Curtis. *The Anglican Experience in Upper Canada, 1791–1853*. Ottawa, 1991.

Fenn, Elizabeth. *Pox Americana*. New York, 2001.

Fitch, Asa. *Early History of the Town of Salem*. Salem, Mass., 1927.

Fitzpatrick, John, ed. *The Writings of George Washington from the Original Manuscript Sources*. Charlottesville, Va., 1931–44.

Force, Peter, ed. *American Archives: Documents of the American Revolution, 1774–1776*. 1837–53.

Foster, Jane. "Always a Loyal Man." In *Bath, on the Bay of Quinte*, 1–7. Bath, Ontario, 1996.

Foster, William Henry. *The Captors' Narrative: Catholic Women and Their Puritan Men on the Early American Frontier*. Ithaca, N.Y., 2003.

Fraser, Alexander, ed. *Second Report of the Bureau of Archives for the Province of Ontario*. Toronto, 1904.

Fraser, Duncan. "Sir John Johnson's Rent Roll of the Kingsborough Patent." *Ontario History* 52:3, 176–89.

Fraser, J. *Skulking for the King: A Loyalist Plot*. Erin, Ont., 1985.

Frazier, Patrick. *The Mohicans of Stockbridge*. Lincoln, Neb., 1992.

Frey, Sylvia. *The British Soldier in America: A Social History of Military Life in the Revolutionary Period*. Austin, Tex., 1981.

———. *Water from the Rock: Black Resistance in a Revolutionary Age.* Princeton, N.J., 1991.

Fryer, Mary Beacock. *Buckskin Pimpernel: The Exploits of Justice Sherwood, Loyalist Spy.* Toronto, 1981.

———. *King's Men: The Soldier Founders of Ontario.* Toronto, 1980.

———. *Loyalist Spy: The Experiences of Captain John Walden Meyers during the American Revolution.* Toronto, 1983.

———. "Sarah Sherwood: Wife and Mother, an 'Invisible Loyalist.'" In Phyllis Blakeley and John Grant, eds., *Eleven Exiles*, 245–62. Toronto, 1982.

Fryer, Mary Beacock, and Christopher Dracott. *John Graves Simcoe, 1752–1806.* Toronto, 1998.

Gerlach, Don. *Proud Patriot: Philip Schuyler and the War for Independence, 1775–1783.* Syracuse, N.Y., 1987.

———. "Philip Schuyler and the New York Frontier in 1781." *The New-York Historical Society Quarterly* 53 (Apr. 1969): 148–81.

———. *Philip Schuyler and the American Revolution in New York, 1733–1777.* Lincoln, Neb., 1964.

Glatthaar, Joseph, and James Kirby Martin. *Forgotten Allies: The Oneida Indians and the American Revolution.* New York, 2006.

Goodrich, John, ed. *Rolls of the Soldiers in the Revolutionary War, 1775 to 1783.* Rutland, Vt., 1904).

Goodwin, Neil. *We Go as Captives: The Royalton Raid and the Shadow War on the Revolutionary Frontier.* Barre, Vt., 2010.

Grant, Anne. *Memoirs of an American Lady.* New York, 1909.

Grant, Charles. *Democracy in the Connecticut Frontier Town of Kent.* New York, 1961.

Graymont, Barbara. *The Iroquois in the American Revolution.* Syracuse, N.Y., 1972.

Greenleaf, Thomas, ed. *Greenleaf's Laws of New York from the First to the . . . Session Inclusive.* New York, 1792.

Greven, Philip. *Four Generations: Population, Land, and Family in Colonial Andover, Massachusetts.* Ithaca, N.Y., 1970.

Gross, Robert, ed. *In Debt to Shays: The Bicentennial of an Agrarian Rebellion.* Charlottesville, Va., 1993.

———. *The Minutemen and Their World.* New York, 1976.

Gruber, Ira. *The Howe Brothers and the American Revolution.* Chapel Hill, N.C., 1972.

Hale, Nathan, to Abigail Hale, June 6, 1777. www.worldpath.net/~rwhite/histarchive/hale/6-21-77/trans.htm (printout in author's possession).

Halevi, Sharon, ed. *The Other Daughters of the Revolution: The Narrative of K. White (1809) and the Memoirs Elizabeth Fisher (1810)*, 75–84. Albany, N.Y., 2006.

Hall, Charles. *Life and Letters of General Samuel Holden Parsons.* Binghamton, N.Y., 1905.

Hanson, Willis. *A History of Schenectady During the Revolution.* Schenectady, N.Y., 1916.

Head, Carolyn. *The Irish Palatines in Ontario.* Milton, Ont., 2009.

Hemenway, Abby, ed. *Vermont Gazetteer.* Burlington, 1868–91.

Henderson, John. "The Witch of Salem, New York," Dec. 1996–Jan. 2006, 3–8.

Herwig, Miriam, and Wes Herwig, eds. *Jonathan Carpenter's Journal.* Randolph Center, Vt., 1994.

Higginbotham, Don. "The American Militia: A Traditional Institution with Revolutionary Responsibilities." In Don Higginbotham, ed., *Reconsiderations on the Revolutionary War: Selected Essays,* 83–103. Westport, Conn., 1978.

———. *Daniel Morgan.* Chapel Hill, N.C., 1961.

Hill, William. *Old Fort Edward before 1800.* Fort Edward, N.Y., 1929.

Hille, Julius Friedrich von. *The American Revolution: Garrison Life in French Canada and New York, Journal of an Officer in Prinz Friedrich Regiment, 1776–1783,* trans. Helga Doblin. Westport, Conn., 1993.

Hoerder, Dirk. *Crowd Action in Revolutionary Massachusetts 1765–1780.* New York, 1977.

Hollister, Heil. *Pawlet for One Hundred Years.* Albany, N.Y., 1867.

Hough, Franklin. *A History of the St. Lawrence and Franklin Counties, New York.* Albany, N.Y., 1853.

Howe, Archibald. *Colonel John Brown of Pittsfield, Massachusetts.* Boston, 1908.

Howson, Gerald. *Burgoyne of Saratoga.* New York, 1979.

Hoyt, Edwin. *The Damndest Yankees: Ethan Allan and His Clan.* Brattleboro, Vt., 1976.

Hubbard, R. H. *Thomas Davies in Early Canada.* N.p., n.d.

Hudleston, F. J. *Misadventures of an English General in the Revolution.* Indianapolis, 1927.

Hughes, Thomas *A Journal by Thomas Hughes,* Kennikat edition. Port Washington, N.Y., 1970.

Huston, Reeve. *Land and Freedom, Rural Society, Popular Protest, and Party Politics in Antebellum New York.* New York, 2000.

Jackson, H. M. *Rogers' Rangers.* Ottawa, 1953.

Jellison, Charles. *Ethan Allen: Frontier Rebel.* Syracuse, 1983.

Jennings, Francis, William Fenton, Mary Duke, and David Miller, David, eds. *The History and Culture of Iroquois Diplomacy.* Syracuse, N.Y., 1985.

Jepson, George. *Herrick's Rangers.* Bennington, Vt., 1977.

Jessup, Henry Griswold. *Edward Jessup of West Farms, Westchester Co., New York and His Descendants.* Cambridge, Mass., 1887.

Johnson, Crisfield. *History of Washington Co., New York.* Philadelphia, 1878.

Johnson, Curtis, and Elsa Gilbertson. "Castleton." In *The Historic Architecture of Rutland County,* 67–73. Montpelier, Vt., 1988.

Jones, Douglas Lamar. *Village and Seaport: Migration and Society in Eighteenth-Century Massachusetts.* Hanover, N.H., 1981.

Jones, Electra. *Stockbridge, Past and Present: Memories of a Mission Station.* Boston, 1857.

Jones, Matt Bushnell. *Vermont in the Making, 1750–1777.* Cambridge, Mass., 1939.

Jones, Robert. *"The King of the Alley": William Duer, Politician, Entrepreneur, and Speculator, 1768–1799.* Philadelphia, 1992.

Jones, Thomas. *History of New York during the Revolutionary War.* New York, 1968.

Judd, Jacob, ed. "Memoir." In *The Revolutionary War Memoir and Selected Correspondence of Philip Van Cortlandt.* Tarrytown, N.Y., 1976.

Kalinoski, Sarah. "Sequestration, Confiscation, and the 'Tory' in the Vermont Revolution." *Vermont History* 45 (1977): 236–46.

Kelly, Edward. "The Reverend John McKenna, Loyalist Chaplain." *Canadian Catholic Historical Association Report,* 1933, 31–44.

Kelsay, Isabel. *Joseph Brant, 1743–1807: Man of Two Worlds.* Syracuse, 1984.

Ketchum, Richard. *Saratoga: Turning Point in America's Revolutionary War.* New York, 1997.

Kierner, Cynthia. *Traders and Gentlefolk: The Livingstons of New York, 1675–1790.* Ithaca, N.Y., 1992.

Kim, Sung Bok. *Landlord and Tenant in Colonial New York: Manorial Society, 1664–1775.* Chapel Hill, N.C., 1978.

Klopet, Beth. "Schaghticoke." *Hudson Valley Regional Review* 2 (1985): 29–40.

Knopf, Richard, ed. *Anthony Wayne: A Name in Arms.* Pittsburgh, 1960.

Lapp, Eula. *To Their Heirs Forever.* Picton, Ont., 1970.

Lasselle, Doris Putnam. "Remembering Jane McCrea: A Newly-discovered Correspondence from the 1850s." *Journal of the Washington County Historical Society* (Fort Edward, N.Y, 2007), 68–83.

"List of Estates Ordered Confiscated by Court of Confiscation," Apr. 23, 1778, *Official Journal of the Northern New York American-Canadian Genealogical Society* 4:1 (Spring 1987), 77–78.

Logusz, Michael. *With Musket and Tomahawk: The Saratoga Campaign and the Wilderness War of 1777.* Philadelphia, 2010.

Lord, Philip, Jr. *War over Walloomscoik: Land Use and Settlement Pattern on the Bennington Battlefield—1777.* Albany, N.Y., 1989.

"The Loyalists of Sorel." *The Loyalist Gazette,* June 1985, 6–7.

Luzader, John. *Saratoga: A Military History of the Decisive Campaign of the American Revolution.* New York, 2008.

Lynd, Staughton. "The Tenant Rising at Livingston Manor, 1777" and "The Tenant Rising of 1766 and the Origin of Party Conflict." In *Anti-Federalism in Dutchess County,* 37–54, 170–82. Chicago, 1962.

MacLeod, D. Peter. *The Canadian Iroquois and the Seven Years' War.* Toronto, 1966.

MacMaster, Richard. "Parish in Arms: A Study of Father John MacKenna and the Mohawk Valley Loyalists, 1773–1778." *Catholic Historical Review,* 107–25.

MacNaughton, James, Jr. *The MacNaughtons of Argyle.* Glens Falls, N.Y., 1994.

Manley, Patricia. *Geophysical Reconnaissance in the Mount Independence Area.* Middlebury, Vt., 1995).

Martin, James Kirby. *Benedict Arnold, Revolutionary War Hero: An American Warrior Reconsidered.* New York, 1997.

Mayo, Lawrence. *John Langdon of New Hampshire.* Reprint of 1932. New York, 1970).

Mattern, David. *Benjamin Lincoln and the American Revolution.* Columbia, S.C., 1998.

McAnear, Beverly. "The Albany Stamp Act Riots." *William and Mary Quarterly* 4 (Oct. 1947): 486–98.

McCabe, George. "Inhabitants of the Embury Wilson Patent who were Obliged to quit their farms during the Revolutionary War." washington.nygenweb.net/Embury.

McCulloch, Ian Macpherson. *Sons of the Mountains: The Highland regiments in the French and Indian War, 1756–1767.* Fleischmanns, N.Y., 2006.

McIlwraith, Jean. *Sir Frederick Haldimand.* London, 1905.

McLean, Marianne. *The People of Glengarry: Highlanders in Transition, 1745–1820.* Montreal, 1991.

Meany, Joseph. "Merchant and Redcoat: The Papers of John Macomb, July 1757 to June 1760." PhD diss., Fordam University, 1990.

Mevers, Frank, ed. *The Papers of Josiah Bartlett.* Hanover, N.H., 1979.

Michelson, Gunther. "Iroquois Population Statistics. *Man in the Northeast* 14 (Fall 1977): 2–4.

Minot, George. *History of the Insurrections in Massachusetts.* Boston, 1810.

Mintz, Max. *The Generals of Saratoga: John Burgoyne and Horatio Gates.* New Haven, Conn., 1992.

———. *Gouverneur Morris and the American Revolution.* Norman, Okla., 1970.

Moffat, Riley. *Population History of Eastern U.S. Cities and Town, 1790–1870.* Metuchen, N.J., 1992.

Moody, Robert. "Samuel Ely: Forerunner of Shays." *New England Quarterly* 5 (1932): 105–34.

Morton, Doris Begor. *Philip Skene of Skenesborough.* Granville, N.Y., 1959.

Mott, Edward. "Journal of Captain Edward Mott," Collections of the Connecticut Historical Society I (1860), 163–188.

Muller, H. N. "Vermont's Constitution Bred Stability." *The Sunday Rutland Herald and the Sunday Times Argus,* July 3, 1977, sec. 3:1, 3.

Naval Documents of the American Revolution. Washington, D.C., 1996.

Nelson, James. *Benedict Arnold's Navy.* Camden, Me., 2006.

Nelson, Paul. *William Tryon and the Course of Empire.* Chapel Hill, N.C., 1990.

———. *General Horatio Gates, A Biography.* Baton Rouge, 1976.

Newcomer, Lee. "Yankee Rebels of Inland Massachusetts. *William and Mary Quarterly* 9, no. 2 (1952): 156–65.

New York State. *18th Century Crown Point Maps.* Crown Point, N.Y., 1971.

———. *The Colonial Laws of New York.* Albany, 1894–96.

Nickerson, Hoffman. *Turning Point of the Revolution.* Cambridge, Mass., 1928.

Neilson, Charles. *An Original, Compiled and Corrected Account of Burgoyne's Campaign,* Kennikat ed. Port Washington, N.Y., 1970; orig. 1844.

Niles, Grace Greylock. *The Hoosic Valley: Its Legends and Its History.* New York, 1912.

Nobles, Gregory. "Shays's Neighbors; The Context of Rebellion in Pelham, Massachusetts." In Robert Gross, *In Debt to Shays: The Bicentennial of an Agrarian Rebellion,* 185–203. Charlottesville, Va., 1993.

———. *Divisions throughout the Whole Politics and Society in Hampshire County, Massachusetts, 1740–1775.* New York, 1983.

Nye, Mary Greene, ed. *Sequestration, Confiscation and Sale of Estates, State Papers of Vermont*. Montpelier, 1941.

O'Callaghan, Edmund B., ed. *Documentary History of the State of New York*. Albany, 1849–51.

Otto, Stephen. *Maitland: "A Very Neat Village Indeed."* Erin, Ont., 1985.

Paine, Thomas. *Common Sense*. In Philip Foner, ed., *The Complete Works of Thomas Paine*. New York, 1945.

Palmer, Gregory. *Biographical Sketches of Loyalists in the American Revolution*. Westport, Conn., 1984.

Paltsits, Victor, ed. *Minutes of the Commissioners for Detecting and Defeating Conspiracies in the State of New York*. Boston, 1972.

Parks, Robert. *History of Wells, Vermont*. Rutland, Vt., 1869.

Pell, John. *Ethan Allen*. Boston, 1929.

Pell, Joshua. "Diary of Joshua Pell, Junior, Officer of the British Army in America." *Magazine of American History* 2 (1878): 107.

Pemberton, Ian. "The British Secret Service in the Champlain Valley during the Haldimand Negotiations, 1780–1783." *Vermont History* 44 (1976): 129–40.

Pencak, William. "The Fine Theoretic Government of Massachusetts." In Robert Gross, *In Debt to Shays: The Bicentennial of an Agrarian Rebellion*, 121–43. Charlottesville, Va., 1993.

Penrose, Maryly, ed. *Indian Affairs Papers: American Revolution*. Franklin Park, N.J., 1981.

Perry, A. L. "The Scotch-Irish in America." *Proceedings and Addresses of the Second Congress at Pittsburg, Pennsylvania, May 29–June 1, 1890*, n.p.

Petersen, James. *Seth Warner*. Middlebury, Vt., 2001.

Pierce, Lorne. "Dr. Solomon Jones: United Empire Loyalist." *Queen's Quarterly* 36 (1929): 437–38.

Potter-MacKinnon, Janice. *While the Women Only Wept: Loyalist Refugee Women in Eastern Ontario*. Montreal, 1993.

Preston, Richard, ed. *Kingston before the War of 1812: A Collection of Documents*. Toronto, 1959.

Pryde, George. "Scottish Colonization in the Province of New York." *New York History* 16 (April 1935): 138–57.

Queen's School of Urban and Regional Planning. *History and Architecture of the Village of Bath, Ontario*. Kingston, Ont., 1976.

Rae, E. Stuart. "Jessup's Rangers as a Factor in Loyalist Settlement." In *Three History Theses*, 1–135. Toronto, 1961.

Reid, Arthur. *Reminiscences of the Revolution, or, Le Loup's Bloody Trail from Salem to Fort Edward*. Utica, N.Y., 1859.

"Reminiscences of Jonathan Elkins." *Proceedings of the Vermont Historical Society, 1919–1920*, 185–211.

Reubens, Beatrice. "Pre-Emptive Rights in the Disposition of a Confiscated Estate: Philipsburgh Manor, New York." *William and Mary Quarterly* 3rd Series, 22, no. 3: 435–55.

Reynolds, Paul. *Guy Carleton: A Biography*. Toronto, 1980.

Richter, Daniel. *Ordeal of the Long House: Peoples of the Iroquois League in the Era of European Colonization*. Chapel Hill, N.C., 1992.

Roberts, Kenneth. *Rabble in Arms.* Garden City, N.Y., 1947.

Rogers, Horatio, ed. *A Journal Kept in Canada and upon Burgoyne's Campaign in 1776 and 1777 by Lieut. James Hadden.* Freeport, N.Y., 1970.

Rorison, Arda Bates, and John Boucher. *Major-General Arthur St. Clair.* New York, 2009.

Roth, Randolph. *The Democratic Dilemma: Religion, Reform and the Social Order in the Connecticut River Valley of Vermont, 1791–1850.* New York, 2003.

Runk, Emma Ten Broeck. *Ten Broeck Genealogy, Being the Records and Annals of Dirck Wesselse Ten Broeck of Albany and His Descendants.* New York, 1897.

Saillant, John. *Black Puritan, Black Republican: The Life and Thought of Lemuel Haynes, 1753–1833.* New York, 2003.

Salsig, Doyen, ed. *Parole: Quebec; Countersign: Ticonderoga, Second New Jersey Orderly Book.* Rutherford, N.J.: 1980.

Saratoga National Historical Park. "Neilson House" brochure, n.d., n.p.

Schuyler, George W. *Colonial New York: Philip Schuyler and his Family.* New York, 1885.

Shalhope, Robert. *Bennington and the Green Mountain Boys: The Emergence of Liberal Democracy in Vermont, 1760–1850.* Baltimore, 1996.

Shannon, Timothy. *Iroquois Diplomacy on the Early American Frontier.* New York, 2008.

Sherwood, Justus. "Justus Sherwood Journal." *Vermont History* 24 (April and July 1956): 101–109, 211–20.

Shomette, Donald. *Pirates on the Chesapeake.* Centreville, Md., 1985.

Shy, John. *A People Numerous and Armed.* New York, 1976.

———. "The Loyalist Problem in the Lower Hudson Valley: The British Perspective." In Robert East and Jacob Judd, eds., *The Loyalist Americans: A Focus on Greater New York*, 3–13. Tarrytown, N.Y., 1975.

———. *Toward Lexington: The Role of the British Army in the Coming of the American Revolution.* Princeton, N.J., 1965.

Siebert, William. "The Temporary Settlement of Loyalists at Machiche, P.Q." *Proceedings and Transactions of the Royal Society of Canada*, 3rd Series, 7 (May 1914): 407–14.

Sketcher, William. "Haverhill in the War of the Revolution." Annual Meeting of the New Hampshire Historical Society, May 14, 1912.

Slade, William, ed. *State Papers of Vermont.* Middlebury, 1823.

Smallwood, Frank. *Thomas Chittenden: Vermont's First Statesman.* Shelburne, Vt., 1997.

Smith, Helen Everson. *Colonial Days and Ways.* New York, 1900.

Smith, Joseph Edward Adams. *The History of Pittsfield, Massachusetts from the Year 1734 to the Year 1800.* Boston, 1868.

Smith, Paul. *Loyalists and Redcoats: A Study in British Revolutionary Policy.* New York, 1972.

———. "Sir Guy Carleton: Soldier Statesman." In George Billias, ed., *George Washington's Opponents: British Generals and Admirals in the American Revolution.* New York, 1969, 103–41.

Smith, Richard. *A Tour of the Four Great Rivers: The Hudson, Mohawk, Susquehanna and Delaware in 1769*, ed. Francis Hawley. New York, 1906.

Smith, Richard B. *The Revolutionary War in Bennington County.* Charleston, S.C., 2008.

Smith, William, ed. *The St. Clair Papers.* New York, 1971.

Sparks, Jared. *Memoir of Colonel Ethan Allen*, Legacy Reprint Series. Middlebury, Vt., 1848.

———. *The Life of Gouverneur Morris with Selections from His Correspondence and Miscellaneous Papers.* Boston, 1832.

Spaulding, E. Wilder. *His Excellency George Clinton: Critic of the Constitution.* New York, 1938.

Stanley, George, ed. *For Want of a Horse.* Sackville, N.B., 1961.

Stark, Caleb, ed. *Memoir and Official Correspondence of General John Stark.* Concord, N.H., 1860, 119–21.

Starna, William. "Mohawk Iroquois Populations: A Revision." *Ethnohistory* 27 (Fall 1980): 371–82.

Stephenson, Michael. *Patriot Battles: How the War of Independence Was Fought.* New York, 2007.

Stevens, Paul L. "His Majesty's 'Savage Allies.'" PhD diss., State University of New York at Buffalo, 1984.

Stone, William L. *Washington County New York: Its History to the Close of the Nineteenth Century.* New York, 1901.

———. *Visits to Saratoga Battle Grounds.* Albany, N.Y., 1895.

———. *Ballads and Poems Relating to the Burgoyne Campaign.* Port Washington, N.Y., 1970; orig. 1893.

———. *The Campaign of Lieut. Gen. John Burgoyne.* Albany, N.Y., 1877.

———. *Life of Joseph Brant–Thayendanegea.* New York, 1838.

———, ed. *Journal of Captain Pausch.* New York, 1971.

———, ed. *Memoirs, Letters, and Journals of Major General Riedesel.* New York, 1969.

———, trans. and ed. *Letters of Brunswick and Hessian Officers during the American Revolution.* Albany, 1891.

Strach, Stephen. "A Memoir of the Exploits of Captain Alexander Fraser and his Company of British Marksmen, 1776–1777." *Journal of the Society for Army Historical Research* 63 (1985): 1–22.

———. "A New Look at the Regimental Colors of the Second New Hampshire Regiment, 1777." *Military Collector and Historian* 3 (Fall 1985): 127–34.

———. "Notes on the Family of Sarah Dunham Jones 1734–1818, Loyalist." Unpublished paper at Saratoga National Historic Park, 1980.

Sullivan, James, ed. *Minutes of the Albany Committee of Correspondence, 1775–1778.* Albany, N.Y., 1923.

Sylvester, Nathaniel. *History of Saratoga County, New York.* Philadelphia, 1878.

Szatmary, David. *Shays's Rebellion: The Making of an Agrarian Insurrection.* Amherst, Mass., 1980.

Talman, James J., ed. *Loyalist Narratives from Upper Canada.* Toronto, 1946.

Tatum, George. *Philadelphia Georgian.* Middletown, Conn., 1976.

Taylor, Alan. *The Divided Ground: Indians, Settlers, and the Northern Borderland of the American Revolution.* New York, 2006.

———. "Regulators and White Indians: The Agrarian Resistance in Post-Revolutionary New England." In Robert Gross, *In Debt to Shays: The Bicentennial of an Agrarian Rebellion*, 147–49. Charlottesville, Va., 1993.

Thomas, Earle. *Sir John Johnson, Loyalist Baronet.* Toronto, 1986.

Thompson, Zadock. *History of the State of Vermont, Natural, Civil, and Statistical.* Burlington, 1842.

Tomasi, Katherine. *The Village of Salem, 1761–1994.* Glens Falls, N.Y. 1995.

Trinterud, Leonard. *The Forming of the American Tradition: A Re-examination of Colonial Presbyterianism.* Philadelphia, 1959.

Turner, Larry. *Ernestown: Rural Spaces, Urban Places.* Toronto, 1993.

Turner, Lynn. *The Ninth State: New Hampshire's Formative Years.* Chapel Hill, N.C., 1983.

Ulrich, Laurel Thatcher. *Good Wives: Images and Reality in the Lives of Women in Northern New England, 1650–1750.* New York, 1982.

Upton, Leslie F. S., ed. *Revolutionary Versus Loyalist, The First American Civil War: 1774–1784.* Waltham, Mass., 1968.

Urban, Mark. *Fusiliers, The Saga of a British Redcoat Regiment in the American Revolution.* New York, 2007.

Valentine, Alan. *Lord Stirling.* New York, 1969.

Van Wagenen, Jared, Jr. *The Golden Age of Homespun.* New York, 1963.

Wallace, Audrey. "The American Revolution and Cambridge." In Robert Clay, Carleton Foster, Robert Raymond, and David Thornton, eds., *Old Cambridge (1788–1988)*, 100–102. Cambridge, N.Y., 1988.

Waltman, Maria. "From Soldier to Settler: Patterns of Loyalist Settlement in Upper Canada, 1783–1785." MA thesis, Queen's University, Kingston, Ont., 1981.

Walton, E. P., ed. *Records of the Council of Safety and Governor and Council of the State of Vermont.* Montpelier, 1873–1880.

Ward, Christopher. *The War of the Revolution.* New York, 1952.

Warren, Mercy Otis. *History of the Rise, Progress and Termination of the American Revolution.* Indianapolis, 1989; orig. Boston, 1805.

Washington, Ida, and Paul Washington. *Carleton's Raid.* Canaan, N.H., 1977.

Watson, Elkanah, Jr. *Pioneer History of the Champlain Valley.* Albany, N.Y. 1863.

Watt, Gavin. *A Dirty, Trifling Piece of Business.* Vol. 1, *The Revolutionary War as Waged from Canada in 1781.* Toronto, 2009.

———. *Rebellion in the Mohawk Valley: The St. Leger Expedition of 1777.* Toronto, 2002.

———. *Burning of the Valleys: Daring Raids from Canada against the New York Frontier in the Fall of 1780.* Toronto, 1997.

Webster, J. Clarence, ed. *The Journal of Jeffrey Amherst.* Chicago, 1934.

Wells, Robert. *The Population of the British Colonies in America before 1776.* Princeton, N.J., 1975.

White, Richard. *The Middle Ground: Indians, Empires, and Republics in the Great Lakes Region, 1650–1815.* Cambridge, 1991.

Wilbur, James Benjamin. *Ira Allen: Founder of Vermont, 1751–1814.* Boston, 1928.

Wilcox, William B. "Too Many Cooks: British Planning Before Saratoga." *Journal of British Studies* 2 (Nov. 1962): 56–90.

———., ed. *The American Rebellion: Sir Henry Clinton's Narrative of Campaigns, 1775–1782*. New Haven, 1954.

Wilkinson, James. *Memoirs of My Own Time*. Philadelphia, 1816.

Willey, George, ed. "Enoch Poor." *State Builders*, 7–10. Manchester, N.H., 1903.

Williams, John. *The Battle of Hubbardton*. Montpelier, Vt., 1988.

Williams, John A., ed., *The Public Papers of Governor Thomas Chittenden, 1778–1789, 1790–1797*, vol. 17. Montpelier, 1969.

Williams, Samuel. *Natural and Civil History of Vermont*. Schenectady, N.Y., 1794.

Wilson, David. *The Life of Jane McCrea with an Account of Burgoyne's Expedition in 1777*. New York, 1853.

Winks, Robin. *The Blacks in Canada: A History*. Montreal, 1997.

Worrall, Arthur J. *Quakers in the Colonial Northeast*. Lebanon, N.H., 1980.

Wraxall, Peter. *An Abridgement of Indian Affairs*, ed. Charles Howard McIlwain. New York, 1968.

Wright, Esmond. "The New York Loyalists: A Cross-section of Colonial Society." In Robert East and Jacob Judd, eds., *The Loyalist Americans: A Focus on Greater New York*, 74–94. Tarrytown, N.Y., 1975.

Yoshpe, Harry. *The Distribution of Estates in Southern New York*. New York, 1939.

INDEX